Consumer Reports

ELECTRONICS BUYING GUIDE 2006

Today's Best Buys in...
- DESKTOP & LAPTOP COMPUTERS
- DIGITAL CAMERAS & CAMCORDERS
- BIG-SCREEN TVs & VIDEO GEAR
- CELL PHONES & MORE

THE EDITORS OF CONSUMER REPORTS

PUBLISHED BY CONSUMER REPORTS ▶ A DIVISION OF CONSUMERS UNION ▶ YONKERS, NY

CONSUMER REPORTS PUBLICATIONS DEVELOPMENT

Editor	David Schiff
Group Managing Editor	Nancy Crowfoot
Coordinating Editor, Master Content	Merideth Mergel
Project Editor	Greg Daugherty
Coordinating Editor	Robin Melén
Contributing Editors	Michael Gikas, Eileen McCooey, Ed Perratore, Paul Reynolds
Technology Editor, Consumer Reports	Jeff Fox
Design Manager	Rosemary Simmons
Art Director	Joseph Ulatowski
Contributing Art Director	Virginia Rubel
Technology Specialist	Jennifer Dixon
Production Associate	Letitia Hughes
Editorial Assistant	Joan Daviet
Illustrations	Trevor Johnston

CONSUMER REPORTS ELECTRONICS DEPARTMENT

Vice President and Technical Director	Jeffrey A. Asher
Assistant Technical Director	Alan Lefkow
Senior Director of Testing	Evon Beckford
Manager	Gerard Catapano
Program Leaders	Dean Gallea, Richard Sulin
Senior Project Leaders	Christopher Bucsko, Maurice Wynn, Joseph Lazzaro
Project Leaders	Kerry Allen, James Langehennig, Claudio Ciacci, Robert Lew, Ernst St. Louis, Charles Davidman
Assistant Project Leaders	Susan Daino, Artur Pietruch
Technicians	Samuel Ahn, Elias Arias, Larry Greene, Maria Grimaldi, Thomas Maung, Miguel Rivera, William South

CONSUMER REPORTS

Editor/Senior Director	Margot Slade
Deputy Editorial Director	Kimberly Kleman
Director, Editorial Operations	David Fox
Design Director, Consumers Union	George Arthur
Creative Director, Consumer Reports	Tim LaPalme
Director, Survey Research	Charles Daviet
Product Manager, Retail Products	Lesley Greene
Retail Marketing Director	Tracy Bowen
Manufacturing/Distribution	Mark Yatarola

CONSUMERS UNION

President	James Guest
Executive Vice President	Joel Gurin

First printing, September 2005
Copyright © 2005 by Consumers Union of United States, Inc., Yonkers, New York 10703.
Published by Consumers Union of United States, Inc., Yonkers, New York 10703.
All rights reserved, including the right of reproduction in whole or in part in any form.

ISBN: 0-97553-881-0
Manufactured in the United States of America.

CONTENTS

INTRODUCTION
- **5** Use this book and our Web site to get best value
- **6** How Consumer Reports tests

CHAPTER 01 | WHERE TO BUY
- **8** You'll pay more to get good service
- **9** Ratings of electronics stores
- **10** Online is the best place to buy a computer
- **11** Ratings of computer stores

Where to buy, p. 8

CHAPTER 02 | YOUR NETWORKED HOME
- **14** Wired and wireless can work in tandem
- **15** Ratings of home-networking choices

CHAPTER 03 | DIGITAL CAMERAS & CAMCORDERS
- **18** Match the camera to how you'll use it
- **19** Enhancing photos is easier than ever
- **20** Flatbed scanners digitize film photos
- **21** Printing your pics
- **22** Digital camcorders
- **23** Buying Advice: Digital cameras
- **26** Buying Advice: Scanners
- **27** Buying Advice: Camcorders

Digital cameras, p. 18

Camcorders, p. 22

CHAPTER 04 | COMPUTERS & THE INTERNET
- **32** Laptops & desktops
- **33** Computer monitors
- **34** Save your computer from online attack
- **36** Ratings of antispam programs
- **38** Ratings of antivirus programs
- **39** Ratings of antispyware
- **41** Find the provider that's best for you
- **43** Ratings of providers
- **45** Today's PDAs link up to your network
- **46** Buying Advice: Desktop computers
- **49** Buying Advice: Laptop computers
- **52** Buying Advice: Monitors
- **55** Buying Advice: PDAs

Laptops, p. 32

CONTENTS

CHAPTER 05 | PRINTERS
58 Choose a printer to suit your tasks
59 Buying Advice: Printers
61 Buying Advice: Multifunction devices

CHAPTER 06 | TVs
64 Step by step guide to choosing a set
67 Picture-tube TVS
68 LCD TVs get bigger
69 Plasma TVs get better
70 Rear-projection TVs
71 Buying Advice: Picture-tube televisions
73 Buying Advice: LCD TVs
75 Buying Advice: Plasma TVs
79 Buying Advice: Rear-projection TVs

CHAPTER 07 | VIDEO GEAR
84 Video recording
86 Get great sound with home theater
88 Buying Advice: DVD players
91 Buying Advice: DVD recorders
93 Buying Advice: Digital video recorders
95 Buying Advice: Home theater in a box
96 Buying Advice: Receivers
99 Buying Advice: Speakers

Speakers, p. 99

Satellite radio, p. 104

CHAPTER 08 | MP3 PLAYERS
102 The ABCs of MP3
103 Your computer as digital jukebox
104 Computers replace most CD recorders
104 Satellite radio: Reception an issue
106 Buying Advice: MP3 Players

CHAPTER 09 | PHONES & PHONE SERVICES
110 Getting the best cellular service
111 Choosing a phone that fits your needs
113 Headsets let you free up your hands
114 Master the minutes to slash your bills
117 Internet phoning is not for everyone
119 Find the cordless that's best for you
120 Buying Advice: Cell phones
123 Buying Advice: Cordless phones

Cell phones, p. 111

RATINGS & REFERENCE
127 Ratings
183 Brand locator
185 Glossary
206 Index

USE THIS BOOK AND OUR WEB SITE TO GET BEST VALUE

This new edition of the CONSUMER REPORTS Electronics Buying Guide is designed to be used in two ways. You can use it by itself to choose specific brands and models, following our step-by-step buying advice and Ratings. Or you can use it in tandem with our Web site, *www.ConsumerReports.org*, where you'll find information on models too new to have been included when this book went to press.

Most of the products referred to in this book should still be in stores until about December 2005. However, because the home electronics marketplace is constantly changing, this book also entitles you to free, 30-day trial access to *www.ConsumerReports.org* (see the inside front cover of this book for details). On our Web site you can read our testers' latest Ratings and other advice to help you choose the best products at the best prices.

WHAT'S NEW IN ELECTRONICS?

The digital revolution continues to change not only the physical products we use but also the ways that many of us spend our work and leisure time. You can read about the latest developments for specific types of products later in this book. But a few overarching trends are worth noting before you venture into the electronics bazaar.

1. Products are getting cheaper in many categories, as their technology matures. This could be a good excuse to buy that gleaming gizmo you want now and, perhaps, to congratulate yourself for not getting one sooner.

2. Products are becoming slimmer, smaller, and lighter too.

3. Many products now do things that once required several different devices. Cell phones increasingly include a digital camera. Some laptop computers play movies on DVD. Multifunction units for your home office may incorporate a printer, copier, fax, and scanner—all at a price that's less than you might have paid for any of those functions separately just a few years ago.

4. Products are becoming more portable. Multifunction handheld devices (cell phones with video and music, game players that also play music and movies) can put a world of information and entertainment literally in your hand. Wireless technology is liberating computers and other devices so that they can now be used just about anywhere—all over your house or all over the planet.

Some laptops now double as multimedia players, while many phones take photos.

Screen test: Our experts look for subtle differences among TVs. Below, an engineer assesses cell-phone sound quality.

The digital revolution has its darker sides, of course. The wireless wonders that have freed us on the one hand have also made us reachable wherever and whenever someone (the boss, for example) wants to reach us. Spyware, spam, phishing, and other unfortunate developments have given the criminally inclined some powerful new tools and the rest of us a few new things to worry about.

This book will tell you how to protect yourself from the latest digital dangers as well as how to get the most value and most fun from all of these exciting new electronic products.

HOW CONSUMER REPORTS TESTS

Equipment rated in this book is tested at CONSUMER REPORTS' labs in Yonkers, N.Y. The products are bought at retail, just as a consumer would acquire them. Our shoppers buy specific models based on which are top sellers or innovative designs.

CONSUMER REPORTS' tests are rigorous and objective, using constantly refined procedures. In the case of home computers, for example, benchmarks are used to assess how quickly machines can simultaneously run a number of applications, including a word processor, a spreadsheet, and a Web browser. Much of the work done in the computer

labs mimics the way a piece of equipment would be used in your home. Engineers read the owner's manual, try out all the switches, and experiment with the features. They try to answer likely consumer questions: How easy is the system to set up? Can components be replaced with industry standard parts? Are the manuals comprehensive and easy to read? If the computer is marketed for game devotees, how smooth is its 3D graphics capability?

To find the best printers, testers compare text, photos, and graphics, and they gauge the printers' speeds. To assess the image clarity of monitors, engineers do side-by-side comparisons. The quality of digital cameras, scanners, and other imaging equipment is assessed by comparing images created using the product. For instance, engineers inspect glossy 8x10-inch prints created by each digital camera tested, using its best-photo mode. They use the model's supplied software and output all prints to the same photo printer.

For every piece of equipment, testers carefully assess features—do they add to usability or just make an item more complicated? They check ergonomic functions—how does the camera feel in the hand?—and assess battery life.

After all these tests, our engineers analyze the data and results to arrive at the comprehensive Ratings that are published in CONSUMER REPORTS magazine, on www.ConsumerReports.org, and in this book.

Some of the products tested and reviewed here were already being replaced by new models as this book was going to press in the summer of 2005. CONSUMER REPORTS tests many of these products throughout the year, however. Look for the latest test results in monthly issues of CONSUMER REPORTS or online at our Web site. And don't forget to see the inside front cover of this book for information on how to activate your free, 30-day trial subscription to www.ConsumerReports.org.

WHERE TO BUY

- **8** You'll pay more to get good service
- **9** Ratings of electronics stores
- **10** Online is best place to buy a computer
- **11** Ratings of computer stores

CHAPTER 01

Buying electronic products is as easy as finding hay in a haystack. These days they're in almost every store you visit, from local merchants to giant discounters, not to mention at a mountain of Web sites.

For consumers, that looks like good news. Presumably, with more stores competing for your electronics dollar, you get more choice, better service, and lower prices. But when we polled 4,708 ConsumerReports.org subscribers about their experiences shopping for home electronics, they told us that not all stores are created equal on those criteria. Ratings of the retailers, based on 7,830 different shopping experiences, appear on page 9. Since buying computers poses different challenges, we queried 43,384 ConsumerReports.org subscribers about where they shopped for desktop models. Those Ratings are on page 11. We plan to update these Ratings in the December 2005 issue of CONSUMER REPORTS.

▶▶ We surveyed thousands of readers to find out there they got the best selection, prices, and service. Here's what they told us.

01 WHERE TO BUY

YOU'LL PAY MORE TO GET GOOD SERVICE

Discount retailers are often short on sales help.

Knowledgeable sales help can make the process of shopping for electronics faster and easier. Fortunately, as we found in our 2004 survey of almost 5,000 CONSUMER REPORTS readers, such help is widely available—if you know where to look. Of the respondents to that survey who relied on sales help, 78 percent said the staff knew the products, and 72 percent said the salespeople were interested in helping.

A knowledgeable salesperson can be a plus, but that help comes at a price. If you don't need advice, a price club or online retailer can save you money.

Many retailers, particularly price clubs, however, did not have an adequate staff. Indeed, the primary complaint among our readers (about 19 percent) was that they couldn't find anyone to answer their questions. The Ratings on page 9 show how major electronics retailers stacked up in terms of service and other factors. (The Ratings for buying electronics are based on the following purchases: camcorders; cameras [digital and nondigital]; DVD players and recorders; PDAs; and televisions. Computer purchases are treated separately in the next section.)

One complication is that not all stores carry all brands or models. Nor is it always clear whether different retailers are carrying the same brands and models. At the behest of large retailers and their huge purchasing power, manufacturers may vary a product slightly and alter the model number, allowing a retailer to sell what may be essentially the same item at a particular price, according to Geoff Wissman, vice president specializing in product distribution for Retail Forward, a consumer products market-research firm.

Some retailers also sell electronics under their own house name. Target sells a line of Sony CD players under the brand name LIV, for example; their sleek design was developed to appeal to women's tastes, says Ellen Glassman, Sony's general manager of design and strategy and creator of the line. The guts of such items may or may not be the same as those of the comparable Sony models.

Despite those challenges, you should be able to find the items you seek at the prices you expect to pay. Most readers did. But they also seem to have done their research before they bought. Indeed, of the small portion of respondents who paid more than expected, 70 percent said they did so to get features they wanted, and 30 percent said they had underestimated prices.

All of this suggests that settling on a brand and model, and knowing prices before you begin shopping, will help you stay on budget.

SHOPPING STRATEGIES

In our survey, no retailers received top marks across the board for price, selection, and service. Amazon.com did get top marks in both price and selection—the only outlet to do so. Not surprisingly, however, Amazon.com consumers sacrificed personal service, and typically bought lightweight objects that are relatively inexpensive to ship, not 500-pound TV sets.

In most cases, then, you should decide whether price, selection, or service is your priority. After you have picked stores that rated high on selection, for instance, you can narrow them down by how well each does on your second most important factor, say, price.

If price is your No. 1 consideration, you'll get the best deals at Amazon.com and, as you might expect, from giant discounters and price clubs, such as Costco and Sam's Club. The trade-off in this case: Discounters and price clubs received lower marks for selection and service. If you shop online, the selection is vast, but you have to rely on the telephone or e-mail to get your questions answered.

Hit the stores. If eyeballing a vast selection of products is crucial, a big electronics store is more likely to satisfy you. Besides Amazon.com and BestBuy.com, respondents to our most recent survey said they found the greatest selection at independent retailers. The trade-off here, however, is that you will often pay more than you would at most discounters and price clubs.

If you can't decide what you want and you feel the need for sales help, head to your locally owned electronics stores or to the electronics chains; that's where our readers usually found good service. Among the chains, they cited Ritz Camera in partic-

WHERE TO BUY

CR Quick Recommendations

Electronics stores

The Reader scores are based on our readers' overall satisfaction with the shopping experience. Our readers gave only one outlet the highest marks for both price and selection: Amazon.com. The performance of other stores was uneven.

Quick Picks

For the best prices:
1. Amazon.com
4. Costco
8. Sam's Club

If you're looking for the widest selection of brands and models and good service:
2. Locally owned businesses
3. Ritz Camera (in cameras only)

Ratings

Better ⬤ ◐ ○ ◒ ⬤ Worse

	Store	Reader score	Price	Selection	Quality of product	Service	Checkout
1	Amazon.com	91	⬤	⬤	○	–	–
2	Independent Stores	88	○	◐	○	⬤	⬤
3	Ritz Camera	87	○	◐	○	⬤	⬤
4	Costco	85	⬤	●	○	●	◒
5	Dell.com	84	◐	●	○	–	–
6	Staples	81	○	◒	○	○	⬤
7	Sears	80	○	○	○	◐	◐
8	Sam's Club	79	⬤	●	◒	●	◒
9	Circuit City	78	○	○	○	○	◐
10	Best Buy.com	76	○	◐	○	–	–
11	Best Buy	76	○	○	○	○	○
12	Fry's Electronics	74	○	○	○	●	●
13	Wal-Mart	73	○	●	●	●	◒
14	CompUSA	72	○	○	○	○	○

Guide to the Ratings

READER SCORE reflects readers' assessment of the overall experience of buying electronics. **A READER SCORE OF 100** would mean all respondents had been completely satisfied with their experience; 80 means very satisfied on average; 60 means fairly well-satisfied. A difference of less than 6 points isn't meaningful. These results, which are based on Consumer Reports Online subscribers, may not reflect the experiences of the general public. **PRICE, SELECTION, QUALITY OF PRODUCT, SERVICE,** and **CHECKOUT** scores reflect the percentage who rated the store as excellent or very good on each item. Higher scores mean the chain was rated more favorably compared with the mean score; lower scores mean it was rated less favorably.

ular. Sears was rated better than most stores for service.

Shop online. If you don't need to see or handle the item you want, go to the Web. CONSUMER REPORTS readers gave Amazon.com very high marks. Of course, with many online retailers, you have to delay gratification for a few days until the item arrives—unless you use one (Best Buy or Circuit City, for example) that allow you to order through their Web sites and pick up purchases at a local store.

Try a bot. Short for "robot," a bot is a Web site that allows you to compare prices across dozens or sometimes hundreds of retailers. Some bots, such as Shopper.cnet.com and StreetPrices.com, specialize in electronics and are available at no charge. (Subscribers to ConsumerReports.org can connect to a bot provided by Yahoo to shop for items including digital cameras and TVs.)

Call for prices. If prices do not vary from store to store, you might have found an item that is subject to MAP, or minimum advertised pricing. Some manufacturers demand that retailers not advertise their goods below a certain amount in exchange for an allowance that defrays the cost of advertising. If the retailer violates the MAP agreement, it loses the allowance and may find products yanked from its shelves.

In that case, look for retailers who say "call for price" or "prices too low to mention" in their ads, or Web sites that will not give a price until you put the item in your shopping cart. Those are indications that the stores might offer a better deal than what they can advertise. Sometimes, however, that special price you're quoted on the phone differs little from the MAP. You still need to compare.

Best months to buy

If you're not in a rush to buy, shop when the item you want tends to go on sale. In the spring, for example, you'll find the best deals on digital cameras and camcorders; camcorders also go on sale in winter. Shop for DVD players in April and July. You'll often find lower prices on TVs in July and November.

Digital cameras and camcorders often go on sale in the spring.

01 WHERE TO BUY

ONLINE IS BEST PLACE TO BUY A COMPUTER

Want exactly the right computer? Go configure.

Desktop computers differ from almost all other electronics in the simple fact that you can customize them. All buying choices flow from the decision whether or not to customize—in computer lingo, "configure."

Though you can customize your computer through some brick-and-mortar stores, you're likely to get better service dealing directly with a manufacturer. If you decide on a model that is already configured, you can buy just about anywhere.

Either way, you can count on our help. The tech support, repair history, and Ratings in Chapter 4 can help you choose a brand. Starting on page 48 you'll find buying advice on what you need to know about buying a computer.

Choosing the right vendor involves a number of considerations. For instance, few brick-and-mortar store sells Dell computers. Conversely, only retailers sell eMachines. And as we found out with the help of 43,384 CONSUMER REPORTS subscribers who helped us in our 2004 Annual Questionnaire rate 21 outlets, satisfaction with price, selection, help, and salespeople's knowledge of the product varies from vendor to vendor.

Interestingly, readers who bought at brick-and-mortar stores were generally less satisfied than those who bought at other outlets. Another plus to buying online: You're likely to see offers for free shipping and free upgrades, especially during the holiday season.

THE CUSTOM ADVANTAGE

Customizing is a strategy we recommend for getting optimal features at the lowest cost. Sixty percent of our survey respondents purchased from Dell, which primarily sells custom-configured computers. Twelve percent more patronized other manufacturers, all of which make configuration available via Web sites, phone services, or catalogs. Readers who purchased directly from manufacturers were among the most satisfied with their buying experience overall. Sony was the only direct seller to receive a poor mark, for its relatively high prices.

Manufacturers have made custom computer shopping easy for those who use the Web. You can choose a basic machine and then add or subtract what you do or don't want. And within days you can repeat the exercise to see whether prices have fallen.

Readers who needed help, whether by phone or e-mail, generally found manufacturers' staffs to be very knowledgeable, particularly at Apple and IBM.

THE READY-MADE OPTION

Shopping for an off-the-shelf

Brick-and-mortar stores offer a hands-on experience, but online retailers satisfied more of our readers.

WHERE TO BUY

CR Quick Recommendations

Computer stores

For superior help and savvy via Web or phone:
- 1 Apple
- 2 IBM
- 18 PC/Mac Connection

Apple's Web site (1) was rated tops overall. Staffers at IBM (2) were deemed extremely helpful and knowledgeable, though selection was not as extensive. PC Connection and Mac Connection (18), operated by a single company, rated better on prices than manufacturers.

For knowledgeable face-to-face help:
- 9 Micro Center

This retailer allows you to custom-configure; you can also order online and pick up your computer in the store. A major drawback: the small number of outlets.

For the best prices:
- 8 Costco
- 18 PC/Mac Connection

If you want a basic computer package right now and don't care about service or selection, the thin offerings at Costco (8) will do. If you need more choices and can wait, try PC/Mac Connection (18).

A customized system lets you pick just the components you want.

package deal isn't as easy as it sounds. Deciding between a computer that has, say, more memory and one that has a faster hard drive can give you a headache. And retailers aren't always clear about what's really included.

At one chain store we visited, for example, many of the monitors on display that appeared to be part of package deals were flat-panel LCDs. These units typically cost $300 to $700. The monitors that were actually part of the promoted packages were flat-screen CRTs—old-style TV-type monitors that have flat-screen surfaces. They cost less, generally from $100 to $400.

SHOPPING STRATEGIES

Start with the brand, not a specific model, since model numbers change often.

Ratings

Better ● ◐ ○ ◑ ● Worse

Within types, in order of reader score for desktop computer purchases.

	Outlet	Reader score (0-100)	Help	Savvy	Selection	Prices
MANUFACTURER WEB SITE/CATALOG						
1	Apple	92	●	●	●	○
2	IBM	86	●	●	◐	○
3	Dell	84	○	◐	●	○
4	HP	83	○	◐	◐	○
5	Gateway	83	○	◐	◐	○
6	Sony	82	-	-	◐	●
7	Compaq [1]	81	○	○	◐	○
RETAIL STORE						
8	Costco	82	◑	●	●	◐
9	Micro Center	81	○	◐	○	○
10	Office Depot	80	○	○	●	○
11	Sam's Club	79	●	○	●	○
12	Staples	77	○	○	●	◑
13	Circuit City	76	○	○	●	◑
14	Fry's Electronics	75	●	◑	●	○
15	CompUSA	74	○	○	○	◑
16	Best Buy	73	◑	○	●	○
17	Wal-Mart	73	●	○	●	○
RETAIL WEB SITE/MAIL ORDER						
18	PC/Mac Connection	91	●	●	●	◐
19	CDW	87	-	-	●	○
20	PC/Mac Mall	84	○	◐	●	○
21	TigerDirect	83	-	-	○	◐

- Denotes insufficient sample size. [1] Merged with HP; purchasers are redirected to the HP Web site.

Guide to the Ratings

Based on 43,384 responses to our online 2004 Annual Questionnaire covering household desktop computers bought new in 2003 and the first half of 2004. In the **RETAIL STORE** category, we counted only in-store purchases, not those made on retailers' Web sites. Differences of 4 points or more in READER SCORE are meaningful. (**READER SCORE** reflects readers' assessment of the overall experience of buying computers. A SCORE OF 100 would mean all respondents had been completely satisfied with their experience; 80 means very satisfied on average; 60 means fairly well satisfied.) **HELP** tracks the salesperson's helpfulness. **SAVVY** gives judgments of the sales staff's knowledge. **SELECTION** reflects opinions of the range of products offered. **PRICES** reflects how competitive readers found prices to be.

01 | WHERE TO BUY

If you want a flat-panel LCD monitor, make sure it (and not an old-style CRT) is part of the package.

Weighing the odds of repair

Product	Repair rate (%)
Desktop PC	37%
Laptop PC	33%
Projection TV	16%
Camcorder	8%
Digital Camera	8%
TV: 30- to 36-inch	7%
TV: 25- to 27-inch	5%

Source: Consumer Reports 2004 Annual Questionnaire, based on three-year-old products

IF YOU CUSTOMIZE:
• Buy directly from the manufacturer. Retail Web site/mail-order operations in our Ratings scored well as a whole, but they don't customize the brand-name computers in our Ratings. Several brick-and-mortar retailers do let you customize but didn't rate as well overall as manufacturers. We can't say whether customer satisfaction with manufacturers extends to direct-sell kiosks, which makers like Dell and Hewlett-Packard have in some retail locations.
• Unbundle. Even computers that you configure yourself may come with a cheap monitor. If you already have a monitor, you may save by not taking the new one. On the day we shopped the Dell site, eliminating the monitor saved about $40.
• Track prices. They bounce around, as promotional offers come and go. For example, we compared identically configured models from Dell; the same model that cost $1,736 one month was just $1,299 two months later. Two days later, however, the price rose to $1,325.

IF YOU BUY OFF THE SHELF:
• Decide which features you want so you can hunt for packages that approximate your needs.
• Use a shopping bot. Both Shopping.com and Bizrate.com allow you to compare prices at stores and Web sites. We shopped for a preconfigured HP computer on Shopping.com and found prices that ranged from $785 to $900.
 The shopping bots also calculate tax and shipping costs, which in our case ranged from zero to $88.
• When prices are close, consider a retailer on other important attributes.

Extended warranties aren't worth the cost—with possible exceptions

On the way to the check-out counter, you have no doubt been waylaid by a sales clerk extolling the benefits of buying an extended warranty. An extended warranty kicks in after the manufacturer's warranty runs out. The insurer pays to repair or replace the item for a specified period of time, usually two to five years from the date of purchase. (Some start on the date of purchase, even though the manufacturer's warranty is also in effect.)

A variation, the replacement plan, is usually offered on less expensive merchandise and promises to give you a new or rebuilt product (or store credit) if the unit you bought conks out while the plan is in effect.

Once offered on costly appliances, extended warranties have trickled down to just about everything on the shelves. For retailers, that makes perfect sense. When profit margins on the products themselves are being squeezed, extended warranties yield 40 to 80 percent profit, according to industry sources. But if these extended plans are a cash cow, just who's getting milked?

You may already know the answer. For years, CONSUMER REPORTS has cautioned against buying this costly coverage. Survey data from thousands of readers have shown that, generally, extended warranties cost not much less than the average repair. That's if you need a repair at all. As you can see in the box above, many electronics products are unlikely to need repairs within the first three years.

When it comes to plasma and liquid-crystal display (LCD) TVs, however, the decision is more difficult. Preliminary data from our user surveys show no unusual rate of repair for flat screen plasma and LCD TVs in the first year, but long-term reliability is still unknown.

Before you say yes to an extended warranty on any product, see whether your credit card provides similar coverage. Such plans, most often found on gold and platinum cards, typically lengthen the original manufacturer's warranty by up to one year. If you use a MasterCard, look in the fine print for the words "extended warranty." Visa calls its program Warranty Manager Service.

YOUR NETWORKED HOME

INSIDE INFO

14 Wired and wireless can work in tandem

15 Ratings of home-networking choices

16 Making Wi-Fi work better

CHAPTER 02

If you have broadband Internet service and more than one computer in your home, there's a good reason to link them to create a home network. A network allows a single broadband account to be shared throughout the home. Alas, such networking is impractical with dial-up Internet service—one of several reasons to consider broadband.

Home networking is also getting a boost from improvements in the range, speed, and cost of wireless networks. Linked to a laptop computer that has wireless capability, a wireless network now allows you to browse the Web at broadband speeds from virtually anywhere in your home or yard.

If you are considering networking your computers, this chapter will help you decide whether a wired Ethernet connection or a wireless Wi-Fi connection—or both—is the way to go.

 It's easier than ever to link up all your home-computer gear.

02 INSIDE INFO YOUR NETWORKED HOME

WIRED AND WIRELESS CAN WORK IN TANDEM

A hybrid system may be your simplest and cheapest solution.

Wireless technology may be all the rage, but wired networking is far from obsolete, since it still provides the most secure and reliable connections. Indeed, for many households the best solution for sharing a broadband connection—or a printer, music files, or digital photos—among multiple computers may be a network that includes both wired and wireless.

Such hybrids are easier and cheaper to assemble than they used to be. Routers, the boxes that connect computers and other equipment to the Internet, increasingly support both Ethernet, the primary technology used in wired networks, and Wi-Fi, its wireless counterpart. They typically cost less than $100.

HOW TO CHOOSE
Home-networking equipment has reached a consistently high standard. We tested more than 35 home-networking devices and found little difference in price and performance among them. You can safely assemble a network by choosing gear of the type and technology you need.

Plan your network. You'll probably want to locate the router near the source of your broadband service—usually a cable or DSL modem. The router and the modem will be connected by Ethernet wires. But the connections between the router and the computers in the network may be either wired or wireless. See First Things First, below, for guidance on deciding which connection to choose for each computer.

Select a wireless router. Most models support both Ethernet and Wi-Fi. Leading brands include D-Link, Netgear, and

First Things First

For each computer, decide on a wired or a wireless connection to the network. Here are the considerations to weigh as you make your choice between a wired Ethernet and a wireless Wi-Fi connection for each of the computers in your network. (There is a third networking technology, a wired option known as HomePlug, but its high cost and low speed make it the networking technology of last resort, as we explain in CR Quick Recommendations, page 15.)

1 Ethernet (wired)

Advantages Very secure; no special security measures necessary. Most reliable; not subject to interference. Fastest data transfer—up to 93 megabits per second, enough for virtually any data application.
Disadvantages Doesn't allow you to easily move your computer around the home. Routing cables throughout home can be a hassle or expensive.
Cost $100 or less for one router and a cable to connect two fairly new computers. Also, possible costs for routing cable through the home.
Best choice for desktops near an Internet connection or computers swapping large files, including video.

2 Wi-Fi (wireless)

Advantages No cables to connect or route. Minimal installation costs. Unrivaled mobility—supplies signals virtually anywhere around the home.
Disadvantages Security requires additional steps, without which your data are vulnerable to hackers. Thick walls can reduce the signal level. Subject to interference from cordless phones, baby monitors, and other wireless devices on the same frequency band (2.4 GHz). Only 20 percent as fast as Ethernet but still fine for typical networking uses.
Cost $150 or less for a router and client cards to allow two computers to use the network wirelessly (to connect additional computers, $50 to $60 each).
Best choice for the mobility and versatility demanded by laptop users. Also a good choice for desktops at opposite ends of the home.

INSIDE INFO YOUR NETWORKED HOME

Linksys. Even if you don't need wireless capability now, acquiring it costs little extra (perhaps $10 or so) compared with a wired or wireless model and might spare your having to replace the router if you want to add a wireless device to it in the future.

Choose the 802.11g wireless standard. Wi-Fi is continually evolving, with new standards designed to increase broadcast range and speed, thus increasing the network's ability to handle more demanding applications.

The name of the standard is usually listed on the router's package, as a letter suffix to the technical term for Wi-Fi, which is 802.11. Currently the most common standard is known as 802.11g. We think it's the best choice for most people.

The 802.11g networks we tested all had sufficient range and speed to provide coverage throughout most homes. The data speeds we measured fell short of the standard speed for 802.11g, as shown on the boxes. But all routers were at least as fast as the typical speed of a broadband Internet connection.

If you already have a wireless network that uses 802.11a or 802.11b, two older standards, consider upgrading only if you find the range, speed, or reliability of your network wanting.

At the other end of the standards spectrum are routers that use early variants of the latest Wi-Fi standard, 802.11n. They are frequently referred to with terms such as "MIMO," "SuperG," or "Pre-N." While those models may seem to offer insurance against obsolescence, quite the opposite may be the case, since there's no guarantee that they will be compatible with the actual "n" standard, which is due in 2006.

Consider one of these new routers only if you now need to frequently transfer large files or have range problems that can't be solved in other ways. In our tests, they were better at penetrating walls than 802.11g routers, and some offered data speeds that were twice as fast. But they were just as vulnerable to interference from cordless phones and other devices.

Weigh whether and how you'll share a printer. A network lets you avoid the cost of putting a printer in every room by sharing one. To do this, you can use a printer with built-in network capability. Networked laser print-

CR Quick Recommendations

Under the best of conditions, all three home-networking technologies provide adequate speed, reliability, and security for sharing a broadband Internet connection. But most people should set aside HomePlug as a networking technology. HomePlug's main advantage is that it can be used in any room with an electrical outlet, making it useful in some places that Wi-Fi may not reach. But that advantage is offset by its high price and low speed. We found it too slow for transmitting standard-definition video and sluggish when displaying digital-photo slide shows or copying large files from one computer to another.

When deciding how to connect each computer on your network, most should apply this rule of thumb: Use Ethernet where possible and Wi-Fi where necessary. Ethernet is best suited for computers that you'll never need to move, so you'll probably use it for a desktop computer located next to or near the router. It provides the fastest, most secure, and most reliable connections for the lowest cost. Installation is usually simple. But running Ethernet cable to some parts of the house can be difficult and expensive.

Wi-Fi offers the greatest mobility, making it ideal for laptops, and is the easiest way to provide access to a hard-to-reach part of the home. But you'll need to take extra steps to ensure security (see What You Can Do, next page). Despite your best efforts, you'll also have to live with occasional interference from other devices or even the odd lost connection.

Ratings

Excellent ● Very good ◑ Good ○ Fair ◐ Poor ●

Listed in order of data-transfer speed.

System	Price		Test results						Comments
	Router	Adapter	Speed	Setup	Equipment installation	Mobility	Reliability	Security	
Ethernet (wired)	$50-$60	$20-$25	●	●	◑	●	●	●	Best for reliability and speed.
Wi-Fi 802.11g (wireless)	60-70	50-60	◑	○	◑	●	○	◑	Best for mobility and versatility.
HomePlug (power line)	110-150[1]	60-90	◐	◑	◑	◐	◑	◑	Slowest and costliest.

[1] Includes router plus powerline adapter—a required additional component.

Guide to the Ratings

ROUTER refers to the typical hardware cost for this component. **ADAPTER** reflects the cost of this add-on card, needed for each computer that doesn't have built-in support that's being added to the network (most newer computers do not need a network adapter). For HomePlug, price is for a bridge. **SPEED** rates the network's data transfer speed—important when moving large files or streaming video from one device to another. **SETUP** rates the ease of setting up and maintaining the network using included software and instructions. **EQUIPMENT INSTALLATION** rates the ease of connecting network hardware. **MOBILITY** rates the freedom to move devices and maintain a connection to the network. **RELIABILITY** rates the overall integrity of the network connection. **SECURITY** rates the effort needed to protect network data, as well as the effectiveness of that protection. For Wi-Fi, the score assumes the activation of WPA security, the best protection.

02 INSIDE INFO YOUR NETWORKED HOME

Close up

Making Wi-Fi work better

Today's Wi-Fi networks perform much better and are easier to set up than in the past, but interference and dropped connections still come with the territory. Here are some tips for eliminating annoying interruptions—or at least reducing their frequency:

Rotate the antennas. Sometimes even a slight nudge to a router or network adapter can make a noticeable improvement in signal strength.

Stay up to date. Make sure network adapter drivers and router firmware are the latest versions. Often manufacturers add new features that address performance issues (consult your owner's manual for step-by-step instructions).

Find better locations. Move the computer and/or router. Keep the distances between your computers and router as short as possible. If you can, avoid such obstructions as thick walls, floors, and large metal objects.

Minimize interference. Cordless devices like phones and baby monitors may broadcast on the same 2.4 GHz range as Wi-Fi. Buy ones that use other ranges, such as 900 MHz or 5.8 GHz. Some 2.4 GHz phones are 802.11-friendly and are less likely to interfere.

Change the channel. If your cordless phone or baby monitor interferes with your network, change its channels. If that doesn't work, change the router's channel.

Extend your range. You can do it two ways: Replace one of the router's antennas with a high-gain antenna. Or place an extender between the router and computer. An extender acts as a middleman, relaying Wi-Fi signals to extend network range.

ers start roughly $50 more than regular models; network-ready color inkjets start at about $130.

It's possible to share a non-networked printer by attaching it to the network via a print server, a device that costs $70 to $100 and is the size of a large paperback. But when we tested two of them, they sometimes interfered with the printer software. Any PC connected to a printer can also serve as a print server for the other computers on the network, though you must leave that computer on when you're printing.

Consider networking issues for other devices. An increasing number of devices that typically connect to a single computer—PDAs, printers, and video-game consoles—are now Wi-Fi compatible. If you plan to connect any of them to your network, make sure they're compatible with the network security you set up (see "What You Can Do," below).

Check whether your computers need adapters. Every computer on your network will require an adapter to allow it to communicate with the network. If you're using Ethernet to connect a computer bought within the past three years or so, the adapter will most likely be built into the unit. The same applies to recent-vintage laptops with a Wi-Fi connection.

If you need to buy an adapter for your desktop, you can choose an internal PCI-card version, which requires opening the computer case for installation, or a USB version, which plugs into a USB port. Laptops can use either a PCI-card or USB adapter. In all cases, the cost should be no more than $60.

Skip professional installation help. Computer retailers may try to sell you on professional installation for your new network, starting at a cost of $150 or so. But wiring aside, today's networks are so easy to set up that you shouldn't take them up on their offer if you're comfortable with technology.

Network gear comes with instructions and access to free 24/7 technical support. And you always have the option of coming back to the retailer to help you troubleshoot the network if necessary.

What You Can Do

Protecting your wireless connection against computer hackers

Wi-Fi's greatest strength is also its weakness. Virtually every network action you take, whether downloading Web pages or printing files, is broadcast a few hundred feet in every direction. In closely spaced homes or apartment buildings, that can be a serious security problem. The most common consequence of using an unsecured wireless network is that a neighbor encroaches upon your broadband connection to surf the Web or send e-mail. That may sound harmless, but it's not if the poacher engages in illegal activities or hogs your bandwidth. A hacker might go further by stealing personal information right off your hard drive or turning your computer into a high-speed spamming machine. Here are the steps for setting up protection of your wireless network:

Activate encryption. Encryption makes all wireless communications look like gibberish to outsiders. No encryption is 100 percent safe. But a technology called Wi-Fi Protected Access (WPA) offers the best protection against hackers. Another, Wired Equivalent Privacy (WEP), will prevent most neighbors from using your connection. But it won't stop even a novice hacker. Make sure your network personal ID and password are hacker resistant: They should each be at least 10 characters long and include both letters and digits.

Change your router's default password. All routers protect their system settings and other controls with factory-set user names and passwords. Since most hackers know them, you must change them at the same time you set up your network.

Disguise your network. Wi-Fi networks continually broadcast a signal called a security set identifier (SSID) so that any Wi-Fi-equipped computer can find them when it comes within range. You should change the default, factory-assigned SSID, which gives away more details about your network than it should. Make sure the one you choose is not based on a password or other personal information. You can also prevent hackers from seeing your network by disabling SSID broadcast. But that will also make it harder for you to set up your network.

Create a computer "guest list." MAC (Media Access Control) filtering is a network protection scheme that takes a different approach. Instead of making communications hard to decipher, you tell the network to pay attention to just the devices you identify. Identification consists of obtaining and entering into your router the unique code built into every Wi-Fi-enabled computer, PDA, or other device you want to network.

DIGITAL CAMERAS & CAMCORDERS

INSIDE INFO
- **18** Match the camera to how you'll use it
- **19** Enhancing photos is easier than ever
- **20** Flatbed scanners digitize film photos
- **21** Printing your pics
- **22** Digital camcorders

BUYING ADVICE
- **23** Digital cameras
- **26** Scanners
- **27** Camcorders

CHAPTER **03**

Now that digital photography has moved from gee-whiz innovation into the mainstream, you have an unprecedented range of options for shooting, altering, and printing your images. You can exert as much, or as little, control over the photos and printing as you wish. Digital cameras offer point-and-shoot simplicity, and many allow you to set shutter speed, exposure, and the like when you'd prefer to be more in charge. When you want prints, you can go online, head to the neighborhood pharmacy, or stay home and use your own printer.

You can expect very good—sometimes excellent—results no matter what set of options you choose. The trick comes in knowing which options best fit with your level of interest in photography and your priorities. This chapter shows how to find the best digital camera or camcorder for your needs. It also takes a look at scanners, an increasingly inexpensive option for bringing your favorite old photos into the digital age.

▶▶ **Smart ways to get the results you want from the latest still and video cameras and accessories.**

Ratings: Camcorders, p. 129; digital cameras, p. 136; scanners, p. 164

03 | INSIDE INFO DIGITAL CAMERAS & CAMCORDERS

MATCH THE CAMERA TO HOW YOU'LL USE IT

First consider what you shoot and how big you print.

Digital camera makers brag about megapixels the way car makers once did about horsepower. But just as you don't need a Ferrari for your Saturday grocery run, you may not want an overpowered digital camera for your family snapshots. Not only will it be needlessly expensive, but the large image files it creates will hog considerably more storage space, and so fill the camera's storage space more rapidly.

So the first question to ask yourself is how you plan to use the camera.

First Things First

Canon

1. If you're a casual photographer who shoots strictly snapshots, look for a camera with:

- 3 to 4 megapixels
- Settings for specific types of scenes (sunsets, for example)
- AA-battery power
- Cradle to easily upload photos to computer
- PictBridge capability for printing without a computer

Extras you might need:
- 128-MB or greater memory card
- Memory-card reader
- 4x6 photo printer
- Rechargeable AAs and charger

Expect to spend $250 or less.

Kodak

2. If you're a more serious photographer who likes to get creative, look for a camera with:

- 3 to 6 megapixels
- Settings for specific types of scenes (sunsets, for example)
- AA-battery power
- Zoom range of 4x or greater
- Some manual controls
- Continuous frames to help capture fast action
- PictBridge capability for printing without a computer

Extras you might need:
- 256-MB or greater memory card
- Memory-card reader
- Basic editing software
- Inexpensive photo printer
- Rechargeable AAs and charger

Expect to spend $250 to $800.

Fujifilm

3. If you're an advanced photographer who considers photography a passion, look for a camera with:

- 6 to 8 megapixels
- Zoom range of 4x or greater
- Image stabilizer
- Full manual controls
- ISO (light sensitivity) of 800 or higher to capture fast motion
- Metering modes for tricky lighting situations

Extras you might need:
- 512-MB or greater memory card
- Memory-card reader
- Spare battery and charger
- Full-featured editing software
- Lens hood, tripod
- Top-of-the-line photo printer

Expect to spend $250 to $800.

▶▶ For more detailed buying advice on digital cameras, see page 23.

INSIDE INFO DIGITAL CAMERAS & CAMCORDERS

Talk the Talk

Digital cameras have their own special terminology. Here's a brief guide to some of the terms you'll encounter:

Burst mode. Allows you to take multiple rapid-fire shots with one touch of the shutter button.

Compression. What the camera does to make an image file smaller, hence faster to download or send via e-mail. Many cameras let you choose the level of compression, often with abbreviations such as HQ (high quality, or highly compressed) and SHQ (super high quality, or lightly compressed).

ISO-equivalent speed. The higher the ISO number, the more light-sensitive the camera will be.

Megapixels. The number of picture elements (pixels) the image sensor has. A megapixel equals 1 million pixels.

Memory card. The digital equivalent of a roll of film. A card that can hold 128 megabytes (MB) of data is the minimum practical size these days.

Resolution. The amount of detail the image contains. Resolution of 2 megapixels provides enough detail for 4x6 prints or full-frame enlargements; 8-megapixel resolution provides four times as much detail, allowing you to make sharp enlargements of only a portion of the original image.

ENHANCING PHOTOS IS EASIER THAN EVER

Free software can help you make your pictures perfect.

Most digital cameras no longer come with full photo-editing software. At best, you get an application for transferring images to your computer. But you can still find no-cost tools to help you crop, correct color, brighten, and sharpen images—the kind of editing that many people want to do to improve the photos they take. In fact, you could already have the tools you need on your computer's hard drive or even in your camera.

If all you want are 4x6 snapshots, you may be able to make any necessary adjustments right in the camera, without editing software. A few cameras can remove red eye, crop images at the edges, or rotate a picture from portrait (vertical) to landscape (horizontal).

The camera alone can't usually correct exposure or color balance. But if you have photo-editing software that came with an older camera, that's all you need for routine fix-ups. If not, try these options:

For serious editing, start with free software. The first choice for Windows users should be a free download called IrfanView (*www.irfanview.com*). IrfanView isn't available for Macintosh. For Mac users, the iPhoto program supplied free with new Macs is a good alternative.

IrfanView has an easy-to-use interface and many useful features, including one that corrects the color balance of photos shot in artificial or dim light, and another that adjusts brightness and contrast. IrfanView can resize files, needed for e-mailing or posting them to the Internet. But IrfanView lacks some advanced features and the panoply of touch-up tools that commercial software offers. And don't expect much technical support.

For advanced uses, buy an editing program. Consider Adobe Photoshop Elements or Corel Paint Shop Pro 9, two widely used, moderately priced editing packages that have done well in our tests. Photoshop Elements sells for $80 to $100 and works with Windows and Macintosh. Paint Shop Pro works with Windows only and sells for about $100. Both have features unavailable in a download such as IrfanView. The "fill flash" tool, for example, brightens areas of an image. Other features include sharpening or editing selected portions of an image, 16-bit color depth to render a wider range of colors, and the ability to process RAW files, which are images stored as the camera's sensors captured them.

You computer may already have all the photo editing tools you need.

03 | INSIDE INFO DIGITAL CAMERAS & CAMCORDERS

FLATBED SCANNERS DIGITIZE FILM PHOTOS

New scanners offer higher resolution and more versatility.

Flatbed scanners are no longer restricted to making digital copies of printed originals. Our tests show that the best flatbeds are now a match for pricey film scanners when it comes to digitizing slides and negatives.

No small accomplishment, this trend reflects improvements to the resolution that new scanners deliver plus better accessories to hold film strips or slides securely for sharp, accurate scans.

Flatbed scanners are for people whose needs are broader than just photos; they can handle 8½x11-inch originals—text documents, original artwork, and the like—as well as transparent material of various sizes. They sell for $200 or less.

Most film scanners, as their name implies, can handle only 35mm negatives or slides. The more-capable units sell for $400 or more and are best for people with very specific needs.

▶▶ For detailed buying advice on scanners, see page 26.

Flatbeds scanner can handle text and artwork in addition to photos.

The greater the resolution of your scanner, the greater the cost.

Getting the most from your scanner's capabilities

Flatbed scanners have three to eight buttons that can automate routine tasks such as faxing or e-mailing an image. To make use of the scanner's full capabilities, however, plan to bypass the buttons and work with the scan-utility software that comes with every unit. When you install the software, you designate a program where scanned images will be routed for editing and storage. The destination program can be one supplied with the scanner or another, such as Adobe Photoshop. Once the scanner is running, you can access its settings either through the scan utility or from the program with which you'll view or edit the scanned image.

The software for some scanners will initially display only those features aimed at basic users. For more-refined tools, choose "advanced" settings from the onscreen menus. These let you change resolution, reduce defects from dust and scratches, correct faded originals, or adjust the brightness and contrast of the scanned image.

For the most control, bypass the buttons (left) and use the software (right).

20 CONSUMER REPORTS ● ELECTRONICS BUYING GUIDE 2006   Expert • Independent • Nonprofit

INSIDE INFO DIGITAL CAMERAS & CAMCORDERS

PRINTING YOUR PICS

You can do it yourself, farm it out to a professional lab, or both.

Making prints of your digital photos is easier than ever. The hardest part may be deciding which of the several methods you should use. This isn't an all-or-nothing decision, of course. You'll probably want to use some combination of these services, depending on such factors as whether you plan to edit your images and how quickly you need your prints.

PRINTING AT HOME

By producing your own prints, you'll have maximum control over how your pictures look. However, the process can be time-consuming, and it isn't always your cheapest option. Expect to pay about 20 to 60 cents per 4x6 print.

For printing snapshots at home, a speedy 4x6 snapshot printer is more convenient, but less versatile, than a full-sized inkjet model. Like a growing number of full-sized printers, many of these 4x6 printers can hook up directly via cable to a digital camera through the PictBridge connection. This is the simplest and quickest way to print at home, provided you don't want to edit the photos beforehand.

▶▶ Printers are covered in Chapter 5 of this book, on page 57.

USING AN IN-STORE PHOTOFINISHER

Retail photofinishing has made a fast, successful transition from film to digital. You can have prints made at pharmacy chains as well as big-box retailers such as Target and Wal-Mart. At most stores with a photofinishing department, you can use a stand-alone kiosk to make prints on the spot, having them dispensed like fresh twenties at an ATM. Or, often using a different kiosk nearby, you can send images to the store's minilab, which will produce prints in about an hour or two.

The main difference is in the way prints are made. Stand-alone

We found a number of in-store kiosks that did a good job with photos.

kiosks generate dye-sublimation prints, using the same process as most home snapshot printers. The minilabs use a chemical process that's akin to film printing. Either way, expect to pay 17 to 39 cents per 4x6 print.

We asked staff members of Consumers Union, publisher of CONSUMER REPORTS, in 15 cities to try in-store photofinishing to help us better understand what you can expect. Our staffers obtained higher-quality photos and the most consistent results at Costco, Ritz, Walgreens, and Wal-Mart, where they could use a Fuji kiosk tied to the store's minilab. Prints from stand-alone Fuji kiosks weren't as good. Kodak equipment produced results that varied considerably. Kodak has announced, however, that it will be converting its store kiosks to use its Perfect Touch processing and paper, which it already uses for its Picture Center online photofinishing services. In our tests of a dozen online photofinishing sites, Perfect Touch processing consistently delivered very good prints.

USING AN ONLINE LAB

The first question to ask yourself before choosing an Internet photofinisher is how quickly you want your photos back. Stand-alone photofinishing sites such as Shutterfly or EZ Prints will mail your prints. Processing typically takes one to three days;

03 INSIDE INFO DIGITAL CAMERAS & CAMCORDERS

shipping can add three days or more. (As with ordering almost anything on line, the faster you want delivery, the more you'll have to pay for it.) Those sites also let you store photos free so that friends and family can view them. If you aren't in a rush for prints but want to share images, consider a stand-alone site.

A faster option is to upload your photos to a Web site such as Wal-Mart's or Kodak's EasyShare Gallery and then pick up your prints at a nearby store. This service isn't available everywhere, and the site may limit the size of prints you can order this way.

Online services work best if you have a high-speed Internet connection. Uploading photos on a dial-up connection is possible, but painfully slow. Most online services also offer some editing tools, but they're fairly rudimentary. Expect to pay 17 to 39 cents per 4x6 print, plus shipping.

DIGITAL CAMCORDERS

Today's models pack higher quality in smaller packages.

Nearly all the camcorders on the market today are digital. Only a few older analog models remain. Digital dominates because it delivers consistent picture quality—no falloff at slow taping speed—and a wealth of options. With digital, you can record on tapes, discs, or memory cards. A growing number of camcorders can also take snapshots, although they don't yet achieve the image quality of 4- to 5-megapixel cameras.

In our tests, we've found that MiniDV camcorders offer the best combination of price and performance. If you're replacing an older camcorder, you'll find some features that weren't around a few years ago. Most models are probably smaller than your old one; some are downright tiny. Image stabilization is practically universal and can take some of the "shakes" out of handheld shots. Digital zoom ranges approach stratospheric levels. Many models tell you approximately how many minutes of shooting are left in the battery.

▶▶ For more detailed buying advice on camcorders, see page 27.

Look for an LCD viewer that's big enough and free from glare.

Three ways to keep your home videos playable for years to come

Maybe you bought your original camcorder so you could record your children's first steps and first words. The kids now have their learner's permits, and the old camcorder has played its last tape. What can you do to preserve those old videos?

Tape won't last forever, even with proper archival care. DVDs are considered inherently more stable. And as tape wanes and the machines to play it disappear, DVD will be the only playback option. If you want to transfer tapes to disks, these are your choices:

Make your own DVD copies. With the right hardware and cables to connect everything, you can transfer old videos to DVD. You'll need a DVD recorder (see page 84) or a computer with a DVD-R/RW or DVD+R/RW drive. (The -R and +R formats play on most other recorders and players.)

Archive as you go. If you have a digital camcorder and a reasonably new computer equipped with video-editing software and a DVD burner, you can back up each new tape to a DVD.

Pay for the service. There are hundreds of services nationwide that will transfer tape to DVD. Local camera stores or photofinishing outlets may handle the work (check the phone book); you can also find mail-order services via the Internet. Prices we've seen range from $18.95 to $39.50 and more (depending on what extras you want) for a 60-minute tape. The biggest risk of using a service: The original tape could be lost, damaged, or erased before the copy is made.

To guard against mishaps, make a backup tape first and think twice before entrusting original tapes to an unknown company.

Whether they're originals or duplicates, store all home videos properly to make sure they last. Avoid dust and extremes of temperature and humidity. Keep the tapes or disks in their cases so they don't get damaged. If you really want to be thorough, our experts recommend keeping duplicate disks. As future technologies emerge, consider upgrading to the newest format.

BUYING ADVICE DIGITAL CAMERAS

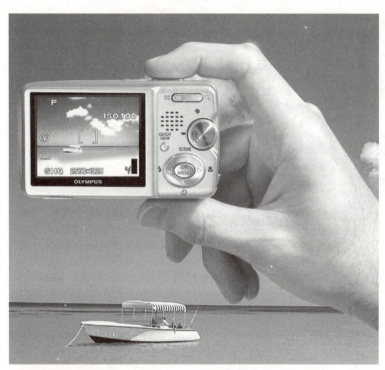

An LCD viewfinder will frame photos accurately but may be tough to see in sunlight.

BUYING ADVICE
Digital cameras

▶ Digital photography allows you to be more easily involved in the creation of the print than film photography.

Digital cameras, which employ reusable memory cards instead of film, give you far easier creative control than film cameras can. With a digital camera, you can transfer shots to your computer, then crop, adjust color and contrast, and add textures and other special effects. Final results can be made into cards or T-shirts, or sent via e-mail, all using the software that usually comes with the camera. You can make prints on a color inkjet printer, or by dropping off the memory card at one of a growing number of photofinishers. You can upload the file to a photo-sharing Web site for storage, viewing, and sharing with others.

Like camcorders, digital cameras have LCD viewers. Some camcorders can be used to take still pictures, but a typical camcorder's resolution is no match for a good still camera's.

WHAT'S AVAILABLE

The leading brands are Canon, Fujifilm, HP, Kodak, Olympus, and Sony; other brands come from consumer-electronics, computer, and traditional camera and film companies.

Digital cameras are categorized by how many pixels, or picture elements, the image sensor contains. One megapixel equals 1 million picture elements. A 3-megapixel camera can make excellent 8x10s and pleasing 11x14s. There are also 4- to 8-megapixel models, including point-and-shoot ones; these are well-suited for making larger prints or for maintaining sharpness if you want to use only a portion of the original image. Professional digital cameras use as many as 14 megapixels. **Price range:** $200 to $400 for 3 megapixels; $250 to $400 for 4 and 5 megapixels; $300 to $1,000 for 6 to 8 megapixels.

FEATURES THAT COUNT

Most digital cameras are highly automated, with features such as **automatic exposure control** (which manages the shutter speed, aperture, or both according to available light) and **autofocus**.

Instead of film, digital cameras typically record their shots onto **flash-memory cards**. Compact Flash and SecureDigital (SD) are the most widely used. Once quite expensive, such cards have tumbled in price—a 128-megabyte card can now cost less than $20. Other types of memory cards used by cameras include MemoryStick, SmartMedia and xD-picture card. A few cameras, mainly some Sony models, use 3¼-inch CD-R or CD-RW discs.

To save images, you transfer them to a computer, typically by connecting the camera to the computer's USB or FireWire port or inserting the memory card into a special reader. Some printers can take memory cards and make prints without putting the images on a computer first. **Image-handling software**, such as Adobe Photoshop Elements, Jasc Paint Shop, Microsoft Picture It, and ACDSee, lets you size, touch up, and crop digital images using your computer. Most digital cameras work with both Windows and Macintosh machines.

Small isn't all. Roughly the size of a credit card and less than an inch thick, the smallest digital cameras are marvels of miniaturization but may feel awkward to hold. Medium-sized models are often easier to handle.

03 BUYING ADVICE DIGITAL CAMERAS

Point-and-shoot cameras often have short zoom lenses.

The file format commonly used for photos is JPEG, which is a compressed format. Some cameras can save photos in the uncompressed TIFF format, but this setting yields enormous files. Other high-end cameras have a RAW file format, which yields the image data with no processing from the camera and is also uncompressed.

Digital cameras typically have both an **optical viewfinder** and a **small color LCD viewer**. LCD viewers are very accurate in framing the actual image you get—better than most of the optical viewfinders—but they use more battery power and may be hard to see in bright sunlight. You can also view shots you've already taken on the LCD viewer. Many digital cameras provide a video output, so you can view your pictures on a TV set.

Certain cameras let you record an audio clip with a picture. But these clips use additional storage space. Some allow you to record limited video, but the frame rate is often slow and the resolution poor.

A **zoom lens** provides flexibility in framing shots and closes the distance between you and your subject—ideal if you want to quickly switch to a close shot. The typical 3x zoom on mainstream cameras goes from a moderately wide-angle view (35 mm) to moderate telephoto (105 mm). You can find cameras with extended zoom ranges between 8x and 12x, giving added versatility for outdoor photography. Other new cameras go down to 24 or 28 mm at the wide-angle end, making it easier to take in an entire scene in close quarters, such as a crowded party.

Optical zooms are superior to **digital zooms**, which merely magnify the center of the frame without actually increasing picture detail, resulting in a somewhat coarser view.

Sensors in digital cameras are typically about as light-sensitive as ISO 100 film, though some let you increase that setting. (At ISO 100, you'll likely need to use a flash indoors and in low outdoor light.) A camera's **flash range** tells you how far from the camera the flash will provide proper exposure: If the subject is out of range, you'll know to close the distance. But digital cameras can tolerate some underexposure before the image suffers noticeably.

Red-eye reduction shines a light toward your subject just before the main flash. (A camera whose flash unit is farther from the lens reduces the risk of red eye. Computer editing of the image may also correct red eye.) With **automatic flash mode**, the camera fires the flash whenever the light entering the camera registers as insufficient. A few new cameras have built-in red-eye correction capability.

Some cameras that have powerful telephoto lenses now come with **image stabilizers**. These compensate for camera shake, letting you use a slower shutter speed than you otherwise could for following movement. But an image stabilizer won't compensate for the motion of subjects.

Testing reflexes: What $800 to $900 will buy

If you're in the market for a high-end digital camera, you have a choice between point-and-shoot models and an entry-level digital single-lens reflex (SLR) camera. Expect to pay between $800 and $900, whichever you opt for. Here's how the two types compare:

Digital reflexes look a lot like their film counterparts and often accept the same lenses.

Image quality. You can expect any camera in the 6- to 8-megapixel range to deliver excellent image quality at light-sensitivity settings up to ISO 200. But the SLRs can deliver even at ISO 1,600, a setting that makes them very light-sensitive.

Lenses. SLRs accept a range of lenses. Point-and-shoots don't. Choose an SLR if you need the versatility of interchangeable lenses. If you have an old film SLR camera, you may be able to use its lenses on a digital. If not, expect to pay $200 and up for a high-quality, name-brand lens.

Weight. SLRs are heavier and bulkier than even the biggest point-and-shoot.

Settings. SLRs can be set to full automatic mode, but they are really meant for people who like to choose their own shutter speed, lens opening, ISO speed, and more. Novices may find them daunting.

Shot delay. SLRs have essentially no delay. With point-and-shoots, you can expect a delay of at least 1 to 2 seconds.

BUYING ADVICE DIGITAL CAMERAS

Most new 6- to 8-megapixel cameras come with full **manual controls**, including independent controls for shutter and aperture. That gives serious shutterbugs control over depth of field, shooting action, or shooting scenes with tricky lighting.

HOW TO CHOOSE

The first step is to determine how you will use the camera most of the time. Consider these two questions:

How much flexibility to enlarge images do you need? If you mainly want to make 4x6 snapshots, a camera with 3- or 4-megapixel resolution will be fine. Such a camera will also make an 8x10 print of an entire image without alteration that looks as sharp as one from a 6- or 8-megapixel model. But to enlarge the image more or enlarge only part of it, you'll want a 6- to 8-megapixel camera.

How much control do you want over exposure and composition? Cameras meant for automatic point-and-shoot photos, with a 3x-zoom lens, will serve snapshooters as well as dedicated hobbyists much of the time. The full-featured cameras in the 6- to 8-megapixel range offer capabilities that more-dedicated photographers will want to have. Two of the more important capabilities are a zoom range of 5x to 10x or more, which lets you bring distant outdoor subjects close and also lets you shoot candid portraits without getting right in your subject's face, and a full complement of manual controls that let you determine the shutter speed and lens opening.

Once you've established the performance priorities that you need from a camera, you can narrow your choices further by considering these convenience factors:

SMALL
Canon SD300

COMPACT
HP Photosmart M307

MEDIUM
Canon A95

LARGE
Olympus C-7070

Size and weight. The smallest, lightest models aren't necessarily inexpensive 3-megapixel cameras. And the biggest and heaviest aren't necessarily found at the high end. If possible, try cameras at the store before you buy. That way, you'll know which one fits your hand best and which can be securely gripped. In our tests, we have found that some of the smallest don't leave much room even for small fingers.

Battery type and life. All digital cameras run on rechargeable batteries, either an expensive battery pack or a set of AAs. In our tests, neither type had a clear performance advantage. The best-performing cameras offer upward of 300 shots on a charge, while the worst manage only about 50. We think it's more convenient to own a camera that accepts AA batteries. You can buy economical, rechargeable cells (plus a charger) and drop in a set of disposable lithium or alkaline batteries if the rechargeables run down in the middle of the day's shooting.

Camera speed. With point-and-shoot cameras like the ones we tested, you must wait after each shot as the camera processes the image. Most models let you shoot an image every few seconds, but a few make you wait 5 seconds or more. They may frustrate you when you're taking photos in sequence.

Your other cameras. If you're adding a camera to your lineup or trading up to a more versatile model, look first for one that's compatible with the other cameras. If it is, you can share memory cards and batteries. Designs within a camera brand line are often similar. So staying with the brand you have lowers the learning curve on the new camera for family members who switch between cameras.

> **Did You Know?**
> Digital camera makers may advertise two types of zoom: optical and digital. When shopping, focus on a camera's optical zoom. Digital zoom is a feature that's of very little use.

03 BUYING ADVICE SCANNERS

Flatbed scanners can also convert printed pages into files for word processing.

For digitizing negatives and slides, the best flatbeds are now a match for costlier film scanners.

BUYING ADVICE
Scanners

▶ A scanner is a simple, cheap way to digitize images for printing, editing on your computer, or sending via e-mail.

You don't need a digital camera to take advantage of the computer's ability to edit photos. Continuing improvements in scanners have made it cheaper and easier to turn photos into digital images that you can enhance, resize, and share. And flatbed scanners are no longer restricted to printed originals. Our tests show that the best flatbeds are now a match for pricey film scanners when it comes to digitizing slides and negatives. That's no small accomplishment, reflecting improvements to the resolution that new scanners deliver and better accessories to hold film strips or slides securely for sharp, accurate scans.

WHAT'S AVAILABLE
A number of scanners come from companies, including Microtek and Visioneer, that made their name in scanning technology. Other brands include computer makers and photo specialists such as Canon, Epson, Hewlett-Packard, and Nikon.

Which type of scanner you should consider—flatbed, sheet-fed, or film—depends largely on how you will use it. If you're short on space, consider a multi-function device.

Flatbed scanners. More than 90 percent of the scanners on the market are flatbeds. They work well for text, graphics, photos, and anything else that is flat, including a kindergartner's latest drawing. Flatbeds include optical-character-recognition (OCR) software, which converts words on a printed page into a word-processing file in your computer. They also include basic image-editing software. Some stores may throw in a flatbed scanner for free, or for a few dollars extra, when you purchase a desktop computer.

A key specification for a scanner is its maximum optical resolution, measured in dots per inch (dpi). You'll pay more for greater resolution. **Price range:** less than $100 for 600x1,200 dpi; $100 to $500 for models with greater resolution.

Sheet-fed models. Sheet-fed models can automatically scan a stack of loose pages, but they sometimes damage pages that pass through their innards. And they can't scan anything much thicker than a sheet of paper (meaning an old photo might be too thick). This type of scanner is often the one that comes as part of a multifunction device that can also print, send, and receive faxes. An increasing percentage of multifunction devices, however, include a flatbed scanner. Sheet-fed scanners also use OCR software. **Price range:** $100 to $600.

Film scanners. Serious photographers may want a film-only scanner that scans directly from an original slide (transparency) or negative. Some can accept small prints as well. **Price range:** $400 to $800.

FEATURES THAT COUNT
While the quality of images a scanner produces depends in part on the software included with it, there are several hardware features to consider.

You start scanning by running **driver software** that comes with the scanner or by pressing a preprogrammed button. Models with buttons automate routine tasks to let you operate your scanner as you would other office equipment. On some models you can customize the functions of the buttons. Any of these tasks can also be performed through the scanner's software without using buttons. A **copy/print button** initiates a scan and sends a command to print the results on your printer, effectively making the two devices act as a copier. Other button functions found on some models include **scan to a file, scan to a fax modem, scan to e-mail, scan to Web, scan to OCR, cancel scan, power save, start scanner software,** and **power on/off**.

You can also start the driver software from within an application, such as a word processor, that adheres to an industry standard known as TWAIN. A scanner's driver software allows you to **preview** a scan onscreen and crop it or adjust **contrast** and **brightness**. Once you're satisfied with the edited image, you can perform a final scan and pass the image to a running program or save it on your computer. You can make more extensive

BUYING ADVICE SCANNERS, CAMCORDERS

changes to an image with specialized **image-editing software**. And to scan text from a book or letter into a word-processing file in your computer, you run **OCR software**.

Many documents combine text with graphic elements, such as photographs and drawings. A handy software feature that's found on many scanners, called **multiple-scan mode**, lets you break down such hybrids into different sections that can be processed separately in a single scan. You can designate, for example, that the sections of a magazine article that are pure text go to the OCR software independently of the article's graphic elements. Other scanners would require a separate scan for each section of the document.

Some flatbed models come with **film adapters** designed to scan film or slides, but if you need to scan from film or slides often, you're better off getting a separate film scanner.

HOW TO CHOOSE

Consider how much resolution you need. If you want a scanner solely for printed originals, look mainly at models that deliver 1,200-dot-per-inch (dpi) resolution; they are generally the least expensive models. You can always set a scanner to work at less than its maximum resolution. In fact, most scans of photos, graphics, and text need only 150 to 300 dpi. (For images to be viewed onscreen, 75 dpi will suffice.) Higher-resolution scans take longer and create bigger files but usually add little.

For film and negatives, you'll want resolution of at least 2,400 dpi. Such a high setting is needed to capture enough detail so that an image created from a 35mm original can be enlarged.

When comparing specs, focus on the native optical resolution. It's more important than the "interpolated" or "enhanced" resolution, which comes in handy only when scanning line art.

Consider color-bit depth for film. If you plan to make enlargements of prints or to scan negatives or slides, pay attention to a specification known as color-bit depth. The greater the color-bit depth (24-bit is basic, 48-bit is tops), the better the scanner can differentiate among subtle gradations of light and dark.

Consider a multifunction unit. If you won't make heavy demands on a scanner (for instance, you cannot scan film or slides) and you need a general-use printer, especially for a tight space, a multifunction printer/scanner/copier may serve.

Don't sweat quality and speed. The majority of the scanners we recently tested were judged very good based on their ability to reproduce a color photo at maximum optical resolution. The rest were judged good, which means their scans were less crisp with less-accurate colors.

Speed matters if you expect to be scanning regularly. In our recent tests, the fastest took about 10 seconds to scan an 8x10-inch photo at 300 dpi, while the slowest needed about 40 seconds.

Don't sweat the software. All the scanners we recently tested came with software for scanning, image editing, and optical character recognition (which lets you scan text directly into a word-processing program). Some had software for making digital photo albums or other projects. All models also included software, often built into the hardware, that can repair image flaws caused by damaged originals.

BUYING ADVICE
Camcorders

▶ Fine picture quality and easy editing have improved the functionality of these moviemakers, especially for digital models.

Those grainy, jumpy home movies of yesteryear are long gone—replaced by home movies shot on digital or analog camcorders. You can edit and embellish the footage with music using your computer, then play it back on your VCR; you can even send it via e-mail.

Digital camcorders, now the dominant type, generally offer very good to excellent picture quality, along with very good sound capability, compactness, and ease of handling. Making copies of a digital recording won't

Camcorders let you edit images and even e-mail them.

03 BUYING ADVICE CAMCORDERS

result in a loss of picture or sound quality. You can even take rudimentary still photos with some digital camcorders.

Analog camcorders, now a small part of the market, generally have good picture and sound quality and are less expensive. Some analog units are about as compact and easy to handle as digital models, while others are a bit bigger and bulkier.

DVD camcorders put your home movies on a durable disc.

WHAT'S AVAILABLE

Sony dominates the camcorder market, with multiple models in a number of formats. Other top brands include Canon, JVC, Panasonic, and Samsung.

Most digital models come in the MiniDV format. Formats such as the disc-based DVD-RAM and DVD-R have also appeared. Some digital models weigh as little as one pound.

MiniDV. Don't let their small size deceive you. Although some models can be slipped into a large pocket, MiniDV camcorders can record very high-quality images. They use a unique tape cassette, and the typical recording time is 60 minutes at standard play (SP) speed. Expect to pay $6.50 for a 60-minute tape. You'll need to use the camcorder for playback—it converts its recording to an analog signal, so it can be played directly into a TV or VCR. If the TV or VCR has an S-video input jack, use it to get a high-quality picture. **Price range:** $350 to more than $2,000.

Digital 8. Also known as D8, this format gives you digital quality on Hi8 or 8mm cassettes, which cost $6.50 and $3.50, respectively. The Digital 8 format records with a faster tape speed, so a "120-minute" cassette lasts only 60 minutes at SP. Most models can also play your old analog Hi8 or 8mm tapes. **Price range:** $350 to $800.

Disc-based. Capitalizing on the explosive growth and capabilities of DVD movie discs, these formats offer benefits tape can't provide: long-term durability, a compact medium, and random access to scenes as with a DVD. The 3¼-inch discs record standard MPEG-2 video, the same format used in commercial DVD videos.

The amount of recording time varies according to the quality level you select: from 20 minutes per side at the highest-quality setting for DVD-RAM up to about 60 minutes per side at the lowest setting. DVD-RAM discs are not compatible with most DVD players, but the discs can be reused. DVD-R is supposed to be compatible with most DVD players and computer DVD drives, but the discs are write-once. We paid about $25 at a local retailer for a blank DVD-RW. **Price range:** $700 to $1,000.

Most analog camcorders now use the Hi8 format; VHS-C and Super VHS-C are fading from the market. Blank tapes range in price from $3.50 to $6.50. Analog camcorders usually weigh around 2 pounds. Picture quality is generally good, though a notch below that of digital. **Price range:** $225 to $500.

FEATURES THAT COUNT

A flip-out **liquid-crystal-display** (LCD) viewer is becoming commonplace on all but the lowest-priced camcorders. You'll find it useful for reviewing footage you've shot and easier to use than the eyepiece viewfinder for certain shooting poses. Some LCD viewers are hard to use in sunlight, a drawback on models that have only a viewer and no eyepiece.

Screens vary from 2½ to 4 inches measured diagonally, with a larger screen offered as a step-up feature on higher-priced models. Since an LCD viewer uses batteries faster than an eyepiece viewfinder does, you don't have as much recording time when the LCD is in use.

An **image stabilizer** automatically reduces most of the shaking that occurs from holding the camcorder as you record a scene. Most

Give your camcorder a checkup if it has been sitting around awhile

Camcorders are used an average of an hour a month. If you leave your camcorder idle for an extended period, our experts recommend this post-hibernation check: Charge the battery. Clean the lens with a lint-free cloth or tissue made for that purpose. Clean the tape heads with a special cassette or spray cleaner. Be sure the tape mechanism will let you load and eject a cassette.

BUYING ADVICE CAMCORDERS

stabilizers are electronic; a few are optical. Either type can be effective, though mounting the camcorder on a tripod is the surest way to get steady images. If you're not using a tripod, you can try holding the camcorder with both hands and propping both elbows against your body.

Full auto switch essentially lets you point and shoot. The camcorder automatically adjusts the color balance, shutter speed, focus, and aperture (also called the "iris" or "f-stop" with camcorders).

Autofocus adjusts for maximum sharpness; **manual focus override** may be needed for problem situations, such as low light. (With some camcorders, you may have to tap buttons repeatedly to get the focus just right.) With many models, you can also control exposure, shutter speed, and white balance.

The **zoom** is typically a finger control—press one way to zoom in, the other way to widen the view. The rate at which the zoom changes will depend on how hard you press the switch. Typical optical zoom ratios range from 10:1 to 26:1. The zoom relies on optical lenses, just like a film camera (hence the term "optical zoom"). Many camcorders offer a digital zoom to extend the range to 400:1 or more, but at a lower picture quality.

For tape-based formats, analog or digital, every camcorder displays **tape speeds** the same way a VCR does. Every model, for example, includes an SP (standard play) speed. Digitals have a slower, LP (long play) speed that adds 50 percent to the recording time. A few 8mm and Hi8 models have an LP speed that doubles the recording time. All VHS-C and S-VHS-C camcorders have an even slower EP (extended play) speed that triples the

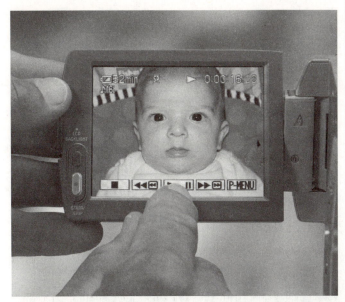

Some LCD viewers, such as the one on this Sony camcorder, have touch-screen controls (top). A video light (below) can help in dark places.

recording time. With analog camcorders, slower speeds worsen picture quality. Slow speed usually doesn't reduce picture quality on digital camcorders. But using slow speed means sacrificing some seldom-used editing options and may restrict playback on other camcorders.

Disc-based formats have a variety of modes that trade off recording time for image quality.

Quick review lets you view the last few seconds of a scene without having to press a lot of buttons.

For special lighting situations, preset **auto-exposure** settings can be helpful. A "snow & sand" setting, for example, adjusts shutter speed or aperture to accommo-

Did You Know?

The typical memory card included with the camera won't hold more than a few shots at the camera's highest resolution. For 3- to 5-megapixel cameras, buy a 128-megabyte card, about $25. For 6- to 8-megapixel cameras, get at least a 256-MB card, about $40.

03 BUYING ADVICE CAMCORDERS

date high reflectivity.

A **light** provides some illumination for close shots when the image would otherwise be too dark. **Backlight compensation** increases the exposure slightly when your subject is lit from behind and silhouetted. An **infrared-sensitive recording**

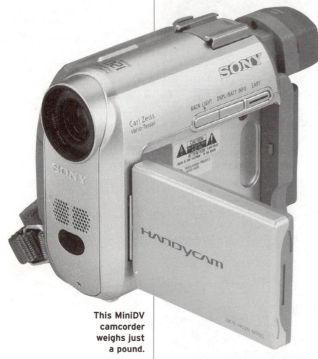

This MiniDV camcorder weighs just a pound.

mode (also known as night vision, zero lux, or MagicVu) allows shooting in very dim or dark situations, using infrared emitters. You can use it for nighttime shots, although colors won't register accurately in this mode.

Audio/video inputs let you record material from another camcorder or from a VCR, useful for copying part of another video onto your own. (A digital camcorder must have such an input jack if you want to record analog material digitally.) Unlike a built-in microphone, an **external microphone** that is plugged into a microphone jack won't pick up noises from the camcorder itself, and it typically improves audio performance.

A camcorder with **digital still** capability lets you take snapshots, which can be downloaded to your computer. The photo quality is generally inferior to that of a still camera.

Features that may aid editing include a built-in **title generator, a time-and-date stamp**, and a **time code**, which is a frame reference of exactly where you are on a tape—the hour, minute, second, and frame. A **remote control** helps when you're using the camcorder as a playback device or when you're using a tripod. **Programmed recording** (a self-timer) starts the camcorder recording at a preset time.

HOW TO CHOOSE

Pick your price range and format. The least-expensive camcorders on the market are analog. All the rest are digital.

Once you've decided which part of the price spectrum to explore, you need to pick a specific recording format. That determines not only how much you'll be spending for tapes or discs, but also how much recording time you'll get. The tape-based formats are typically superior in picture quality.

With analog, you can get 120 to 300 minutes of recording on a Hi8 cassette; with the S-VHS-C or VHS-C formats, you can get only 30 to 120 minutes.

With digital formats that use MiniDV, Digital 8, or MicroMV tapes, you can get at least 60 minutes of recording on a standard cassette. MiniDV and D8 cassettes are the least expensive and easiest to find.

Digital DVD camcorders from Panasonic and Hitachi can accommodate DVD-RAM discs, which can be reused but aren't compatible with all DVD players. All brands also use DVD-R, one-use discs that work in most DVD players. The standard setting yields 60 minutes of recording; the "fine" setting, 30 minutes.

If you're replacing an older camcorder, think about what you'll do with the tapes you've accumulated. If you don't stay with the same format you've been using, you will probably want to transfer the old tapes to an easily viewed medium, such as a DVD.

If you're buying your first camcorder, concentrate on finding the best one for your budget, regardless of format.

Check the size, weight, and controls. In the store, try different camcorders to make sure they fit your hand and are comfortable to use. Some models can feel disconcertingly tiny. (You'll need to use a tripod if you want rock-steady video, no matter which camcorder you choose.) Most camcorders are designed so that the most frequently used controls—the switch to zoom in and out, and the record button—fall readily to hand. Make sure that the controls are convenient and that you can change the tape or DVD and remove the battery.

Check the flip-out LCD viewer. Most measure 2.5 inches on the diagonal, but some are larger, adding about $100 to the price. If the viewer seems small and difficult to use or suffers from too much glare, consider trading up to a similar model or a different brand to get a better screen.

Think about the lighting. A camcorder isn't always used outdoors or in a brightly lit room. You can shoot video in dim light, but don't expect miracles. In our tests, using the camcorders' default mode, most produced only fair or poor images in very low light. Many camcorders have settings that can improve performance but can be a challenge to use.

COMPUTERS & THE INTERNET

CHAPTER 04

INSIDE INFO
- **32** Laptops and desktops
- **33** Computer monitors
- **34** Save your computer from online attack
- **41** Find the provider that's best for you
- **45** Today's PDAs link up to your network

BUYING ADVICE
- **46** Desktop computers
- **49** Laptop computers
- **52** Monitors
- **55** PDAs

Security might not be foremost in your mind when you're shopping for a computer, but it should play a part in your decision. Your choice of hardware and software can affect your ability to deflect intruders and defend your data. That's why we've devoted a considerable portion of this chapter to these important issues.

Viruses and spyware are far more likely to target Windows PCs than Macs. It's too soon to know, however, whether new Macs will be more vulnerable to attack once Apple begins its switch to Intel processors, the type used in Windows PCs, next year.

Whether you opt for a Windows PC or a Mac, you should use antivirus, firewall, and antispyware programs, as we explain later in the chapter. Many computers include software such as Norton Internet Security or McAfee AntiSpyware, but those are often limited to 30 to 90 days of use. Plan to upgrade and update these starter packages as necessary or replace them to maintain protection over the long haul.

▶▶ **Security technology keeps improving. So, unfortunately, do the skills of spammers, phishers, and other bad guys.**

Ratings: Desktops, p. 132; laptops, p. 134; monitors, p. 146; PDAs, p. 152.

04 INSIDE INFO COMPUTERS & THE INTERNET

LAPTOPS & DESKTOPS

Before you buy, take a hard look at the maker's tech support.

If you're in the market for a new laptop or desktop computer, the Buying Advice sections that begin on pages 46 and 49 will walk you through the essential steps for choosing one model over another. Fortunately, these days it's hard to go too far wrong; the performance and reliability of today's computers are uniformly quite high across the brands.

As a result, technical support may be a deciding factor in which manufacturer gets your business. Tech support remains a hot-button issue, judging from our latest subscriber survey of desktop-computer users. Apple has maintained its lead in tech support. Other brands continue to show only so-so performance and face some chronic support woes.

Our subscribers still say that "tech support" is at risk of becoming an oxymoron. The biggest complaint is that the support people simply can't solve the problem. Either they don't seem knowledgeable or they have trouble communicating clearly, our subscribers say. Compaq earned the lowest reader scores for desktops, while Compaq and Sony earned the lowest scores among laptop-computer users.

Online or e-mail support still doesn't measure up. Of those who tried to find support information on the company's Web site, more than 66 percent said they left empty-handed. Nearly 30 percent reported that they followed instructions that didn't work. Of those who used e-mail for support, 9 percent said they never received a reply. Almost half of those who got an answer said that it was of no help.

Our survey also underscored the severity of problems with malicious software that unscrupulous companies or identity thieves try to plant on people's computers. Thirteen percent of the tech-support diagnoses were related to virus or spyware infections, a topic we take up later in this chapter.

Details of our surveys of reliability and tech support are on page 52.

OTHER NEWS FROM THE COMPUTER FRONT

Laptops lose battery life. Perhaps owing to the wider, brighter screens and faster processors in the latest laptops, battery life has dwindled significantly. The most recently tested models averaged less than 2½ hours on a charge, far short of what we saw only six months ago.

Desktops gear up for multimedia and networking. You're likely to see more high-end desktop computers designed to be the hub of a home media center. The new models will include larger hard drives and additional bays for other drives that can be devoted to heavy-use tasks such as TV-program storage and DVD burning.

You will also see computers with dual processors, a design aimed at increasing speed and

Budget desktops now sell for about $600.

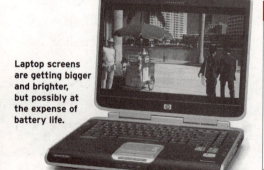

Laptop screens are getting bigger and brighter, but possibly at the expense of battery life.

You Need To Know

The hidden costs of laptop living

Laptop prices continue to tumble, but price tags usually exclude the cost of accessories that some people may consider essentials. For example, frequent travelers may well need a padded carrying case ($50 and up), extra battery ($100 to $200), and spare power adapter ($80 and up). Useful add-ons for work at home include a USB mouse ($30) and cable lock ($40). Laptops don't always come with as wide an array of drives as do desktops. But some have modular bays that let you swap one drive for another, such as a DVD drive for a memory-card reader. One extra drive costs $50 or more.

INSIDE INFO COMPUTERS & THE INTERNET

making it easier for two or more users to access the computer over a home network. In theory, for example, you could use a remote control and some form of console device in the living room to play audio or video stored across the network—on a PC in the bedroom—while your child plays a game on that same PC and notices no slowdown of activity.

But if you're in the market for new hardware, you don't have to wait for those new machines to come on the market. Budget and workhorse computers you can buy today (see Ratings) will serve most users very well.

▶▶ Buying advice on desktop computers begins on page 46. For laptops, see page 49.

COMPUTER MONITORS

LCDs dominate, offering more screen for less money.

In computer monitors, as in TVs, models with LCD technology are becoming bigger, cheaper, and more dominant in the marketplace.

About a year ago, the liquid-crystal display market shifted distinctly from 15-inch monitors to 17- and 19-inch models. Prices for 17-inch models, the size most people buy, now start at around $300, compared with $450 last year. And 60 percent of the computer monitors now sold in the U.S. are LCDs.

LCDs are beginning to dominate the monitor market for practical reasons: They take up far less desk space than a CRT, or cathode-ray tube, monitor and weigh about 15 pounds, vs. 30 to 50 pounds for a CRT. But a CRT still has some advantages (see the box at right).

Here's what we found in our latest tests of LCD monitors:

They're getting wider. More LCDs have screens with a wide shape that is handy for viewing and editing photos and running multiple programs.

They're more versatile. More than half the models we tested had stands that allow you to lift, lower, or tilt the screen. That's useful because LCD screens are less bright and sharp when viewed at an extreme angle. More LCDs can rotate from a landscape to portrait orientation—handy for viewing documents or Web pages.

Convergence with TVs isn't here yet. Computer equipment and TV sets are becoming a little more alike. Samsung, Sony, and others now offer monitors with TV tuners and LCD TVs with computer connections. But big differences between the two types of devices still remain. While both share LCD technology, monitors designed for computer use generally display computer content more clearly than TV sets do. Computer monitors with built-in TV tuners cost $100 to $200 more than those without and can't decode digital broadcasts.

▶▶ For buying advice on monitors, see page 52.

For most users, a 17-inch monitor will do the job.

CRT monitors: down but not out

Big and bulky, a CRT monitor can gobble up a huge section of your desktop, be difficult to maneuver or move, and consume twice as much energy—up to 80 watts—as a comparably-sized LCD. Nevertheless, for some people, it may still be worth considering, for these reasons:

A CRT offers the most screen for the money. A 19-inch model can be on your desk for less than $200, compared with $350 and up for an LCD.

It may perform very well. Two 17-inch models with 16-inch viewable-image sizes we tested performed better overall than half the LCDs in the Ratings.

It's superior for photographers, designers, and gamers. CRTs generally deliver slightly truer colors, making them the preferred medium for graphic designers and digital photographers. They also render fast-moving objects better than LCDs, making them attractive to serious gamers. Unlike LCDs, they can be readily viewed from extreme angles.

For most CRTs, depth equals screen size.

04 | INSIDE INFO COMPUTERS & THE INTERNET

SAVE YOUR COMPUTER FROM ONLINE ATTACK

Here's how to protect against viruses and spyware.

Use the Internet at home and you have a one-in-three chance of suffering computer damage, financial loss, or both in the near future because of a computer virus or spyware—sneaky software that plants itself on your computer. That's one of several unsettling findings from our 2005 Consumer Reports State of the Net survey of online consumers.

What else did we discover? Despite having spent more than $2.6 billion over the past two years for protection software, American consumers lost more than $9 billion during that same period to computer repairs, parts, and replacement because of viruses and spyware. Equipment damage from those two hazards is so extensive, we found, that it accounted for more than 7 percent of all consumer computer purchases in 2003 and 2004.

The results of our survey also highlight the risks of both spam and the scams known as phishing— fraudulent e-mail that solicits confidential information by impersonating a reputable institution. Future surveys will continue to track those growing consumer threats.

As our survey results indicate, the Internet is no longer the urbane information motorway it was five years ago. It's more like a no-holds-barred raceway teeming with unsavory drivers and with hardly a police car in sight.

Macintosh computers are less vulnerable because most viruses and spyware are written for Windows-based PCs.

Individual consumers now face assaults through e-mail, Web sites, messaging services, and downloads. Large institutions aren't faring much better, as millions of MasterCard and Visa cardholders learned when their personal information was stolen over the Internet, exposing them to identity theft.

To help you cope with the Internet's growing catalog of hazards, we interviewed experts from government, industry, and public interest groups. We studied hundreds of pieces of spam and intentionally infected computers with the latest spyware. And we tested three types of security software you need to protect yourself. We found that the software is better than ever (see the Ratings starting on page 38).

Our survey and investigation found that as a result of government inertia and consumers' imprudent practices, and despite industry's efforts, most online threats are worse than they were a year ago. We also found that well-known brands are supporting spyware by using it as an advertising medium. Until the institutions that can clean up the Internet provide more effective solutions to its security problems, most of the burden for online security will continue to fall on millions of consumers.

HERE ARE THE SPECIFICS FROM OUR SURVEY:

• In a nationally representative

INSIDE INFO COMPUTERS & THE INTERNET

What you can do to stop threats

Protection software isn't perfect. Taking the right precautions yourself can greatly reduce exposure to online hazards. Here are the measures our experts consider most effective now, and recommended continuing practices:

IMMEDIATE STEPS

1 Consider switching to a Mac. Most viruses and spyware are written for Windows-based PCs.

2 Upgrade your PC operating system. If you're a Windows XP user and haven't done so, enable the automatic Windows Update feature. Go to *www.microsoft.com/protect* and download and install Service Pack 2, which provides enhanced security. Consider upgrading to the next version of Windows when it becomes available to gain added security features. For earlier versions of Windows, run Windows Update from the Start menu. For Macintosh, go to the Software Update Control Panel. Also regularly update your Web browser and other major software, using the manufacturers' update instructions or features.

3 Use a firewall. If you use Windows XP, enable its built-in firewall. If you use an older version of Windows or if you have a Mac, install either a software or hardware firewall, especially if you have a high-speed Internet connection. A software firewall costs $30 to $40. The firewall should provide both incoming and outgoing protection. If you have a home network, your router most likely has a built-in firewall. Change its default password and disable "remote administration" to prevent hackers from seizing control of the router.

4 Adjust browser security settings. If you use Internet Explorer 6, keep its security level at medium or higher to block Web sites from downloading programs without your authorization or automatically running Windows active scripts. Consider upgrading to Internet Explorer 7 when it becomes available, for stronger security features.

5 Consider an ISP or e-mail provider that offers security. AOL, EarthLink, MSN, and Yahoo all offer spam filtering, virus scanning for e-mail, and antiphishing protections at no extra charge for dial-up users. Use them as one layer of a multilayer defense. You can check other ISPs' sites to find out what they provide.

6 Use antivirus software. You can obtain additional virus protection from ISPs, directly from a manufacturer's site, or at a retail store. Enable the auto-protect and automatic update features and keep your subscription current.

7 Use more than one antispyware program. None of the products we've tested catches every spyware variant. Using more than one product boosts your coverage, even if the second product is a free one. If you use more than one, you should enable the real-time protection for only one product. Download and install the free Microsoft AntiSpyware beta from *www.microsoft.com/protect*, but avoid free antispyware not listed in the Ratings on page 39. Keep your subscription to new spyware definitions current and regularly update the definitions or use the automatic update feature.

GOOD ONLINE PRACTICES

8 Regularly back up personal files. This safeguards your data in case of a security problem. Consider using a plug-in external hard drive as your main or backup storage, so that if the computer becomes disabled, you'll already have your files off the machine.

9 Beware while browsing. Download only from online sources you trust. Be wary of ad-sponsored or "free" screen savers, games, videos, toolbars, music and movie file-sharing programs, and other purported giveaways; they probably include spyware that may damage your PC if it gets through your security. Children who share and download files should do so on a PC that doesn't contain confidential information or valuable data, such as financial records.

10 Avoid short passwords. To foil password-cracking software, use passwords that are at least eight characters long, including at least a numeral and a symbol, such as #. Avoid common words, and never disclose a password online. With a broadband connection, shut off the computer or modem when you aren't using it. Don't post your e-mail address in its normal form on a publicly accessible Web page. Use a form, such as "Jane AT isp DOT com," that spammers' address-harvesting software can't easily read.

11 Use e-mail cautiously. Never open an attachment, even from someone you know, that you weren't expecting. Never respond to an e-mail asking for personal information. Forward fraudulent spam to the Anti-Phishing Working Group at *reportphishing @antiphishing.org*. Don't reply to spam or click on its "unsubscribe" link. That tells the sender that your e-mail address is valid.

12 Use multiple e-mail addresses. Have one e-mail address for family and friends, another for everyone else. You can get a free address from Hotmail, Yahoo, or a disposable-forwarding-address service such as SpamMotel. When an address attracts too much spam, drop it. Instead of an e-mail address like *janedoe@isp.com*, select one with embedded digits, like *jane8doe2@isp.com*. Report spam to your ISP to improve its filtering.

13 Take a stand. Don't buy anything promoted in a spam message. Even if the offer isn't a scam, you are helping to finance and encourage spam. If you receive spam that promotes a brand, complain to the company behind the brand.

14 Look for secure Web sites. To check whether a site is secure, look at the bottom of your browser's window, not the Web page itself, for an icon of an unbroken key or a lock that's closed, golden, or glowing. And make sure that the site's address begins with "https:" Double-click on the lock to display the site's certificate, and make sure it matches the company you think you're connected to.

04 INSIDE INFO COMPUTERS & THE INTERNET

survey of more than 3,200 households with at-home Internet access, half reported a spyware infection in the past six months. Of those, 18 percent reported having had an infection so serious that they had to erase their hard drives. To avoid spyware, 51 percent of all online users reported being much more careful visiting Web sites, and 38 percent said they download free programs less frequently.

- Sixty-four percent of survey respondents said they had detected viruses on their computer in the past two years. Four percent found them at least 50 times.
- Almost half of our respondents reported an increase in spam in the past year, but 30 percent reported a decline. People who used a spam filter were more likely to report less spam. Thirteen percent said that the need to avoid spam and e-mail scams had induced them to shop online less.
- Six percent of respondents had submitted personal information in response to a phishing scam. Financial losses were rare—only 0.5 percent said they had lost money—but costly: They averaged nearly $400, and a few topped $1,000.
- Macs are safer than Windows PCs for some online hazards. Only 20 percent of Mac owners surveyed reported detecting a virus in the past two years, compared with 66 percent of Windows PC owners. Just 8 percent of Mac users reported a spyware infection in the past six months vs. 54 percent of Windows PC users.

Through good practices (see "What you can do to stop threats," page 35) and the use of protection software (see Ratings, page 36), you can greatly reduce your exposure online. Protecting yourself takes effort. Our survey shows that consumers are starting to make that effort. Compared with last year, fewer are engaging in behaviors likely to encourage more spam, such as clicking on links within a spam message to get more information or replying to spam to be taken off the mailing list. More consumers are using antispyware, and more of those who use antivirus software rely on a product that automatically downloads the newest remedies.

Ratings ANTISPAM PROGRAMS

Within types, in performance order.

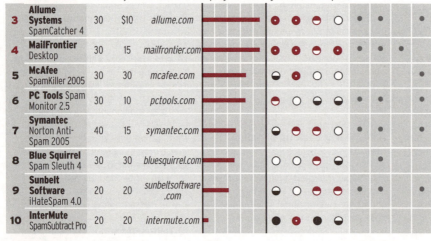

Guide to the Ratings

Overall score is based on the ability to recognize valid e-mail and spam. **DELIVERS VALID E-MAIL** indicates how well a product correctly identified e-mail that wasn't spam, based on 333 valid messages. Because the software requires a training period to learn how to better differentiate valid e-mail from spam, one-third of the messages were used for training. Products scored excellent recognized more than 95 percent. The product that scored poor misidentified 57 percent. **DETECTS SPAM** indicates how well each product correctly identified spam, based on 1,000 spam messages, one-third of which were used for training the filters. Products scored excellent recognized 86 percent or more. A product that **INTEGRATES WITH MAILER** blends its own controls with the e-mail program's. A product that **LEARNS** identifies patterns in your e-mail, providing you tell the software which messages are spam and which are not. Using this process over time, it can continue to improve its ability to discern spam. One that uses **ONLINE COLLABORATION** checks messages against a "live" Internet list of signatures of reported spam messages to improve accuracy. A product that **TAGS SPAM** inserts a label into the Subject field of e-mail deemed spam. **PRICE** is approximate retail. **ANNUAL FEE** is for continued use after the first year.

INSIDE INFO COMPUTERS & THE INTERNET

ROOM TO IMPROVE
- Seventeen percent of our survey respondents don't use antivirus software.
- Ten percent of those with high-speed broadband access—prime targets for hackers—said they don't have firewall protection that would block online intruders. Nationally, that's the equivalent of 3.6 million unprotected households.
- About 1.4 million online households helped keep spammers in business by purchasing a product or service advertised through spam.

Consumer awareness needs to be higher. Last year, in a study of 329 Internet users by America Online and the National Cyber Security Alliance, computer scans revealed that 80 percent had some form of spyware on their computer, but only 53 percent of the users surveyed knew that it was present.

ONLINE ROGUE'S GALLERY
Here is a rundown of the major online threats you need to know about, plus the latest news on the battle between ISPs and software makers and the spammers and scammers.

Viruses and worms. They are the most destructive online hazards and have plagued Internet users for nearly two decades now. They typically infiltrate a PC via e-mail attachments or files downloaded from Web sites; seize control, spread by e-mailing copies of themselves to listings in your address book; and can destroy critical files and disable your computer. Some use your computer to send large volumes of spam or to attack specific Web sites.

Broadband users in our survey were significantly more likely to catch a virus than those with dial-up service. Of those infected, 40 percent suffered noticeable operating problems or permanently lost files. Once the product of techno-geek malcontents, viruses are increasingly used for criminal purposes. Over the second half of 2004, viruses aimed at stealing confidential information accounted for 54 percent of the top 50 viruses, according to Symantec, maker of Norton Antivirus.

Spyware. This is a fast-growing and complex threat. As the Federal Trade Commission defines it, spyware gathers data from your PC, which it may then transmit, or asserts control over your PC all without your knowledge or consent.

By that standard, adware, which interferes with Web browsing by popping up paid advertisements, is spyware if it was installed without proper consent. Often, consent is obtained deceptively or not at all. Companies that make or distribute such soft-

---

CR Quick Recommendations

Internet protection programs

Online users should run updated antivirus software and at least one antispyware program. Just one antispyware should have its real-time protection enabled; all products in the Ratings have that feature. Only users whose spam has become excessive need an antispam. Among all three types of software, higher-priced products didn't necessarily outperform lower-priced or even free ones.

Antispam software. If your Internet provider offers spam blocking, enable it as a first line of defense. If you use free Web-based e-mail services such as Hotmail or Gmail, add-on products in the Ratings will usually not work with them. But those services do have built-in blockers. Otherwise, to eliminate the costs and hassles of using a separate e-mail program and spam blocker, use an e-mail program with integrated blocking: Microsoft (1) for Windows or Apple (2). Both were rated excellent.

If you prefer an add-on blocker, performance is so important in choosing a spam blocker that you should limit your choice to the products in the Quick Picks.

Antivirus software. Properly updated, all rated products will detect viruses or worms that have been circulating for more than a few days. But they may fail to detect new ones until remedies are distributed. So it's essential to practice good online hygiene (see "What You Can Do" on page 35).

Antispyware. If you use a Mac, it's apt to be less of a target for spyware than a Windows PC. Obtain software only from the official sites listed because similar software offered at other sites may actually be spyware. If you surf the Web often but haven't checked your PC for spyware, download a free product, such as the one offered by Microsoft (1), and remove whatever may have accumulated. Because no product offers perfect protection, you should complement your main antispyware with at least one other recommended product. **Ratings** rank products by performance and features. **Quick Picks** highlight models that we consider an especially attractive value.

Quick Picks

Antispam programs

If you use an older version of Microsoft Outlook or Apple Mail:

1 Microsoft $90
2 Apple $130

Upgrade to these tested versions, which provide significantly better protection than their predecessors. Microsoft's product (1) also blocks pictures but can let them in either manually or from designated friends. Apple (2) also blocks Web bugs and HTML in spam.

If you use an e-mail program other than Microsoft Outlook or Apple Mail:

3 Allume Systems $30
4 MailFrontier $30

These are the best choices in add-on programs. Allume Systems (3) tags spam to help you delete it quickly but provides no phone support. MailFrontier (4) is easier to set up, blocks Windows Messenger pop-ups, lets you set categories, identifies fraudulent e-mail, and can report it to authorities.

(continued)

04 INSIDE INFO COMPUTERS & THE INTERNET

Ratings ANTIVIRUS PROGRAMS

Legend: ● Excellent ◕ Very good ○ Good ◐ Fair ● Poor

In performance order.

Key number	Brand & model	Price	Annual fee	Overall score (0–100)	Versatility	Ease of use	Scan speed	Scheduled scan	Firewall/hacker blocking
1	Trend Micro PC-cillin Internet Security 2005	$50	$25	VG	●	●	●	●	●
2	Kaspersky Lab Anti-Virus Personal 5.0	35	30	VG	●	●	◕	●	●
3	Softwin SRL Bitdefender 8 Std	30	15	G	●	◕	◕	●	
4	Symantec Norton AV 2005	50	30	G	●	●	◕	●	
5	Alwil Avast! Antivirus	free	free	G	◕	◕	●	●	
6	McAfee VirusScan 2005 9.0	50	25	G	●	◕	○	●	●
7	Panda Software Titanium AV 2005	50	40	G	◕	◕	◕		●
8	Computer Associates eTrust EZ Antivirus 2005	30	20	F	○	◐	●	●	

Guide to the Ratings

VERSATILITY indicates how many useful features are included. **EASE OF USE** indicates how appropriate default settings are and how easy the product is to use. **SCAN SPEED** is how quickly the product scans a typical hard drive. **SCHEDULED SCAN** means that you can set up automatic scans. **FIREWALL/HACKER BLOCKING** indicates whether the product also provides a firewall to block hackers. **PRICE** is approximate retail; **ANNUAL FEE** is for protection after the first year.

CR Quick Recommendations

Internet protection programs (continued)

Quick Picks

Antivirus programs

If you have no antivirus program:

1 Trend Micro $50
2 Kaspersky Labs $35

Both are easy to use and offer full technical support. Trend Micro (1) has a button to disconnect from the Internet; Web mail scan that works with AOL, Yahoo, and MSN; antispam and privacy protection; vulnerability scan; and a Web filter. Kaspersky Labs (2) has few options but includes spyware and adware detection (which we did not test), "network attack" protection, and an extended database to scan for malicious software programs.

If you already own one of these major-brand products:

4 Symantec $50
6 McAfee $50

Both are bundled with new computers and worth staying with. Symantec (4) includes worm blocking, spyware and keylogger detection, and an MS Office document scan. McAfee (6) includes a firewall but has a confusing interface.

Free protection but limited support:

5 Alwil

Alwil (5) provides full-featured protection and is relatively easy to use. But there's no phone support, only e-mail support. The download site is at www.avast.com

Antispyware

For an excellent main antispyware program with real-time protection:

1 Microsoft (free download)

Microsoft says it will offer the final version of the beta software we tested free to licensed Windows users.

To complement your main antispyware, consider one or more of these:

2 Webroot $30
3 eTrust $30
5 Spybot (free download)
6 Ad-Aware $25

Webroot (2) and eTrust (3) offer better detection than the free Spybot (5). Webroot (2) has many features and is easy to use. eTrust (3) is very good but doesn't protect browser settings from being changed. It scans cookies slowly. Spybot (5) is full-featured. We also tested a free version of Ad-Aware (6). It lacks real-time protection but is worth using as a second line of defense. Don't download free software not listed in the Ratings. It may be malicious software in disguise.

---

ware often embrace the label "adware" to avoid the stigma associated with spyware.

Whatever the name, it can infiltrate your computer through e-mail attachments, files downloaded from Web sites, and instant-messaging programs. A common way to unwittingly infect your PC with such software is to download free games, utilities, or ad-supported software; the spyware piggybacks on the freebie. Some sites alert you to the extras, but such notice isn't always prominent or explicit.

Spyware can affect you in these ways:

A rare type, called a keylogger, can record and transmit to others over the Internet every character you type, thus capturing user names, passwords, and the like. Some spyware can capture screen shots of, say, your electronically filed tax return, your online checkbook, and your Quicken household budget or assets inventory. Other variants can

INSIDE INFO COMPUTERS & THE INTERNET

literally eavesdrop on you and your family via your PC's webcam and microphone.

Spyware can track your online activities, such as which sites you visit, and report your behavior to marketers. Some of the most widespread pestware generates pop-up ads and interferes with your browser's behavior. Should enough of this infest your computer, it can bring the PC to a halt. That's probably why, among the respondents to our survey who had detected spyware recently, 5 percent had to replace hardware such as a hard drive and 3 percent replaced the computer. Microsoft estimates that spyware is responsible for up to half of all PC crashes.

Companies that create so-called "adware" make no apologies. "The bargain is, we'll give you free software in exchange for your agreement to receive ads," says Reed Freeman, chief privacy officer for Claria Corp., which offers free Kazaa file-sharing software, GotSmiley icons, and screen savers.

But in practice, it can be hard for a consumer to learn the full terms of such an agreement. When we downloaded Kazaa, Claria's license agreement appeared on the screen, but we couldn't print it out. Information about advertising was buried within the more than 9,000 words of the combined Kazaa and Claria agreements. In all those words, there was no notice that the person agreeing must be at least 18 years old to legally give consent, despite the fact that this software is widely used by minors.

Companies are constantly creating new spyware variants. Computer Associates, maker of eTrust Pest Patrol Anti-Spyware, says 350 new samples and 250 variations on existing samples turn up each week. "The mutation rate for spyware is high because companies are behind this, and they are actively working not to be detected by spyware programs," says Sam Curry, a vice president at Computer Associates.

Most spyware operates under the cloak of legitimate business, complete with corporate headquarters, legal departments, publicists, Washington lobbyists, and millions in revenues to fund the assault on your computer. "Spyware is written by the very best teams of hackers and virus writers," says Rick Carlson, president of Aluria, publisher of Spyware Eliminator software.

Big-name companies pay spyware purveyors big money for space in those pop-up windows: Circuit City, Dell Computer, Expedia, FTD.com, ING Direct Securities, JPMorgan Chase, Orbitz, Sprint PCS, Travelocity, Verizon, and Vonage are just a few. "Lots of big, seemingly respectable companies get involved in this mess," says Ben Edelman, a spyware researcher who has served as an expert witness in lawsuits against spyware companies.

More threats, such as those combining virus technology with spyware, are appearing. "About 18 months ago, you could keep a new PC online for 45 to 55 minutes before it was attacked by something," says Kraig Lane, group product manager at Symantec. "Now it takes just 4 to 5 minutes."

Spam. This constitutes most Internet e-mail. Fifty-three percent of respondents in our survey said that at least half of their e-mail was spam, and 33 percent

Ratings ANTISPYWARE

Listed mainly in order of detection.

Key number	Brand & model	Price	Annual fee	Official download site	Test results		Features			
					Detection	Ease of use	Auto updates	Can ignore cookies	Protects browser settings	Scheduled scan
1	**Microsoft** AntiSpyware (beta)	Free	None	microsoft.com	◓	●	•	•	•	•
2	**Webroot** Spy Sweeper	$30	$20	webroot.com	◓	◓	•	•	•	•
3	**Computer Associates** eTrust PestPatrol 2005	30	20	pestpatrol.com	◓	◓	•	•	•	•
4	**Spybot** Search & Destroy	Free	None	spybot.info	○	◓		•	•	•
5	**Ad-Aware** SE Plus	25	10	lavasoft.de	○	○				
6	**McAfee** AntiSpyware	40	30	mcafee.com	◐	◓				
7	**Trend Micro** PC-cillin Internet Security 2005	50	25	trendmicro.com	◐	○	•			
8	**Allume** Internet Cleanup	30	10	allume.com	○	◐			•	

Guide to the Ratings

DETECTION indicates how well a product identified spyware on a badly infected PC. **EASE OF USE** indicates how intuitive the interface is and how easy it is to perform common functions. A product that **CAN IGNORE COOKIES** can exclude certain browser data files from a hard-drive scan, speeding it up and making it easier to spot true spyware. **PROTECTS BROWSER SETTINGS** means that the product prevents spyware from changing your home page and redirecting your Web searches. **SCHEDULED SCAN** lets you set computer scans to run at a designated time. **PRICE** is approximate retail. All paid products require an **ANNUAL FEE** for updates and new spyware definitions after the first year.

04 INSIDE INFO COMPUTERS & THE INTERNET

Internet protection programs repel viruses.

Antispyware programs protect privacy.

Antispam software can keep out most junk e-mail.

said they were getting much more than they did a year ago.

The biggest consequence of spam by far is time wasted sorting through it, deleting it, and for those with a slower, dial-up connection, downloading it. Eighty-two percent of spam recipients in our survey complained about wasted time. Nearly 20 percent said spam interfered with their browser, which suggests that it planted spyware, and 47 percent said they received pornographic or other objectionable spam. Based on our survey, we estimate that more than 2 million children nationwide inadvertently viewed pornographic spam.

Phishing scams. The criminal variant of spam, phishing e-mail, appears to come from a legitimate financial institution or company, requesting personal information such as a password or PIN code. You're asked to click on a link, but when you do so you're connected to a fraudulent look-alike Web site. Fifty-two percent of the Internet users we surveyed said they received what looked like a fraudulent solicitation.

More than 2,800 active fraudulent Web sites were operating last March, a 64 percent jump from only three months earlier, according to the Anti-Phishing Working Group, an industry association. Symantec says its antifraud filters blocked an average of 33 million phishing e-mail messages per week late last year versus 9 million per week nearly 6 months earlier.

The latest development in phishing is the use of blank e-mail—no text message and no suspicious link. When you open it on an unprotected PC, a silent script is released onto your computer that does nothing until the next time you try to bank online. Then it automatically redirects you to the fraudulent site. Even more insidious is a script that operates while you use the legitimate banking Web site, sending your personal information to identity thieves.

HELP ON THE WAY?
The most immediate help for beleaguered consumers is from some leading Internet service providers, notably AOL and EarthLink. They provide antivirus protection and filter out spam and phishing e-mail before it reaches the user. Some offer to download free antispyware to your desktop. Other ISPs generally don't provide those extras.

ISPs and phone companies have also banded together and formed the Messaging Anti-Abuse Working Group to shut down known spammers' accounts and block access to fraudulent phishing Web sites in the U.S. and overseas. Even if you unwittingly click on a phishing link, you'll receive a warning from your ISP and won't be able to connect to it.

EarthLink has been especially aggressive in suing spammers. It has prosecuted more than 100 in civil court since 1997. "Our goal is to put the spammers permanently out of business," says Carla Shaw, an EarthLink spokeswoman. "We seek permanent injunctions." In 2003, EarthLink won a $16.4 million judgment against Howard Carmack, a Buffalo, N.Y., spammer. Microsoft has also aggressively litigated against spammers and phishers, involving itself in more than 200 suits.

Microsoft, whose dominant Windows operating system and browser have been criticized for security vulnerabilities, has become more serious about securing its products over the past few years. The latest version of Windows automatically downloads security fixes and checks your PC for vulnerabilities. Microsoft is also expected to release a public beta version of an antivirus, antispyware, antispam product later in 2005 called Windows OneCare, which will be subscription-based. But no price or release date has been set. Right now, Windows users can download free antispyware from Microsoft.

For all that Microsoft has done to tighten its software's security, its recent actions to reduce spam have generated controversy: Progress against spam requires a major redesign of the Internet's decades-old public e-mail system. Microsoft is currently experimenting with a new design, called Sender ID, in which it says it has a proprietary interest.

In mid-2005, it announced a new policy: If an e-mail sent to the hundreds of millions of users of its Hotmail e-mail service didn't conform to Sender ID, that would increase the likelihood of its being labeled as spam by Hotmail. Some industry observers view this as an attempt to pressure Internet services that haven't adopted Sender ID into adopting it. Microsoft says that its purpose is to help reduce spam for its customers.

Government has also geared up against Internet threats. Congress and 27 states are working on antispyware legislation. But Congress's online security track record isn't encouraging. It took seven years to pass an antispam bill. The one it passed, the Can-Spam Act of 2003, was opposed by 44 state attorneys general and has done little to reduce spam while legitimizing some types of spam, pre-empting strong state law, and prohibiting consumers from suing spammers.

The Federal Trade Commission has a lead role in enforcing Can-Spam and other laws designed to

INSIDE INFO COMPUTERS & THE INTERNET

protect online consumers. But since the late 1990s it has brought only 69 cases against spammers. Lydia Parnes, acting director of the FTC's Bureau of Consumer Protection, says she needs more resources. Since the agency was given major new responsibility for Can-Spam in 2003, it has added only one person to the enforcement staff.

An antispyware bill sponsored by Senator George Allen of Virginia would give the FTC a needed $10 million more per year to crack down on spammers and spyware purveyors, as well as authority it now lacks to work with other nations' law enforcers, essential since the Internet knows no borders. A bill already passed in the House, HR 29, sponsored by California Representative Mary Bono, is similar, imposing limited disclosure requirements on spyware makers and distributors. Both the House and Senate bills prohibit consumers from suing spyware makers.

The U.S. Secret Service has 3,300 agents worldwide pursuing hackers, identity thieves, and other Internet defrauders, as part of their duties. And some state attorneys general have aggressively pursued online predators. In April 2005, New York Attorney General Elliott Spitzer charged Intermix Media with deceptively bundling spyware with pictures of Jennifer Lopez, and with software downloaded by millions of unsuspecting users.

FIND THE PROVIDER THAT'S BEST FOR YOU

Broadband has advantages, but providers vary widely.

These days, if you spend much time online you're probably using a broadband Internet connection to your home—or are thinking seriously about getting one. Broadband offers near-instantaneous connections and swifter downloads than slower, albeit cheaper, dial-up Internet service.

But if broadband service is becoming almost a utility, it isn't yet as predictable and uniform in performance as that term suggests. In a survey of nearly 26,000 Consumer Reports Online subscribers—our largest-ever survey on Internet service and the first to rate broadband providers—we found differences in satisfaction with broadband service.

Here are the highlights of our findings:

There's no best broadband type. Availability of broadband is growing, with virtually all cable-TV companies now offering broadband Internet service and telephone companies wiring more neighborhoods for digital subscriber line (DSL) service. The highest-scoring cable and DSL providers offered comparable, fairly high levels of satisfaction—and the least satisfactory of each got equally ho-hum overall Ratings.

Barraged by broadband offers? Focus on monthly costs, not introductory price.

But the two provider types differed in what made their best ISPs score so high. Subscribers to the better-rated cable-broadband providers were more satisfied than most DSL subscribers with the speed of their service, and with its reliability and tech support. But subscribers to the least pricey of the DSL providers were far more satisfied with their monthly bills (around $30) than were subscribers to cable broadband, who paid about $35 to $45 a month.

There's no question as to the worst provider in our

04 INSIDE INFO COMPUTERS & THE INTERNET

First Things First

Pick a type of provider. Here's a summary of how the three main types of Internet service compare. The fourth option, service via satellite, should be a last resort for those who cannot receive broadband by any other means (see CR Quick Recommendations, below).

1 Cable-Internet service

Cost $40 to $50 a month. Modem may be free or an extra $3/month.
Advantages For the highest-rated cable services, speed and reliability. Easy to try out; usually no service commitment.
Disadvantages High cost.
Best for people who also want cable TV and/or voice over Internet phone services (bundled discounts usually apply).

2 DSL service

Cost $30 to $45 a month. Modem may be free or $50 to $100 to buy.
Advantages With some providers, it's the least-expensive broadband service.
Disadvantages Often demands a 12-month commitment and that you also be a landline phone subscriber.
Best for people who also want telephone service from the provider (bundled discounts usually apply).

3 Dialup service

Cost Typically $10 to $25 a month. Usually, no other equipment is needed.
Advantages Low cost. Easy to take your e-mail address with you if you move.
Disadvantages Slower than cable or DSL in time to connect and in download speed. Ties up a phone line.
Best for patient people who mostly use the Web for e-mail and occasional surfing.

CR Quick Recommendations

Our Ratings show a fairly narrow range in overall satisfaction for both cable and DSL providers. With dial-up services, the range of satisfaction is a little broader.

It's unlikely you'll have more than one cable-Internet option where you live. Nor will all of the DSL services likely be available in your area. Bell South, for example, is offered in only 9 southeastern states and Qwest serves only 14 states in the west.

If your only broadband option is DirecWay, which uses satellite transmission, consider dial-up service or WildBlue, a new satellite-broadband provider that launched in June.

The dial-up services are all nationally available, and the best are as reliable as most DSL providers but at a much lower cost. Also, with virtually all of them you can keep your e-mail address for a modest cost if you leave the service—which may help you to decide to upgrade to broadband.

The **Ratings** list Internet providers by overall satisfaction, based on our national survey of subscribers to the services.
Quick Picks highlights services you might want to consider based on how they scored and on other factors such as speed, reliability, and price.

Quick Picks

If high speed is a priority:

Consider the cable-broadband service that's available in your area. For all but the lowest-rated cable services, respondents reported faster connection speeds than DSL. That difference is important if you often download large files, access the Internet with more than one computer at a time, or are hosting a Web site.

Cable will likely cost more than DSL. However, as you compare prices, consider the likely savings if you also get cable-TV service bundled with your Internet, since that might close or eliminate the cost gap with a DSL service.

The best values in broadband service:

11 SBC Yahoo
12 Verizon

There's a good likelihood of one or both of these DSL services being available where you live. Both offer satisfactory broadband service at unusually low cost; our readers paid about $30 a month. Neither provider (nor most other DSL services) yielded the high satisfaction scores with service reliability and tech support of the better cable companies. However, both were reliable enough. Verizon's tech support was more satisfactory than that of SBC Yahoo. The latter has the more aggressive pricing, but be aware that its lowest-priced service, at $19.95 and sometimes $14.95 a month, has speeds as low as 384 kilobits per second—only a few times as fast as dial-up.

The best value in dial-up service:

17 Juno

This service was as satisfactory to subscribers overall as pricier EarthLink, which scored higher for protection. If your Internet needs are limited, there's also a Juno service that offers up to 10 hours of access a month, including e-mail, free. NetZero, owned by the same company as Juno, also offers excellent value, although its reliability was a little lower than its sibling. Unfortunately, we lack sufficient data to score technical support for either provider.

INSIDE INFO COMPUTERS & THE INTERNET

survey. It's DirecWay, the satellite-TV broadband provider, which offers relatively low satisfaction at a very high price—$600 and up for equipment and installation, and $57 a month thereafter for service.

At its best, dial-up service is satisfactory. Cost was again a likely reason. It certainly wasn't speed, which was much slower than the broadband providers for all the dial-ups. In fact, the least expensive service, Juno, was among the top-rated dialups while pricey AOL, the biggest ISP, had one of the lowest overall scores.

HOW TO CHOOSE AN ISP
Know the types of provider. For a summary, see First Things First, at left.

Find out the choices where you live. Your choice in providers depends on where you live—right down to your neighborhood or even street in some cases. Most cable companies now offer broadband, though they may not yet have wired their entire coverage area for the service. Major

Guide to the Ratings

Ratings are based on 25,981 online responses from CONSUMER REPORTS subscribers who completed the Consumer Reports 2005 Annual Questionnaire; they may not be representative of the U.S. population. **PRICE PAID** is the average monthly fee for service, including discounts and promotions, as reported by readers. Prices tend to vary considerably. **READER SCORE** reflects overall satisfaction. If everyone were completely satisfied with their service, the reader score would be 100; 80 would mean respondents were very satisfied, on average; 60 fairly well satisfied. Differences of 5 or more points between scores are meaningful. The following scores are relative and indicate respondents' satisfaction with each ISP compared with the average: **SPEED** reflects satisfaction with Internet connection speed (dial-up ISPs were not included in ratings of speed as they were uniformly lower-rated than broadband providers). **RELIABILITY** reflects satisfaction with the providers' ability to maintain stable, uninterrupted service. **TECHNICAL SUPPORT** reflects satisfaction with the provider's response to service problems. — indicates insufficient data to provide a score. **E-MAIL ONLY** indicates whether the provider has a low-cost plan for keeping an e-mail account active, as when you switch to another ISP.

Ratings

Better ← → Worse

Within types, in order of reader score.

Key number	Service provider	Price	Reader score (0-100)	Speed	Reliability	Technical support	E-mail only
CABLE BROADBAND PROVIDERS							
1	EarthLink earthlink.net [1]	$45	76	◐	◐	○	●
2	Cox cox.com	37	75	◐	◐	◐	
3	Road Runner rr.com [1]	44	74	◐	◐	◐	●
4	Optimum Online optonline.net	44	73	●	●	◐	●
5	Insight insight-com.com	42	71	◐	◐	–	
6	Charter charter.com	39	69	○	○	○	
7	Comcast comcast.com	46	67	○	○	○	
8	Mediacom mediacomcc.com	45	67	○	○	–	
9	Adelphia adelphia.com	43	67	○	○	○	
DSL BROADBAND PROVIDERS							
10	EarthLink earthlink.net	43	72	○	○	○	●
11	SBC Yahoo sbc.com	28	72	○	○	◑	
12	Verizon verizon.com	30	72	○	○	○	
13	BellSouth bellsouth.com	43	71	○	◐	○	●
14	Qwest qwest.com	35	68	◑	○	○	
15	Sprint sprint.com	43	67	○	○	–	
SATELLITE PROVIDER							
16	DirecWay direcway.com	57	55	●	●	–	
DIAL-UP PROVIDERS							
17	Juno juno.com	10	71	–	○	–	●
18	EarthLink earthlink.net	22	69	–	○	○	●
19	AT&T att.net	17	68	–	○	–	●
20	NetZero netzero.net	11	68	–	◑	–	●
21	SBC Yahoo sbc.com	16	63	–	◑	–	
22	MSN msn.com	23	62	–	◑	◑	●
23	AOL aol.com	25	60	–	●	●	●

[1] Ratings are for EarthLink through Time Warner cable, and Road Runner through Time Warner or Bright House Networks. Both are also available through other cable providers.

04 INSIDE INFO COMPUTERS & THE INTERNET

The more time you spend downloading, the more you'll notice broadband's speed.

If you use the Internet mainly for e-mail and occasional Web searches, a dial-up connection may be just fine.

phone companies, too, typically offer DSL service in their most densely populated markets, but not yet in every neighborhood.

Part of the reason for limited choice is that cable companies need not make their networks available for competitors to use—a position that was recently upheld by the Supreme Court. An exception is Time Warner, which as a condition of its 2001 merger with AOL, must allow third-party vendors to access to its cable lines.

The Web sites of most ISP providers allow you to find out what's available by typing in your telephone number or ZIP code. But consider calling instead, in part so that you can ask about how soon service (or improved service) might arrive.

That's especially useful when it comes to DSL. Verizon, SBC Communications, and BellSouth are upgrading their networks to use fiber-optic technology, which promises broadband that's several times faster than cable. But fiber-optic service is available only in about 2 million homes, mostly in affluent areas, and our Ratings may not yet reflect its effect on service quality.

Decide whether broadband is worth it. If you use the Internet mainly to check e-mail and occasionally to surf online, a dial-up connection may suffice.

That said, even casual surfers will notice Web pages loading more quickly with broadband service. And the more time you spend online either downloading large files (poster-size high-resolution digital photos, for example) or uploading data to Web sites, the more you'll notice the speed difference with dial-up service.

Some dialup providers are claiming recent enhancements to the speed of their service. Claims of fivefold speed improvements are overblown, but these ISPs have trimmed download times by storing graphics and other elements of frequently visited Web sites on your computer's hard drive, where they can quickly be summoned when you revisit the site. (Of course, such acceleration doesn't work well the first time you visit a Web site.)

Broadband has the added plus of being always connected; no listening to the pulse of your computer dialing up service each time you want to use the Web.

Select a speed. The scores in our Ratings are only a rough guide to how fast your broadband connection might be. Within any DSL provider, speed declines with distance from the central station, the neighborhood "node" from which service originates; providers can generally specify a data rate for your home. Also, speed will decline if several computers in your home are simultaneously surfing the Web. Finally, almost all broadband services offer several service speeds.

Most people should seek a data speed of 1½ megabits per second for downloads—now the standard speed for most broadband providers. Some broadband services offer speeds less than half as fast, albeit at budget prices.

Providers' superfast tiers offer speeds of 3 or more megabits per second, for anywhere from about $10 to hundreds of dollars more a month. Opt for the extra speed only as an upgrade if you often find your connection slowing from handling large files or when multiple computers in your home are online.

Consider your current cable-TV and telephone service. Chances are good that you're already a subscriber to other services offered by a poten-

INSIDE INFO COMPUTERS & THE INTERNET

tial new broadband provider; that is, you get TV service (and perhaps even Internet phone service) from the cable company and landline or cell-phone service from the phone company that's offering DSL.

At best, that can save you money on your overall telecom expenses, since providers almost invariably offer discounts if you subscribe to several of their services. At worst, it can require you to use them for those other services; for example, most phone companies require that you be a landline phone customer before they'll offer you DSL service. (However, an upcoming Supreme Court ruling and legislative action may change that requirement.)

Consider the standouts for security. ISPs vary in the array of security features they offer, such as antispam, antivirus, and pop-up blocking software. Survey respondents were most satisfied with the security features from Earthlink and AOL. More dial-up survey subscribers took advantage of those services, while broadband users were more likely to use third-party software. We recommend the use of both.

Also, broadband customers in our survey who also subscribed to AOL and MSN (as a $10 to $30 a month add-on) were considerably more satisfied with protection and reported less spam in the past six months compared with broadband subscribers who didn't take either service.

(Note that Consumers Union, publisher of CONSUMER REPORTS, provides online content and sells subscriptions through AOL, MSN, and Yahoo.)

Establish whether you can keep your e-mail address. There are options that allow you to keep your address when you switch service providers. They don't advertise the fact, but many ISPs allow you to keep an e-mail-only account for a much-reduced fee, typically $4.95 a month (see Ratings). You can also switch to a non-ISP-based e-mail service, such as Bigfoot.com, or to one offered by your college or professional organization.

Read the fine print. Sometimes the "introductory" rates only last a few months. You could then end up paying more than if you went with an independent provider. Also, most DSL providers require a 12-month commitment to service, and typically charge a penalty of $100 or more for early termination. Most cable-broadband providers have no such requirement.

TODAY'S PDAS LINK UP TO YOUR NETWORK

They're no longer just a fancy calendar and address book.

The personal digital assistant is evolving in ways that make it easier to use and better able to connect to the Internet and to other devices.

Two types of PDA dominate in sales to U.S. consumers. Seventy percent use the Palm operating system (OS); the rest use Microsoft's Pocket PC software. Here's what the latest models offer:

Designs tailored to the user. Some of the latest models can easily be operated with one hand and wirelessly send and receive e-mail, or readily fit into a pocketbook or shirt pocket. Until they decided to exit the PDA market, Sony had taken the design lead with built-in cameras and bigger screens among Palm OS units.

Better power management. Some Pocket PC units have laptoplike power-saving schemes, but in our most recent tests, only the one in the Toshiba e805 made a difference: You can extend its battery life for an hour by slowing the processing speed.

In some cases, fewer choices. Power-hungry color displays have nearly displaced monochrome; nonreplaceable batteries are standard for Palm OS models.

▶▶ For buying advice on PDAs, see page 55.

A large display, above, can make a PDA easier to use. Some models have an onscreen keyboard, left.

04 BUYING ADVICE DESKTOP COMPUTERS

BUYING ADVICE
Desktop computers

▶ The desktop computer has become just another appliance you use every day. Replacement sales—not first-time purchases—now drive the computer market. Fully loaded desktops selling for less than $800 are common, even among established brands. Even the least-expensive desktop machines deliver impressive performance.

WHAT'S AVAILABLE

There are dozens of companies vying to put a new desktop in your home. Dell, eMachines, Gateway (which merged with eMachines in 2004), Hewlett-Packard (which merged with Compaq in 2002), IBM, and Sony all make machines that use Microsoft's dominant Windows operating system. Apple is the sole maker of Macintosh models. Small mail-order and store brands cater to budget-minded buyers. **Price range:** $400 to $3,000.

> **Given the disk-space requirements** of games, photos, and video files, bigger is better when it comes to hard drives.

FEATURES THAT COUNT

The **processor** houses the "brains" of a computer. Its clock speed, measured in gigahertz (GHz), and the chip's design, termed "architecture," determine how fast the chip can process information. In general, the higher the clock speed, the faster the computer. But not always, since different chip families attain different efficiencies. Manufacturers of Windows machines generally use 1.6- to 3.8-GHz processors with one of the following names: Intel's Pentium or Celeron, or AMD's Athlon or Sempron. Celeron and Sempron are lower-priced processors that equal higher-priced chips in many respects. Intel now assigns "processor numbers" to its chips, de-emphasizing clock speed, while AMD uses a "speed rating" number. Apple's Macintosh machines use 1.25- to 2.7-GHz PowerPC G4 or G5 processors, which are manufactured by IBM. Apple has announced that it will begin a transition to Intel processors in 2006. The system architecture of some families of chips allows them to be as fast as or faster than others with higher clock speeds, so speed comparison by the numbers can be misleading.

All name-brand computers sold today have at least 256 megabytes (MB) of **RAM**, or **random access memory**, the memory the computer uses while in operation. **Video RAM**, also measured in megabytes, is secondary RAM that works with the **graphics processor** to provide smooth video imaging and game play.

The hard drive is your computer's long-term data storage system. Given the disk-space requirements of today's multimedia games, digital photos, and video files, bigger is better. You'll find hard drives ranging in size from 40 to 300 gigabytes (GB).

A **CD-ROM** drive has been standard on most desktops for many years. Commonly supplied now is a CD-RW (CD-rewriteable) drive, also known as a "burner" that lets you create backup files or make music compilations on a compact disc. A **DVD-ROM drive** brings full-length movies or action-packed multimedia games with full-motion video to the desktop. It complements the CD-RW drive on midline and higher-end systems, allowing you to copy CDs directly between the two drives. A DVD drive will also play CDs and CD-ROMs. Combo drives combine CD-writing and DVD-playing in a single drive, saving space. A **DVD-writer**, which lets you transfer home-video footage to a DVD disk, or store as much data as six CDs. There are three competing, incompatible DVD formats—DVD-RW, DVD+RW, and DVD-RAM—as well as drives that can create dual-layer DVDs that store twice as much. Some drives can write in more

By configuring your desktop, you can get just the components you want.

46 CONSUMER REPORTS ● ELECTRONICS BUYING GUIDE 2006   Expert • Independent • Nonprofit

BUYING ADVICE DESKTOP COMPUTERS

than one format, but all can create a disk that will play on standalone DVD players.

Almost gone is the **diskette drive**, where 3.5-inch diskettes are inserted. Most PCs don't have such a drive built in, because it only allows you to read or store relatively small amounts of data. Many people use a CD-RW as a large "diskette" drive to back up or transport files. Many PCs now come with a digital camera memory-card reader that can also serve for file transfer. You can also get external drives or use a USB memory module that holds much more than a diskette.

The computer's **cathode ray tube (CRT)** or **flat-panel liquid crystal display (LCD) monitor** contains the screen and displays the images sent from the graphics processor—internal circuitry that creates the images. Monitors come in sizes (measured diagonally) ranging from 15 to 21 inches and larger. Seventeen-inch monitors are the most common. Apple's eMac and iMac come with built-in monitors, its Mac Mini without one. LCD displays are now the most popular, taking less space and using less power than CRTs. Better LCD displays can use a Digital Video Interface (DVI) connection, found on many newer PCs.

The critical components of a desktop computer are usually housed in a case called a **tower**. A minitower is the typical configuration and can fit either on top of or under a desk. More expensive machines have a midtower, which has extra room for upgrades. A microtower is a space-saving alternative that is usually less expensive. All-in-one computers, such as the Apple iMac, have no tower;

ShopSmart
Configuring your computer

The specifications we use for the computers we buy to test would serve most households well. The chart indicates the specs we decided on for the newest models in the four main categories of computers tested. If you're into extreme gaming or expect to edit video frequently, you may need to bump up the specifications to a higher level than what we've selected.

Note also that older models from previous CR reports will have a slightly slower processor, less system or video memory, a smaller hard drive, and other differences.

Should you wish to configure a computer to order online, onscreen menus typically display all the options and let you see how changing an option affects the overall price.

Computer type	Processor, speed (GHz)	System RAM (memory, in MB)	Hard-drive storage capacity (GB)	Disc writer	Video RAM	Speakers
Budget desktop	Celeron D, 2.8	256	80	CD-RW	64 or 128 MB, integrated	2-piece
Workhorse desktop	Pentium 4, 3.4	512	180	DVD-RW	256 MB, midlevel card	3-piece (subwoofer)
Budget laptop	Celeron M, 1.5	256	40	DVD/CD-RW combo	64 MB	built-in
Workhorse laptop	Pentium M, 1.7	512	80	DVD-RW	128 MB	built-in

Budget computers have slower processors and lower-capacity hard drives than those in other models. Manufacturers use less sophisticated audio-video components and peripherals, and you'll find it more difficult to add features should your needs evolve.

Workhorse computers are versatile, and you can easily expand their capacity and add features. Many offer cards for improved audio and video performance. But some don't have enough muscle for serious video editing or extreme gaming.

everything but the keyboard and mouse is built into a small case that supports the monitor. Apple's Power Mac line of computers has a tower. Apple's newest model, the Mac Mini, has a space-saving design that puts everything but the monitor, keyboard, and mouse in a case about the size of a hardcover book. An "entertainment PC"— one with a TV tuner built in— comes in a case that is more like an audio or video component, made to fit in with other home-entertainment devices.

A **mouse**, a small device that fits under your hand and has a "tail" of wire that connects to the computer, moves the cursor (the pointer on the screen) via a rolling ball or a light sensor on its underside. Alternatives include a trackball, which is rolled with the fingers in the direction you want the cursor to go; a pad, which lets you move the cursor by sliding a finger; a tablet, which uses a penlike stylus for input; and a joystick, used to play computer games.

Most computers come with a standard **keyboard**, although you can also buy one separately. Many keyboards have CD (or DVD) controls to pause playback, change tracks, and so on. Many also have keys to facilitate getting online, starting a search, launching programs, or retrieving e-mail. There are also wireless keyboards and mice that let you move about as you type.

Computers for home use feature a high-fidelity **sound system** that amplifies music from CDs or downloaded music files, synthesized music, game sounds, and DVD-movie soundtracks. Speaker systems with a subwoofer have deeper, more powerful bass. Surround-sound

04 | BUYING ADVICE DESKTOP COMPUTERS

A workhorse desktop can handle gaming, video editing, and more.

systems can turn a PC into a home theater. Some computers come with a **microphone** for recording, or one can be added.

PCs come with a **modem** to allow a dial-up Internet connection. **Parallel** and **serial ports** are the traditional connections for printers and scanners. **Universal serial bus (USB) ports** are designed to replace parallel and serial ports and provide a connection to many other devices. **FireWire** or **IEEE 1394 ports** are used to capture video from digital camcorders and other electronic equipment. An **Ethernet port** or **wireless network card** lets you link several computers in the household to share files, a printer, or a broadband Internet connection. An **S-video output jack** lets you run a video cable from the computer to a television, which lets you use the computer's DVD drive to view a movie on a TV instead of on the computer monitor.

Media Center PCs have a **TV tuner** and a **remote control**, making them a complete entertainment system. They can also record TV programs, just like a TiVo DVR.

HOW TO CHOOSE

First, decide whether to upgrade your current computer. Upgrading, rather than replacing it, may make sense if your additional needs are modest—a second hard drive, say, because you're running out of room for digital photos. Adding memory or a CD burner is usually more cost-effective than buying a whole new machine. If your PC has become unreliable, your want list is more demanding, or if there's software you must run that your system is not up to, a new PC is the logical answer.

Consider a laptop. A desktop computer typically costs hundreds less and is easier to

Moving to a new computer

A little forethought can help you avoid data loss and make moving your personal information from old computer to new relatively painless. Here is some general advice to help you get started:

Making the move. The most important thing to keep in mind when moving information from one computer to another is this: Reinstall programs from scratch on the new computer using the original CDs or diskettes. You can directly copy data files, such as word-processing documents, financial records, photos, and music files.

Transferring data files. If your old files can fit on a few removable CDs or Zip disks, it's easiest to manually copy documents and personal files to disk, then from there to the new PC. You can simplify the transition for yourself by first creating a folder hierarchy on the new computer that's comparable with what's on your old machine.

If you must copy large numbers of files on Windows computers, consider using Windows XP's Files and Settings Transfer Wizard. You can run the Wizard from the Windows XP installation CD or from a diskette. You can connect the two computers via a home network, a serial cable, or simply by manually swapping diskettes between them.

If you are transferring data between two FireWire equipped Macintosh computers, you can use the FireWire Target Disk Mode.

After the move. Leave everything that's on your old computer intact for a few days until you're sure that everything on the new computer is OK. Get everything working again. On the new computer, try out all your programs to be sure they operate as expected. Make sure you can connect to and browse the Internet and send and receive e-mail. You may have to re-enter your account and log-in information.

Protect yourself. Make sure your antivirus program is functioning and that its automatic update feature is enabled.

Update. On a new Windows computer, Windows will prompt you to enable automatic Critical Updates, which we recommend. You should perform a Windows Update (Click on Start, All Programs, Windows Update) or a Mac OS update as soon as possible, to get the latest security and driver updates.

BUYING ADVICE LAPTOP COMPUTERS

Laptop computers

▶ A longtime companion at work, school, and on the road, the laptop has finally come home.

Laptops account for about 25 percent of sales. It's not hard to understand why. Small screens and cramped keyboards have been replaced by bigger, crisper displays and more usable key layouts. Processors have caught up in speed, and innovative new processors provide some real advantages. Fast CD and DVD recording drives are common, as are ample hard drives. And a growing interest in wireless computing plays to the laptop's main strength: its portability. A laptop is the most convenient way to take full advantage of the growing availability of high-speed wireless Internet access at airports, schools, hotels, and even restaurants and coffee shops.

The Centrino technology that's central to Intel's newest laptop processors has wireless capability built in, and it delivers commendably long battery life. The thinnest laptops on the market are less than an inch thick and weigh just 2 to 5 pounds. To get those light, sleek models, however, you'll have to pay a premium and make a few sacrifices.

WHAT'S AVAILABLE

Dell, Gateway, Hewlett-Packard, Compaq (now owned by HP), IBM, Sony, and Toshiba are the leading Windows laptop brands. A laptop can be a secondary computer or your only one. A desktop PC is generally easier to upgrade, expand, and repair. It usually offers better ergonomics, such as a more comfortable keyboard, bigger display, and enhanced audio. But a laptop merits consideration if portability and compactness are priorities.

Pick the right type of desktop. Most manufacturers offer several lines at different price points. Budget computers are the least expensive, yet they are suitable for routine work, such as e-mail, word processing, and Web surfing. You can also do photo editing. Workhorse computers cost a few hundred dollars more but are faster, more versatile, and upgradable. They can run complex 3-D games and edit video. All-in-one models have most of the components in a single case. And entertainment or media PCs include TV tuners, a remote control, and software that give them the functions of a DVR (digital video recorder, such as TiVo).

Choose by brand. Our surveys have consistently shown notable differences in reliability and technical support among computer brands. And some brands are generally more expensive than others. Those factors could help you decide which of two similarly equipped computers is the better buy.

Choose between preconfigured and custom built. You can buy a PC off the shelf in a store or via the Web, configured with features and options the manufacturer pitches to average consumers. Or consider purchasing a desktop that you configure to order, either online or in a store. When you configure a computer to order online, onscreen menus typically show you all the options and let you see how a change in one option affects the overall price.

Wireless technology makes laptops a more useful tool wherever you are.

04 BUYING ADVICE LAPTOP COMPUTERS

Macintosh laptops are made by Apple. Laptops can be grouped into several basic configurations:

Budget models. These have slower processors and lower screen quality than others but are suitable for routine office work and home software. **Price range:** $800 or less.

Workhorse models. These have faster processors and more built-in devices, so there's less need for external attachments. They're not lightweight or battery-efficient enough for frequent travelers. **Price range:** $1,000 and up.

Slim-and-light models. These are for travelers. They can be less than an inch thick and weigh as little as 2 or 3 pounds. They generally require an external drive to read DVDs or burn CDs. **Price range:** $1,500 and up.

Tablet-style. These sit in your hands like a clipboard and have handwriting-recognition software. Some convert to a "normal" laptop with a keyboard. **Price range:** $1,800 and up.

FEATURES THAT COUNT

A **diskette drive** has become a rare option in laptops. As an alternative, you can use a U**SB memory drive** (about $20 and up), which fits on a keychain and holds as much data as numerous diskettes. Or you can save files on a **writeable CD** or **camera memory card**. Most laptops have slots that can read one or more types of memory cards.

Windows laptops generally have a **1.5- to 3.5-GHz processor**. Pentium 4 processors have the higher speed ratings; the new Pentium M and Celeron M processors have a slower rated speed but actually perform on a par with other processors. Macintosh Power PC processors are measured on a different basis altogether. In short, the different types of processors make direct speed comparisons difficult, but any type of processor is likely to deliver all the speed you'll need.

Laptops come with a 40- to 160-gigabyte hard drive and 256 megabytes or more of **random access memory** (RAM) and can be upgraded to 1 gigabyte or more.

Today's laptops use a rechargeable **lithium-ion battery**. In CONSUMER REPORTS tests, batteries provided 2 to 5 hours of continuous use when running office applications. (Laptops go into sleep mode when used intermittently, extending the time between charges.) You can extend battery life somewhat by dimming the display as you work and by removing PC cards and turning off wireless devices when they aren't needed. Playing a DVD movie uses more battery power than usual, but any laptop should be able to play a movie through to the end.

A laptop's **keyboard** can be quite different from that of a desktop computer. The keys themselves may be full-sized (generally only lightweight models pare them down), but they may not feel as solid. Some laptops have extra buttons to expedite your access to e-mail or a Web browser or to control DVD play-

Laptops keys may not feel as solid as those on a desktop keyboard.

Brand repair history

Readers report on more than 140,000 desktop and laptop computers.

The charts at right show the percentage of computers ever needing a repair or having had a serious problem, according to our 2004 Annual Questionnaire. Any brand's repair history includes models that may vary in reliability, and design or manufacturing changes can also affect a brand's repair record. Still, your chances of getting a reliable computer are better when you choose a brand of proven reliability. Gateway was among the more repair-prone brands of desktop; Gateway and Compaq were among the more repair-prone brands of laptop.

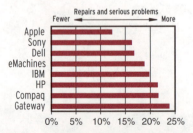

Based on more than 69,000 desktop computers purchased new from 2000 to 2004. Data were standardized to eliminate differences linked to age and use. Differences of less than 4 points are not meaningful.

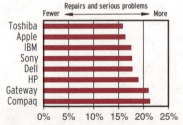

Based on more than 73,000 laptop computers purchased new from 2000 to the first half of 2004. Data were standardized to eliminate differences linked to age and usage. Differences of less than 3 points are not meaningful.

BUYING ADVICE LAPTOP COMPUTERS

back. You can attach an external keyboard, which you may find easier to use.

A 14- to 15-inch **display**, measured diagonally, should suit most people. A few larger models have a 16- or 17-inch display. A resolution of 1,400x1,050 (SXGA+) pixels (picture elements) or more is better than 1,024x768 (XGA) for viewing the fine detail in photographs or video, but may shrink objects on the screen. You can use settings in Windows to make them larger. Many models are now offered with a display that has a "glossy" surface instead of a dull one. Those look better in bright ambient light, as long as you avoid direct reflections.

Most laptops use a small **touch-sensitive pad** in place of a mouse—you slide your finger across the pad to move the cursor. You can also program the pad to respond to a "tap" as a "click," or to scroll as you sweep your index finger along the pad's right edge. An alternative pointing system uses a pencil-eraser-sized joystick in the middle of the keyboard. You can attach an external mouse or trackball if you prefer.

Laptops usually include at least one **PC-card slot** for expansion. You might add a wireless network card or a digital camera memory-card reader, for example, if those are not built in. Many laptops offer a connection for a **docking station**, a $100 or $200 base that makes it easy to connect an external monitor, keyboard, mouse, printer, or phone line. Most laptops let you attach these devices anyway, without the docking station. An external display lets you set up your workspace more ergonomically. At least two USB ports, for easy hookup of, say, a printer, digital camera, or scanner, is standard. A wired network (Ethernet) port is common, as is a FireWire port for digital-video transfer. Many models have a standard or optional internal wireless-network ("Wi-Fi") adapter. The infrared port found on a few models can be used to synchronize data wirelessly between the computer and a personal digital assistant (PDA).

Laptops typically come with less software than desktop computers, although almost all are bundled with a basic home-office suite (such as Microsoft Works) and a personal-finance program. The small speakers built into laptops often sound tinny, with little bass. Headphones or external speakers deliver much better sound.

HOW TO CHOOSE

Decide if a laptop is right for you. If you're on a tight budget and aren't cramped for space, a desktop computer may still be OK. It's also best for heavy users who spend hours at the computer each day. Otherwise, consider a laptop.

Windows vs. Macintosh. Many people choose Windows because it's what they've always used. Apple's iBook will suit you if you're interested in photo editing, music, video, and other multimedia applications. In recent subscriber surveys, CONSUMER REPORTS has found Apple laptops to be among the most reliable and Apple technical support to be top-notch. Apple computers are also less susceptible to viruses and spyware than Windows-based computers. The Apple PowerBook is relatively expensive as laptops go, however.

Buy à la carte. Dell and Gateway pioneered the notion that every computer can be tailored to an individual buyer's needs, much like choosing the options for a car. This configure-to-order model is now common practice for laptops as well as desktops.

You can also purchase a pre-configured computer off the shelf. (You can do the same online if you opt for the default choices of equipment the manufacturer offers.) That's fine if you don't have very strict requirements for how a laptop is outfitted or if you want to take advantage of an attractive sale.

Configure-to-order menus show you all the options and let you see how a change in one affects the overall price. You may decide to use a less-expensive processor, for example, but spend more for wireless capability or better graphics. Configure-to-order will often give you choices you won't get if you buy off the shelf. And configure-to-order means less chance of overlooking important details. But be sure to double-check your choices before ordering and look for unwanted items that some manufacturers include by default.

A workhorse laptop can be a good choice for an at-home computer.

A spare power adapter will run you $30 and up.

04 BUYING ADVICE LAPTOP COMPUTERS, MONITORS

Moving up? What to do with that old computer

You can give it away, you can recycle it, or you can keep it in the attic, just in case

Find a new home for your computer. A computer that's stored in your basement or garage doesn't serve anyone and quickly outlives its usefulness. According to experts at Carnegie Mellon University, PCs lose about 40 percent of their value each year. So the sooner you find a new home for your old computer, the better. Many local, regional, and national organizations will take usable PCs for groups or individuals that can't afford to buy new ones. One such organization is the National Cristina Foundation. It will take PCs that are Pentium 2 or newer and Macs that are G3 or newer. You can tell if your computer is new enough to donate by clicking the Start menu, right clicking My Computer, selecting Properties and looking at the bottom of the window that pops up. At TechSoup you can find a ZIP-code searchable database listing organizations that will take used equipment, those that offer low-cost refurbished products, and other information.

If nobody wants your computer, recycle it. If your computer is just too old (that is, it can't run at least Windows 95 or Mac OS 7.5), it may be destined for the scrap heap. Check with your local waste management agency to find out if your municipality has a recycling program that accepts electronic waste. Many municipalities in states that have banned computer equipment from landfills offer collection or drop-off programs.

Learn more by linking to our Recycling Center at *www.GreenerChoices.org*.

You may find that the company you buy your next computer from will take the old one off your hands, either for free or at a nominal cost. Some companies also provide discounts on new equipment for customers who send old equipment back for recycling.

Major manufacturers with recycling services include Apple, Dell, and HP. Some manufacturers have also teamed with retailers like Best Buy and Office Depot to sponsor limited-time, in-store collection events. In many cases these services are free, but some retailers may charge fees or accept only certain types or brands of equipment.

Consider keeping your monitor. Monitors can often be reused even when a computer cannot. If you find no takers for yours, you may want to save it as a spare. Monitors are the most environmentally hazardous computer component, with pounds of lead-filled glass and other toxins. Some states—Massachusetts was the first—have banned monitors from landfills. Whatever you do, don't simply take your monitor to the curb for trash pickup. Crushing up computer equipment, especially monitors, contaminates other waste, making it more likely that the toxic components will get into the environment. Broken monitors are also more expensive to manage because they must be treated as hazardous waste. Intact monitors are exempt from hazardous-waste management regulations and are cheaper and easier to recycle.

Check out the recycler. Unfortunately, not all the computer equipment returned for recycling ends up at an appropriately managed facility. The Silicon Valley Toxics Coalition has found that some equipment is diverted to uncontrolled landfills or unsafe recycling operations in developing countries. As a result, the local environment in these areas can become contaminated, and local residents, in an effort to reclaim valuable metal components, may be exposed to hazardous materials. Some companies are pledging to track the equipment to keep this from happening. Look for a recycling firm that has taken the Electronics Recyclers' Pledge of True Stewardship. The program is new, but the number of companies that have signed on is growing.

Warning: Whether you donate or discard your old computer, be sure to erase all information stored on its hard drive to protect your privacy.

Downplay the processor speed. Speed is no longer the be-all of personal computers. For years, processors have delivered all the speed most people need. That's still very much the case. Spend the money on more memory instead. A Pentium 4 processor with a speed of 2.4 GHz and a Pentium M at 1.4 GHz earned the same speed score in our tests. The different types of chips now on the market make direct speed comparisons difficult.

Look closely at warranties and insurance. Get the longest manufacturer's warranty you can afford; many offer one or two years above the basic one-year warranty, for a price. If you intend to travel a lot, buy screen insurance from the manufacturer. If you take full advantage of the manufacturer's warranty and insurance, you won't need an extended warranty from the retailer.

BUYING ADVICE
Monitors

▶ Prices are dropping for larger CRT monitors, and for flat-panel LCD displays that free up space on your desktop.

Deciding whether to buy a flat-panel LCD or a standard, fairly fat CRT monitor comes down to this: Do you need more space on the surface of your desk or on the screen? If freeing up space on your desk is the priority, an LCD is the clear choice. But since LCDs are costly, you might still opt for a CRT.

Desktop computers and monitors are often sold as a package. Still, some people buying a new desktop decide to hold on to their old monitor. Others choose to buy a new monitor for their existing computer.

WHAT'S AVAILABLE
Apple, Dell, eMachines (which merged with Gateway in 2004), Gateway, Hewlett-Packard (which merged with Compaq in 2002), IBM, and Sony all market their own brands of monitors for their computers. Other brands of monitors, such as CTX, Envision, Mitsubishi, NEC, Philips, Samsung, and ViewSonic are sold separately. Many brands are manufactured on an outsource basis.

CRT monitors. These typically range from 17 to 21 inches.

BUYING ADVICE MONITORS

To reduce glare, some CRTs have flattened, squared-off screens (not to be confused with flat-panel LCD screens). The nominal image size—the screen size touted in ads—is generally based on the diagonal measurement of the picture tube. The image you see, called the viewable image size (VIS), is usually an inch smaller. Thus a 17-inch CRT has a 16-inch VIS. As a result of a class-action lawsuit, ads must state a CRT's VIS as well as its nominal image, but you may have to squint at the fine print to find it.

Generally the bigger the screen, the more room a CRT takes up on your desk, with depth roughly matching nominal screen size. "Short-depth" models shave an inch or more off the depth.

A 17-inch monitor, the most frequent choice these days, has almost one-third more viewable area than the 15-inch version now vanishing from the market. The larger size is especially useful when you're using the Internet, playing video games, watching DVD movies, editing photos, or working in several windows.

If you regularly work with graphics or sprawling spreadsheets, consider getting a 19-inch monitor. Its viewable area is one-fourth larger than a 17-inch model's. A short-depth 19-inch model doesn't take up much more desktop space than a standard 17-inch.

Aimed at graphics professionals, 21- and 22-inch models provide ample viewing area but they gobble up desktop space. **Price range:** $100 to $200 (17-inch); $175 to $300 (19-inch); $500 to $1,000 (21- to 22-inch).

Flat-panel LCD monitors. These began to outsell CRT monitors in 2003. Because these monitors have a liquid-crystal display rather than a TV-style picture tube, they take up much less desktop space than CRTs. They operate with analog or digital input, or both. Unlike a CRT, the nominal and the viewable image sizes of a flat-panel LCD are the same. Desktop models typically measure 15 inches diagonally and just a few inches deep, and weigh around 15 pounds, compared with 30 to 50 pounds for a CRT. LCDs with a screen 17 inches or larger are available, but they are still somewhat pricey. Wide-screen LCDs with a 17-inch VIS, specially designed for watching wide-format videos, are also available. These screens have an aspect ratio of 16:9, like those found on most digital TVs, and they're also fairly pricey.

Flat-panel displays deliver a very clear image, but they have some inherent quirks. Their range of color is a bit narrower than that of CRT monitors. And you have to view a flat-panel screen straight on; except for wide-screen models, the picture loses contrast as you move off-center. Fine lines may appear grainy. In analog mode you have to tweak the controls in order to get the best picture. **Price range:** $300 to $450 (15-inch); $300 and up (17- to 18-inch).

FEATURES THAT COUNT

A monitor's **resolution** refers to the number of picture elements, or pixels, that make up an image. More pixels mean finer detail. Most monitors can display at several resolutions, generally ranging from 640x480 to 1,600x1,200, depending on the monitor and the graphics card. An LCD usually displays a sharper image than a CRT of comparable size when both are

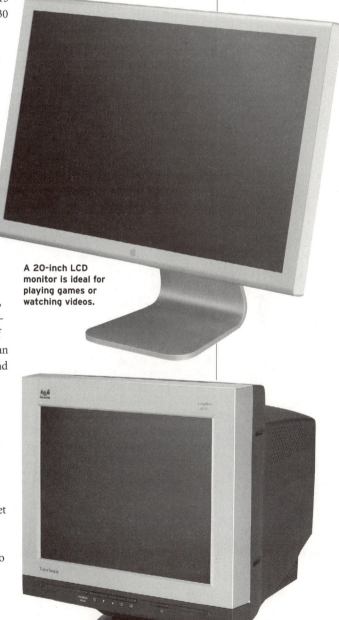

A 20-inch LCD monitor is ideal for playing games or watching videos.

CRTs offer more screen (and bulk) for the money.

04 BUYING ADVICE MONITORS

viewed at identical resolutions. But that's only if the LCD is set to its "native" resolution—1,024x768 pixels for a 15-inch screen; 1,280x1,024 or 1,400x1,050 for a 17-, 18-, or 19-inch model. On both types of monitor, the higher the resolution, the smaller the text and images, so more content fits on the screen. Bigger CRT screens can handle higher resolutions and display more information.

Dot pitch, measured in millimeters, refers to the spacing between a CRT's pixels. All else being equal, a smaller dot pitch produces a more detailed image, though that's no guarantee of an excellent picture. In general, avoid models with a dot pitch larger than 0.28 mm.

A CRT requires a high **refresh rate** (the number of times per second the image is redrawn on the screen) to avoid annoying image flicker. In general, you'll be more comfortable with a 17-inch monitor with a refresh rate of at least 75 hertz (Hz) at the resolution you want. For a 19-inch monitor, you may need an 85-Hz rate to avoid eyestrain, especially at higher resolutions. Refresh rate isn't an issue with flat-panel displays.

Monitors have controls for **brightness and contrast.** Most of them also have controls for color balance (usually called color temperature), **distortion,** and such. Buttons activate onscreen controls and menus.

Bigger CRTs use a considerable amount of juice: about 80 watts for a typical 19-inch model, between 65 to 70 watts for a 17-inch model, and about 20 watts for a 15-inch flat-panel LCD, for example. Most monitors have a **sleep mode** that uses less than 3 watts when the computer is on but not in use.

Some monitors include a microphone, integrated or separate **speakers,** or **composite-video** inputs for viewing the output of a VCR or camcorder.

Plug-and-play capability makes it fairly simple to add a new monitor to an existing computer.

HOW TO CHOOSE

Decide between LCD and CRT monitors. If your computer's monitor is hogging the top of your desk, you can reclaim much of that space by replacing it with an LCD. But doing so will cost you about $200 to $300 more than if you bought a new CRT monitor. And LCD screens have an inherent shortcoming: The image appears to fade as you move left, right, up, or down. However, most LCD monitors in our recent tests had a wider viewing angle than we've seen in the past. If space isn't an issue but budget is, a CRT monitor is a good choice. Because CRTs deliver truer color and render fast-moving objects better, they are a superior choice for photographers, designers, and gamers.

Settle on size. For most people, a 15-inch LCD monitor or a 17-inch CRT is big enough. Larger monitors are best suited for people who need to show photo enlargements or who regularly display multiple windows on the screen.

Consider helpful features. A monitor you can raise or lower can compensate for a desk that's too high or low. It's a feature found on some LCD monitors, but not on CRTs because they're so heavy. Some monitors can be rotated 90 degrees, from a landscape to portrait orientation, with the image automatically adjusting itself. That can be handy for viewing photos and Web pages. Also, look for conveniently placed controls that adjust contrast, brightness, and other settings that affect image.

Look for a long warranty. Many monitors, both LCDs and CRTs, come with a three-year warranty on parts and labor. A warranty that long is worth looking for, especially when purchasing a more expensive model.

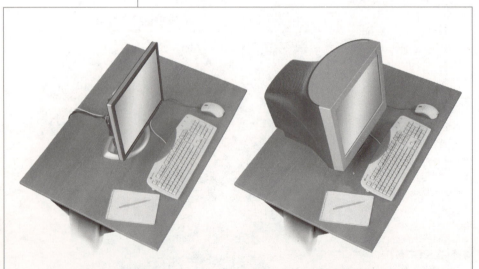

If desk space is at a premium in your office, consider buying an LCD monitor, left. A CRT monitor, right, takes up more space on the desktop, but offers a bigger screen size for the money.

BUYING ADVICE
PDAs

▶ Besides serving as an address book, calendar, and to-do list, many personal digital assistants offer multimedia functions.

PDAs can store thousands of phone numbers, appointments, tasks, and notes. All models can exchange, or synchronize, information with a full-sized computer with PIM (personal information management) software. To do this, you connect the PDA to your computer via a cradle or cable. For models that run on rechargeable batteries, the cradle doubles as a charger. Infrared, Bluetooth, and Wi-Fi let you synchronize your PDA and a computer without the use of wires or a cradle.

Most PDAs can be made to work with both Windows and Macintosh computers, but PDAs with the Pocket PC operating system usually require third-party software for Macs. PDAs with Wi-Fi (wireless) capability can access the Internet. Those without need a separately purchased modem. Most PDAs can record your voice, play videos, display digital photos, and hold maps, city guides, and a novel.

WHAT'S AVAILABLE

Most PDAs on the market are the familiar tablet-with-stylus types that feature a squarish display screen, a design pioneered by Palm Inc. (now called Palm). Today the main choices are models that use the Palm operating system (OS)—mostly PalmOne models—and Pocket PC devices from companies such as Dell and Hewlett-Packard. The latter use a stripped-down version of Microsoft Windows. A few PDAs use a proprietary operating system. Kyocera, Nokia, Samsung, and Sony Ericsson offer units that combine a cell phone and a PDA.

Palm OS systems.
Equipped with software to link with Windows and Macintosh computers, Palm units have a simple user interface. You use a stylus to enter data on the units by tapping an onscreen keyboard or writing in a shorthand known as Graffiti. Or you can download data from your computer. Most Palm OS-based PDAs can synchronize with a variety of desktop e-mail programs, such as Outlook, Outlook Express, and Eudora. Most Palm models come with VersaMail, software good at handling e-mails with attachments. And all include Palm desktop, a basic PIM application for exchanging information with your desktop PC. Palm OS units are easy to use, although navigation between different programs is cumbersome because of the operating system's "single-tasking" nature.

Most Palm OS models make it difficult or impossible to replace the battery yourself. And beyond the warranty period, you can't be sure the manufacturer will do it for you.

Most Palm OS models have expansion slots that let you add memory or attach separately purchased accessories. All Palm OS-based PDAs can be enhanced by adding third-party software applications—the more free memory that a model comes with, the more software it can accommodate. There is a large body of Palm OS-compatible freeware, shareware, and commercial software available for download at such sites as *www.palmgear.com*. Many Palm models come with Documents To Go—word-processing and spreadsheet software

Tapping on the screen with a stylus is just one way of entering data on a personal digital assistant, or PDA.

04 BUYING ADVICE PDAS

similar to that used in Pocket PCs but more versatile. **Price range:** $100 to $800.

One of PalmOne's top-of-the-line models, the Tungsten T5, combines a Palm OS-based PDA with many of the best features of the PocketPC OS. When it's connected to a Windows PC, you can drag and drop files to the T5's built-in "flash drive," even on PCs that don't have Palm's desktop software installed.

Pocket PC systems. These resemble Palm OS-based models but are more like miniature computers. They have a processor with extra horsepower and come with familiar applications such as a word processor and a spreadsheet. Included is a scaled-down version of Internet Explorer, plus voice-recording and perhaps some financial functions. The included e-mail program handles Word and Excel attachments easily. Also standard is an application that plays MP3 music files.

As you might expect, all the application software included in a Pocket PC integrates well with the Windows computer environment. You need to purchase third-party software to use a Mac. And you'll need Microsoft Office programs (Word, Excel, and Outlook) on your computer to exchange data with a PDA. All Pocket PCs include a copy of Outlook for use as a PIM application. Pocket PCs have a color display and rechargeable lithium-ion batteries. Unlike most Palm OS-based PDAs, replacing the battery of most Pocket PCs is straightforward. **Price range:** $200 to $700.

Some PDAs have a keyboard for entering data.

FEATURES THAT COUNT

All PDAs have the tools for basic tasks: a **calendar** to keep track of your appointments, **contact/address software** for addresses and phone numbers, **tasks/to-do lists** for reminders and keeping track of errands, and a **calculator**. A **notes/memo function** lets you make quick notes to yourself. Other capabilities include **word-processing, spreadsheet,** and **e-mail functions**. A **voice recorder**, which uses a built-in microphone and speaker, works like a tape recorder. **MP3 playback** lets you listen to digital-music files stored in that format, and a picture viewer lets you look at digital photos. A few models also include a **built-in digital camera** and **keyboard**.

A PDA's processor is the system's brain. In general, the higher the processing speed of this chip, the faster the PDA will execute tasks—and the more expensive it will be. But higher-speed processors may require more battery power and thus deplete batteries more quickly. Processing speeds are 16 to 600 megahertz (MHz), and models typically have 8 to 64 megabytes (MB) of user memory. Even the smallest amount in that range should be more than enough for most people.

Nearly every PDA offers an **expansion slot** for some form of removable memory card: CompactFlash, MultiMedia card (slots also accept SecureDigital cards), or Memory Stick. Models with two expansion slots can accommodate a peripheral device, such as a Wi-Fi wireless networking card, as well as removable memory. If you plan to transfer photos from a digital camera to your PDA, make sure the two devices use the same type of card.

Some PDAs offer **wireless connectivity**. Models with a capability known as Bluetooth can connect wirelessly over short distances to a properly equipped computer or peripheral such as a printer or modem. Models with Wi-Fi can connect over medium distances to a Wi-Fi-enabled home network or to the Internet at "hotspots" in certain airports, coffee shops, and hotels. A PDA combined with a cell phone can make voice calls or directly connect to the Internet via a wireless Internet service provider. It's possible for a single PDA to have more than one of these three types of wireless connectivity.

HOW TO CHOOSE

Consider your ties to a computer. Pocket PCs provide a Windows-like interface that allows simple PC-to-PDA file transfer with drag-and-drop capability. They're also more convenient than Palm OS models for setting up a Wi-Fi (wireless) e-mail connection. Most have replaceable batteries, along with accessible flash memory to which you can back up data.

Palm OS models run a wider range of third-party software applications than do Pocket PCs. For the basics, they're still easier to use. While all PDAs can sync with Macintoshes, only Palm models do so out of the box. The Missing Sync (available at *www.markspace.com*) and PocketMac (*www.pocketmac.net*) connect a Pocket PC to a Mac. Both are priced under $50.

Small size vs. extra features. As a rule, a model with a larger display or physical keyboard won't be the lightest or smallest. A PDA with two slots for memory and peripherals is more expandable but will tend to be larger.

PRINTERS

INSIDE INFO
58 Choose a printer to suit your tasks

BUYING ADVICE
59 Printers
61 Multifunction devices

CHAPTER 05

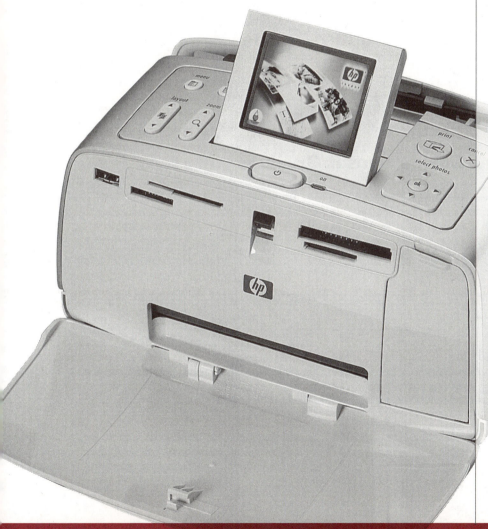

Paired with a PC and the right software, today's inkjet printers offer unmatched versatility: You can switch at will from color to black-and-white, from photos to text, or to elaborate combinations of all of those. Little wonder that they are the best-selling type of printer.

But that doesn't mean inkjets are right for everybody. For one thing, printing photos on an inkjet can be more expensive and more time-consuming than simply taking them to your local one-hour lab. What's more, it typically costs more to print black-and-white text with an inkjet than with a laser printer, which could be a consideration even if you aren't, say, Stephen King or someone equally prolific.

Of course, all the major types of printers continue to evolve, and they may have changed significantly since you last shopped for one. In the pages that follow, we'll cover what you need to know to pick the perfect printer (or multifunction device) now.

 Some printers are ideal for text, some for photos, and some can handle both. Multifunction units do all that and more.

Ratings: Printers, p. 160

05 INSIDE INFO PRINTERS

CHOOSE A PRINTER TO SUIT YOUR TASKS

Prices and functions vary. Here's how to get best value.

The first question you need to ask yourself is what you expect to print with your new printer—text, photos, or some combination of the two. Here's a quick rundown of the four basic types, with some of their pros and cons. More detailed buying advice follows later in this chapter.

First Things First

1 Text Only

Your best choice: A laser printer.
Pros: Nothing beats a laser for fine, fast text printing. The best inkjet can match the excellent text quality, but lasers print text more quickly and cheaply than most inkjets. As an added plus, lasers are often quieter than inkjets too.
Cons: While tops for text, lasers aren't as versatile as inkjets and they're not suited for printing photos. Even models that can print in color aren't intended for use with glossy photo stock or other specialty papers. They also cost more to buy than inkjets, although you'll probably spend less on supplies over time.
Price range: $150 and up for black-and-white printers. Multifunction models start at $250, color ones at about $400.
The bottom line: A laser printer will be your best choice for fast, low-cost, top-quality black-and-white text. But you'll still need an inkjet or 4x6 model if you plan to print photos.

2 Text Plus Color Photos & Graphics

Your best choice: A regular inkjet printer.
Pros: Many regular inkjet printers offer excellent print quality for both photos and text, and will accept a variety of paper types and sizes. Most can print photos directly from a digital camera.
Cons: Supply costs can be high. Inkjet speeds can also be slow, ranging from 1½ to 21 minutes for an 8x10-inch photo.
Price: $80 and up.
The bottom line: Inkjets remain your best all-around choice for printing photos, text, and color graphics, such as greeting cards and Web pages.

3 Text, Photos, & Graphics Plus Copying & Scanning

Your best choice: A multifunction inkjet printer.
Pros: Multifunction machines combine printing, scanning, and copying in one unit and may be cheaper than buying several separate devices. The best of them can produce excellent color photos and text, and most will print photos without a PC.
Cons: The print quality of some multifunction machines may not match that of a regular printer, especially for photos. They may also have fewer features than stand-alone printers, and, unlike many stand-alone scanners, most can't scan negatives or slides. As with other electronic devices designed to do more than one job, you'll have to repair or replace the entire unit if one part of it breaks down.
Price: $100 and up.
The bottom line: Check out multifunction machines if you need a printer, scanner, and copier, but lack the space for separate units.

4 Snapshots Only

Your best choice: A 4x6 photo printer.
Pros: 4x6 photo printers are small and fast, with speeds as quick as a minute per snapshot. Some portable types can run on batteries, handy for use on the road. All can print photos from a digital camera or memory card, without requiring a computer. Many models use dye-sublimation (dye-sub) technology to make prints that are more water-resistant than those from inkjets.
Cons: 4x6 photo printers use pre-cut photo paper, and they are not for printing text or graphics. In our tests, they didn't provide the photo quality of the better regular inkjets, and these printers tend to be more costly. Supplies for the dye-sublimation models are also expensive.
Price: $140 to $200.
The bottom line: 4x6 photo printers are speedy and convenient, but you'll sacrifice flexibility and some print quality.

BUYING ADVICE PRINTERS

Our tests have found that brand-name ink cartridges generally deliver the best print quality.

BUYING ADVICE
Printers

▶ New, inexpensive inkjets print color superbly, and they do it faster than ever. Laser printers excel at printing black-and-white text.

Inkjet printers are now the standard for home-computer output. They can turn out color photos nearly indistinguishable from lab-processed photos, along with banners, stickers, transparencies, T-shirt transfers, and greeting cards. Many produce excellent black-and-white text. With some very good models going for less than $200, inkjets account for the vast majority of printers sold for home use.

Laser printers still have their place in home offices. If you print reams of black-and-white text documents, you probably need the quality, speed, and low per-copy cost of a laser printer.

Printers use a computer's microprocessor and memory to process data. The latest inkjets and lasers are so fast partly because computers themselves have become more powerful and contain much more memory than before.

WHAT'S AVAILABLE

The printer market is dominated by a handful of well-established brands. Hewlett-Packard is the market leader. Other major brands include Brother, Canon, Epson, and Lexmark.

The type of computer a printer can serve depends on its ports. A Universal Serial Bus (USB) port lets a printer connect to Windows or Macintosh computers. A few models have a parallel port, which lets the printer work with older Windows computers. All these printers lack a serial port, which means they won't work with older Macs.

INKJET PRINTERS

Inkjets use droplets of ink to form letters, graphics, and photos. Some printers have one cartridge that holds the cyan (greenish-

The latest printers are so fast partly because computers themselves have become more powerful and contain much more memory than before.

Inkjet printers are versatile and inexpensive.

More colors, more cartridges
To improve the rendering of color or shades of gray, some manufacturers have increased the number of inks in their printers to as many as nine.

Many printers have separate cartridges for each ink color. One potential benefit of this approach is economic: Individual colors are typically consumed at different rates. When one color in a multicolor cartridge runs out, you must replace the entire cartridge—a waste of the other, unused inks. Having a cartridge for each color can reduce that waste, although it won't necessarily save you any money. In our tests of printers over the past few years, models with individual cartridges haven't always produced photos more economically than those using multicolor cartridges.

05 BUYING ADVICE PRINTERS

An LCD screen (center) lets you preview and crop your images.

Printing color inkjet photos on special paper at a higher dpi setting can produce smoother shading of colors, but it can also slow printing significantly.

blue), magenta, and yellow inks, and a second cartridge for the black ink. Others have an individual cartridge for each ink. For photos, many inkjets also have additional cartridges that contain lighter shades of cyan and magenta inks; some have added red, gray, blue, or green inks. Most inkjets print at 2½ to 11 pages per minute (ppm) for black-and-white text but are much slower for color photos, taking 1½ to 21 minutes to print a single 8x10. The cost of printing a black-and-white page with an inkjet varies considerably from model to model—ranging from 3 to 7.5 cents. The cost of printing a color 8x10 photo can range from 80 cents to $1.50. **Price range:** $80 to $700.

LASER PRINTERS
These work much like plain-paper copiers, forming images by transferring toner (powdered ink) to paper passing over an electrically charged drum. The process yields sharp black-and-white text and graphics. Laser printers usually outrun inkjets, cranking out black-and-white text at a rate of 12 to 18 ppm. Black-and-white laser printers generally cost about as much as midpriced inkjets, but they're cheaper to operate. Laser cartridges, about $50 to $100, can print thousands of black-and-white pages for a per-page cost of 2 to 4 cents. Color laser printers are also available. **Price range:** $150 to $1,000 (black-and-white); $400 and up (color).

FEATURES THAT COUNT
Printers differ in the fineness of detail they can produce.

Resolution, expressed in dots per inch (dpi), is often touted as the main measure of print quality. But other factors, such as the way dot patterns are formed by software instructions from the printer driver, count, too. At their default settings—where they're usually expected to run—inkjets currently on the market typically have a resolution of 600x600 dpi. For color photos the dpi can be increased. Some printers go up to 5,760x1,440 dpi. Laser printers for home use typically offer 600 or 1,200 dpi. Printing color inkjet photos on special paper at a higher dpi setting can produce smoother shading of colors but can slow printing significantly.

Most inkjet printers have an **ink monitor** to warn when you're running low. Generic ink cartridges usually costs less, but most produce far fewer prints than the brand-name inks, so per-print costs may not be any lower. And print quality and fade-resistance may not be as good.

For **double-sided printing**, you can print the odd-numbered pages of a document first, then flip those pages over to print the even-numbered pages on a second pass through the printer. A few printers can automatically print on both sides, but doing so slows down printing.

HOW TO CHOOSE
Be skeptical about advertised speeds. Print speed varies depending on what you're printing and at what quality, but the speeds you see in ads are generally higher than you're likely to achieve in normal use. You can't reliably compare speeds for different brands because each company uses its own methods to measure speed. We run the same tests on all models, printing text pages and photos that are similar to what you might print. As a result, our scores are realistic and can be compared across brands.

Don't get hung up on resolution. A printer's resolution, expressed in dots per inch, is another potential source of confusion. All things being equal, the more ink dots a printer puts on the paper, the more detailed the image. But dot size, shape, and placement also affect quality, so don't base your decision solely on resolution.

Consider supply costs as well as a printer's price. High

Pricedrop Alert

Affordable color lasers are here, but ...

Laser printers still have their place in home offices, especially if you churn out reams of black-and-white text documents. Recently, color lasers have become more affordable, with several manufacturers offering models starting at about $400, down from the four-figure prices of several years ago. While their graphics quality makes them suitable for jobs such as newsletters or flyers, their photo quality is lower than that of color inkjets. And given their slowness at color printing compared to the faster inkjets, we see no reason yet to recommend them.

BUYING ADVICE MULTIFUNCTION DEVICES

ink-cartridge costs can make a bargain-priced printer a bad deal in the long run. Shop around for the best cartridge prices but be wary of off-brands; we have found brand-name cartridges to have better print quality overall, and per-page costs are often comparable.

Glossy photo paper costs about 25 to 75 cents a sheet, so use plain paper for works in progress and save the good stuff for the final results. We've gotten the best results using the recommended brand of paper. You may be tempted to buy a cheaper brand, but bear in mind that lower-grade paper can reduce photo quality and may not be as fade resistant.

Decide if you want to print photos without using a computer. Printing without a computer saves you an extra step and a little time. Features such as memory-card support, PictBridge support (a standard that allows a compatible camera to be connected directly to the printer), or a wireless interface are convenient. But when you print directly from camera to printer, you compromise on what may have attracted you to digital photography in the first place—the ability to tweak size, color, brightness, and other image attributes. And with a 4x6 printer, you give up the ability to print on larger media.

Weigh convenience features. Most printers make borderless prints like those from a photo developer. This matters most if you're printing to the full size of the paper, as you might with 4x6-inch sheets. Otherwise you can trim the edges off.

If you plan to use 4x6-inch paper regularly, look for a printer with a 4x6-inch tray, which makes it easier to feed paper of this size. With these small sheets, though, the cost per photo may be higher than ganging up a few images on 8½x11-inch paper.

With some models, if you want to use the photo inks to get the best picture quality, you have to remove the black ink cartridge and replace it with the photo-ink cartridge. Then you have to replace the black for text or graphics. This can get tedious. Models that hold all the ink tanks simultaneously eliminate that hassle.

Consider connections. Printers with USB 2.0 ports are now fairly common. However, they don't enable much faster print speeds than plain USB. All new computers and printers have either USB or USB 2.0 ports, both of which are compatible. Computers more than six years old may have only a parallel port.

Decide whether you need scanning and copying. A multifunction unit provides scanning and color copying while saving space. The downside is that multifunction units' scanners may have lower resolution than the latest stand-alone scanners. Stand-alone scanners are best for handling negatives and slides. And if one part of the unit breaks, the whole unit must be repaired or replaced.

BUYING ADVICE
Multi-function devices

▶ A multifunction device gives you a printer, scanner, copier, and sometimes a fax machine in a single unit, often for less than $200 for an inkjet model. Laser multifunctions can start around $180, but rise considerably with color capability.

Multifunctions offer versatility and affordability. You get a printer, scanner, copier, and sometimes a fax machine in a package that's just a little larger than a regular printer. These devices have improved over the past few years, so even a home office user may be satisfied with their print quality.

A multifunction device offers versatility and affordability. You get a printer, scanner, copier, and sometimes a fax machine in a package that's just a little larger than a regular printer.

Memory cards let you bypass the computer.

Will your new printer & old camera communicate?

The ability to print snapshots directly from a digital camera or its memory card can make life easier for those of us who want our prints without having to fuss with computer programs.

Many newer models, especially those marketed as "photo" printers, have slots for memory cards or support for PictBridge, a standard that allows a suitable camera to be connected directly to the printer.

Unfortunately, digital cameras that are more than about a year old probably don't have PictBridge support. As a result, you may not be able to use your camera's USB port to transfer images directly to the printer, though you can use it to send them to your computer for later printing.

If you'll be using your printer with a digital camera and printing lots of photos, make sure the printer has all the features you need, including a memory-card slot. If you aren't sure, check the manufacturer's Web site or inspect a floor model at a retailer.

05 BUYING ADVICE MULTIFUNCTION DEVICES

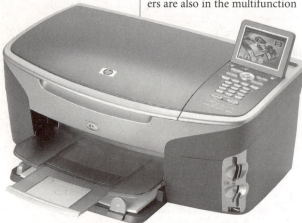

Multifunction inkjet printers can print, copy, and scan.

*The included scanners, which have resolution ranging from **600 to 2,400 dpi,** delivered quality similar to that of the stand-alone scanners in our last tests but were slower.*

WHAT'S AVAILABLE
Most major printer manufacturers are also in the multifunction business. The key brands in the category are Brother, Canon, Dell, Epson, Hewlett-Packard, and Lexmark.

The two types are inkjet and laser. Inkjet models can print and copy in color. Most laser models print and copy only in black and white. More expensive models can print in color, but they're expensive—$800. Most multifunction devices support both Windows and Macintosh computers, but because these units don't have a serial port, they will not work with Macs manufactured before mid-1998. **Price range:** $100 to $400.

FEATURES THAT COUNT
All these devices are TWAIN-compliant. (TWAIN refers to an interface between image-processing software and a scanner or digital camera.) As with printers, a selling point is maximum resolution, or maximum dpi, used when printing photos. But a model with a high maximum dpi does not necessarily produce the highest-quality output. Most multifunction devices can reduce or enlarge images.

Multifunction devices that can fax do so in black and white, but most can also **fax in color** to a color-enabled device. Most current models have a **flatbed scanner**. After scanning, text must be "read" by an **optical-character-recognition (OCR) program** before it's edited on the computer. Images can be used immediately either by a graphics program that comes with the scanner or one you buy separately.

HOW TO CHOOSE
Consider space. Printers that also scan and copy can save space compared with having a separate unit for each. But keep in mind that most multifunctions are larger than regular printers and require more vertical clearance to lift the lid. If a basic inkjet printer and a separate fax machine are all you need, you can get these for about $200.

Weigh a multifunction's limitations. Photo quality from multifunction printers may not match that of regular printers. The included scanners, which have resolution ranging from 600 to 2,400 dpi, delivered quality similar to that of the stand-alone scanners in our last tests but were slower. If you choose an all-in-one, check to see whether it can make copies when the computer is off.

Consider your future needs. If you decide to use one machine to do everything, you will sacrifice some future flexibility: You can't upgrade just one function in a multifunction device. And if a major part breaks down, the entire machine may be out of service.

Choose between inkjet and laser. If you scan and print mostly color photos or graphics, look for an inkjet model. But if you plan to print or copy only black-and-white text, a black-and-white laser multifunction device is the more appropriate choice.

Printing at less princely prices

Buying a printer is just the beginning of your printing costs, of course. Supplies can quickly add to the total. Here are some simple ways to get the most value from your printer.

Ink: Shop around and stock up.

- Shop around for the best deals on consumables such as ink and paper, but don't venture too far from name brands. In our experience, third-party brands of paper and ink may deliver photos that aren't as vivid and are more prone to fading. We have also found that off-brand inks do not always yield lower per-photo printing costs.
- Print snapshots to a 3½ x 5-inch size. That's a standard snapshot format, and it allows you to squeeze four onto one 8½ x 11-inch sheet.
- If you're printing from your computer, crop and edit before printing to improve your odds of getting the image you want on the first try.
- Print your works in progress on plain paper, in draft mode when possible.

- Print Web pages in black-and-white unless you have an obvious reason for using color. For example: if the page contains a photo or graphic, such as a chart, that can be understood only if it's printed in color.
- Choose a type of paper that resists fading. While all photos will fade eventually if displayed, some paper brands are especially prone to premature fading. In our most recent fade tests, we used the recommended brand-name ink and photo paper for each model and subjected photos to round-the-clock, daylight-balanced fluorescent light for six weeks. Photos printed on Dell, Epson, HP, and Kodak models showed no visible fading. Those from Canon, Lexmark, and Sony models faded slightly.

TVs

INSIDE INFO

- **64** Step-by-step guide to choosing a set
- **67** Picture-tube TVs
- **68** LCD TVs get bigger
- **69** Plasmas get better
- **70** Rear-projection TVs

BUYING ADVICE

- **71** Picture-tube televisions
- **73** LCD televisions
- **75** Plasma televisions
- **79** Rear-projection televisions

CHAPTER 06

If you're thinking of buying a new TV set, now is the time to think big. Sky-high costs may have scared you away from large-screen high-definition (HD) TVs in the past, but prices have dropped sharply and could continue to go down.

Even with prices falling, a big-screen TV is still a four-figure investment—probably the most challenging you've made since your first home computer. There are a host of new display technologies to consider, and there is a a growing list of manufacturers to consider, some who are better known for computers.

Deciding how big to go is its own issue. Is a 36-inch television large enough, or would you prefer a truly jumbo screen that spans 60 inches or even more? This chapter can help you answer that and all the other important questions you'll need to consider.

 The big news in television: larger screens, better picture quality, and more flat screens, all at lower prices.

Ratings: LCD TVs, p. 166; picture-tube TVs, p. 172; plasma TVs, p. 178

06 | INSIDE INFO TVS

STEP-BY-STEP GUIDE TO CHOOSING A SET

These questions can help you zero in on your next TV.

Be forewarned: Any large TV is likely to look more massive in your home than it did at the store.

Most HD sets have wide screens like this one. Regular TV programming will show up with bars on both sides unless you modify it.

STEP 1: HOW BIG A SCREEN?

Don't let cost alone drive your decision on screen size. Think about where you'll be watching the TV. In general, the bigger the screen, the more room you need—for the set itself and for viewing distance. If you sit too close to any screen, you'll see the picture elements (lines or pixels) that make up the images.

When you're in the store, step back from a TV until you can't see the scan lines or pixels that make up the picture. That's the minimum distance to strive for at home. With HD sets, allow at least 5 feet for a 36-inch or smaller set, 6 to 9 feet for larger screens. You need even more distance for analog sets.

The screen size you decide on may help narrow your choice of technology. For example, you're unlikely to find a traditional picture-tube TV with a screen larger than 36 inches or a rear-projection TV with a screen smaller than 40 inches.

Screen shape, or aspect ratio, has become almost moot. Most HD sets are now 16:9 models, designed for the wide-screen format of most HD broadcasts and movies on DVD. You'll find squarish (4:3) screens only on some HD sets using picture-tube or LCD technology and on some analog sets. We believe 16:9 screens are better for most buyers of HD sets, because more programming will shift to wide-screen format as time goes on.

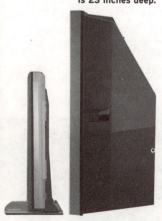

Two extremes: Flat panels like the 42-inch plasma set at left have a screen that's less than six inches thick. The 51-inch rear-projection TV at right is 23 inches deep.

STEP 2: THICK OR THIN?

Today's TVs range from a few inches to a few feet deep, so you can opt for a set that's svelte, stocky, or somewhere in between. In most cases, the thinner the profile, the fatter the price.

LCD and plasma flat-panel TVs are the trimmest and the priciest; these screens measure less than 6 inches thick, and they can be wall-mounted.

Rear-projection models using LCD, DLP, or LCoS technology offer a middle ground for both size and price. Most of these sets are about 15 to 20 inches deep, though RCA has introduced a 7-inch-deep set.

Rear-projection sets and traditional TVs using CRTs (cathode-ray tubes, commonly called picture tubes) are the bulkiest at about 24 to 30 inches deep. They're also the cheapest.

Samsung recently introduced a SlimFit tube TV that's only 16 inches deep. LG Electronics is expected to offer a similar product as well.

Floor space is an important consideration with bulkier TVs. The largest rear-projection sets can take up as much space as a loveseat. Even if such a behemoth fits in your room, you might not like the way it looks.

Bear in mind that any large television set will look more massive in your home than in a spacious showroom.

64 CONSUMER REPORTS • ELECTRONICS BUYING GUIDE 2006 Expert • Independent • Nonprofit

INSIDE INFO TVS

STEP 3: WHICH TYPE OF DISPLAY?
Here's a quick overview of your current choices and the trade-offs.

PICTURE-TUBE (CRT) TVs

Best choice if you want a midsized HD set at a fairly low price and if the bulk doesn't bother you.
Screen sizes: 26 to 36 inches.
Typical prices: About $800 for a 32-inch 4:3 set, $1,200 for a 34-inch wide-screen model. (Estimates are based on TVs in our Ratings and prices advertised by major retailers in early January 2005. Prices may have changed since.)
Pros: Mature technology with proven reliability and long life. The best sets have top-notch picture quality, with excellent detail, color, and contrast. Picture doesn't appear dimmer if viewed from off center. They also have the lowest prices of all HD sets.
Cons: Maximum screen size limited to 36 inches. Most are bulky, at 2 feet deep or more. Heavy, often 100 pounds or more. Shiny surface can produce annoying reflections in brightly lit rooms.
▶▶ For more about picture-tube TVs, see page 67.

Picture-tube (CRT) TV

LCD FLAT-PANEL TVs

Best choice if you want a smaller flat-screen set.
Screen sizes: 15 to 50-plus inches.
Typical prices: About $1,600 for a 26-inch wide-screen HD-ready set, $2,500 for a 32-inch TV. Prices could drop soon.
Pros: Thin, light, sleek sets that can be wall-mounted. The best are capable of displaying very good, bright HD images. They maintain good contrast in bright lighting and pose no risk of screen burn-in.
Cons: Price goes up sharply as screens get bigger. Most sets can't render deep black, and some can't distinguish subtle shades of gray and black. Fast motion may blur. Picture may appear dimmer or washed out as your viewing position angles away from the center on some models. Their reliability is not yet known.
▶▶ For more about LCD TVs, see page 68.

LCD flat-panel TV

PLASMA FLAT-PANEL TVs

Best choice if you want a very big, very thin set without the complexity of a front-projection setup.
Screen sizes: 32 to 60-plus inches.
Typical prices: About $3,500 for a 42-inch HD-ready set.
Pros: Thin, sleek sets that can be wall-mounted. The best display excellent HD images. Picture doesn't appear dimmer if viewed from off center. Bigger sizes are cheaper than LCD TVs of comparable size.
Cons: Shiny surface can produce annoying reflections in brightly lit rooms. Uses a lot of power and generates a lot of heat. Stationary images displayed for long periods may leave a ghosted image. Some models are simply monitors—they don't include a tuner or speakers. Their reliability is not yet known.
▶▶ For more about plasma TVs, see page 69.

Plasma flat-panel TV

REAR-PROJECTION TVs

Best choice if you want a jumbo TV for less than the cost of a plasma set.
Screen sizes: 40 to 60-plus inches.
Typical prices: About $1,200 for 51-inch CRT-based HD-ready set, $3,000 for 50-inch LCD-based HD-ready set.
Pros: Lowest-cost jumbo screens. The best are capable of a very good HD picture. CRT-based models are low-priced and generally reliable. Models using LCD, DLP, and LCoS technology are thinner than CRT sets.
Cons: Picture may appear dimmer or washed out when viewed off center. CRT-based sets are big and heavy; fixed items displayed for long periods can leave a ghosted image. Shiny surface on some models can produce annoying reflections in brightly lit rooms. For LCD, DLP, and LCoS sets, reliability is not yet known, and the lamp must be replaced periodically.
▶▶ For more about rear-projection TVs, see page 70.

Rear-projection TV

FRONT PROJECTORS

Best if you want a theater-like experience on a giant screen and are willing to deal with a complex setup.
Screen sizes: Projector with a 9-by-12-inch or smaller footprint can be used with very large screens.
Typical price: $1,500 and up for HD projector only.
Pros: Picture size and characteristics most closely resemble a movie theater's.
Cons: TV tuner and speakers are not included. Your viewing room must be completely dark to achieve deep black and maximum contrast. Screen affects brightness, viewing angle, and picture quality. The projector may require periodic lamp replacement. Professional installation for the projector and screen can be costly.

Front projector

06 INSIDE INFO TVS

STEP 4: HD OR NOT?

If you're thinking of springing for a new television set, we recommend that you buy a digital, HD-capable model.

Those sets have the highest native resolution—the number of picture elements the screen contains—so they can display the sharpest and most detailed images.

Standard-definition television sets, the type many of us have watched for decades, display much less detail.

With plasma TVs, you might want to consider an enhanced-definition (ED) model. This type of set's resolution is technically a step down from HD, but you might not notice the difference unless you're sitting up close—say, five feet or less.

The best ED plasma sets that we have tested did well displaying HD content at a lower resolution, and they're usually cheaper than true HD sets.

> **If you'll be getting HD** via cable or satellite, you can save by buying an HD-ready set while they're still available in large sizes.

STEP 5: HD-READY OR BUILT-IN TUNER?

Some HD televisions contain a digital tuner that can receive digital broadcasts of all types, HD as well as standard definition (SD) and enhanced definition (ED). But most HD sets on the market are HD-ready, meaning they need an external digital tuner—an HD cable or satellite box or a set-top box used with an antenna—to decode HD broadcasts. They are the least expensive type of HD-capable TV.

Integrated HDTVs have built-in digital tuners and can get broadcast and other digital programming—but no ESPN or other cable or satellite channels—via antenna. To get HD via satellite or cable, most of these sets require a special cable box or satellite receiver, just as HD-ready sets do. Starting in July 2005, all new TVs 36 inches and larger were required to have a built-in digital tuner to comply with a government ruling. Smaller sets must have a built-in digital tuner within a year or two.

Digital-cable-ready (DCR) TVs are a new type of integrated HDTV. They can not only get digital broadcasts by antenna but also receive unencrypted digital-cable programming without using a box. For digital HD and premium cable programming, which is encrypted, you must insert a CableCard into a slot on the set. (Some cable companies encrypt all or most digital programming, so you may need a card for virtually everything.) These TVs cost more, and you usually have to pay a few dollars a month to rent a card. Many integrated HDTVs coming out now are digital-cable ready.

If you will be getting HD via cable or satellite, you can save by buying an HD-ready set while they're still available in large sizes. An integrated set is a fine choice, but it will cost more.

Don't rush to buy a digital-cable-ready TV. Current, first-generation CableCard TVs are one-way, so they don't provide an interactive program guide, video on demand, or pay-per-view ordering via the remote control. For those, you'll still need a cable box. Second-generation DCR TVs and CableCards should be here soon. They should have two-way capability, allowing for interactive features.

Card trick: CableCards can receive HD signals without a cable box, but you'll lose the interactive program guide and other features.

Talk the Talk: Definition defined

Digital and HD television have their own special terminology. Here's a brief guide to some of the jargon.

Enhanced definition. ED refers to 480p, a spec between standard and high definition. Some ED plasma sets (and, less commonly, LCD TVs) do a very good job down-converting HD signals to a resolution they can display.

HD-ready. These sets have no built-in digital tuner, so they're usually cheaper than integrated sets. They require an HD-capable digital-cable box or satellite receiver to get HD via cable or satellite. (Some of those devices can get HD from an antenna.) To get HD signals free with these sets, you need a digital set-top tuner (several hundred dollars) and an antenna.

High definition. HDTVs display digital TV signals, in 1080i or 720p definition—two technical specs for true HD. Images of both types are sharper and more detailed than standard-definition images.

Native resolution. The number of pixels on an LCD (liquid-crystal display) or plasma screen or in LCD, LCoS (Liquid Crystal on Silicon, a form of projection TV), and DLP (Digital Light Processing) rear-projection TVs and front projectors. Expressed as horizontal by vertical pixels, such as 1,280x720 or 852x480. On HDTVs, the second number is 720 and above; on ED sets, the vertical resolution is 480.

Standard definition. Refers to the analog signals in the 480i format, which regular TV content has used for decades.

INSIDE INFO TVS

PICTURE-TUBE TVs

Many models now offer wide screens and slimmer profiles.

Big-screen suitors may be winning over more TV buyers, but the tubby and dependable picture-tube TV is still a sensible, if somewhat stodgy, choice for many buyers. These sets offer great performance and proven reliability at a comparatively low price.

Not that the tube TV isn't undergoing an evolution of its own. A growing number of picture-tube TVs with 26- to 36-inch screens are high-definition sets, many of them with wide screens rather than the usual squarish ones.

Slimmer sets are also arriving as manufacturers address a major objection to picture-tube TVs—their roughly 2-foot depth. Mimicking a trend that swept computer-monitor lines some years back, slimmer, though probably not lighter, 26- to 36-inch models with picture tubes 16 inches deep or less should be in stores this year.

Overall, it looks like there will be fewer of the biggest tube TVs on the shelves. With prices becoming more competitive for LCD and plasma TVs, which are easier for retailers to ship or store in volume, some manufacturers are discontinuing their 36-inch picture-tube sets.

▶▶ For more detailed buying advice on high-definition picture tube TVs, see page 71.

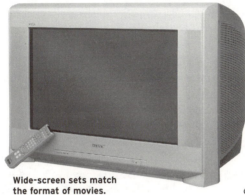
Wide-screen sets match the format of movies.

Brand Repair History

Picture-tube TVs

You can minimize potential problems by choosing a reliable brand. Our brand-repair histories have been quite consistent over the years, though they are not infallible predictors. Repair rates for specific models may vary, and products can, of course, change in how they're designed and made.

These graphs show the percentage of 25- to 27-inch and 30- to 36-inch conventional (picture-tube) TV sets purchased new from 1999 to 2004 that were ever repaired or had a serious problem that wasn't resolved. RCA and Samsung were among the more repair-prone brands of 25- to 27-inch sets. RCA and Zenith were among the more repair-prone brands of 30- to 36-inch sets. RCA was the least reliable brand of 34- to 36-inch TVs. Both graphs include digital HD sets as well as analog sets. (To date the two types have shown no significant difference in reliability, but since HD sets are much newer than basic models, we will continue to monitor their repair record closely in the years to come.) Data do not apply to LCD, plasma, or rear-projection TVs.

A 36-inch picture-tube, like this Panasonic, is a reliable way to get a big screen.

25- to 27-inch TVs

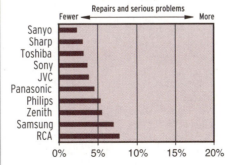

30- to 36-inch TVs

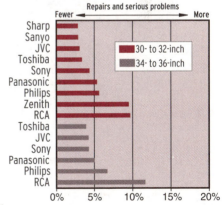

Data for 25- to 27-inch sets are based on more than 75,000 responses to our 2004 Annual Questionnaire; data for 30- to 32-inch and 34- to 36-inch sets are based on nearly 71,000 responses. Data for the two charts are not directly comparable. Repair rates for specific models may vary, and changes in design and manufacturing may affect reliability. Still, you increase your chances of getting a reliable TV by choosing among brands that have proven reliable in the past. Data have been standardized to eliminate any differences attributable to age. Differences of less than 3 percentage points are not meaningful.

06 | INSIDE INFO TVS

LCD TVs GET BIGGER

New models are becoming easier to view and to afford.

While plasma TVs generally have screens 42 inches or larger, many LCD sets top out at a relatively small 32 inches, making them something of a little brother to the competing flat-screen technology. That's changing, however. There are now more 37- to 46-inch LCD screens, with even bigger sizes coming, making LCD TVs increasingly competitive with plasma TVs.

The best of today's LCD TVs—mostly high-definition (HD) models—have the very good picture quality you'd want in a big screen. Viewing angles have improved, so many new models display a better image from off-center than older sets did—a must if a TV will be watched by several people at once.

Price is becoming less of an issue as well. The largest LCD screens have been very expensive—considerably more than comparably sized plasma sets—but prices could drop as much as 25 to 30 percent below last year's, according to the market-research firm iSuppli. We've already seen a few HD LCD sets with 30- to 34-inch screens advertised for less than $2,000, a sharp drop from last year's lows.

LCD sets we've tested to date haven't equalled the better picture-tube and plasma TVs at displaying deep black levels and fast motion.

▶▶ **For more detailed buying advice on LCD TVs, see page 73.**

Some LCD TVs, like this Sony, don't have HDTV tuners.

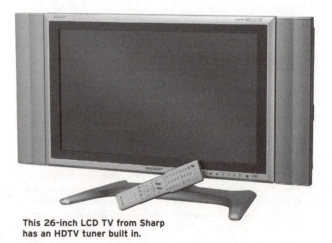

This 26-inch LCD TV from Sharp has an HDTV tuner built in.

The high-def difference

A better picture (usually). While true HD programming should look great on a good HD set of any type, some so-called HD programming may not. Content that was recorded at lower resolution and up-converted to simulate HD has lower picture quality.

In addition, you'll probably watch a fair amount of standard-definition content for a few years. Given a clean, strong analog signal, some HD sets make regular programming look better than it does on an analog TV. But with a poor signal, which sometimes occurs with cable, the picture can actually look worse.

DVDs look very good on decent standard-definition sets and can look better on HDTVs. You'll see a bigger improvement with HD sets when high-definition DVDs (in either Blu-ray or HD-DVD format) and the players that support them arrive, probably in 2005 or 2006.

More complex setup. Even with a basic setup, you'll probably have your HD set hooked up to a digital-cable box or satellite receiver, a DVD player, a VCR, and other components. For that, a lot of inputs and outputs need to be connected to the TV.

To change video sources on some remotes—say, from cable box to DVD player—you have to press the Input or Video button repeatedly to cycle through the inputs until you reach the desired source. Other remotes have designated buttons for each input.

Ask the installer, if you use one, to program the remote for you and to draw a diagram explaining the hookup. It could be a lifesaver if you have to disconnect things at some point. And be sure to try it out and determine that everything works the way you want it to before the installer leaves.

INSIDE INFO TVS

PLASMAS GET BETTER

Their pictures are improving, but reliability remains a question.

Plasma TVs display bright, colorful images that are eye-catching, especially in high definition. No matter how big the screen, they're only 4 to 6 inches thick. Prices have dropped sharply over the past year or two, making these flat-panel sets look even more attractive.

Most HD-ready models with 42-inch screens, the best-selling size, have been going for $3,000 to $5,000 or more. Enhanced-definition sets of this size, which have lower native resolution, generally cost about $1,000 less. Larger HD sets with screens of 50 inches or more have been hampered by high prices, typically $5,000 and up.

In coming months, prices of all these plasma TVs could fall by as much as 25 percent, according to the market-research firm iSuppli, based in El Segundo, Calif.

Overall, it will be easier to find top-notch picture quality. Plasma technology has gradually improved, and the best of the models we have tested can display excellent or very good images with all types of programming—HD, DVDs, and even regular TV content. The best picture-tube TVs still do slightly better with fine detail and subtle gradations of black and gray, but plasma technology has gradually narrowed the gap.

Because plasma televisions are fairly new, long-term reliability is still a question. The repair histories we have for other types of TVs don't apply. We can offer a few caveats: Plasma TVs use more power and generate more heat than other types of TVs, and bright images from, say, a video game or news "zipper" may burn a permanent impression into the screen over time.

▶▶ For more detailed buying advice on plasma TV sets, see page 75.

Plasma TVs now compare favorably with picture-tube models in image quality.

Digital dollars-and-cents strategies

Beware loan gotchas. To drive sales of higher-priced TVs and other electronics, some retailers now offer zero-interest loans for up to two years. If you opt for one, be sure you keep up with payments. Most retailers make you sign up for a credit card that carries a high annual interest rate—up to 29 percent. If you don't repay the loan in full before the term expires, you could be socked with interest from the date of purchase. With some loans, missing three payments in a row triggers the same hefty penalty.

So even if you've paid $7,000 toward the price of an $8,000 plasma TV, you could be charged interest on the original $8,000 over the full loan period. On a two-year loan with a 24 percent rate, that would tack thousands more onto what was a $1,000 balance.

Weigh extended-warranty costs. For most products, extended warranties aren't worth it. Appliances and electronic gear, such as conventional TVs, camcorders, and digital cameras, aren't likely to break down during the warranty period. And even if they do, the typical repair costs roughly the same as a warranty.

But an extended warranty might be worthwhile for high-priced plasma and LCD TVs and rear-projection sets using LCD, DLP, or LCoS. Preliminary data from our user surveys show no unusual rate of repair for flat-screen plasma and LCD TVs in the first year, but their long-term reliability remains a question mark.

Extended warranties typically cover parts and labor for two to five years from the date of purchase—or one to four years beyond the standard one-year warranty. Costs vary by the type of TV, its price, and the length of the warranty. At Best Buy, a four-year service plan on LCD TVs 13 inches and larger recently cost $200 to $400, depending on size. For a plasma TV, a four-year plan recently cost $400 to $600, depending on the TV's price. We've seen other service plans that cost as much as $1,000.

Find out exactly what is covered by any plan. Typically, TVs with screens smaller than 25 or 27 inches have to be carried in or shipped to a store or repair center, while larger sets are serviced in-home. If a set can't be repaired, make sure that a plan will provide a replacement.

Consider paying a pro installer. If you're daunted by the idea of moving a huge TV and connecting it to all your gear, hire a pro to do the job for you. Large retailers like Best Buy, Circuit City, and Sears offer several levels of in-home installation. Prices start at $100 to hook up a cable box and a VCR or a DVD player; they can top $1,000 to wall-mount a plasma or LCD TV, connect numerous audio/video components, and hide wiring behind walls or under floors. Big-box chains, such as Costco and Wal-Mart, generally don't offer installation. To find a third-party installer, contact the Custom Electronic Design & Installation Association (800-669-5329 or www.cedia.org), an industry group that offers vetted, experienced installers.

INSIDE INFO TVS

REAR-PROJECTION TVs

They deliver a big-screen experience at a bargain price.

If you want to enjoy HD programming on a 50-inch-plus screen, a rear-projection TV is your best value. With prices dropping, slimmer sets proliferating, and more models offering fine picture quality, rear-projection TVs have emerged as serious candidates for anyone who wants a high-definition television with a jumbo screen. Here's a look at some of the trends heating up this category.

Tight for space? "Microdisplay" sets shave some of the depth off conventional rear-projection TVs, but they also cost more.

CRT-based sets are bargains. A rear-projection CRT-based TV—the type that uses picture tubes—is the least-expensive way to watch HD on a big screen. You can buy an HD-ready TV with a 50-inch-plus screen for $1,500 or less. We've seen some sets advertised for $1,000. The well-known drawback to these TVs is their bulk: Most are 24 to 30 inches deep. Still, if you have the space, they're real values.

Slimmer models come on strong. A new breed of projection TV has started to show up in force. Called "microdisplays" by some manufacturers, these use LCD, DLP, or LCoS technology. That shaves a foot or more off the depth of a CRT-based set. But at 15 to 20 inches deep, most aren't as "micro" as the name might suggest. Nor are they cheap. Prices start at about $2,500 for a set with a 50-inch screen. Thinner TVs are beginning to arrive, including a 61-inch, 7-inch-deep RCA DLP set that sells for under $7,000 and did well in our tests. Microdisplays are likely to dominate the category before long, as manufacturers, including Panasonic, stop making CRT-based rear-projection TVs.

Prices keep dropping. CRT-based models are even better buys. Prices have dropped by as much as one-third in some cases. Prices of LCD, DLP, and LCoS sets should continue to decrease.

Picture quality has improved. Virtually all the sets now being sold are digital, HD-capable TVs, which have much better picture quality than analog sets. New microdisplay technologies are also proving to have fine picture quality. As a result, many of the models we tested displayed very good picture quality with HD content and good picture quality for DVDs and regular TV programming. Still, none of them equaled the excellence of the best plasma TVs. We didn't find that any one projection technology was consistently better than another for picture quality. On some models, the picture may appear dimmer or washed out if viewed from off center, especially in the vertical direction.

The bar for picture quality may be set even higher with the introduction of more microdisplay projection TVs with a native resolution of 1920x1080. Most current sets have lower resolution than that. Screens with higher native resolution theoretically should be able to display finer, sharper detail, although many factors affect picture quality.

▶▶ **For more detailed buying advice on rear-projection TV sets, see page 79.**

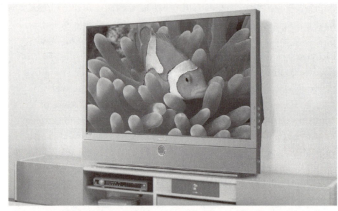

Some rear-projection models, like this DLP set, are slimmer than smaller conventional, picture-tube televisions, and prices are dropping.

A CRT-based rear-projection set typically measures 24 to 30 inches deep.

Expert • Independent • Nonprofit

BUYING ADVICE PICTURE-TUBE TVS

BUYING ADVICE
Picture-tube televisions

▶ You have more (and better) viewing choices than before, including HD models, at ever-lower prices.

Conventional TVs with picture tubes are still big sellers. Many of these sets offer outstanding performance and proven reliability at low prices. A growing number of tube TVs are high-definition (HD) models, which offer the best picture quality.

WHAT'S AVAILABLE

Among the better-selling brands are JVC, Magnavox, Philips, RCA, Samsung, Sanyo, Sharp, Sony, and Toshiba. Picture-tube TVs can be either analog (the kind of set you've been watching for years) or digital models (including HD sets). Analog TVs can display only standard-definition signals, like those used for most TV broadcasts. Standard definition is called 480i because images contain up to 480 lines that are drawn onscreen in an interlaced pattern (hence the letter "i"), first the odd lines and then the even, 30 times a second.

Most digital sets can display HD signals with resolution of 1080i (1,080 lines with an interlaced scan) or 720p (720 lines scanned progressively, in one sweep). These HD images are much sharper and more detailed than standard definition. Some manufacturers, such as RCA, have introduced standard-definition (SD) digital models, not to be confused with HDTVs. These sets can display only 480i, but picture quality may be slightly better than with an analog set because digital signals tend to be cleaner than analog.

Size and shape. Most picture-tube TVs have a screen that measures 13 inches to 32 inches diagonally; there are fewer of the largest sets, with 36-inch screens, possibly because other technologies such as plasma and rear-projection are coming on strong. HD sets generally have screens 24 inches or larger. On analog sets, the screens are usually squarish, with an aspect ratio of 4:3, meaning they're four units wide for every three units high. Some HD sets have a 4:3 screen, but more have a 16:9 wide screen with proportions similar to that of a movie-theater screen. One of the downsides to picture-tube sets is that they're relatively bulky and heavy, about 2 feet deep and more than 100 pounds in larger sizes. A few slimmer sets that measure about 16 inches deep were recently introduced. Samsung's 30-inch wide-screen SlimFit HDTV

sells for about $1,000, $100 more than a comparable standard model. Though slimmer, these sets are no lighter.

Features. Generally, the larger the screen, the higher the price and the more features and inputs for other video devices. Most sets with screens measuring 24 inches and larger have flat screens, high-quality video inputs, universal remotes, and simulated surround sound.

Price. Analog tube TVs that display only standard definition are the lowest-cost type of set, but they're becoming less common as HD models attract more interest.
Price range: Analog 13-inch sets start at $75 or so; 27-inch sets start at about $200; 32-inch sets start at about $350; 36-inch sets start at $600. A 27-inch HDTV monitor capable of displaying HD typically sells for $400 to $600. Most 30-inch wide-screen HDTVs start at about $800.

Facts about HD-capable TVs. Within the HD category, there are two types of TV sets. HD-ready sets, also known as HDTV monitors, can receive standard-definition analog programs on their own. To receive any digital signals, including HD, they require an external tuner/decoder. Many consumers use an HD cable box or satellite receiver to get such signals via cable or satellite; some of those devices can also get digital signals from a rooftop antenna. To receive HD signals without paying for cable or satellite, you'll need a separate digital-TV receiver, which costs several hundred dollars, and a rooftop antenna. (These digital-TV receivers are sometimes called ATSC tuners, which stands for Advanced Television Systems Committee.) Depending on your location, an antenna may be able to pull in the major broadcast networks' HD offerings.

Integrated HD sets, also called HDTVs, have a built-in ATSC digi-

A big screen on a picture-tube TV means a big footprint.

06 BUYING ADVICE PICTURE-TUBE TVS

tal tuner that lets them decode over-the-air HD signals received via a roof antenna. Although they have their own tuner, most of these TVs still require an HD-capable cable box or satellite receiver to get cable or satellite. Some new integrated models, called digital-cable-ready (DCR) or plug-and-play sets, can receive digital-cable programming without using a set-top box. For HD and premium cable programming—and possibly for any digital programming—you must insert a CableCard into a slot on the set. You usually have to pay a few dollars a month to rent the card from the cable company. First-generation DCR CableCards and TVs are not interactive, so they can't provide features such as an interactive program guide, video on demand, or pay-per-view ordering via remote. Second-generation DCR TVs and CableCards should be here within the next year or two, and they're expected to have two-way capability, allowing for interactive features. Integrated sets typically cost more than HD-ready sets, with digital-cable-ready models costing the most.

FEATURES THAT COUNT

Many new TVs, and all HD models, have a **flat-front-screen CRT**, which reduces reflections and glare but doesn't necessarily improve picture quality. **Adjustable color temperature** lets you shade the picture toward the blue range ("cooler," better for images with outdoor light) or the red ("warmer," preferred for movie-theater-like realism). Some sets can memorize custom picture settings for each video input, useful as signal qualities often differ when you switch video sources, say from a DVD player to a cable box or antenna.

Picture-in-picture (PIP) lets you watch two channels at once, one in a small picture alongside the full-screen image. A **single-tuner** TV requires another device with a tuner, such as a VCR or cable box, to display two programs at once; **dual-tuner** models can display two programs simultaneously on their own.

Stereo sound is standard on sets 27 inches or larger, but you'll generally hear little stereo separation from a TV's built-in speakers. **Ambient sound** is often termed "surround sound," but it isn't true surround like that from a multi-speaker home-theater system. It's an effect created by special audio processing. You can turn it off if you don't like it. For a better stereo effect or true surround sound, route the signals to a sound system. **Automatic volume leveler** compensates for the volume jumps that often accompany commercials or changes in channel.

Most TVs have several types of inputs that handle varying levels of quality. A **cable/antenna**, or radio frequency (RF), **input** is the most basic connection, and it can be used with almost any video source. A **composite-video input** will give you slightly better picture quality and is often used with a VCR or regular cable box. An **S-video input** lets you take advantage of the still-better picture quality from a digital-cable box, a satellite-dish system, a DVD player, or a digital camcorder. A **component-video input** offers superior quality, making this a good choice for progressive-scan DVD players, high-definition satellite receivers, and HD digital-cable boxes that have the corresponding output. HDTVs have **DVI (Digital Visual Interface)** or **HDMI (High-Definition Multimedia Interface) inputs**, which provide a high-quality digital connection to devices such as DVD players, digital-cable boxes, and satellite receivers. HDMI carries both audio and video on one cable; DVI inputs carry video only, so you need separate audio inputs. These connections may allow the content providers to control your ability to record certain programming. Many sets have more than one of a given type of input. Having two or three S-video or component-video inputs is a plus. For a camcorder or video game, **front-panel A/V inputs** are helpful. A headphone jack lets you watch (and listen) without disturbing others. HD sets also have a Dolby-Digital audio output for surround sound, available in some digital broadcasts.

HD sets may have a **film-mode feature**, sometimes referred to as 3:2 pulldown compensation or by brand-specific names such as CineMotion. This can make moving images that were converted from film to video look less jerky, with less jaggedness around the edges of objects. On 16:9 sets, **stretch and zoom** modes will expand or compress an image to better fill the screen shape. This helps to reduce the dark bands that can appear around images if you watch content formatted for a screen shape other than 16:9. (The picture may be distorted or cut off a bit in the process of stretching or zooming.)

HOW TO CHOOSE

TVs using the familiar picture-tube technology are the least-expensive option, and these still offer the best picture quality.

Decide on a screen size. TVs with small screens (less than 27 inches) are likely to have fewer bells and whistles than larger sets. Medium screens (27 to 36 inches) are the most popular in households, so the category has a large number of choices in terms of features, price, and brand. You also need to consider the size of your room to allow for enough distance so that you don't see the lines that make up the images.

> **Stereo sound** is standard on sets 27 inches or larger, but don't expect to hear much separation from the TV's built-in speakers.

BUYING ADVICE LCD TVs

Decide whether you want HD image quality. Digital HDTVs can display sharper, finer images than conventional analog TVs, whether you're watching HDTV programming, standard TV programming, or DVD movies. Even with standard (non-HD) signals from a good cable connection, a satellite signal, or a DVD player, the picture quality can be better than a conventional set's. But with a poor signal, like the worst channels from cable, an HDTV can make the images look worse because the digital circuitry can't always differentiate the noise from the real signal.

While standard-definition TVs can't match HD for picture quality, some offer very good or excellent non-HD images that may suit you fine. Only firsthand experience will enable you to decide whether the extra quality of HD is worth the extra cost. Though HD sets cost less than they used to, they still command a premium—usually hundreds more than a comparable analog set.

Most parts of the U.S. have access to a fair amount of HD content, but offerings vary by locale and the reception method you'll use—antenna, digital cable, or satellite. You can receive programming via an antenna only if you're close enough to the transmitter, with an unobstructed view. Digital cable currently offers more HD content than satellite, but both are constantly adding more programming, so check with your provider.

Decide between an HD-ready set and an integrated HDTV. As of July 2005, all new TVs 36 inches and larger were required to have a built-in digital tuner to comply with a government ruling, and smaller sets must have a built-in tuner within the next year or two. If you're among the majority of consumers who get their HD via cable or satellite, you can save money by buying an HD-ready set while they're still available. Integrated sets cost more, and they generally require a cable box or satellite receiver anyway. The new plug-and-play sets that use CableCards are the most expensive type, and as noted above, this first generation doesn't offer interactive program guides or video-on-demand via remote control.

Consider the shape. A regular screen with the familiar 4:3 aspect ratio is a good choice for regular TV programming, which is formatted for this squarish shape. Most DVD movies and a growing number of HDTV programs are formatted for wide screen. We believe a wide-screen TV will give you a better HD experience now and be preferable for all viewing a few years from now. But 4:3 sets cost less and might suit you if a lower price is important. Content formatted for one screen shape has to be modified to fit the other, so you may see bars on two sides of the image. Most 16:9 HD sets can stretch or crop images to eliminate the bars, but such measures often distort the picture.

BUYING ADVICE LCD TVs

▶ LCD TVs pack a lot of bang for a lot of bucks. Their svelte profile is the main attraction.

Once available only with small screens, LCD (liquid-crystal display) TVs now come with screens as large as 50 inches (and climbing), which makes them suitable for a household's primary TV set. Regardless of screen size, these TVs are only a few inches thick, giving them a small footprint. They're also relatively lightweight, often as little as 30 pounds or less, so they can be wall-mounted.

Prices are heading downward, but inch for inch, LCD TVs are relatively expensive. In larger sizes, they cost more than comparably sized plasma sets, for instance. The picture quality on the best LCD TVs we've tested has been very good. Recent improvements in LCDs intend to address earlier weaknesses at displaying deep black levels, accurate colors, and fast motion.

WHAT'S AVAILABLE

Strong brands include Panasonic, Philips, Samsung, Sharp, and Sony, along with many computer-display manufacturers. The entry of computer makers Dell and Gateway into the LCD TV market has accelerated price competition.

LCD TVs are available in standard-definition (analog), enhanced-definition (ED), and high-definition (HD) models. ED and HD sets are digital TVs. Analog TVs can display only standard-definition signals, like those used for most TV broadcasts. ED sets can also accept the higher-quality 480p signals like those from a progressive-scan DVD player. HD images are the sharpest and most detailed. These models can accept all signals from DVD

Some digital-cable-ready plasma TVs, like this one, can receive some cable programs without using a cable box.

06 BUYING ADVICE LCD TVs

players and HD signals from digital-video players/recorders. Within the HD category, there are three types of TV sets:

HD-ready sets. Also called HDTV monitors, these sets can display standard-definition programs (which still account for most non-prime-time TV broadcasts) on their own. To display digital programs, they require a digital tuner to decode those broadcasts. If you're getting your HD programming from cable or satellite, your digital cable box or satellite receiver has the appropriate digital decoder built in. All you have to do is connect your HD-ready TV to the box and you're all set. Cable companies charge a small rental fee for digital or HD-capable boxes. To receive HD via satellite, you need an HD receiver and special dish antenna(e). Together, these cost about $300, but you may be able to get them

LCD and plasma sets are typically 3 to 6 inches deep.

from the satellite company at little or no charge as part of a promotion.

You can also get digital broadcasts, including HD, over the air, via an antenna. To do so, you'll have to buy a digital tuner called an ATSC (Advanced Television Systems Committee) tuner—the external box costs a few hundred dollars. However, there's no charge for service as there is with cable or satellite. Some satellite receivers also offer a built-in ATSC digital tuner. To receive digital programming via antenna, you must be fairly close to a transmitter, with an unobstructed view. With digital signals, you'll either have a clear, strong signal or none at all.

Integrated HDTV sets. These have the ATSC digital tuner built in, which enables them to decode any digital signals, including HD with no additional equipment when used with a roof antenna. You may be able to receive the major networks' HD offerings transmitted over the air in your area, but you won't get the premium channels available on satellite and cable. To get HD via cable or satellite, integrated sets require an HD-capable cable box, CableCard, or satellite receiver—the built-in digital tuner only works for off-air digital broadcasts.

Starting in July of 2005, all new TVs with 36-inch or larger screens—a category covering the largest LCD TVs—were required to have a built-in digital tuner to comply with a government ruling. Smaller sets must have such tuners within a year or two.

Digital-Cable-Ready (DCR). Some new integrated models, called digital-cable-ready (DCR) or plug-and-play sets, can receive digital-cable programming without using a set-top box. For HD and premium cable programming—and possibly for any digital programming—you must insert a CableCard into a slot on the set. You usually have to pay a few dollars a month to rent the card from the cable company. Current DCR TVs are not interactive, so even with a CableCard in the slot they can't provide features such as an interactive program guide, video on demand, or pay-per-view ordering via remote. Second-generation DCR TVs and CableCards should be here soon, and they're expected to have two-way capability, allowing for interactive features. Integrated sets typically cost more than HD-ready sets, with digital-cable-ready models costing the most.

Major-brand LCD sets with 13-inch screens of ED-ready resolution (equivalent to progressive-scan DVD, average about $400 to $500. Prices for 15- to 18-inch HD models start at less than $800, while 20-inchers cost $1,200 or more—several times what you'd pay for a conventional TV with the same screen size. HD-ready LCD TVs with 23- to 30-inch screens typically cost between $1,600 and $3,000. There is a growing number of LCD TVs with even larger screens—up to 50 inches or more—and prices go up along with size.

FEATURES THAT COUNT

LCD TVs typically have all the usual features you expect on a TV. If you watch many movies, look for a **film mode feature** on HD sets. This feature is also called 3:2 pulldown compensation or brand-specific names such as CineMotion and Film Mode. This can make moving images that were converted from film to video look less jerky, with less jaggedness around the edges. On 16:9 sets, **stretch and zoom modes** will expand or compress an image to better fill the screen shape. This helps to reduce the dark bands that can appear around images if you watch content that isn't formatted for a wide-screen TV. (The picture may be distorted or cut off a bit in the process of stretching or zooming).

Most TVs have several types

BUYING ADVICE PLASMA TVs

of inputs that handle varying levels of quality. See "Hooking Up" on next page.

Audio outputs let you direct a TV's audio signal to a receiver or self-powered speakers. Integrated digital TVs usually have a Dolby Digital output for surround sound (available from some broadcasts). An **automatic volume leveler** compensates for the jarring volume jumps that often accompany commercials or changes in channel. A **headphone jack,** if available, lets you watch (and listen) without disturbing others.

HOW TO CHOOSE

Think twice before buying an ED set. An ED set may cost a bit less than an HD model, but the tradeoffs aren't worth it with LCD sets. The picture quality almost certainly won't be as good as that you'll get with an HD set. We'd recommend an ED or standard-definition LCD TV only for uses such as casual viewing in the kitchen, where you wouldn't want the cable or satellite box you generally need to receive HD signals. For a main TV or one you'll watch often, we'd strongly recommend an HD set. The best are capable of very good picture quality, although deep blacks may not quite match those of a good tube-based set.

Check the viewing angle. Viewing angles have improved, so many new models display a better image from off-center than older sets did—a must if a TV will be watched by several people at once. Some sets have wider viewing angles than others. Before buying one, see how the picture looks if you step off to the side or move up and down. With some, you'll see a dimmer, somewhat washed-out image as your view-

LCD TVs now come with screens as large as 50 inches. This one is 17 inches wide.

ing position angles away, particularly in a vertical direction.

Look for easy-to-use inputs. On many LCD televisions, the connections are on the side or rear of the panel and might be hard to reach. Some larger models have separate control units that connect to the LCD panel via cables. Devices such as a cable box or DVD player are connected to the control unit, so there are fewer cables running to the panel—a plus for wall-mounting—and the inputs may be easier to access. But it does give you another box to contend with.

Consider a set that doubles as a computer display. If you need a computer display as well as a TV, check out the connectivity options. We recommend an HD set since it's most suitable for computer use. A standard VGA connection will work with all computers; a Digital Visual Interface (DVI) input would be compatible with newer mid-range computers.

Weigh the merits of an extended warranty. While extended warranties aren't worthwhile for most products, they may be for high-priced devices using new technologies. Because LCD TVs are costly items that haven't yet established a track record for reliability, check into the cost of a service plan. Find out whether in-home service is covered and whether a replacement is provided if a set can't be repaired.

BUYING ADVICE
Plasma televisions

▶ Plasma TVs boast bright, colorful displays and a wide viewing angle, but there are a few issues you should consider before buying one.

Plasma TVs make a blockbuster first impression. A scant 6 inches thick or less, these sleek flat panels display bright images on screens measuring about 3 to 5 feet diagonally.

A plasma screen is made up of thousands of pixels containing gas that's converted into "plasma" by an electrical charge. The plas-

06 | BUYING ADVICE PLASMA TVs

ma causes phosphors to glow red, green, or blue, as dictated by a video signal. The result: a colorful display with high brightness and a wider viewing angle than most rear-projection sets and LCD TVs. Thanks to steady improvements in plasma technology, the best of these sets have excellent or very good picture quality. Some picture-tube TVs still do slightly better with fine detail and subtle gradations of black and gray, but plasma TVs are coming closer.

However, the picture isn't all rosy. Like projection TVs using CRT (cathode-ray tube) technology, plasma sets may be vulnerable to screen burn-in. Also, when watching bright programs, plasma sets run hotter and consume more power than any other type of TV. Because plasma sets are relatively new, their long-term reliability is still a question.

WHAT'S AVAILABLE

When buying a plasma TV, you'll face a choice between HD (high definition) and ED (enhanced definition) sets, which cost less. The two types differ in native resolution, meaning the fixed number of pixels on the screen. In a spec like 852x480, note the second number. If it's 480, the set is ED; 720 or higher, it's HD. Both types of sets should be capable of up- or down-converting signals to match their native resolution. ED sets can display the full detail of 480p signals such as those output by a DVD player. When connected to an HD tuner, many can down-convert HD signals (which are 720p or 1080i) to suit their lower-resolution screens. While you won't see true HD, the picture quality can be very good. If you sit too close to an ED set, though, images may appear coarser than on an HD set, as if you were looking through a screen door.

There's another major choice. Within the HD category, there are three types of TV sets:

HD-ready sets. Also called HDTV monitors, these sets can display standard-definition analog programs (which still account for most non-prime-time TV broadcasts) on their

Hooking up your new TV: Which wire goes where, and why

New TV sets have different types of inputs that handle varying levels of quality. That's because manufacturers have added new connections as higher-quality signals have become available and left the other inputs in place to work with older equipment. Using the appropriate input can improve picture quality. HD signals can be carried by a component-video, DVI, or HDMI input, or by an RF input on an integrated HDTV (with built-in digital tuner) used with an antenna. From most basic to best, here are the inputs you're apt to see:

Antenna/cable, VHF/UHF, or RF (radio frequency), inputs are the most basic, and they can be used with almost any video source. An RF input may be the only way to connect an antenna and some older cable boxes and VCRs. It's one of the few inputs (along with HDMI) that carries both picture and sound. The others require separate audio inputs for the sound.
Composite-video inputs carry only the video signal, providing better picture quality than RF. They're often used to connect a VCR, cable box, camcorder, or game console.
S-video inputs split the video signal into two parts, color and luminance. This lets you take advantage of the improved picture quality from a satellite system, DVD player, or digital camcorder.
Component-video inputs split the video signal into three parts: two for color and one for luminance. This provides slightly better picture quality than S-video. These inputs are often used with DVD players, high-definition satellite receivers, and cable boxes.

DVI and HDMI inputs provide a high-quality digital connection to DVD players, satellite receivers, and other digital devices. DVI signals carry only video; HDMI signals carry audio and video on one cable. The digital-to-digital connection may ensure optimal picture quality. These inputs may also allow content providers to control your ability to record certain programming.
VGA inputs let the TV accept signals from a computer. That's especially important if you want to use an LCD TV as a computer display.
Front-mounted A/V inputs are a handy way to connect camcorders or video games.
Audio outputs let you direct a stereo TV's sound to a receiver or self-powered speakers. Integrated Digital TVs also include a Dolby Digital Audio output for Surround Sound (available from some digital broadcasts).

Composite-video

S-video

Component video

DVI

HDMI

BUYING ADVICE PLASMA TVs

own. To display digital programs, they require a digital tuner to decode those broadcasts. If you're getting your HD programming from cable or satellite, your digital cable box or satellite receiver has the appropriate digital decoder built in. All you have to do is connect your HD-ready TV to the box and you're all set. Cable companies charge a small rental fee for digital or HD-capable boxes. To receive HD via satellite, you need an HD receiver and special dish antenna(e). Together, these cost about $300, but you may be able to get them from the satellite company at little or no charge as part of a promotion.

You can also get digital broadcasts, including HD, over the air, via an antenna. To do so, you'll have to buy a digital tuner called an ATSC (Advanced Television Systems Committee) tuner—the external box costs a few hundred dollars. However, there's no charge for service as there is with cable or satellite. Some satellite receivers also offer a built-in ATSC digital tuner. To receive digital programming via antenna, you must be fairly close to a transmitter, with an unobstructed view. With digital signals, you'll either have a clear, strong signal or none at all.

Integrated HDTV sets. These have the ATSC digital tuner built in, which enables them to decode any digital signal, including HD, with no additional equipment when used with a roof antenna. You may be able to receive the major networks' HD offerings transmitted over the air in your area, but you won't get the premium channels available on satellite and cable. To get HD via cable or satellite, integrated sets require an HD-capable cable box, CableCard, or satellite receiver—the built-in digital tuner only works for off-air digital broadcasts. As of July 2005, all new TVs 36 inches and larger—a category covering most plasma TVs—were required have a built-in digital tuner to comply with a government ruling. Although integrated HDTVs have a digital tuner for off-air programs, most of these sets still require an HD-capable cable box or satellite receiver to get cable or satellite.

Digital-Cable-Ready (DCR) sets. Some new integrated models, called digital-cable-ready (DCR) or plug-and-play sets, can receive digital-cable programming without using a set-top box. For HD and premium cable programming—and possibly for any digital programming—you must insert a CableCard into a slot on the set. You usually have to pay a few dollars a month to rent the card from the cable company. Current DCR TVs are not interactive, so even with a CableCard in the slot they can't provide features such as an interactive program guide, video on demand, or pay-per-view ordering via remote. Second-generation DCR TVs and CableCards should be here soon, and they're expected to have two-way capability, allowing for interactive features. Integrated sets typically cost

Enhanced-definition (ED) sets typically cost less than HD models.

Cable, satellite, or antenna: Three ways to receive HD programs

How much HD programming is available in your area depends, in part, on how you receive the signals. You can get HD from a cable or satellite company, provided that they transmit it in HD, or over the air via antenna. To see what's available in HD locally, check www.hdtvpub.com.

Cable. Cable currently offers more HD programming than the two major satellite companies, but the amount varies greatly by cable provider. You'll need digital cable to get HD, because HD signals are digital and can't be carried over regular cable service, which is analog. Contact your cable company to see how much HD it offers as part of its digital-cable service and whether there is an extra cost for an HD-capable box or an HD programming package.
Satellite. The two major satellite providers, Dish and DirecTV, currently offer only a handful of channels of HD programming and charge about $10 or so a month for the programming package. You'll need a special satellite dish or a second dish. For more information, visit www.dishnetwork.com or www.directv.com.

If your cable or satellite company doesn't offer as much HD as you'd like, you may be able to connect the box they provide to an antenna to pull in over-the-air HD network broadcasts as well.
Antenna. If you get HD via antenna, you'll get only broadcast network fare, not cable and satellite stations such as Discovery HD. You must be close enough to a station transmitting in HD, with an unobstructed view, to get the HD signals. With digital signals, reception is all or nothing: You'll either have a clear, strong signal or none at all. To find out about digital TV stations in your area, visit www.fcc.gov/mb/video/files/dtvonair.html.
For more on choosing and using an antenna, visit www.antennaweb.org.

06 | BUYING ADVICE PLASMA TVs

more than HD-ready sets, with digital-cable-ready models costing the most.

Among the brands in the plasma TV category are Hitachi, Panasonic, Philips, Pioneer, Samsung, Sharp, Sony, and Toshiba. Prices have dropped sharply over the past year or two. At publication time, HD-ready models with 40- to 44-inch screens, the best-selling size, were going for $3,000 to $5,000 or more. TVs with 50-inch or larger screens were selling for $4,500 and up. Look for prices to fall further, now that companies such as Dell and ViewSonic have expanded from the computer arena into TVs with aggressive pricing.

Some plasma TVs are only monitors, without a tuner or speakers.

FEATURES THAT COUNT

Plasma TVs have most of the features that are now standard on direct-view, CRT-based TVs; plus some features that are less common. These include **picture-in-picture (PIP)**, which lets you watch two channels at once, one in a small box, the other a full-screen image. It's useful if you want to browse the onscreen guide while keeping an eye on the program you're watching. A single-tuner TV requires another device with a tuner, such as a VCR or cable box, to display two programs at once; dual-tuner models can display two programs simultaneously on their own.

Most TVs have several types of inputs that handle varying levels of quality. See "Hooking up" on page 76.

Audio outputs let you direct a TV's audio signal to a receiver or to self-powered speakers. Integrated digital TVs also include a Dolby Digital audio output for surround sound (available from some digital broadcasts). An **automatic volume leveler** compensates for the jarring volume jumps that often accompany commercials or changes in channel. Some plasma sets have a separate control unit—a video receiver, in effect, that accepts connections more easily than a panel you've had mounted onto a wall.

If you watch many movies, look for **film mode** feature on ED and HD sets. This feature is also called **3:2 pulldown compensation** or brand-specific names such as CineMotion. This can make moving images that were converted from film to video look less jerky, with less jaggedness at the edges of objects. On 16:9 sets, **stretch and zoom modes** will expand or compress an image to better fill the screen shape. This helps to reduce the dark bands that can appear around images if you watch content formatted for one screen shape on a TV that has the other shape. (The picture may be distorted or cut off a bit in the process of stretching and zooming). Those bars make the picture slightly smaller and use the phosphors unevenly, which may leave ghosted images on the screen over time. This "burn-in" may be also a risk with any images—say from a stock ticker—left on the screen for long periods.

HOW TO CHOOSE

Decide whether you want true HD or the next best thing. HD sets generally perform better than ED sets with all types of signals. They may be worth the higher cost if you're a purist who wants the best image quality. Most ED plasma sets can down-convert an HD signal to fit their lower resolution, so you can still enjoy HD programming. While it won't be true HD quality, it can be very good. Minor differences in resolution between two HD sets or two ED sets won't necessarily determine overall image quality. Other factors affect the picture, such as the way a TV converts a signal to fit the screen and its ability to render subtle shading. Note that the shiny surface of a plasma TV can produce annoying reflections, especially in brightly lit rooms. Many of these sets look best in low light.

Weigh screen size against price. If you're buying a plasma TV, an important question is how much screen you can afford. All other things being equal, the bigger the screen, the bigger the price tag, and the greater the viewing distance you need to see optimal picture quality. You'll enjoy the best viewing experience if you sit at least 6 feet away from a 42-inch HD set, and a little farther from an ED set or larger screen.

Beware of burn-in and burnout. Plasma TVs may be prone to burn-in, much like CRT-based rear-projection TVs. Over time, static images from fixed items displayed for long periods (such as a video game or a stock ticker) may leave permanent ghosted impressions on-screen, so minimize the risk as much as you can.

You may have seen reports, in print or online, suggesting that plasma TVs may not last as long as other types of TVs. Overall longevity and reliability is an open question because the technology is so new. Major manufacturers now tout 60,000 hours of use or more before a recent-model plasma screen loses half its brightness. Even in heavy use (40 hours a week), that's about 29 years.

Don't get hung up on specs. Ads touting high contrast ratios and brightness (cd/m2, or candelas per square meter) may sway you to one set

BUYING ADVICE REAR-PROJECTION TVs

or another. Don't pay much heed. Manufacturers arrive at specs differently, so they may not be comparable. Try adjusting sets in the store yourself to compare contrast and brightness.

Determine what's included when comparing prices. Most other types of TVs come with speakers and a tuner at least for standard channels. (A digital tuner for HD isn't included with any HD-ready or ED-ready set.) Some plasmas are purely monitors only, sold with no sound capabilities whatsoever; they don't include speakers or a tuner for any type of TV signal. You won't have to pay for a tuner if you'll be using a cable box or satellite receiver, which would serve as the tuner for all programming. Otherwise you'll need a set-top box to work with an antenna. You'll have to pay extra for optional speakers unless you plan to connect the set to your existing sound system.

Consider the logistics. Ads for plasma TVs may not show any wires, but you'll probably be connecting a cable box or satellite receiver and a DVD player, and possibly a DVR, DVD recorder, VCR and audio receiver as well. You can tuck wires behind the TV if you place it on a stand. With wall-mounting, you can run the wires behind the wall or through conduits, a task that might be best handled by a professional. Often weighing 100 pounds or more, plasma TVs need adequate support and ample ventilation because of the heat they can generate. Ask the retailer to recommend an installer or contact the Custom Electronic Design & Installation Association (800-669-5329 or www.cedia.net). Figure on $300 to $1,000 for labor, plus a few hundred dollars for mounting brackets.

Weigh the merits of an extended warranty. While extended warranties aren't worthwhile for most products, they may be for high-priced devices using new technologies. Because plasma TVs are costly items that haven't yet established a track record for reliability, check into the cost of a service plan. Find out whether in-home service is covered and whether a replacement is provided if a set can't be repaired.

BUYING ADVICE
Rear-projection televisions

The least expensive—and most common—type of jumbo TV is a rear-projection set. Some projection sets have three cathode-ray picture tubes (CRTs), smaller versions of the tubes used in conventional sets. The images from those small tubes are projected onto the back of a 42- to 70-plus-inch screen, hence the name rear-projection TV. Microdisplay sets use liquid-crystal display (LCD), digital light processing (DLP), or liquid crystal on silicon (LCoS) technology in place of CRTs. These TVs are slimmer, lighter, and more expensive than comparable CRT-based sets. More of them are appearing in stores, and their prices are starting to drop.

WHAT'S AVAILABLE

Major brands include Hitachi, Mitsubishi, Panasonic, Philips, RCA, Samsung, Sony, and Toshiba.

The smallest sets, measuring about 42 inches diagonally, offer only a few more inches of screen than a conventional 36-inch set. Rear-projection sets with 50- to 60-inch screens are the best sellers. The largest of these TVs have screens measuring 70 inches or more. Keep in mind that a set with a 57-inch screen could be overwhelming in a modest-sized room. CRT-based sets are floor-standing units about 24 to 30 inches deep that take up about 8 square feet of floor space. They weigh about 200 pounds and are mounted on wheels.

Microdisplay models may require a stand. Most are about 15 to 20 inches deep and weigh about 100 pounds.

Most rear-projection sets now on the market are digital (HD-capable) sets, but there may still be a few analog models. Both types can accept regular TV signals, but HD-capable sets can best display the superior images you get from DVD players and from HD sources (antenna, satel-

Most CRT-based models sit on the floor and require about eight square feet of floor space.

06 BUYING ADVICE REAR-PROJECTION TVs

lite, digital cable, or digital-video players/recorders). HD-capable sets generally cost a few hundred dollars more than comparably sized analog models. Most have a wide-screen 16:9 aspect ratio that resembles a movie-theater screen.

Within the HD category, there are three types of TV sets:

HD-ready sets. Also called HDTV monitors, these sets can display standard-definition analog programs (which still account for most non-prime-time TV broadcasts) on their own. To display digital programs, they require a digital tuner to decode those broadcasts. If you're getting your HD programming from cable or satellite, your digital cable box or satellite receiver has the appropriate digital decoder built in. All you have to do is connect your HD-ready TV to the box and you're all set. Cable companies charge a small rental fee for digital or HD-capable boxes. To receive HD via satellite, you need an HD receiver and special dish antenna(e). Together, these cost about $300, but you may be able to get them from the satellite company at little or no charge as part of a promotion.

You can also get digital broadcasts, including HD, over the air, via an antenna. To do so, you'll have to buy a digital tuner called an ATSC (Advanced Television Systems Committee) tuner—the external box costs a few hundred dollars. However, there's no charge for service as there is with cable or satellite. Some satellite receivers also offer a built-in ATSC digital tuner. To receive digital programming via antenna, you must be fairly close to a transmitter, with an unobstructed view. With digital signals, you'll either have a clear, strong signal or none at all.

Integrated HDTV sets. Also called HDTVs, these have the ATSC digital tuner built in, which enables them to decode any digital signals, including HD, with no additional equipment when used with a roof antenna. You may be able to receive the major networks' HD offerings transmitted over the air in your area, but you won't get the premium channels available on satellite and cable. To get HD via cable or satellite, integrated sets require an HD-capable cable box, CableCard, or satellite receiver—the built-in digital tuner only works for off-air digital broadcasts.

Starting in July of 2005, all new TVs with 36-inch or larger screens—a category covering virtually all projection TVs—were required to have a built-in digital tuner to comply with a government ruling.

Digital-Cable-Ready (DCR) sets. Some new integrated models, called digital-cable-ready (DCR) or plug-and-play sets, can receive digital-cable programming without using a set-top box. For HD and premium cable programming—and possibly for any digital programming—you must insert a CableCard into a slot on the set. You usually have to pay a few dollars a month to rent the card from the cable company. Current DCR TVs are not interactive, so even with a CableCard in the slot they can't provide features such as an interactive program guide, video on demand, or pay-per-view ordering via remote. Second-generation DCR TVs and CableCards should be here soon, and they're expected to have two-way capability, allowing for interactive features. Integrated sets typically cost more than HD-ready sets, with digital-cable-ready models costing the most.

IMPORTANT FEATURES

Virtually all projection TVs have the features that are now standard on regular 27-inch and larger TVs, plus some features that aren't so common—such as **pic-**

Brand Repair History

Projection TVs

Choosing a brand with a good repair history can improve your odds of getting a reliable TV. The graph at right shows the percentage of rear-projection TVs that were ever repaired or had a serious problem that was not resolved. RCA was among the more repair-prone brands. The data apply primarily to CRT-based models and may not apply to projection sets employing LCD, DLP, or LCoS technology, which are relatively new to the market. The vast majority of the TVs in the sample are HD sets; the rest were analog. The two types showed no difference in reliability. Note that repair rates for specific models may vary, and changes in design and manufacturing may affect reliability.

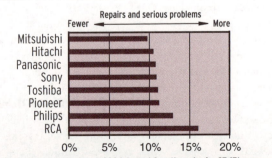

Based on responses to our 2004 Annual Questionnaire for 27,671 rear-projection TVs purchased new between 2000 and 2004. Data have been standardized to eliminate any differences linked to age. Differences of less than 4 points are not meaningful.

BUYING ADVICE REAR PROJECTION TVs

ture-in-picture (PIP) or a variant side-by-side picture mode.

Most TVs have several types of inputs that handle varying levels of quality.

Audio outputs let you direct a TV's audio signal to a receiver or to self-powered speakers. Integrated digital TVs also include a Dolby Digital audio output for surround sound (available from some digital broadcasts). An **automatic volume leveler** compensates for the jarring volume jumps that often accompany commercials or changes in channel.

Auto convergence provides a one-touch adjustment to automatically align the three CRTs' images to form an accurate picture. It's much more convenient than manual convergence, which can require time-consuming adjustments. Manual convergence does allow finer control, though. The best bet is a set that has both manual and automatic convergence. (Convergence is not necessary on LCD, DLP, or LCoS models.)

Stretch and zoom modes on wide-screen sets will expand or compress an image to better fill the screen shape. This helps to reduce the dark bands that can appear above, below, or on the sides of the image if you watch content that's not formatted for 16:9 screens. (The picture may be distorted or cut off a bit in the process of stretching or zooming.) Those bars make the picture slightly smaller. On CRT sets (but not LCD, LCoS, or DLP models), the bars can leave "burn in" ghosted images on the screen over time, as can any image—say, from a stock ticker or station logos—left on the screen for long periods.

If you watch many movies, look for a feature called **3:2 pull-down compensation** or brand-specific names such as CineMotion and Film mode. This can make moving images that were converted from film to video look less jerky, with less jaggedness at the edges of objects.

HOW TO CHOOSE

Here are some points to consider in choosing a rear-projection TV:

Consider space before settling on screen size. Most rear-projection TVs have screens measuring 42 to 65 inches. You might be tempted by the biggest screens, which can span as much as 70 inches or more, but take a breath—and some measurements—first. Figure out how much floor space you can spare, and plan to view the TV from about 7 to 9 feet away for optimal picture quality.

Weigh depth and price in choosing a display type. Once you know how much room you have, decide whether size or price is more important. CRT-based sets are floor-standing models with deep cabinets mounted on casters. Some take up as much space as an armchair or loveseat. Most microdisplays are tabletop units. You buy a stand separate-

Before you buy a rear-projection TV, figure out how much floor space you can spare.

Talk the Talk: Projection TV terms & technologies

If high-definition television has a special language (see page 66), projection TV speaks its own dialect. Even the term for the category can be a puzzle. You might wonder why rear-projection sets are called that, given that there's no projector anywhere in sight. It's because the projector is inside the cabinet. An image is created within the set and projected onto the rear surface of the screen (hence the name "rear projection"). By contrast, direct-view sets (picture-tube TVs and flat-panel LCD and plasma displays) create images right on the screen, not internally.

Several different technologies are used to create the images on projection TVs:
CRT models. This type of projection TV contains three CRTs, or cathode ray tubes—one each for red, green, and blue—making the cabinet big and heavy. Three beams converge on the inside of the screen to form an image. You must periodically align the CRTs, using the TV's controls, to ensure a sharp image. This is known as convergence. All but the cheapest sets now have an automatic convergence feature that makes this a quick and easy process. Manual convergence usually allows for finer tweaks.
Microdisplays. This is an industry term sometimes used to describe rear-projection sets using LCD (liquid-crystal display), DLP (digital light-processing), or LCoS (liquid-crystal on silicon) chips and a bright lamp to create images. This space-saving "light-engine" technology makes microdisplays slimmer and lighter than **CRT-based sets.** Most microdisplays are tabletop sets 15 to 20 inches deep that weigh about 100 pounds. CRTs are floor-standing sets 24 or more inches deep, and many weigh about 200 pounds. Here's a look at the three types of microdisplays:
LCD. These TVs have three tiny LCD panels inside. Don't confuse LCD-based rear-projection TVs with LCD flat panels, though. These big TVs are more than a foot deep. The best of the LCD-based projection sets we've tested displayed very good picture quality. None of the sets, however, were able to display the deep black levels of TVs using other technologies, and the contrast wasn't as good as we've seen on other types of TVs.
DLP. These sets create images using a digital light-processing chip with thousands of tiny mirrors. Rear-projection DLP sets have one chip and a rotating color wheel, which may cause occasional annoying flashes of color visible to some viewers—what's called the rainbow effect. Some high-end front projectors have three chips; they don't have that problem. The best of the DLP projection sets we've tested displayed very good picture quality.
LCoS. These sets share some attributes with LCD and DLP, using both tiny mirrors and liquid-crystal technology. The technology's rollout has been hampered by production problems and costs, prompting companies such as Intel and Philips to abandon their LCoS plans. Because LCoS sets have been slow to reach the market, we've tested only two so far. Both had good picture quality. JVC has an LCoS variant that it calls HD-ILA, using Direct-drive Image Light Amplifier technology.

06 | BUYING ADVICE REAR-PROJECTION TVs

ly for a few hundred dollars or more. Would you prefer to save money with a bulkier CRT set or spend more for a slimmer microdisplay?

Consider reliability. CRT technology has been used in rear-projection TVs for years and has generally been quite reliable. Note, though, that any pattern left on a CRT screen for long periods—such as a stock ticker or video game—can burn into the tubes of a CRT-based model, producing a permanent ghosted image on the screen. Most warranties don't cover burn-in. This problem doesn't affect other types of rear-projection TVs. Microdisplay technologies are newer and haven't established a track record for long-term reliability, but they're not vulnerable to screen burn-in. They may require lamp replacement, however, which can cost a few hundred dollars. Factor these considerations into your decision.

Focus on picture quality. It's a little harder to find top picture quality in rear-projection TVs than in plasma TVs, so you'll have to be choosy. The best sets can deliver very good picture quality with HD content and good picture quality for DVDs and regular TV programming. Microdisplays are likely to provide better picture quality than CRT-based models. Within the microdisplay category, we haven't found that any one projection technology was consistently better than another.

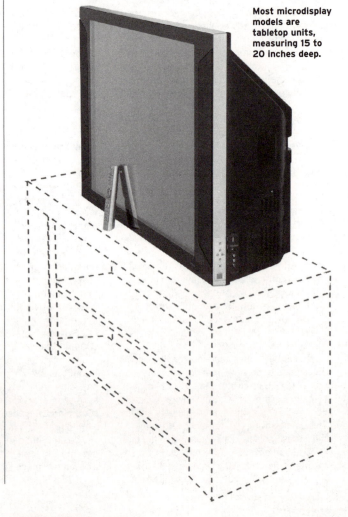

Most microdisplay models are tabletop units, measuring 15 to 20 inches deep.

Check the viewing angle. Some new models display a better image from off-center than older sets did—a must if a TV will be watched by several people at once. Some sets have wider viewing angles than others. Before buying one, see how the picture looks if you step off to the side or move up and down. With some, you'll see a dimmer, somewhat washed-out image as your viewing position angles away, particularly in a vertical direction.

Expect fine sound quality. Many people connect big-screen TVs to an audio system to provide surround sound, so the quality of the TV's speakers may not be an issue. It may reassure you to know that virtually all the sets we've tested recently produced excellent sound. That's largely because projection sets have bigger speakers than direct-view TVs and bigger cabinets with superior acoustical properties.

Consider installation. Because rear-projection sets are floor-standing units, installation is easier than with front-projection systems or wall-mounted plasma TVs. Still, rear-projection sets are larger and may be somewhat harder to set up than regular TVs, so consider having a professional install your TV.

Weigh the merits of an extended warranty. While extended warranties aren't worthwhile for most products, they may be for high-priced devices using new technologies. Because microdisplay TVs are costly items that haven't yet established a track record for reliability, check into the cost of a service plan. Find out whether in-home service is covered and whether a replacement is provided if a set can't be repaired.

VIDEO GEAR

INSIDE INFO
84 Video recording

86 Get great sound with home theater

BUYING ADVICE
88 DVD players

91 DVD recorders

93 Digital video recorders

95 Home theater in a box

96 Receivers

99 Speakers

CHAPTER 07

If you're replacing an aging VCR this year, a digital recorder should be at the top of your list. Not only can its picture quality exceed that of a VCR, but it can offer functions and versatility that no VCR can match. These devices record on DVDs, hard drives, or sometimes both.

With digital recording, there's no more trolling back and forth through a videocassette in search of the start of that big game. A few button clicks through an onscreen menu, and the gridiron fills the screen. Some digital recorders also let you pause live TV and resume watching where you left off, or watch a previously recorded program while the device records a new one.

Much more expensive than VCRs just a few years ago, some digital recorders now cost under $200 or so—although you can still spend far more. In this chapter we look at digital recording options, along with plain DVD players, including portable models. We also explain how to set up a home theater to get the full benefit from all your entertainment gear.

▶▶ Digital recording sends the VCR toward retirement.

Ratings: DVD recorders, p. 142; Home theater in a box, p. 145

07 INSIDE INFO VIDEO GEAR

VIDEO RECORDING

Digital recorders have two ways to work, alone or in combination.

There are at least a half-dozen types of digital video hardware competing for your dollar today. DVD players dominate the market, but various types of player-recorders are gaining, including some that accept both videotape and discs, and other that use hard drives. Our tests show that some players come close to being a universal machine that can handle just about any disc format.

Recording onto blank DVDs gives you many of the familiar advantages of videotape recording. You can easily keep a recording once you've made it—by simply removing the disc from the machine and storing it. And while not all types of recordable DVDs play in all DVD drives, many types should play on virtually all DVD players and computer DVD-ROM drives.

Models that use a hard drive have many of the same capabilities as a computer. That begins with large storage capacity—from 40 to 100 hours or more of video for digital recorders—and the ability to search through and easily access programs on the drive, using the remote and an onscreen menu that shows a list of recordings.

You can simply program one-time recordings, as with any VCR or DVD recorder. Some hard-drive video recorders can be programmed to continuously comb through hundreds of TV channels, automatically recording the programs you've specified as being of interest to you. To get that functionality, you'll likely be paying a monthly fee—either to a programming service such as TiVo and ReplayTV or to your cable or satellite provider, to rent a box with a built-in hard-drive recorder that works with the provider's program guide.

HOW TO CHOOSE

You can expect fine performance from virtually any digital recorder. First Things First, at right, summarizes the recorder types and the requirements they meet. These questions will help you determine your requirements:

What's important when it comes to programmed TV recording? If you're seeking only the familiar functionality of a VCR, with its ability to make timed recordings to blank media, a plain DVD recorder will fill the bill. If you want something more sophisticated—such as a machine that does some of the programming work for you—consider a hard-drive recorder.

Is it a priority to easily save copies of some TV recordings? Archiving a cherished TV show from a hard-drive-only recorder requires the hassle of connecting another recorder to the unit. A DVD recorder makes it easy to archive an entire show by saving the disc on which it was recorded. A recorder with both hard drive and DVD recording allows you to record shows onto the hard drive and then selectively transfer them to disc.

Are you integrating a recorder with a TV set-top box? Contact your TV provider to see if you can rent (from cable companies) or buy (from satellite providers) an integrated TV decoder box/digital recorder.

Do you want to use your recorder to store camcorder videos? Any digital recorder also allows you to make backup copies of home movies recorded on a digital or analog camcorder.

But only one kind of recorder provides the features and functionality you'll want if you'll often make such video transfers. It's a recorder that records both to DVD and to a hard drive but is not allied with either the TiVo or ReplayTV services.

Such units have more sophisticated editing tools and better input options for digital camcorders. But they cost a little more than other combination recorders and lack the sophisticated programming-search recording capabilities of the TiVo or ReplayTV units. And editing a home video on a digital recorder is more difficult than with a computer, mouse, and keyboard, so you shouldn't buy a recorder solely to work on home videos.

Be skeptical of premium-priced connections that purport to maximize picture quality with high-definition TV sets.

A DVD player, like this Pioneer model, will also play music CDs.

INSIDE INFO VIDEO GEAR

First Things First

1 DVD player
Pros: Low price, especially for single-disc models. Multi-disc players offer continuous music from audio CDs and DVDs.
Cons: Not designed to record.
Choose first if: You want a DVD machine only to watch prerecorded movies or to listen to music.
Price range: $80 to $150 for most.

2 DVD player with built-in VCR
Pros: Plays all prerecorded media. The least-expensive type of recorder.
Cons: Less versatile than DVD/VCR recorder; you can only record to tape. You can't transfer copy-protected DVDs to tape.
Choose first if: You want a low-priced unit that plays and records.
Price range: $110 to $170 for most.

3 DVD-only recorder
Pros: The least-expensive way to record on DVDs. Also serves as a DVD player.
Cons: Lacks editing versatility of DVD/hard-drive units.
Choose first if: You want the lowest-cost digital recorder.
Price range: $300 to $500 for most.

4 DVD recorder with built-in VCR
Pros: Plays all prerecorded media. Handy for transferring home video from tape to DVD and vice versa.
Cons: Relatively expensive. Loss of picture quality if you copy a DVD to tape. You can't transfer copy-protected tapes or DVDs.
Choose first if: You want a unit that does almost everything.
Price range: $370 to $400 for most.

5 DVD/hard-drive recorder
Pros: Can hold many hours of video. Flexible editing and archiving capability.
Cons: Expensive.
Choose first if: You want the most flexible and generous digital recording.
Price range: $500 to $800 for most.

6 Stand-alone hard-drive recorder
Pros: Depending on model, hard drive can hold up to 100 hours or more of video. Some models combined with cable/satellite receiver can record high definition. Versatile and very easy to use for recording TV programs, allows you to pause and rewind "live" TV. Those combined with cable/satellite receiver eliminate extra box and remote.
Cons: Archiving requires connecting a VCR or DVD recorder. Typically have to pay for program guide (DVR will not function, or functionality is very limited, without it). Some models require a phone connection (but not a separate line) to update program guide. Can't edit recordings. Those combined with cable/satellite receiver will record only TV programs.
Choose first if: You are exclusively interested in TV recording, especially of HD programs, and want ample storage.
Price range: $99 and up for TiVo or ReplayTV, plus one-time ($299) or monthly ($13) fee for TV program guide. About $10 a month from cable provider.

For more detailed buying advice on video recording, see page 91.

07 | INSIDE INFO VIDEO GEAR

GET GREAT SOUND WITH HOME THEATER

You can buy one in a box or create your own, piece by piece.

Even the priciest digital TV can't convey the rich multichannel sound you'll find on most DVD movies and high-definition television programs. To remedy that, you have two basic choices: You can buy components and assemble your own system (also integrating equipment you already have) or opt for a home-theater-in-a-box system.

The biggest selling point of prepackaged systems: their simplicity. You won't have to spend your time auditioning separate components.

With your home theater, you can enjoy the movies you want without paying $6 for popcorn.

Home theater systems such as this one from Yamaha provide everything you need in one package.

The latter option is the cheapest, easiest way to envelop yourself with surround sound. Most of these pre-picked packages are more compact than a system with stand-alone components, and many have designs that are quite stylish.

The biggest selling point may be simplicity. The speakers are matched for sound, saving you the work of auditioning separate components. The packages include the wires to connect everything, and color-coding and labeling simplify setup. The downside: You generally can't replace components or add new ones to the mix.

You'll find a wide selection of systems in mass-market stores, starting at less than $300. The typical system bundles a receiver and the speakers for a Dolby Digital 5.1 surround setup: two front and two rear speakers, a center-channel speaker, and a subwoofer. Most packages include a progressive-scan DVD player.

Some new models offer more than the usual bundle. In the $500-and-up range, you may get Dolby Digital 6.1 surround sound and a third rear speaker to carry the additional surround channel. Other systems, even some in the $300- to-$400 range, include a VCR and a DVD player.

There are differences worth noting. The receiver and DVD player (and VCR, if included) are often combined in one unit, especially on lower-priced models. Combo devices save space, but they usually have fewer inputs than a separate receiver and DVD player. The controls can be tricky to use because each button may control several functions.

86 CONSUMER REPORTS • ELECTRONICS BUYING GUIDE 2006 Expert • Independent • Nonprofit

INSIDE INFO VIDEO GEAR

Other variations include systems with wireless rear speakers, which don't require cables stretching from the receiver to the back of a room. Instead, the rear speakers are wired to and powered by a separate box containing an antenna. The antenna communicates with the receiver via radio frequency (RF) or infrared. RF models may suffer interference from cordless phones or baby monitors operating on the same frequency, often 2.4 GHz. An infrared connection requires an unobstructed line of sight between the receiver and antenna.

You can cut clutter by getting a system that builds the subwoofer, and sometimes the surround speakers, into the front speakers. This eliminates the need to find a place for a bulky bass unit and rear speakers and their wires. The trade-off is some compromise in bass performance and the surround effect.

▶▶ For more detailed buying advice on home-theater-in-a-box systems, see page 95. For buying advice on separate receivers, see page 96. For speakers, page 99.

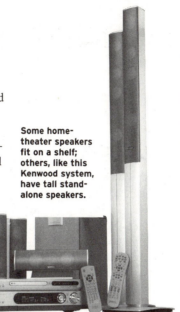

Some home-theater speakers fit on a shelf; others, like this Kenwood system, have tall stand-alone speakers.

Setting up your home theater for the best possible sound

FIND THE SWEET SPOT
The trick in setting up a home theater is arranging components in a way that maximizes their capabilities. The room you choose has a fundamental bearing on sound quality. For the best sound, try to strike a balance between acoustically "live" (bare floor and walls) and "dead" (carpeted floor and curtained walls).

Upholstered furniture, wall hangings, and stocked bookshelves can help deaden the front of a room, where the TV is. The back of the room, where the rear-channel speakers are, should be live. The size and shape of room also matter. A 17-foot by 11-foot room with an 8-foot ceiling is good. A square room can make bass sound boomy or uneven. The diagrams here show "sweet spots" for various shapes of rooms.

HOOK IT ALL UP
When hooking up components, go from left to right across the back of the receiver. Here are steps to follow:
1. Connect the receiver to the audio devices with the appropriate cables.
2. Connect the video devices, using the best video signal that your TV set, receiver, and DVD player have—component video, if you have that; S-video, if you have that; or composite, in all video equipment.
3. With speakers, start with as close to the ideal as you can. The main speakers should approximately form an equilateral triangle with you, the listener, and should be at the same height as your ears. The center speaker should be atop or below the TV and aligned with, or only slightly behind, the main speakers. The best place for your surround speakers will depend on the room's acoustics. You may have to experiment with their positions and directions. The surround speakers may be placed alongside the seating position or facing each other or the back wall. The subwoofer can go anywhere convenient.
4. Connect the speakers, observing polarity; connect the power cords.
5. Experiment with the speaker locations and tweak the tone controls. Moving the subwoofer out of the corner or away from the wall may make it sound less boomy.

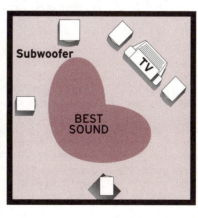

The shape of the room will influence where you should place your components. From left: A rectangular, square, and L-shaped room.

07 BUYING ADVICE DVD PLAYERS

BUYING ADVICE
DVD players

These devices play high-quality videos and CDs, and prices are lower than ever.

The DVD has come to dominate video even more quickly than the CD conquered audio in the 1980s. Along with changing what we watch—discs rather than tapes—DVDs are changing how we watch. The digital format makes it easy to go directly to desired sections of a movie, and the picture and sound quality surpass what you'll get with a videotape. One DVD can store a complete two-hour-plus movie with a Dolby Digital or DTS soundtrack containing up to eight audio channels. There's also room for extra material such as multiple languages, behind-the-scenes documentaries, and commentary by the director or actors.

High-definition DVD players are expected to hit the market by the beginning of 2006.

DVD players can play standard audio CDs, and some models fully support DVD-Audio or SACD, two competing high-resolution audio formats offering multichannel sound.

While DVD players are playback-only devices, DVD recorders record as well as play. Prices of recorders have dropped considerably in the past few years, with entry-level models now selling for less than $200.

WHAT'S AVAILABLE

Apex, Panasonic, Sony, and Toshiba are among the biggest-selling brands of DVD players. Virtually all new DVD players are progressive-scan models. When used with a conventional TV, these players provide the usual high DVD picture quality. With a TV that can display high-definition (HD) or enhanced-definition (ED) images, image quality is slightly better. (That's because HD and ED sets support the player's progressive-scan 480p mode, drawing 480 consecutive lines on the screen. By comparison, with a conventional TV, every other line is drawn and then interlaced or combined, a resolution referred to as 480i.) A player can be connected directly to your TV for viewing movies or routed through your receiver to play movies and audio CDs on your sound system. Progressive-scan models come in single-disc and multidisc versions. The few non-progressive-scan players now on the market are mostly single-disc models; these tend to be the cheapest type.

Single-disc consoles. Even low-end models usually include all the video outputs you might want. **Price range:** less than $60 to more than $300.

Multidisc consoles. Like CD changers, these players accommodate more than one disc at a time, typically five. DVD jukeboxes that hold 400 or so discs are also available. **Price range:** $100 to $800.

Portables. These DVD players generally come with a small wide-screen-format LCD screen and batteries that claim to provide three hours or more of playback. Some low-priced models don't come with a screen; they're intended for users who plan to connect the device

---

Portable DVD players are lightweight and inexpensive
If you want to take the show on the road, pick up a portable DVD player.

These devices resemble small laptop computers minus the keyboard, but they cost much less. Some now sell for less than $150.

Weigh screen size against portability and price. Screens that measure 4 to 6 inches diagonally are too small for comfortable viewing. A 7-inch screen is the smallest we'd recommend. Players with 9- or 10-inch screens are heavier and more expensive but worth considering if several people will be watching a movie.

Be realistic about picture quality. The LCD screens on portable players don't offer the excellent picture quality that DVD technology can produce on a good LCD TV set. Better portables should be fine for watching DVDs in your car or on a plane, but the picture tends to wash out in bright light.

Listen before you buy. The sound from the built-in speakers is usually just OK. You can get very good sound by using headphones, generally not included. Bring them along to audition players. Dual headphone jacks make it easy for two people to listen simultaneously.

Check battery life. Most movies run about 2 hours, so make sure the built-in battery can last at least that long without recharging. In our limited testing, most players lasted 2.5 hours or more. A car adapter is handy for longer stints.

Consider construction and warranties. Some models have flimsy lids, and pressure on the lid may cause DVDs to misplay. Warranties are usually 12 months on parts and 3 months on labor. Avoid those with only 3 months on parts.

Play it safe. If you plan to use a portable DVD player in a car, buy a mount ($20 to $40) to secure it on the center armrest or suspend it between the front seats, to keep it from flying around if you stop short.

BUYING ADVICE DVD PLAYERS

to a television. You pay extra for portability either way. **Price range:** $150 to $800.

FEATURES THAT COUNT

DVD-based movies often come in various formats. **Aspect-ratio control** lets you choose between the 4:3 viewing format of conventional TVs (4 inches wide for every 3 inches high) and the 16:9 ratio of newer, wide-screen sets.

A DVD player gives you all sorts of control over the picture—control you may never have known you needed. **Picture zoom** lets you zoom in on a specific frame. **Black-level adjustment** brings out the detail in dark parts of the screen image. If you've ever wanted to see certain action scenes from different angles, **multi-angle capability** gives you that opportunity. Note that this feature and some others work only with certain discs.

A DVD player enables you to navigate the disc in a number of ways. Unlike a VHS tape, most DVDs are sectioned. **Chapter preview** lets you scan the opening seconds of each section or chapter until you find what you want; a related feature, **chapter gallery,** shows thumbnails of section or chapter opening scenes. **Go-to by time** lets you enter how many hours and minutes into the disc you'd like to skip to. **Marker functions** allow easy indexing of specific sections.

To get the most from a DVD player, you need to hook it up to the TV with the best available connection. A **composite-video connection** to the TV can produce a very good picture, but there will be some loss of detail and some color artifacts such as adjacent colors bleeding into each other. Using the TV's **S-video input** can improve picture quality. It keeps the black-and-white and the color portions of the signal separated, producing more picture detail and fewer color defects than composite-video.

Component-video, sometimes not provided on the lowest-end models, improves on S-video by splitting the color signal, resulting in a wider range of color. If you connect a DVD player via an S-video or component connection, don't be surprised if you have to adjust the television-picture setup when you switch to a picture coming from a VCR or a cable box that uses a **radio-frequency** (RF, also called antenna/cable) **connection** or a composite connection.

Two newer outputs found on some players, **Digital Video**

VCRs: Buy by price & features

Old-hat as they may seem in today's digital world, VCRs still offer a serviceable way to record TV programs, play back prerecorded tapes, and transfer home camcorder movies onto a convenient viewing format. The recorders and blank tapes are inexpensive and have the advantages of familiarity and universal compatibility—no format wars as with DVD recordings.

We haven't found many performance differences among VCRs. Most models, even inexpensive ones, are capable of good picture quality. Base your decision more on price and features.

Get a hi-fi model for home theaters. These are much better for TVs with stereo sound or for connection to a receiver that can process surround sound.

For easy programming, look for an onscreen menu and VCR Plus. An onscreen menu accessed by the remote control lets you avoid fiddling with small buttons and squinting at a tiny display. VCR Plus lets you record a show by entering a numerical code from TV listings instead of the date, time, duration, and channel.

Consider ease-of-use features. Index search fast-forwards or rewinds the tape to a specific point set by the machine at the start of a recording. Commercial advance lets you bypass commercials by fast-forwarding in 30- to 60-second intervals. Some models can automatically switch from SP to EP speed, a feature called auto speed-switching, to extend recording time, helpful if you're near the end of a tape.

Think twice about paying extra for S-VHS. Inexpensive Super VHS models are not much better than common VHS models, but pricier models offer better picture quality when playing back S-VHS tapes recorded on the same machine. No S-VHS model will improve picture quality on commercial VHS tapes.

If you want to edit recordings, look for these editing features: Shuttle and jog controls let you scan large segments or move forward or backward a frame at a time to find a precise spot. Audio dub lets you add music or narration. A flying erase head lets you insert a segment without noticeable video glitches.

Brand Repair History

DVD players

This graph shows the percentage of single-disc and multidisc DVD players, purchased new from 2000 to 2004, that were ever repaired or had a serious problem that was not resolved. Because many people discard rather than repair a broken DVD player, our data include broken models no longer in use. (We lacked sufficient data on portable, jukebox-changer, and combination players and on recorders.) Repair rates for specific models may vary, and changes in design and manufacturing may affect reliability. Still, you can increase your chances of getting a reliable DVD player by choosing a brand that has been reliable in the past.

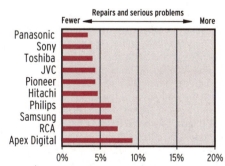

Data, based on nearly 81,000 responses to our 2004 Annual Questionnaire, have been standardized to eliminate differences between brands attributable to age. Differences of less than 3 points are not meaningful.

07 | BUYING ADVICE DVD PLAYERS

Interface (DVI) and **High Definition Multimedia Interface (HDMI),** are intended for use with digital TVs with corresponding inputs. They may be used to pass digital 480p and up-converted higher-resolution video signals. These connections potentially allow the content providers to control your ability to record the content.

Another benefit of DVD players is the ability to enjoy movies with **multichannel surround sound**. To reap the full sound experience of the audio encoded into DVD titles, you'll need a Dolby Digital receiver and six speakers, including a subwoofer. (For 6.1 and 7.1 soundtracks, you'll need seven or eight speakers.) **Dolby Digital decoding built-in** refers to a DVD player that decodes the multichannel audio before the audio receiver; without the built-in circuitry, you'd need to have the decoder built into the receiver or, in rare instances, use a separate decoder box to take advantage of the audio. (A Dolby Digital receiver will decode an older format, Dolby Pro Logic, as well.) Most players also support **Digital Theater System (DTS)** decoding for titles using that six- or seven-channel encoding format. When you're watching DVD-based movies, **dynamic audio-range control** helps keep explosions and other noisy sound effects from seeming too loud.

In addition to commercial DVD titles, DVD players often support playback or display of numerous other disc formats. They include CD-R/RW recordings of standard audio CDs; the recordable DVD formats DVD+R/RW, DVD-R/RW, and DVD-RAM; Video CD (VCD); and DVD-Audio and Super Audio CD (SACD). They can also play CD-R/RW discs containing MP3 and Windows Media Audio (WMA) files and JPEG picture files. Make sure a model you're considering plays the discs and formats you use now, or may want to use in the future.

DVD players also provide features such as **multilingual support**, which lets you choose dialog or subtitles in different languages for a given movie. **Parental control** lets parents "lock out" films by their rating code.

HOW TO CHOOSE

Buy a progressive-scan model unless the lowest price is your highest priority. Although you won't see progressive-scan picture quality on a conventional analog TV, it's worth spending a little extra for a progressive-scan player if you might get a digital (probably HD) TV at some point. You'll have a wider choice of products as well, since almost all new players are progressive-scan. It's definitely worth getting a progressive-scan player for use with a digital TV, which is capable of displaying the smoother picture these players can deliver.

Choose a multidisc model if you want continuous music. A single-disc player is fine for movies and CDs one at a time. If you want this to be your main music player, consider a multidisc player. Note, though, that multidisc models are typically about 1 to 2 inches taller and 6 to 7 inches deeper than single-disc players.

Make sure there are enough connections of the types you want. Virtually all DVD players now have outputs for optimal connection to most TV sets. A few players have DVI or HDMI connectors that are compatible with some new TVs, though these don't necessarily offer improved picture quality. If you want to use digital-audio connections from the DVD player to a receiver, make sure the DVD player's digital-audio outputs match the receiver's inputs. Some receivers use a coaxial input; others, an optical input. If you have an older receiver that lacks 5.1 surround-sound decoding, look for a player with a decoder for Dolby Digital.

Consider which, if any, special playback formats matter. All DVD players can play prerecorded DVDs and CDs. Most models also play several types of discs you record yourself, such as DVD-R, DVD+R, and CD-R/-RW. Most can read DVD+RW, but the ability to read DVD-RW discs depends on how they were recorded. Some can also play DVD-RAM discs. Most models play CD-audio and MP3 music recorded on discs you burn yourself. You'll need to shop around more if you want to

---

Deciphering the DVD formats

DVDs come in five different varieties: DVD-R, DVD-RW, DVD+R, DVD+RW, and DVD-RAM. If you want to record on discs that are compatible with the most DVD players, only two matter: DVD-R and DVD+R. Their main limitation is that you can record on them only once.

The multirecordable formats, DVD-RW and DVD+RW, are more expensive and may not be compatible with older players. But they can save money if you reuse them as you would a tape. DVD-RAM discs, which are also rerecordable, are the least compatible. However they do play on Panasonic models, a growing number of players from JVC, Toshiba, and others, and on some computer drives. Forget about high-definition DVD recording—for now. Today's discs and recorders lack the capacity to provide adequate playing time at HD resolution. HD DVD formats, such as Blu-ray and HD-DVD, may begin to be available by the end of 2005. When they do arrive, expect high prices and renewed format wars. HD-ready recorders that record on a hard drive are already available, either for purchase or via monthly rental from some satellite provider or local cable companies.

BUYING ADVICE DVD RECORDERS

play Windows Media Audio (WMA) files, video CD, and high-resolution SACD and DVD-Audio discs in their original format.

Do you want to present slide shows on your TV? Then choose a model that can read the memory card for your camera or JPEG image files from a digital camera or scanner that you have burned onto a disc.

BUYING ADVICE
DVD recorders

While DVD players are playback-only devices, DVD recorders record onto these removable discs as well as playing them. Prices have dropped considerably in the past few years, with entry-level models now selling for less than $150. At the highest-quality setting, the quality of most DVD video recordings is better than that of a VCR. DVD recorders also offer more ways to navigate recordings, with no need to rewind or fast-forward. With certain disc types, DVD recorders can perform functions that no VCR can match, such as letting you watch a program from the beginning while recording is already under way. They also offer a way to convert camcorder tapes or homemade VCR recordings to a digital format. The DVD recorder market is still in its early stages, so it's likely there will be further changes involving disc types, and prices for machines and for blank storage media may drop further. At press time, there were no DVD recorders capable of recording high-definition (HD) content. HD DVD recorders are in development and could be on the market in 2006. (There are some digital video recorders capable of recording HD TV programs. They are mainly available from satellite and cable companies. However, these use hard discs, not removable DVDs.)

WHAT'S AVAILABLE

DVD recorders are available from many of the same manufacturers that make DVD players. Apex Digital, Panasonic, Philips, Sony, and Toshiba are among the biggest brands. Some DVD recorders store content only on DVDs. Others can also use VHS tapes, hard drives, or both. **Price range:** DVD-only recording, about $150 and up.

FEATURES THAT COUNT

As with any other video recorder—including digital cameras—a recorder's **storage capacity** varies in actual usage. DVD recorders store content at different **compression settings** and thus at different quality levels. For the best image quality, you have to record programming at the device's lowest level of compression, yielding as little as one hour of recording time. To get the maximum capacity advertised—typically six or eight hours—you have to use the highest level of compression, which gives the lowest quality.

All rewriteable DVD formats let you edit, to varying extents, what you've recorded. DVD-RW (in VR mode) and DVD-RAM recorders let you edit more extensively than does DVD+RW. Besides letting you watch one program while recording another, recorders with DVD-RAM capability and some with DVD-RW in VR mode let you watch an earlier section of a program while you're still recording it.

As with VCRs, DVD recorders may use **VCR Plus** to ease the setup of time-shift recordings. Some also come with **Gemstar** or **TV Guide On-Screen**, free interactive program guides that get three days of listings at a time from your TV signal. They offer point-and-click setup of recording events.

In addition to commercial DVD titles, DVD recorders often support playback or display of numerous other disc formats. They include CD-R/RW discs containing standard CD-audio information; the recordable DVD formats DVD+R/RW, DVD-R/RW, and DVD-RAM; Video CD (VCD); and DVD-Audio and Super Audio CD (SACD). They can also play CD-R/RW discs containing MP3 and Windows Media Audio (WMA) files and JPEG picture files. Make sure a model you're considering plays the discs and formats you use now, or may want to use in the future.

DVD-based movies often come in various formats. **Aspect-ratio control** lets you choose between the 4:3 viewing format of conventional TVs (4 inches wide for every 3 inches high) and the 16:9 ratio of newer, widescreen sets.

A DVD recorder gives you all sorts of control over the picture—control you may never have known you needed. **Picture zoom** lets you zoom in on a specific frame. **Black-level adjustment** brings out the detail in dark parts of the screen image. If you've ever wanted to see certain action scenes from different angles, **multi-angle capability** gives you that opportunity. Note that this feature and some others work only with certain discs.

A DVD recorder enables you to navigate the disc in a number

07 BUYING ADVICE DVD RECORDERS

A 'time slip' DVD recorder will let you pause viewing while the unit continues to record, or you can watch a previously recorded program while you're recording another one.

of ways. Unlike a VHS tape, most DVDs are sectioned. **Chapter preview** lets you scan the opening seconds of each section or chapter until you find what you want; a related feature, **chapter gallery**, shows thumbnails of section or chapter opening scenes. **Go-to by time** lets you enter how many hours and minutes into the disc you'd like to skip to. **Marker functions** allow easy indexing of specific sections.

To get the best picture quality when playing DVDs, you need to hook up the recorder/player to the TV with the best available connection. A **composite-video connection** to the TV can produce a very good picture, but there will be some loss of detail and some color artifacts such as adjacent colors bleeding into each other. Using the **S-video output** can improve picture quality. It keeps the black-and-white and the color portions of the signal separated, producing more picture detail and fewer color defects than standard composite video.

Component-video, sometimes not provided on the lowest-end models, improves on S-video by splitting the color signal, resulting in a wider range of color. If you connect a DVD recorder via an S-video or component connection, don't be surprised if you have to adjust the television-picture setup when you switch to a picture coming from a VCR or a cable box that uses a **radio-frequency (RF, also called antenna/cable) connection** or a composite connection.

Two newer outputs found on some models, **Digital Video Interface (DVI)** and **High Definition Multimedia Interface (HDMI)**, are intended for use with digital TVs with DVI or HDMI inputs. They may be used to pass digital 480p and up-converted higher-resolution video signals. Those outputs potentially allow content providers to control your ability to record the content.

Another benefit of DVD recorders is the ability to enjoy movies with **multichannel surround sound**. To reap the full sound experience of the audio encoded into DVD titles, you'll need a Dolby Digital receiver and six speakers, including a subwoofer. (For 6.1 and 7.1 soundtracks, you'll need seven or eight speakers.) **Dolby Digital decoding built-in** refers to a DVD player that decodes the multichannel audio before the audio receiver; without the built-in circuitry, you'd need to have the decoder built into the receiver or, in rare instances, use a separate decoder box to take advantage of the audio. (A Dolby Digital receiver will decode an older format, Dolby Pro Logic, as well.) Most recorders also support **Digital Theater System (DTS)** decoding for titles using the six- or seven-channel encoding format. When you're watching DVD-based movies, **dynamic audio-range control** helps keep explosions and other noisy sound effects from seeming too loud.

DVD recorders also provide features such as **multilingual support**, which lets you choose dialog or subtitles in different languages for a given movie. **Parental control** lets parents "lock out" commercial films by their rating code.

HOW TO CHOOSE

Decide whether you want to record on removable media. DVD recording is the best option for those who want to share video recordings with other users or to have unlimited storage, allowing recordings to be saved indefinitely. They're also space-efficient, since they can play pre-recorded movies, replacing a separate DVD player. But if none of these attributes is important to you, consider a hard-drive-based DVR instead. If you've decided on DVD recording, here's what to consider in selecting a unit:

Choose between a DVD-only recorder or a combo unit. DVD-only models can cost about half the price of units with a second recording platform such as a hard drive or VCR. The combos are pricier and bulkier but more versatile.

Look for "time slip" capability. It allows you to

You can archive home videos on DVD.

BUYING ADVICE DIGITAL VIDEO RECORDERS

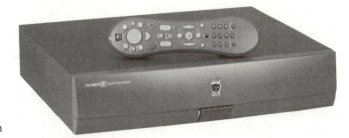

Some DVRs, such as this TiVo unit, have only a hard drive.

Other DVRs, like this one, have both a hard drive and a DVD.

pause your viewing of a TV program you're recording, while the unit continues to record. You can resume viewing where you left off. Time-slip models also let you view a previously recorded program while recording another. An inherent feature of all hard-drive-equipped recorders, time slip is also available on stand-alone DVD recorders that record to DVD-RAM discs, one of five disc types recorders use. (All models use at least one write-once and one rewriteable disc type; DVD-RAM discs are rewriteable.) But there's a downside to DVD-RAM discs: They can be played on fewer other recorders or players than discs using formats that are more widely compatible. Some models that record to DVD-RW discs in VR mode also have time-slip capability.

Decide what kind of TV-programming capabilities you want. When it comes to programmed recording, a typical DVD recorder can do everything a VCR can. And as with VCRs, some DVD recorders can control a cable or satellite box, allowing you to program the unit to record from various channels without setting the box to the correct channel before each recording. DVD/hard-drive recorders designed to work with TiVo, the subscription programming service, also offer automatic recording of your favorite shows (or performers) whenever or wherever they're on. But that added functionality has a cost: a monthly fee of about $13 or a one-time fee of about $300 (at time of publication). TV Guide On-Screen is a free interactive program guide that is available on some models. While not as versatile as the TiVo programming guide, it does offer point-and-click recording ability.

Decide the importance of video editing. A DVD-only model that records to DVD-RAM discs or to DVD-RW discs in VR mode allows scenes to be subdivided and rearranged onscreen. But the discs aren't compatible with all players, and even if they do play, edits you make on those discs might not show up. DVD/hard-drive models, except for tested models allied with the TiVo service, give you the ability to edit video on the hard drive. You can then burn images to a range of disc types for maximum compatibility with other players.

BUYING ADVICE
Digital video recorders

▶ Avid TV watchers are prime candidates for these devices. DVRs are also a good bet for anyone who hates sitting through commercials.

DVRs don't have a slot for removable discs or tapes; they record only on the hard drive and can't play prerecorded media. Some combination units pair a DVR with a DVD player/recorder so you can play (and copy to) removable media. Some cable boxes or satellite TV receivers also have built-in DVRs. Digital video recorders offer recording capability with the convenience of a TV program guide. They have a hard drive much like the one in a computer, generally with space for 100 hours or more of programming. Models that are not combined with a cable box or satellite receiver let you trade more recording time for lower video quality.

You can get a stand-alone DVR or one that's integrated into a digital-cable box, satellite-TV receiver, off-air digital TV decoder, or DVD player/recorder. Depending on which type you choose, you may pay for the service as well as the equipment—either a one-time activation charge or a monthly fee on top of your current cable or satellite-TV bill.

Because they can record and play at the same time, DVRs allow you to pause (and rewind or fast-forward) the current show

For the best image quality, use your DVR's lowest level of compression when you're recording.

07 BUYING ADVICE DIGITAL VIDEO RECORDERS

you're watching, picking up where you left off. If you pause a one-hour show for 10 or 15 minutes at the beginning, you can resume watching it, skip past all the commercials, and catch up to the actual "live" broadcast by the end of the show. Dual-tuner models can record two programs at once, even as you're watching a third recorded program.

Onscreen TV program guides are customized according to which broadcast channels are available in your area and to which cable or satellite service you subscribe. A DVR does not replace your usual programming source. You must still get broadcasts via cable, satellite service, or antenna.

WHAT'S AVAILABLE

If you get your DVR functionality in a digital-cable box leased from your cable company, you're typically limited to the cable operator's choice of hardware. For hard-drive recording in a satellite receiver, you may be abe to buy or lease the hardware directly from the Dish Network or DirecTV, or buy it from a retailer, depending on the model you choose.

For stand-alone DVRs, there are two main service providers: TiVo and ReplayTV. Hardware prices depend mostly on how many hours of programming you can store; service charges vary. The DVRs intended for use with one provider will not work with the other. You can buy TiVo equipment directly from TiVo or a number of electronics retailers. TiVo functionality is incorporated into DVRs from Sony, Toshiba, Pioneer, and Humax. Basic TiVo service is included with some of those products at no additional charge, but TiVo's regular subscription rates (see below) apply for full functionality. **Price range:** about $250 to more than $1,000.

TiVo service requires a paid subscription of $13 per month, or $299 for the life of the DVR (transferable if you sell it). You can also get a DirecTV satellite receiver that incorporates TiVo capability.

ReplayTV offers some models bundled with lifetime service included in the equipment price. With other models, service is separate; you can pay a one-time activation fee of $299 or a monthly charge of $13. In either case, you must buy equipment directly from the company. **Price range:** $150 to $800.

Some manufacturers, such as Panasonic, make combination DVD recorder/DVR models that use a free program guide service, such as TV Guide On-Screen.

FEATURES THAT COUNT

Most DVRs resemble VCRs in size and shape but don't have a slot for a tape or disc. (The internal hard drive is not removable.) Combination units that add a DVD player or recorder will have the requisite media slots. All these units connect to your television using **composite**, **S-video component**, or possibly **RF antenna outputs** to match the input of your set.

A recorder's hard-drive capacity varies in actual usage. Like digital cameras, many DVRs record at different compression settings and thus at different quality levels. For the best image quality, you have to record programming at the DVR's lowest level of compression. To get the maximum capacity advertised, you have to use the highest level of compression, which gives the lowest quality. For example, a model that advertises a 30-hour maximum capacity will fit only about nine hours at its best-quality setting.

The **program guide** is an interactive list of TV programs that can be recorded by the DVR for the next three to 14 days, depending on the program guide source. You can use it to select the show currently being broadcast to watch or record, or you can search it by title, artist, or show type for programs you want to record automatically in the future.

Custom channels, available with some models, are individualized groupings of programs that interest you. The feature allows you to set up your own "channel" of your favorites, such as crime dramas or appearances by William Shatner, whether on "Star Trek" or a talk show. A DVR can also record a specified show every time it runs.

A **remote control** is standard. Common features include instant replay, fast-forward, rewind, and pause of either recorded or live programs.

HOW TO CHOOSE

Ultimately, the DVR's picture quality, like the VCR's, depends on the quality of the signal coming in, whether that's via your cable, satellite provider, or antenna.

Do you want the most programming features? The services from TiVo and ReplayTV may have more features and functionality than some of the offerings of cable and satellite companies. But you will have to buy another box, deal with another remote, and possibly have another monthly fee.

Would you prefer to have fewer boxes and service providers to contend with? Inquire whether a cable box

BUYING ADVICE HOME THEATER IN A BOX

equipped with DVR functionality is available. If satellite service is an option, consider getting a receiver that includes a DVR. Keep in mind that you may have to pay a separate fee for the DVR service. Note that some satellite and cable DVRs work only with the service provider's programming and won't record from other sources, such as an antenna.

Do you want to edit recordings or store camcorder video? Then you need a DVD recorder or DVD recorder/hard-drive combo like those on page 85. You won't get both capabilities in a box allied with TiVo or ReplayTV or the cable or satellite companies.

BUYING ADVICE
Home theater in a box

▶ All-in-one systems that hook up to your TV and DVD player can minimize the setup hassle.

Good speakers and the components for a home-theater system cost less than ever. But selecting all those components can be time consuming, and connecting them a challenge—even for audiophiles. You can avoid some hassle by buying an all-in-one "home theater in a box" system that combines a receiver with a speaker set, wiring, and often a DVD player. Unless you're very demanding, you'll compromise little on quality.

WHAT'S AVAILABLE
Panasonic and Sony are among the best-selling brands in the market. Home theater packages include a receiver that can decode digital-audio soundtracks and six to eight compact, matched speakers—two front, one center, two to four surround speakers for the rear, and a subwoofer. You also get all the cables and wiring you need, usually color-coded and sometimes labeled for easy setup. Most systems now include a progressive-scan DVD player (either a separate component or built into the receiver) and a powered subwoofer. **Price range:** $275 to $1,000 for typical systems with a DVD player and powered subwoofer, and $2,000 or more for systems aimed at audiophiles.

FEATURES THAT COUNT
The receivers in home-theater-in-a-box systems tend to be on the simple side. They usually include both **Dolby Digital** and **DTS decoders**. Controls should be easy to use. Look for a front panel with displays and controls grouped by function and labeled clearly. An **onscreen display** lets you control the receiver via a television screen.

Switched AC outlets let you plug in other components and turn on the whole system with one button. The receivers have about 20 or more **presets** you can use for AM and FM stations. Most receivers also offer a **sleep timer**, which turns them on or off at a preset time. **Remote controls** are most useful when they have clear labels and different-shaped and color-coded buttons grouped by function. A universal remote can control a number of devices.

A component-video output on the receiver that can connect to a relatively high-end TV allows for better picture quality if you choose to switch video signals through your receiver; however, not many receivers have such an output. Instead, most have S-video output, which is better than a composite-video or RF (antenna) connection.

Look also for an S-video input, which lets you pipe signals from an external DVD player, digital camcorder, or certain cable or satellite boxes through the system. Any player that you might want to connect will need the same digital-audio connections, either optical or coaxial, as those of the included receiver. And if you want to make occasional connections at the front—perhaps for a camcorder or an MP3 player—you'll need front-panel inputs.

DSP (for digital signal processor) modes use digital circuitry to duplicate the sound measurements of, say, a concert

Some home theaters, such as this Sony model, will play up to five DVDs or CDs.

07 BUYING ADVICE HOME THEATER IN A BOX

hall. Each mode represents a different listening environment. A **bass-boost switch** amplifies the deepest sounds.

A **subwoofer** may be powered or unpowered. Either type will do the job, but a powered subwoofer provides more control over bass and lets a powered receiver drive the other speakers.

An **integrated DVD player**, available with some models, typically has fewer features than does a stand-alone DVD player. Features to expect are **track programmability** (more useful for playing CDs than DVDs), **track repeat**, and **disc repeat**. If you want more features, a stand-alone DVD player may be the wiser choice.

HOW TO CHOOSE

Decide whether you want a DVD player. If not, you may save money by buying a system without one. If you want a DVD in the bundle, consider whether you need a multidisc model that will provide uninterrupted play of music CDs and DVD movies. Most systems have a progressive-scan player. These offer regular DVD picture quality when used with a conventional TV but can deliver a smoother image when paired with a TV capable of displaying high-definition (HD) signals. Some bundled DVD players offer support for multichannel DVD-Audio and SACD music discs, although not in their original, high-resolution format.

Do you want a separate DVD player or one integrated with the receiver? Systems with separate DVD players and receivers tend to offer fuller functionality and more connections than those that integrate both units in one box. Integrated units are somewhat simpler to set up, but they tend to be bulkier and may not allow you to connect video devices other than a TV to the receiver. Any other devices would have to be hooked up directly to the TV.

Make sure there are enough inputs. Most home-theater systems have enough audio and video inputs for an external DVD player, a VCR, a CD player, and a cable box or satellite receiver. See if a model you're considering has enough of the type of inputs you want, given that each type is capable of conveying a different level of video quality. With audio inputs, there are two points to check. Choose a model that matches the output on your CD or DVD player, digital-cable box, or satellite receiver. If you want to connect a turntable, you'll need a phono input—hard to come by. And if you want to make occasional connections at the front—perhaps for a camcorder or an MP3 player—you'll need front-panel inputs.

Get features that suit your needs. With any system, you can be assured of basics such as AM/FM tuners and Dolby Digital and DTS surround-sound support. You almost always get Dolby Pro Logic II, which offers basic surround sound from TV and VHS programs and music CDs.

Features such as front-panel inputs and onscreen displays for making adjustments on the TV screen are less common than on component receivers, so make sure a system has what you want. A few models offer newer Dolby and DTS surround formats that process 6.1 or 7.1 channels. Those formats aren't widely used in movies at this point but could become more common in the future.

> **Most receivers** are designed for the six-channel surround-sound formats encoded in most DVDs and some television programs.

BUYING ADVICE
Receivers

▶ For a home-theater surround-sound system, look for a receiver that can decode Dolby Digital and DTS soundtracks.

The receiver is the brain of a home-entertainment system. It provides AM and FM radio tuners, stereo and surround sound, and switching capabilities. It's also the heart of the setup. Most of the devices in a home-entertainment system connect to it, including audio components such as speakers, a CD player, cassette deck, and turntable, as well as video sources such as a TV, DVD player, VCR, and cable and satellite boxes. Even as receivers take on a bigger role in home entertainment, they're losing some audio-related features

At 135 watts per channel, this Pioneer receiver will fill any room in your house with sound.

BUYING ADVICE RECEIVERS

that were common years back, such as tape monitors and phono inputs. Manufacturers say they must eliminate those less-used features to make room for others.

WHAT'S AVAILABLE

Sony is by far the biggest-selling brand. Other top-selling brands include Denon, JVC, Kenwood, Onkyo, Panasonic, Pioneer, RCA, and Yamaha. Most models now are digital, designed for the six-channel surround-sound formats encoded in most DVDs and some TV fare, such as high-definition (HD) programming. Here are the types you'll see, from least to most expensive:

Stereo. Basic receivers accept the analog stereo signals from a tape deck, CD player, or turntable. They provide two channels that power a pair of stereo speakers. For a simple music setup, add a DVD or CD player to play CDs, or a cassette deck for tapes. For rudimentary home theater, add a TV and DVD player or VCR. Power typically runs 50 to 100 watts per channel. **Price range:** $125 to $250.

Dolby Pro Logic. Dolby Pro Logic, Pro Logic II, and Pro Logic IIx are the analog home-theater surround-sound standard. Receivers that support it can take a Dolby-encoded two-channel stereo source from your TV, DVD player, or hi-fi VCR and output it to four to six speakers—three in front, and one to three in back. Power for Dolby Pro Logic models is typically 60 to 150 watts per channel. **Price range:** $150 to $300 or more.

Dolby Digital. Currently the prevailing digital surround-sound standard, a Dolby Digital 5.1 receiver has a built-in decoder for six-channel audio capability—front left and right, front center, two rear, and a powered subwoofer for low-frequency, or bass, effects (that's where the ".1" comes in). Dolby Digital is the sound format for most DVDs, HDTV, digital cable TV, and some satellite-TV broadcast systems. Newer versions of Dolby Digital add one or two back surround channels for a total of seven-channel (6.1) and eight-channel (7.1) sound, respectively. To take advantage of true surround-sound capability, you'll need speakers that do a good job of reproducing full-spectrum sound. Dolby Digital is backward-compatible and supports earlier versions of Dolby such as Pro Logic. Power for Dolby Digital receivers is typically 75 to 150 watts per channel. **Price range:** $200 to $500 or more.

DTS. A rival to Dolby Digital 5.1, Digital Theater Systems also offers six channels, and newer versions have additional rear channels. It's a less common form of digital surround sound that is used in some movie tracks. Both DTS and Dolby Digital are often found on the same receivers. Power for DTS models is typically 75 to 150 watts per channel. **Price range:** $200 to $500 or more.

THX-certified. The high-end receivers that meet this quality standard include full support for Dolby Pro Logic, Dolby Digital, and DTS. THX Select is the standard for components designed for small and average-sized rooms; THX Ultra is for larger rooms. Power for THX models is typically 100 to 170 watts per channel. **Price range:** $500 to $2,500 and up.

FEATURES THAT COUNT

Controls should be easy to use. Look for a front panel with displays and controls clearly labeled and grouped by function. **Onscreen display** lets you control the receiver via a TV screen, a squint-free alternative to using the receiver's tiny LED or LCD display. **Switched AC outlets** (expect one or two) let you plug in other components and turn the whole system on and off with one button.

Remote controls are most useful when they have clear labels and buttons that light up for use in dim rooms. It's best if the buttons have different shapes and are color-coded and grouped by function—a goal seldom achieved in receiver remotes. A **learning remote** can receive programming data for other devices via their remotes' infrared signal; on some remotes, the necessary codes for other manufacturers' devices are built-in.

Input/output jacks matter more on a receiver than on any other component of your home theater. Clear labeling, color-coding, and logical groupings of the many jacks on the rear panel can help avert glitches during setup such as reversed speaker polarities and mixed-up inputs and outputs. Input jacks situated on the front panel make for easy

Although slim, this Panasonic receiver has enough inputs and power to serve a sophisticated setup.

07 BUYING ADVICE RECEIVERS

connections to camcorders, video games, MP3 players, digital cameras, MiniDisc players, and PDAs.

A stereo receiver will give you audio inputs and no video jacks. Digital receivers with Dolby Pro Logic will have several types of video inputs, including composite and S-video and sometimes component-video. **S-video** and **component-video jacks** allow you to route signals from DVD players and other high-quality video sources through the receiver to the TV. Digital receivers also have analog **5.1 audio inputs**. These accept input from a DVD player with its own built-in Dolby Digital decoder, an outboard decoder, or other components with multichannel analog signals, such as a DVD-Audio or SACD player. This enables the receiver to convey up to six channels of sound or music to your speakers. Dolby Digital and DTS receivers have the most complete array of audio and video inputs, often with several of a given type to accommodate multiple components.

Tone controls adjust bass and treble, allowing you to correct room acoustics and satisfy your personal preferences. A **graphic equalizer** breaks the sound spectrum into three or more sections, giving you slightly more control over the full audio spectrum. Instead of tone controls, some receivers come with tone presets such as Jazz, Classical, or Rock, each accentuating a different frequency pattern; often you can craft your own styles.

DSP (digital signal processor) modes use a computer chip to duplicate the sound characteristics of a concert hall and other listening environments. A **bass-boost** switch amplifies the deepest sounds, and **midnight mode** reduces loud sounds and amplifies quiet ones in music or soundtracks.

Sometimes called "one touch," a **settings memory** lets you store settings for each source to minimize differences in volume, tone, and other settings when switching between sources. A similar feature, **loudness memory**, is limited to volume settings alone.

Tape monitor lets you either listen to one source as you record a second on a tape deck or listen to the recording as it's being made. **Automatic radio tuning** includes such features as **seek** (automatic searching for the next in-range station) and 20 to 40 **presets** to call up your favorite stations.

To catch stations too weak for the seek mode, most receivers also have a **manual stepping knob** or buttons, best in one-channel increments. But most models creep in half- or quarter-steps, meaning a lot of button tapping to find the frequency you want. **Direct tuning** of frequencies lets you tune a radio station by entering its frequency on a keypad.

HOW TO CHOOSE

First, don't assume that pricey brands outperform less costly ones. We've found fine performers at all prices. Points to consider:

How many devices do you want to connect? Even low-end digital receivers generally have enough video and audio inputs for a CD or DVD player, a VCR, and a cable box or satellite receiver. Mid- and high-priced models usually have more inputs, so you can connect additional devices, such as a camcorder, a digital video recorder such as a TiVo box, or a game system.

The number of inputs isn't the only issue; the type also matters. Composite-video inputs, the most basic type, can be used with everything from an older VCR to a new DVD player. S-video and component-video inputs are used mostly by digital devices such as DVD players and satellite receivers. If you have such digital devices or may add them, get a receiver with a few S-video and/or component-video inputs. Both can provide better video quality than composite-video.

All these video inputs require a companion audio input. The basic left/right audio inputs can be used with almost any device to provide stereo sound. A turntable requires a phono input, which is available on fewer models than in years past.

To get multichannel sound from DVD players, digital-cable boxes, and satellite receivers, you generally use a digital-audio input. With this input, digitally encoded multichannel sound is relayed on one cable to the receiver, which decodes it into separate channels. The input on the receiver must be the same type—either optical, the more common type, or coaxial—as the output on the other device. You usually must buy cables, about $10 and up, for digital-audio, S-video, and component-video connections. You often have to buy speaker cables as well.

What kind of sound do you want from movies? All new digital receivers support Dolby Digital and DTS, the surround-sound formats used on most movies. Both provide 5.1 channels. Most receivers also support Dolby Pro Logic, Pro Logic II, and sometimes Pro Logic IIx. If you want the latest type of surround sound, look for a receiver that supports Dolby Digital EX and DTS-ES.

BUYING ADVICE SPEAKERS

These offer 6.1 or 7.1 channels, subtly enhancing the rear surround. Fairly few movies using these formats are available, but offerings should increase.

What kind of music do you like? Any receiver can reproduce stereo from regular CDs. Most models have digital signal processing (DSP) modes that process a CD's two channels to simulate a sound environment such as a concert hall. For multichannel music from SACD or DVD-Audio discs, get a receiver with 5.1 analog inputs.

How big is your room? Make sure a receiver has the oomph to provide adequate volume: at least 50 watts per channel in a typical 12-by-20-foot living room, or 85 watts for a 15-by-25-foot space. A huge room, plush furnishings, or a noisy setting all call for more power.

Is the receiver compatible with your speakers? If you like to blast music for hours on end, get a receiver rated to handle your speakers' impedance. Most receivers are rated for 6-ohm and 8-ohm speakers. If used with 4-ohm speakers, such a receiver could overheat and shut down or be damaged.

Is it easy to use? Most receivers have legible displays and well-labeled function buttons. Some add an onscreen menu, which displays settings on your TV screen. An auto-calibration feature adjusts sound levels and balance to improve the surround effect. Models with a test-tone function for setting speaker levels help you balance the sound yourself.

Two tips: When deciding where to place your receiver, allow 4 inches or so of space behind it for cables and at least 2 inches on top for venting to prevent overheating. If setting up a home theater is more than you want to tackle, consider calling in a professional installer. Retailers often offer an installation service or can refer you to one.

BUYING ADVICE
Speakers

Speakers can make or break your audio or video setup. Try to listen to them in a store before buying. And if you can splurge on only part of your system, splurge here.

The best array of audio or video components will let you down if matched with poor-quality speakers. Good speakers don't have to cost a bundle, though it is easy to spend a lot. For a home-theater system, you can start with two or three speakers and add others as need dictates and budget allows. Size is no indication of quality.

WHAT'S AVAILABLE

Among the hundreds of speaker brands available, the major names include Altec, Bose, JBL, KLH, Pioneer, Polk Audio, RCA, Sony, and Yamaha. Speakers are sold through mass merchandisers, audio/video stores, and "boutique" retailers. You can also buy speakers online, but be prepared for shipping charges of up to $100 because speakers can be fairly heavy.

Speakers are sold as pairs for traditional stereo setups, and singly or in sets of three to six for equipping a home theater. To keep a balanced system, buy left and right speakers in pairs, rather than individually. The center-channel speaker should be matched to the front (or main) speakers. For the best effect, the rear speakers should also have a sound similar to the front speakers.

Each type of speaker serves a different purpose. The front speakers are used for stereo music playback; in a home theater set-up, they provide front left and right sounds. The center (or center-channel) speaker chiefly delivers movie dialog and is usually placed on top of or beneath the TV in a home-theater setup. Rear speakers, sometimes called surround or satellite speakers, deliver rear ambient effects such as crowd noise. A subwoofer carries the lowest tones, such as explosions in an action movie.

Bookshelf speakers. These are among the smallest speakers, but at 12 to 18 inches tall, many are still too large to fit on a shelf, despite their name. A pair of bookshelf speakers can serve as the sole speakers in a stereo system or as the front or rear duo in a home-theater setup. One can serve as the center-channel unit, provided it's magnetically shielded so it won't interfere with the TV. Small speakers like these have made strides in their ability to handle deep bass without buzzing or distortion. Any bass-handling limitations would be less of a concern in a multispeaker system that uses a subwoofer to reproduce deep bass. **Price range:** $100 to more than $800.

Floor-standing speakers. Typically about 3 to 4 feet tall, these large speakers can also serve as the sole speakers in a stereo system or as the front pair in a home-theater system. Their big cabinets have the potential to do more justice to deep bass than smaller speakers, but we believe many listeners would be satisfied with smaller speakers that scored well for bass han-

Expensive brands don't always outperform less costly ones, according to our speaker tests.

A tiny cube speaker from Sony.

A slightly bigger speaker from Yamaha.

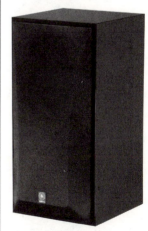

A mid-sized speaker from Yamaha.

07 BUYING ADVICE SPEAKERS

Speakers can make or break your setup. Try to listen to them in the store before buying. And if you can splurge on only part of your system, splurge here.

A tower speaker from Samsung.

dling. Even if floor models do a bit better their size and cost may steer buyers toward smaller, cheaper bookshelf models. **Price range:** $300 to more than $1,000.

Center-channel speaker. In a multichannel setup, the center-channel speaker sits on or below the TV. Because it primarily handles dialog, its frequency range doesn't have to be as full as that of the front pair, but its sound should be similar so all three blend well. Dedicated center-channel speakers are short and wide (6 inches high by 20 inches wide, for instance) so they perch neatly atop a TV. **Price range:** $100 to more than $500.

Rear-surround speakers. Rear speakers in a multichannel setup carry mostly background sound such as crowd noise. Newer multichannel formats such as Dolby Digital, DTS, DVD-Audio, and SACD make fuller use of these speakers than did earlier formats. You'll get the best blend if the rear pair sounds similar to the front pair. Rear speakers tend to be small and light (often 5 to 10 inches high and 3 to 6 pounds) so they can be wall mounted or placed on a shelf. **Price range:** $100 to more than $500.

Three-piece sets. Designed to be used as a stand-alone system or integrated with other speakers, these sets combine two bookshelf or satellite speakers for midrange and higher tones with either a center-channel speaker or a subwoofer for bass. **Price range:** $300 to $800.

Six-piece sets. These systems have four satellites (used for both the front and rear pairs), one center-channel speaker, and a subwoofer. Six-piece sets save you the trouble of matching the distinctive sounds of six speakers. That can be a daunting task at home and even more of a challenge amidst the din of a store that doesn't have a decent listening room. **Price range:** $400 to more than $1,000.

Other shapes and sizes. A "power tower" is a tower speaker, usually priced above $1,000, with a side-firing, powered subwoofer in its base.

FEATURES THAT COUNT

Lovers of loud sound should pay attention to a speaker's **measured impedance**. The speaker impedance should be matched with the receiver; check your receiver manual. **Power range** refers to the power-handling capability of the speaker, usually expressed in RMS (average power) and peak power (maximum surge power). Speakers placed near a TV set should have magnetic shielding so they won't distort the picture; check the literature before buying to make sure.

HOW TO CHOOSE

Consider size. Speakers come in all shapes and sizes, so see how they'll fit in your room. Floor-standing speakers might overwhelm smaller spaces. Bookshelf speakers are often a better fit, but some are quite large, so make sure a model you choose will fit the shelf or niche you've earmarked for it. And don't fear that you're giving up quality for compactness. Many small speakers do a fine job. Style

Speakers generally come in sets that are prematched for sound.

may factor into your decision as well. Some speakers are sleekly shaped, with silver finishes. Others are more conventional black boxes.

Focus on accuracy, not advertising. The most critical attribute of any speaker is accuracy—the ability to reproduce sound frequencies without over- or under-emphasizing any part of the audio range. As our tests have shown time and again, some of the lowest-priced speakers can be among the most accurate. Ads often tout two-way or three-way drivers and the size of the cone inside a speaker, but you can't judge sound quality by these attributes.

Listen for the differences. Even speakers with comparable accuracy scores can sound quite different. One model may overemphasize treble, while another under-emphasizes it. There's no substitute for hearing speakers, so bring a CD with a familiar piece of music to the store. Pay special attention to the front pair, because those speakers do the most work.

Speakers will sound different at home because of your room size, shape, and furnishings, so see if the retailer will allow a home trial or ask about the return policy. If you're torn between two choices, buy the cheaper. Stores may be more open to a return if you want to trade up to a pricier set.

Check impedance. If you like to play music loudly, make sure your receiver is rated to handle the impedance (generally ranging from 4 to 8 ohms) of the front speaker pair.

MP3 PLAYERS & OTHER MUSIC MAKERS

INSIDE INFO

102 The ABCs of MP3

103 Your computer as digital jukebox

104 Computers replace most CD recorders

104 Satellite radio: Reception an issue

BUYING ADVICE

106 MP3 players

CHAPTER 08

Just as music fans over a certain age can get nostalgic about the era of vinyl, people who grew up with CDs may one day be telling their disbelieving grandchildren that the music of their youth came on shiny plastic discs. Given enough distance, they might even find themselves wistfully reminiscing about the hours they spent struggling to remove the tight plastic wrappers from their new CDs.

The digital revolution—in which the CD played a major role—has moved into a new phase, with more and more consumers converting their CDs to digital music files, buying new music on the Internet, and storing their collections on a hard drive. While CDs may still be with us for a some time to come, the sound wave of the future would appear to be the technology now commonly referred to as MP3. This chapter looks at MP3 and other ways to enjoy music digitally.

▶▶ Digital technology can put thousands of tunes in your pocket or your favorite station on the radio when you're a thousand miles from home.

Ratings: MP3 players, p. 148.

08 INSIDE INFO MP3 PLAYERS & OTHER MUSIC MAKERS

THE ABCS OF MP3

Digital audio is changing how and where we listen to music.

Apple's phenomenally successful iPod dragged the digital music player out of geekdom and into the mainstream. Other companies have since tried to match the iPod's enticements, including huge capacity in a compact, stylish box and a hassle-free link to buy music online. While iPods are still the best choices for many people, they aren't the only good performers, as we note in the Ratings on page 148.

In recent years, much of the news about digital music has come out of court rooms rather than electronics labs. But despite copyright-infringement lawsuits by the music industry, free music-sharing Web sites carry on. Online music stores, led by Apple's iTunes, allow users to download music legally for a fee. Downloaded songs from contemporary artists typically cost less than $1 each, or $10 for an entire album. Copy-protection measures prevent these songs from being shared with other people over a network and limit the number of times users can transfer them to MP3 players or burn them onto CDs. That limitation is typically 3 to 10 times, depending on the service.

Other legal online music sources include BuyMusic (WMA), Musicmatch (WMA), and Napster (WMA), retailers such as Wal-Mart (WMA), as well as electronics giant Sony (ATRAC). Some of these sites also offer subscription-based services, typically less than $10 per month, that allow you to listen to music on your computer in real time (streaming). Downloading music that you transfer to an MP3 player or CD costs extra, but fees are generally lower than the ones for nonsubscribers.

Creative Zen Touch, above, and Sony Network, below, each hold about 5,000 songs.

Downloaded songs typically cost less than $1 each, or $10 for an album.

One caveat of these services is that their copy-protected songs won't work with all players. Also keep in mind that while managing MP3 files and using an MP3 player adds flexibility and control to your listening, it is still more demanding than using an audio CD player.

▶▶ For buying advice on MP3 players, see page 106.

INSIDE INFO MP3 PLAYERS & OTHER MUSIC MAKERS

YOUR COMPUTER AS A DIGITAL JUKEBOX

Both a link to the Web and a player in its own right.

Though iPods and other MP3 players may be the most ubiquitous symbols of the digital-music boom these days, the computer retains its edge for versatility. All new computers include a basic application that lets you play music. With the music-management software that's often supplied with an MP3 player you can use your computer to convert audio CDs to MP3 files, which you can then download onto the player. You can also transfer songs you download from the Internet to an MP3 player or simply listen to them via your computer.

To make CDs using your computer, you'll need a CD-burner drive and software, which come standard with most desktop computers. You can also burn CDs with a DVD burner. You can buy a drive and software for an older PC for under $100.

With a CD burner, you can copy entire discs or selected tracks from multiple discs to create your own CD compilations. You can also burn CDs from MP3 files downloaded from the Web.

Computers can record to CD-Rs (discs you can record on only once) or CD-RWs (rewriteable discs that can be erased and rerecorded repeatedly). CD-Rs and CD-RWs play on almost any current CD player, although some older disc players need to have been designed to accept CD-RWs. The sound quality is the same with either type of disc.

The CD-Rs for a computer cost as little as a dime each when purchased in quantity; computer CD-RWs go for about 50 cents and up. Blank discs also differ somewhat in their recording capacity, which ranges from 74 minutes to 80 minutes. Also some cannot accept certain recording speeds. The speed at which you record a CD doesn't affect its quality or capacity, only how long you have to wait for the recording process to be completed.

Another option for copying CDs or other music media is a CD player/recorder, described in the next section. These require CD-Rs meant for audio, which cost a bit more. For buying advice and other information on computers, see Chapter 4.

You will still need a computer to manage your digital music collection.

CDs range in capacity from 74 to 80 minutes.

If your computer didn't come with a CD-burner drive, you can buy one and the necessary software for an older PC for under $100.

08 INSIDE INFO MP3 PLAYERS & OTHER MUSIC MAKERS

COMPUTERS REPLACE MOST CD RECORDERS

Player/recorders are still the easiest way to archive old albums.

A couple of years ago, CD player/recorders and computers equipped with CD burners vied for the affection of consumers who wanted to create their own CDs. In fact, earlier editions of this book discussed their respective pros and cons in some detail—most of which we can spare you this time around. CD player/recorders basically lost that battle, although they may be worth considering in one specific instance: if you plan to record from analog sources, such as converting an old album and cassette-tape collection to CDs. Computers can do this too, although not as conveniently and not without additional equipment. For example, to record an LP you'll need a preamplifier (found in most receivers).

Using a CD player/recorder to record from an LP or cassette tape is much like making an audiotape with a cassette deck. You select an analog external recording mode, pause the recorder, and set the recording levels (a task the recorder does automatically when recording from a digital source). Once recording is under way, you generally insert track numbers between selections, using the remote—another step the recorder does automatically when recording from CDs.

Most recorders come with the optical digital inputs that let you connect another digital audio component—say, a digital audio-tape player—directly to the unit. Some also have the coaxial inputs that some older digital devices use.

If you decide to buy a CD player/recorder, look for one with a multidisc magazine or carousel, rather than a single-disc model. It won't cost much more and will make it easier to record compilation CDs from other CDs or to play uninterrupted music.

Also note that the blank CD-R and CD-RW discs configured for use in a CD player/recorder are slightly more expensive than their computer counterparts. To know what you're buying, look for the words "For Digital Audio Recordings" or "Recordable CD for Music Use" on the box.

For convenience at little extra cost, look for a model with a carousel or multidisc magazine.

SATELLITE RADIO: RECEPTION AN ISSUE

It's no longer just for the car, so it's beginning to take off.

Satellite radio is attracting lots of listeners who don't mind paying to avoid the homogenized playlists and endless ads on local FM and AM stations.

XM's portable radio puts satellite programming wherever you happen to be.

Initially, satellite radio was mainly for cars. Sirius and XM, the two satellite-radio services, have since added programming and expanded at-home listening options, though reception can be a problem.

SATELLITE OR NOT?
Satellite radio is for you if:
▸ Your taste goes far beyond Top 40—to big-band standards, world music, Broadway show tunes, garage-band rock, and more. Satellite delivers what landlocked radio doesn't.
▸ You do plenty of highway driving and want the same channel coast-to-coast.
▸ You don't like ads. The music channels on Sirius and XM are commercial-free, but some of the other channels run ads.

Sirius and XM both cost $12.95 a month and are closely matched programming and receivers. But the services are incompatible, and once you've settled on a service, you're committed. To switch, you have to buy new hardware.

It's easier to get satellite-radio reception in cars than in homes, we've found. During long drives,

INSIDE INFO MP3 PLAYERS & OTHER MUSIC MAKERS

we could nearly always count on strong reception from both services, though overpasses and tunnels interfered. Getting good reception at home depends on positioning the radio's antenna to pick up a strong signal from the satellites. The best reception wasn't always in the room where we wanted the radio. Both services let you preview reception at home before you activate an account.

CHOOSING BETWEEN THEM

Pick programming. Sirius and XM don't have identical channel lists. National Public Radio is only on Sirius, for example, and XM carries Major League baseball games. Sirius has a channel devoted to gay and lesbian issues, as well as play-by-play for the National Football League, National Basketball Association, and National Hockey League.

Both services offer at least 20 rock and pop channels, covering a range of music types. Both have three channels for classical music and three for Christian programming. Both also have continuous traffic and weather information for about 20 metropolitan areas. Before you sign up, you can sample programs at www.sirius.com and www.xmradio.com.

Pick hardware. Satellite radio is often an option in new cars. The most economical way to add it to an older car is with a receiver that connects to the car radio through a built-in wireless FM modulator.

Good choices in hardware:

XM. The Delphi XM SkyFi Receiver SA 10000. It costs $100 and can be used with a car kit or home kit (each $50). It can also work with at-home boom boxes that cost $100 or $200 (the more expensive boom box includes AM, FM, and a CD/MP3 player). For a complete package, try the Delphi XM Roady SA 10035, $125.

Sirius. Among the many options are the Audiovox SIR-PNP1, $90, or PNP2, $100. Kits for car or home use cost $30 to $50. The receivers work with a Sirius SIR-BB1 Boom Box, $100.

CONSIDER A PERSONAL PORTABLE

Subscribers to XM satellite radio can now use the Delphi MyFi XM2Go, $300, a battery-operated personal radio designed to work anywhere. Sirius, XM's competitor, was expected to have a personal portable by the end of 2005.

The MyFi is more than a radio; it also records about five hours of radio programming, which lets you schedule recordings in advance or record on the fly so that you can listen in places with limited or no reception. The MyFi also contains an FM transmitter, which allows you to feed satellite broadcasts through any nearby radio or a home theater system. The MyFi comes with two auxiliary antennas to improve reception and a personal antenna for when you're on the go.

But the MyFi, our tests showed, needs improvement:

Iffy reception. In our tests, reception wasn't a problem on the open road, but it was indoors, such as in malls and office buildings. We also encountered interference when using the MyFi in a hilly, tree-filled suburban area. The personal antenna improved reception only in open spaces. But XM has installed signal repeaters in large cities to improve reception, so you don't need to point the antenna to the southern sky.

Quirky controls. The MyFi has an array of buttons for quick access to features such as one-button recording and station presets, along with a dial you move with your thumb to select any station or recording. But the dial is mounted on MyFi's right side—an awkward position for left-handed users.

The bottom line: We found some reasons to like the MyFi, but we also found flaws that may outweigh the radio's merits. With competitors on the horizon, it may be worth waiting until you can comparison shop.

> **Satellite radio is often** an option in new cars. The most economical way to add it to an older car is with a receiver that connects to the car radio through a built-in wireless FM modulator.

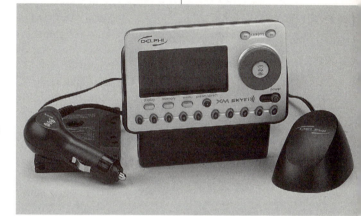

The SkyFi Receiver for XM (above) and the Audiovox model for Sirius (below), shown with car kits, also connect to home sound systems.

08 BUYING ADVICE MP3s

BUYING ADVICE
MP3 players

Comparing Apples and Apples: The iPod, top, and iPod Shuffle, below.

▶ These devices let you play music you've either downloaded from the Web or "ripped" from your own CD collection.

Portable MP3 players store digital music in their internal memories, on removable storage media, or a combination of both. You don't buy prerecorded discs or tapes but instead create your own digital files on a computer, using software often supplied with a player. You can convert music from your favorite audio CDs, tapes, and even records to digital files—a process known as ripping—or download music from the Internet. In either case you can listen to the files on your computer or transfer them to a portable MP3 player so you have music to go.

The term MP3 has become shorthand for digital audio of every stripe, but it's actually just one of the formats used to encode music. The abbreviation stands for Moving Pictures Expert Group 1 Audio Layer 3, a file format that compresses music to one-tenth to one-twelfth the space it would take in uncompressed form. Other encoding schemes include Windows Media Audio (WMA), the most widely supported; Advanced Audio Codec (AAC), and Adaptive Transform Acoustic Coding (ATRAC), a proprietary format used by Sony products. Most MP3 players can handle formats in addition to MP3, typically WMA. Plus the software that comes with them may convert incompatible files into formats the player can handle.

WHAT'S AVAILABLE

Major brands include Apple, Archos, Creative Labs, Dell, iRiver, Panasonic, Rio, Samsung, and Sony. Other, smaller brands are on the market as well. MP3 playback has been incorporated into other handheld portable products, including CD players, MiniDisc players, cell phones, and personal digital assistants (PDAs).

Flash-memory players. These are solid-state devices with no moving parts, which eliminates skipping, even on a bumpy road or during a grueling jog. They're also the smallest and lightest category, which makes them easier to carry around. Sizes range from as small as a thick matchbook to the size of a large pocket watch. Weight usually ranges from about 1 to 3 ounces. Most of the players have 128 or more megabytes (MB) of internal memory; 256 MB can hold about four hours of MP3-formatted music (about 60 songs) recorded at a CD-quality setting. You can fit more music into memory if you compress songs into smaller files, but that may result in lower audio quality.

Some flash-memory players also have expansion slots to add more memory via card slots or "backpack" modules on the player. Common expansion memory formats include Compact Flash, MultiMedia, Secure Digital, and SmartMedia. Sony players may use a MagicGate Memory Stick, a copyright-protected version of Sony's existing Memory Stick media. Memory-card capacities range from about 32 MB to 1 gigabyte (GB). Memory costs have gradually dropped. **Price range:** about $100 to $200 for the player; $25 to $40 for a 64-MB memory card.

Hard-disk players. These devices have a hard drive that can hold hundreds and even thousands of songs. Storage capacity can reach 80 gigabytes (GB), enough for more than 1,000 hours of music. But often that extra capacity translates into a bulkier, heavier player. Some are bigger than a portable CD player and weigh up to a pound. Hard-disk players hold about 20 GB of music files, are about the size of a deck of cards, and typically weigh half a pound. Smaller still are microdrive players, which tend to be palm-sized and weigh about a quarter-pound. Their drives typically provide about 4 to 6 GB of storage, but that's still enough room for many hours of continuous music. Some also have memory-card slots to transfer files. **Price range:** $180 and up.

Disc players with MP3 compatibility. Flash-memory and hard-disk portable players aren't the only way to enjoy digital music. Many of today's portable CD and MiniDisc players can play digital music saved on their discs, and may support the copyright-protected formats from online music stores.

Controls and displays are comparable to portable MP3 players, and you can group songs on each disc according to artist, genre, and other categories. A CD, with its 650- to 800-MB

106 CONSUMER REPORTS ● ELECTRONICS BUYING GUIDE 2006

Expert • Independent • Nonprofit

BUYING ADVICE MP3s

storage capacity, can hold more than 10 hours of MP3-formatted music at a CD-quality setting. You can create MP3 CDs using your PC's CD burner.

Sony's MiniDisc players, the other disc option, generally have smaller dimensions than portable CD players. MiniDiscs are smaller, removable optical disks protected by a plastic case, similar in size and shape to a 3.5-inch floppy disk. They can be recorded over many times. According to Sony, models that accept a Hi-MD disk can store up to 45 hours of music. **Price range:** $100 to $200 for players; 50 cents to $1 to $4 for blank CDs; $1.50 to $7 for MiniDiscs.

FEATURES THAT COUNT

Software and hardware. Most MP3 players come with music management software to convert your CDs into the audio playback format the player can handle. You can also organize your music collection according to artist, album, genre, and a variety of other categories, as well as create playlists to suit any mood or occasion. All come with software to help you shuttle music between your PC and the player via a Universal Serial Bus (USB) or FireWire connection. All players work with Windows PCs, and many support the Macintosh platform.

Player upgradability. On most models, the firmware—the built-in operating instructions—can be upgraded so the player does not become obsolete. Upgrades can add or enhance features, fix bugs, and add support for other audio formats and operating systems.

Display. Most MP3 players have a liquid crystal display (LCD) screen, sometimes a color one, that allows you to view the song title, track number, amount of memory remaining, battery life indicator, and other functions. Some displays present a list of tracks from which you can easily make a selection, while others show only one track at a time, requiring you to advance through individual tracks to find the one you want. On some of the models you can access the player's function controls via a wired or infrared remote control.

Sound enhancement. Expect some type of equalizer, which allows you to adjust the sound in various ways. A custom setting via separate bass and treble controls or adjustable equalizers gives you the most control over the sound.

Playback controls. Volume, track play/pause, and forward/reverse controls are standard. Most portable MP3 players let you set a play mode so you can repeat one or all music tracks, or play tracks in a random order, also referred to as "shuffle" mode. An A-B repeat feature allows you to set bookmarks and repeat a section of the music track.

Useful extras. In addition to playing music, most MP3 players can function as external hard drives, allowing you to shuttle files from one PC to another. Some allow you to view text files, photos, and videos on their LCD screens. Other convenient features include an FM radio tuner, a built-in microphone or line input for recording, as well as adapters or a line output for patching the player into your car's audio system.

HOW TO CHOOSE

Because digital music players are still a relatively new market, new portable models with more features and greater capabilities are continually coming out. Decide how much you're willing to spend

The Creative Nomad MuVo, a 4-gigabyte player, holds about 1,000 songs.

on a unit you may want to replace in a year or two. Here are some considerations before you buy:

Be sure your computer can handle it. Make certain any player you're considering is compatible with your Windows or Macintosh computer (including the version of the operating system your computer uses). Keep in mind that some operating system upgrades can exceed the price of a player. Your computer must have USB or FireWire ports. Consider high-speed Internet access if you plan on downloading much of your music. Also keep in mind that getting started can be tricky with some players. An older computer may not recognize the player, so you may have to seek help from the manufacturer.

Weigh capacity vs. size. Some MP3 players can serenade you for weeks without repeating a tune—a great feature to have on long excursions but perhaps not as necessary on short visits to the gym. Consider a flash-memory model if a lower price, smaller size, less weight, and long playback time are more

> **Some MP3 players** let you view text files, photos, and videos on their LCD screens.

08 BUYING ADVICE MP3s

Don't forget the batteries. Many flash memory players conveniently use AA or AAA batteries and can accept either standard alkaline or rechargeable types.

important to you than a vast selection of tunes. Look for flash models that can accept external memory cards to expand song capacity. If you have a large music collection that you want to keep with you, determine if a hard-disk player may make more sense. However, a hard-disk player is generally more complicated to manage than a flash-memory player—and more vulnerable to damage if dropped. For some, navigating through the menus or directories (folders) of songs may also take longer.

Most MP3 player headphones use an unobtrusive earbud design.

Hard-disk players range in size, generally in step with capacity. So-called microdrive players are about the size of a credit card, and a 4 GB model can hold about 1,000 songs, whereas models with 20 GB hard disks are about the size of a deck of cards and can hold about 5,000 songs.

Consider download choices. Be aware that online music sources are limited with some models. For example, iPods and Sony players only work with one online music store. Owners of players that support the copy-protected WMA formats, like those from Creative, Rio, and RCA, have access to the greatest number of online stores, and, often, the best deals. Some players won't play music purchased from any online store.

Downloading "free" music from such online sources as peer-to-peer Web sites is another option. But you risk a copyright-infringement lawsuit by the music industry. You'll also increase your exposure to a host of nasty computer viruses and spyware programs that tend to hitch rides on songs swapped on these sites.

Also, note that with most players, you have choices when it comes to software for recording (ripping) music. You can use the software that comes with your computer or player, such as Apple iTunes, MusicMatch, Napster, or Windows Media Player, or download other freeware or shareware applications. If the program has the software plug-in for your player, you can transfer the music to your player directly; otherwise you'll need to use the program that came with your player to perform the transfer.

Ensure upgradability. Regardless of which player you choose, look for one with upgradable firmware for adding or enhancing player features, as well as accommodating newer encoding schemes or variations of compression. Firmware is coded instructions in read-only memory. Upgrading firmware can be a time-consuming and sometimes risky process. MP3 players use several methods for upgrading; one method, which executes the upgrade file on the computer while the player is still attached, can cause permanent damage to the player if there's even a slight interruption during execution. Upgrades can be found at the manufacturer and music-management software application Web sites.

Consider power consumption and battery type. With any portable device, batteries are a consideration. Our tests found a wide variation among the players. Depending on the player settings, some will run out of power after only five hours of play, while others can play music for more than 70 hours before their batteries give out. Flash-memory players tend to have longer playback times than hard-disk players. Many flash memory players use AA or AAA batteries and can accept either standard alkaline or rechargeable batteries—convenient when electrical outlets are hard to find. Other players use a rechargeable nonstandard "block-" or "gumstick-" shaped nickel metal-hydride or lithium-ion removable battery, which is both more expensive and harder to find. Many hard-drive players use a non-removable rechargeable battery. When the battery can no longer hold a charge, the player has to be sent back to the manufacturer for service—a costly procedure if the product is no longer under warranty.

Consider ergonomics and design. Whichever type of MP3 player you choose, make sure you'll be comfortable using the device. Look for a display and controls that are easy to read and that can be worked with one hand. Because sizes and shapes vary widely, check to see that the player fits comfortably in your pockets, and that it's easy to fish it out when you need to access controls.

The RCA Lyra, another 20-gigabyte player, also includes a radio.

PHONES & PHONE SERVICES

INSIDE INFO

- **110** Getting the best cellular service
- **111** Choosing a phone that fits your needs
- **113** Headsets let you free up your hands
- **114** Master the minutes to slash your bills
- **1117** Internet phoning is not for everyone
- **119** Find the cordless that's best for you

BUYING ADVICE

- **120** Cell phones
- **123** Cordless phones

CHAPTER 09

Just as the computer has changed our lives at home and at the office, the cell phone has done it for practically all points in between. While cell phones may be one of the most visible—and audible—symbols of today's digital world, they represent just one piece of the larger revolution in telecommunications. Like many revolutions, this one has delivered mixed results: exciting new tools but some bewilderingly complex choices.

Cordless phones are borrowing features from cell phones, but as you'll find in our cordless phone section, digital is not always best.

This chapter aims to make today's new world of phones and phone services a bit less complicated. It will help you choose a cell phone and cellular carrier and show you how to save money on both. For a preview of what could be the next major change in your phone service, be sure to read our section on Internet phoning, a promising technology but one with a few kinks still to be worked out.

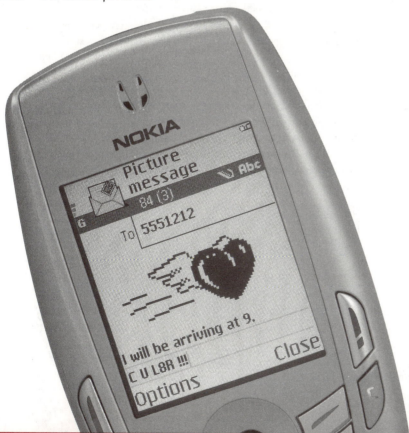

 Your phone may be smaller now, but how about your phone bill? Here's how to get the best deal on both.

Ratings: Cell phones, p. 154; cordless phones, p. 156.

09 INSIDE INFO PHONES & PHONE SERVICES

GETTING THE BEST CELLULAR SERVICE

All carriers have problems, but you can minimize them.

Because the phone you choose must be compatible with your wireless carrier, you'll want to choose the carrier first. However, finding a wireless carrier you'll be happy with may be difficult. Every national carrier has chronic problems with service, billing, and complaint-handling, according to our third annual subscriber survey.

Conducted in September 2004, the survey showed how major carriers compare in 17 major metropolitan areas, based on the experiences of some 39,000 subscribers to our Web site, ConsumerReports.org. CONSUMER REPORTS is planning to update this information in January 2006. Here's what we found in the 2004 survey:

▸ Overall levels of satisfaction are lower than for most other services we measure, such as hotels, retail outlets, and insurance. The overall satisfaction index has changed by only one point in the past three years, from 65 to 66.

▸ Only 45 percent of respondents said they were completely satisfied or very satisfied with their cell-phone service, a very low showing for any service.

▸ Nearly 70 percent of those who use a cell phone frequently had at least one dropped call in the week before the survey. Nearly 60 percent said they had a bad connection.

▸ Only 31 percent said the company's response to a service inquiry was very helpful; 40 percent said responses to billing inquiries were very helpful.

▸ Verizon topped the Ratings in each city, as it did in the previous two surveys. In 10 cities, it wasn't ahead of the pack in a statistically meaningful way, though. And Verizon wasn't problem-free. It simply had fewer problems than other carriers.

Given such results, it's little wonder that 35 percent of our respondents were seriously considering a switch of carrier. Most of those who had already switched said they were after better service.

State officials across the country have begun forcing providers to do better. In July 2004, Verizon Wireless, Cingular, and Sprint PCS settled with attorneys general in 32 states, which were investigating deceptive practices in the wireless industry. The carriers agreed to provide accurate coverage maps and to have their ads describe service more clearly and concisely.

CHOOSING A CARRIER

The carriers have become very competitive with calling plans. Service and satisfaction are more important factors.

Consider our survey findings. Verizon has consistently topped the Ratings and is the obvious first choice for many people. However, Verizon isn't the only choice. In most of the 17 cities in our survey, T-Mobile came in a close second.

Check coverage, based on your own experience and that of your friends. Ask people who travel the same streets that you do whether the cell-phone company they use delivers consistent service. You may find

Look for a carrier that offers coverage where you need it.

INSIDE INFO PHONES & PHONE SERVICES

that another company has better coverage where you need it.

Weigh each company's networks and phones against your needs. The network may make a difference if, for example, you need good service in rural areas. We have also found that GSM and CDMA phones have distinct differences (see box on page 112), which may also help you settle on a carrier.

Weigh each company's rates and plans against your needs. In areas where carriers are closely matched in major respects, you may want to base your choice on factors specific to the carriers. For example, if your usage varies from month to month, you may want to consider Sprint or Cingular, which have plans that allow for monthly fluctuations.

CHOOSING A PHONE THAT FITS YOUR NEEDS

Look first to the basics: voice quality, battery life, and ease of use.

Once you have selected your wireless carrier, you are ready to pick your phone. The good news is that carrier subsidies continue to keep phone prices low. However, carrier rebates and discounts often make comparison shopping impossible.

Folding phones keep keys from being pressed accidentally in your pocket.

The first decision you'll need to make in picking a cell phone is also one of the easiest. Do you want a rectangular (or "candy bar") model or one that folds? Both types, as you might expect, have their own advantages and disadvantages.

With the rectangular models, you can always see who's calling you before answering. The antenna is also usually inside the phone and not susceptible to damage. However, rectangular phones tend to have lower voice quality in noisy surroundings. Their keypad layouts may follow odd designs. And unless you remember to lock the phone, the number keys can be pressed by accident if you keep the phone in your pocket or purse.

Folding phones, on the other hand, tend to offer better voice quality in noisy surroundings. They are more compact when folded, and their cover protects keys from being pressed by acci-

A camera is a fun extra, but it's the basics that count.

dent. Their keypads are also generally laid out in a standard pattern. However, many folding phones have an external antenna that's susceptible to damage. And the extra step of opening the case to make or take a call may annoy some people.

Beyond case style, there are some other phone features to consider. Even many of the lowest-priced phones in the stores will have a color display and a camera, for example. As you move up in price, you'll find fancier cameras and features such as Bluetooth wireless technology. But none of those features count if the phone can't deliver the basics: good voice quality, decent battery life, and a design that's easy to use.

That's where we concentrated our most recent testing. Judging from our tests, there are important differences in basic performance.

**HERE'S WHAT WE FOUND
Very good overall quality, but with some differences.**
None of the phones we tested had severe drawbacks. However, in our critical voice-quality tests, we found that quality was almost always better for talking than for listening. Even the best phones in these tests weren't as good as a landline phone. And we found

09 INSIDE INFO PHONES & PHONE SERVICES

Candy-bar designs usually tuck the antenna inside to keep it safe.

that some phones were easier to use than others.

Your choice of carrier may be influenced by qualities in the phones. As we note later in the chapter, if you live in an area where the companies providing service are fairly closely matched, you may want to narrow the choice based on the networks that the carriers use and the characteristics of the phones themselves.

Phones designed for the CDMA network (used by Verizon and Sprint) have different characteristics from those using the GSM network (Cingular/AT&T and T-Mobile). Battery life is one difference. So is performance outside cities. If you need a phone that's more likely to perform well in rural areas, look to a CDMA phone with analog backup. But if you want a phone that can work in Europe or Asia, look to a GSM phone. See the box below for details.

Numbers are portable; phones aren't. Since November 2003, when the Federal Communications Commission allowed consumers to keep a wireless phone number if they switch carriers, some 10 million people have "ported" their numbers. That invariably means buying a new phone. Cell phones don't work with every carrier, either because of inherent incompatibilities (T-Mobile phones can't work on Sprint's network, for example) or because the carriers have locked the phone's software so that it won't work even with a compatible carrier.

Carrier subsidies continue to keep phone prices low. Substantial rebates and discounts remain commonplace. In fact, the carriers often claim to spend more on a phone than consumers do. Those deals ease the financial burden of switching carriers, but they often make comparison shopping impossible.

Moving phone lists is easier. Until recently, whenever you bought a new phone you usually had to re-enter names and numbers stored in its memory. But more wireless carrier stores have computer setups that can transfer that information quickly, for a fee of $15 or less. Or you can try a computer program such as SnapSync, from FutureDial.com. It automatically downloads contacts and calendar information from the old phone to your computer and then to your new phone, and you can synchronize contact information with Microsoft Outlook. However, SnapSync doesn't support every phone and, including needed cables, can cost up to $100.

▶▶ For detailed buying advice on cell phones, see page 20.

GSM or CDMA: Finding the right digital network

You may not even know which type of network your cell phone uses when you make calls. But whether your phone uses GSM or CDMA, the two main digital networks, could make a difference in performance. (An older network, TDMA, used mainly by Cingular, is being supplanted by GSM.) Here's what you need to know.

GSM phones
• Provide more talk time on a battery charge. In our tests, GSM phones typically lasted more than five hours.
• Do not support analog networks, which may mean spotty coverage if you travel to rural areas. To ensure maximum coverage, look for phones that support both the cellular and PCS digital bands of the GSM network, typically denoted as "850 MHz network compatibility" on the box or in stores.
• Are more "device-centric," packing technologies such as Bluetooth and infrared that allow you to beam pictures directly to a printer and synchronize your phone's address book with a computer or PDA.
• Tend to have more innovative designs. The Nokia 6820, for example, has a diminutive typewriter-style keyboard for messaging as well as a regular phone keypad.

• Are more portable. All of your account information is contained on a single, removable card called a subscriber information module (SIM), which can be easily transferred to a new phone. You can store names and phone numbers on the SIM card, too.
• Can be used in Europe and Asia. GSM is a worldwide standard. If you get a "world phone," you can use it on wireless networks outside the United States.

CDMA phones
• Generally provide less talk time on a charge, typically about three hours in our tests.
• Most CDMA phones provide analog backup for more reliable coverage in rural areas.
• Are more "network-centric." To move data, such as photos, in or out of the phone, you need a network connection. No CDMA phone supports infrared communication from one device to another. And the Bluetooth phones we've tested come with a version of Bluetooth that works only with wireless headsets and handheld devices.
• Tend to have folding-case designs, which, in general, have an edge in voice quality.
• Operate on a true third-generation (3G) wireless network. A 3G network can trim the time it takes to upload and download files.

INSIDE INFO PHONES & PHONE SERVICES

HEADSETS LET YOU FREE UP YOUR HANDS

All deliver decent voice quality, so focus on fit and comfort.

Cell-phone headsets are less conspicuous and come in more styles than they did a few years ago. But no headset in our tests was a standout for comfort, voice quality, and convenience. So, we're talking about some basic trade-offs.

Want a fit that's especially comfortable? You might sacrifice a bit on voice quality. Want the best voice quality? You may have to forgo a few nice features.

We tested 10 headsets: 8 wired models and 2 wireless units that use Bluetooth technology and work with Bluetooth-compatible cell phones or those with a special adapter. In our labs, we assessed how well each headset transmitted and received speech under various conditions. We also asked 12 panelists to wear the headsets and assess fit, comfort, and ease of use.

The good news is that voice quality was at least adequate in all models we tested, meaning that you'll hear and be heard acceptably no matter which model you select. But as First Things First (below) describes, there are differences between headset types that you should consider.

A headset will leave your hands free for more important things.

First Things First

Before you head to the store

Fit and comfort are the most important attributes because voice quality does not vary much. Before considering anything else, choose the style you prefer. Whichever type most appeals to you, size up the headset in the store. If you can't intuitively figure out how to wear it, don't buy it. A headset shouldn't be complicated. Best advice: Try it on. Most headsets are sold in sealed packages. But stores such as Best Buy and Radio Shack allow you to return them if, say, you can't stand the fit. Check the retailer's return policy before you buy. Basically, you have three choices:

1 In-Ear

The earpiece fits in your ear.
Pros: Easy to put on with one hand. Small and unobtrusive. Some earpieces are available in various sizes, making it easier to get a comfortable fit.
Cons: Some people don't like the feel of an earpiece in their ear. Our panelists said it can fall out more easily than other types.
Cost: $20 to $25.

IN-EAR
Jabra EarBoom

2 Over-the-Ear

A hook over the ear holds the unit in place. The earpiece rests in or just outside your ear.
Pros: Some models are easy to put on with one hand. It fits securely, so it's less likely to fall out. This style may be more comfortable for people who don't like wearing an earpiece.
Cons: Heavier than in-ear design, although weight is evenly distributed. Bulkier and more visible than in-ear designs.
Cost: $20 to $25.

OVER-THE-EAR
Jabra EarWave Boom

3 Lobe Clip

The earpiece fits in your ear, while a clip on your earlobe holds it in place.
Pros: This model can be easy to clip on the ear with one hand.
Cons: Some people don't like the feel of an earpiece. Weight is not evenly distributed, so the clip can feel heavier the longer you wear it. A clip is difficult to wear with earrings. This style is also bulkier than in-ear design.
Cost: $20 to $35.

LOBE CLIP
Plantronics MX150

09 INSIDE INFO PHONES & PHONE SERVICES

Headset features that count

Those we like include the following:

Adjustable-boom microphone. These are better than fixed microphones at masking background noise.

Ear gels. Some earpieces have gel caps that fit over the earpiece. Some models come with ear gels of varying sizes so that you can experiment for the best fit.

Answer/end switch. Several models we tested allow you to answer or end a call by pressing a switch on the cord, rather than fumbling for your cell phone. The wireless models we tested also had this function.

Volume control. For adjusting the headset's sound level to suit the situation.

You still can't have it all. A model most panelists judged highly comfortable, the Jabra EarWave Boom, had reasonable voice quality but not the best. Moreover, features that make headsets easy to use, such as a switch on the cord to answer and end calls, and attributes that improve voice quality, such as an adjustable boom microphone, are not widely available. The most fully featured models in our tests were wireless headsets, which also had very good voice quality. But they're at least five times the price of wired headsets, and they work with few cell phones unless you buy an adapter.

HEADS UP ON SAFETY

One reason people buy headsets is to talk on a cell phone while driving. In some states, it's illegal for motorists to talk on cell phones without using a headset. We don't recommend talking while driving, with a headset or without, because talking itself is a distraction from minding the road.

Another reason consumers buy headsets is to reduce their direct exposure to the energy emitted by a cell phone. (Wireless headsets also emit energy, although less than cell phones.) A recent Swedish study linked using a cell phone for 10 or more years to an increased risk of developing a type of slow-growing benign head tumor. But the data are based on people who used analog cell phones, which emit twice the energy of today's digital phones.

How to avoid some common cell-service gotchas

A resounding 83 percent of the subscribers we surveyed last year had at least some trouble shopping for wireless phone service. For example, 52 percent complained that they had to sign up for a long contract to get the best price on a phone; 48 percent said it was hard to compare plans from competing carriers. And 43 percent said it was hard to figure out the true cost of the service. Here's how you can get the best deal:

Take advantage of the trial period. Before signing a contract, find out how much of a trial period you have. The national carriers offer trial periods of two weeks to a month. Use that time to assess the service carefully.

Sign up for the shortest contract. We usually recommend a one-year contract, even if that means paying more for the phone, because it gives you a faster way out if service deteriorates. Early-termination penalties typically range from $150 to $200. Consider a two-year contract if you're renewing with a carrier that has given you good service.

Read the fine print. Read all the terms and conditions before you sign up. If you don't understand something, ask; if you don't like one of the terms and the carrier won't budge, consider another carrier.

If you shop in a store or at a Web site run by a company other than the carrier, be extremely cautious. We found two agents on the Web that have their own $350 early cancellation fee on top of the carrier's $200 fee.

MASTER THE MINUTES TO SLASH YOUR BILLS

Whether you use your phone a little or a lot, you can save big.

You may think of your phone bill as relatively fixed, varying mainly in the number of calls you make. In fact, the phone bill is pliable. It probably has a good deal of fat in it, and you can find meaningful cuts without trimming the number of calls you make or the extra services you actually use.

The trick is to think minutes. Time is what you're buying, and knowing the number and type of minutes you use is critical to paying the least possible.

Phone companies have plenty of ways to fog your true per-minute costs. For example, a home long-distance plan that charges 5 cents a minute may seem a bargain, even if it also carries a $3.95 monthly fee. But if you use only 30 long-distance minutes a month ($1.50 of talking time), the actual per-minute charge is 18 cents, once you factor in the monthly fee. Over a year you'll overpay by at least $47, compared with what you could get in a plan with no monthly fee.

You might also be paying too much if you haven't mastered the cornucopia of choices. You can get phone service from your cable

INSIDE INFO PHONES & PHONE SERVICES

company, a wireless carrier, a Voice over Internet Protocol (VoIP) newcomer, or a company that buys phone time wholesale and sells it.

Based on the rates we found while shopping for better deals for several CONSUMER REPORTS readers who sent us their phone bills, you're probably overpaying if you spend more than these amounts:

▶ 3 to 5 cents per minute with no monthly fee for state-to-state landline calls, 4 to 15 cents per minute for in-state calls.

▶ 3 to 4 cents per minute for a prepaid long-distance card with no connection charge and minutes that don't expire.

▶ 13 cents per minute for weekday nationwide wireless service on a plan with 250 to 400 included minutes; 8 cents on a plan with 900 to 1,000 included minutes; 6 cents on a plan with more than 2,000 included minutes.

It pays to check the way you've allocated phone service among local, long-distance, and wireless carriers and to shop for better deals at least once a year as well as near the end of a wireless-phone contract. Here's what to do:

KNOW HOW MUCH SERVICE YOU USE

Looking at your recent phone bills, consider which of the follow-

Decoding your cell-phone bill in four reasonably easy steps

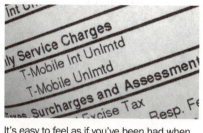

It's easy to feel as if you've been had when you receive your cell-phone bill each month. You chose your service plan for its $29.99 advertised price, not to mention that free nifty flip phone. But all the taxes, fees, and surcharges can add some 20 percent to your monthly tab, and that's on top of any charges for minutes you used over your plan limit.

So just what are all those charges? Here's a quick guide to the fee clutter, broken down into four categories, which may be summarized on one page of your bill.

Note that you might also get hit with hefty one-time penalties for starting a new service—the so-called activation fee (up to $36)—or for terminating a plan before the contract expires (as much as $200), not to mention charges for paying late or for downloading ring tones and games.

1 MONTHLY SERVICE CHARGE. It's what you saw advertised and includes extras you added to your plan, such as unlimited text or photo messaging, which may be listed separately on your bill. Plans can range from $19.99 to $299.99 a month, excluding taxes, depending on the geographical coverage, minute amount, and extra services you choose.

2 USAGE CHARGES. This section can include a wide variety of charges. It might also have a detailed summary of your calls so that you can check the bill's accuracy, but the convenience may cost you a few dollars a month. Here are some usage charges you might find on your bill:

Overage charges: Exceeding your plan minutes can cost 7 to 45 cents per extra minute, plus taxes. To avoid overage charges, find out how your carrier defines the minutes in your plan, which might include night, weekend, peak, and "anytime" minutes. Not all carriers consider 6 a.m. a "peak" time, for example. Also remember that most plans bill for incoming calls and that you might be charged for unanswered calls you make.

Roaming fees: Calls made outside your "home" area could cost 49 cents to 69 cents per minute. You might also get socked with long-distance fees. Make sure you understand the "local" and "regional" areas your plan covers. Carriers define them differently and might not even provide you with an accurate map. Even nationwide plans can hit you with roaming charges if your cell-phone carrier has holes in its network.

Text messaging: Unless you purchased a service plan that includes text messaging, which can add $2.99 to $20 to your monthly bill, carriers will charge you 2 to 10 cents to receive a text message and 5 to 10 cents to send one.

411: The cost of a call to information usually ranges from $1.25 to $1.29.

3 MANDATORY FEES AND TAXES. These fees are set by government authorities.

State, city, county, and district taxes: Amounts are based on your mailing address and bill size.

Federal excise tax: Set at 3 percent.

911 and E911 fees: Charged by local governments to cover fire and rescue services and to upgrade 911 wireless services.

4 DISCRETIONARY SURCHARGES AND FEES. These extras have mushroomed in recent years, but they aren't standardized or well-explained and they're not included in advertised plan prices. (Under a settlement with 32 states, however, a few leading cell-phone companies are now required to disclose these fees on their Web sites and in retail outlet sales materials.) Although they may sound like official fees required by a government authority, they are in fact determined by the carriers, which can up the ante whenever they like to cover their overhead expenses and services that aren't yet available to you.

Federal Universal Service Fund charge (aka federal universal service charge): Phone companies must contribute to this fund to make phone service widely affordable and available. The amount your carrier charges depends on the size of your bill. Cell-phone companies are not required to pass this cost along to consumers, but they always do.

Number-portability and pooling fees: These enable carriers to recover costs related to number-portability rules and the allocation of new numbers. The government allows carriers to collect these fees but doesn't control what they charge. So fees are all over the map and usually get folded into the so-called regulatory fee. Some good news: Sprint and Verizon are cutting number-portability fees.

Regulatory fee: Some carriers consolidate numerous charges associated with government programs under this rubric. They can add $0.45 to $1.55 to your bill.

You can find more information on understanding cell-phone bills as well as tips on lodging complaints about them at *www.hearusnow.org*, a Consumers Union Web site.

09 INSIDE INFO PHONES & PHONE SERVICES

Look for a well-designed display and keypad.

ing three profiles best describes you and read the targeted strategies that follow:

BUDGET CALLERS
Less than 70 long-distance minutes on a landline each month and under 500 minutes wireless, with a current monthly outlay of $30 to $70.

Consider measured local service. Unlimited local service may be a waste of money if you don't make many local calls or if your carrier bills you at long-distance rates for calls beyond a very limited radius. However, unlimited local service is a better bet for budget callers who have dial-up Internet service.

Avoid local/long-distance bundles. Several major carriers offer unlimited local and long-distance packages for a set monthly rate, such as $40 or $70. But if you don't make enough calls to justify that monthly rate, the bundled price is no bargain.

Use prepaid phone cards. If you make very few long-distance calls, consider dropping your long-distance carrier and using a prepaid phone card instead. Prepaid cards are a little inconvenient, however, because you have to enter a toll-free number first, then an authorization code and the number you want to call. Plus, some cards have a hefty per-call connection charge. Check the terms first, and avoid cards with those charges.

Find a better wireless option. If you want a wireless phone for roadside emergencies, consider a prepaid phone, such as TracFone, or limited-local-area cellular. One such provider is MetroPCS, available in the Atlanta area, Sacramento, the San Francisco Bay area, and south Florida. It was recently offering unlimited local calling and long-distance for $40 per month. The phones are not intended for roaming outside their home calling areas.

AVERAGE CALLERS
70 to 110 long-distance minutes on a landline each month and 400 to 900 minutes wireless, with a current monthly outlay of about $120.

Consider prepaid phone cards. Like budget callers, users with average bills might benefit from switching long-distance carriers or using prepaid phone

Not ready for prime time: TV on your cell phone

TV for cell phones is a new and highly hyped service. Most of these video clips aren't live; still, the service is aimed at news nuts.

We tested video services in New York and New Orleans from two major cell-phone providers, Sprint PCS and Verizon. Sprint was the easier to use, though we can't recommend either service. For both, navigation is clumsy. Touch the wrong phone button while downloading a video and it's lost; you have to start all over again. You also can't see a lot on the tiny phone screens.

Only a few pricey phones can accommodate video service.
Here are the details on the two services, Sprint TV and Verizon VCast:

Sprint TV
Availability: Nationwide.
Cost: Basic, $10 a month (Fox News live, updated video clips from Fox Sports, Discovery Channel, the Weather Channel, other networks, and a preview of premium offerings). Premium, $4 to $6 each for a full, live feed from above networks. Prices don't include a required $15-per-month Web access fee.
Pros: Service is available anywhere within the Sprint network. Video clips are easy to access.
Cons: In our tests, calls were sent to voice mail when we watched videos.

Verizon VCast
Availability: 50 markets.
Cost: Basic, $15 a month (clips from 14 sources, such as NBC News, Accuweather, ESPN, Fox Sports, and Comedy Central). Premium, $1 extra for Nascar and NBA clips; $2.50 to $5 extra per 3D game or $7 to $10 for unlimited play.
Pros: You can store downloaded clips. Can take calls when viewing.
Cons: Signing on to the video network is laborious.

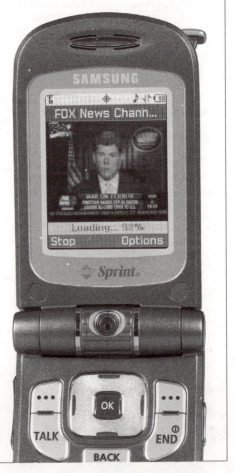

The Samsung MM-A700 cell phone is compatible with Sprint TV service.

INSIDE INFO PHONES & PHONE SERVICES

cards for long-distance.

Drop false "savings" plans. Some companies offer plans that charge a flat fee for a set number of local toll calls—calls to nearby towns billed as long-distance. But if you don't make many local toll calls, you're buying minutes you don't need.

Weigh local/long-distance bundles. The more long-distance calls you make on the landline, the more beneficial a local/long-distance bundle will be. If you're spending more than $40 to $70 a month for local and long-distance plans and no other cost-cutting strategy works for you, then consider a bundle.

Seek a better wireless plan. If you regularly exceed the minutes in your calling plan or pay high roaming charges, switch to a plan with a bigger allotment of minutes. Choose a national (not regional) plan, which typically has no roaming or long-distance charges. If you're ready to change wireless carriers, look for a plan with more minutes than you've had and a lower monthly fee.

Use your wireless phone for long-distance. Many consumers have a wireless calling plan that includes long-distance, yet they often pay for the same service on their home phone. Many cell phone users also don't use up all their allotted monthly minutes. About 25 percent of minutes are left unused each month, according to a 2003 survey by the Yankee Group. On a 500-minute plan, that leaves 125 minutes available. Assuming that you're happy with wireless voice quality, you can use wireless for long-distance and drop the landline long-distance service.

Drop redundant calling features. When we did our most recent report on phone services, we found that Verizon charged New Jersey customers $5.50 a month for voice mail, $4.59 for call waiting, and $7.50 for caller ID, while Verizon Wireless charged nothing for the same features. Customers with a wireless phone could save $211 a year by dropping those extra features from the landline.

HEAVY USERS
110 or more long-distance minutes on a landline each month and more than 1,000 minutes wireless, with a current monthly outlay of $170 or more.

Consider local/long-distance bundles. Such plans are most beneficial to big-time callers and often include free calling features.

Consider phoning over the Internet. If you have a broadband connection, you may want to sign up for VoIP service (see below). It generally costs $25 to $40 a month for unlimited U.S. calling. But VoIP shouldn't be a household's only phone service, because of its uncertain ability to make emergency calls.

> **You may be able to save $200 a year** simply by dropping extra calling services your landline phone company that charges you for but your wireless carrier offers for free.

INTERNET PHONING IS NOT FOR EVERYONE

The price is right, but the quality still lags behind landlines.

By one industry estimate, about 1 million people currently use a new kind of phone service that sends calls over the Internet instead of regular phone lines. The main reason: Internet calling is cheap. But is it for you? We tested it to find out.

Phone service over the Internet, properly known as Voice over Internet Protocol, or VoIP, is now offered by just about every major telecommunications and cable TV company. AT&T, which is retreating from the residential long-distance and local landline markets, now offers VoIP. So do Verizon, the nation's largest phone company; Comcast; Time Warner Cable; and other cable providers. There are also VoIP-only companies, such as Vonage and 8x8 Inc.

VoIP plans offer domestic calling for as little as $15 a month, and unlimited local and domestic long-distance for a flat $25 to $40 a month. That's significantly less than what regular landline companies charge, and providers include in the monthly fee caller ID, call waiting, voice mail, and nearly a dozen other features.

VoIP converts a voice call into "packets," or bits of digital data, routes them over the Internet, reassembles them into a voice signal at the other end, and feeds them into the call recipient's local telephone network.

The conversion is handled by

To send calls over the Internet, you have to plug your phone into an adapter that is linked to a broadband connection.

ConsumerReports.org · CONSUMER REPORTS · ELECTRONICS BUYING GUIDE 2006 · 117

09 INSIDE INFO PHONES & PHONE SERVICES

If you want to try Internet phoning, using a cable connection, rather than DSL, may be the better way to go.

When choosing a cell phone, check that the display is readable in all lighting conditions.

a device called an analog telephone adapter, connected to your phone and to a broadband Internet connection. Any regular wired or cordless phone works with VoIP.

You can choose a new number, and you can use the VoIP adapter away from home if you have broadband access. VoIP doesn't depend on your being in a fixed location. You can be across the country and call your next-door neighbors as if you're making a local call. But if you live in area code 609 and decide you want a 415 phone number, your neighbors will pay long-distance rates to reach you. Some VoIP providers can provide a "virtual" phone number that far-flung callers use to phone you at local rates.

To test VoIP, we recruited 10 volunteers at our Yonkers, N.Y., headquarters and our offices in Washington, D.C., and Austin, Texas, to sign up for service from five leading providers—AT&T, Optimum, Time Warner Cable, Verizon, and Vonage. Only one staffer tried Optimum; at least two staffers tried each of the others, using a mix of cable and DSL connections. We asked the staffers to get a new phone number and use the service at home for a month.

WHAT OUR TESTS SHOWED

Talk is cheap, but it costs more than advertised. VoIP rates exclude the cost of the necessary broadband connection, which can run as much as $40 per month. Of course, if you already have broadband, there's no added expense. Overseas calls are extra; rates vary according to VoIP provider and the country you are calling but are lower than what other long-distance carriers charge. With Vonage, for example, calls to France or Hong Kong are 3 cents per minute.

We think you should figure on an additional expense with VoIP: $20 or so per month to keep landline service for emergency calls. We don't think you should use VoIP as your only phone service, because it may not work in a power outage like landline service does. Keeping the landline also lets you hedge your bets in case the VoIP provider goes bust.

Voice quality may be uneven. Quality was OK most of the time, but some panelists said it didn't quite measure up to traditional landline service. They frequently used words such as "hollow" or "echoing" to describe the voice quality.

Incoming calls may not get through. Two panelists said that they failed to get some incoming calls or that the calls were dropped after a few minutes. One panelist said he once tried six times to call home.

Installing hardware yourself may be frustrating. Some VoIP providers send you the telephone adapter and setup instructions; others, usually the cable companies, will send an installer. Nearly all the staffers who tried installation on their own had to call the provider for help. The do-it-yourselfers generally needed several hours to get VoIP up and running. The pros needed less than an hour.

You may lose convenience and flexibility. The location of the VoIP adapter determines where your main phone goes. That's usually where the broadband service enters the house and may not be where you want a phone. The easiest way to put phones where you want them is to use a cordless phone that can support multiple remote handsets. With most VoIP providers, using existing extensions requires professional installation; Optimum Voice performs the service at no charge.

THE BOTTOM LINE

If you spend more than $60 a month for local and long distance, VoIP may save you money. That's more than you'd pay for unlimited VoIP plus a basic landline for emergencies. One of the few panelists who said he would consider keeping VoIP said its $35 monthly rate would cut his costs nearly in half.

VoIP isn't yet the equal of landline. Judging from our panelists' experiences, installation difficulties, voice quality, and problems with incoming calls put VoIP at a disadvantage at present. Most panelists said they wouldn't want to keep VoIP. For them, the inconvenience outweighed the prospect of lower bills.

Don't rely on VoIP alone. Without backup power, VoIP won't work in a power outage. The Federal Communications Commission issued a ruling in May 2005 that will require some VoIP service providers to make E911 access available this year. VoIP may also not work reliably with a home-security system to dial the security company's office.

If you want VoIP, a cable connection may be the better way to go. More complaints about VoIP service quality came from panelists using a DSL connection. In our test, cable companies seemed to do the best job of providing quick, reliable installation and good voice quality.

INSIDE INFO PHONES & PHONE SERVICES

FIND THE CORDLESS THAT'S BEST FOR YOU

Here's one product where digital isn't necessarily better.

Cordless phones are available in both digital and analog models. Bucking the pervasive "digital is better" trend, phones using analog transmission had the best voice quality in our tests. Many analog phones have another important edge over most digitals, we have found: They aren't likely to interfere with other wireless hardware in the home.

You might think that those advantages would put analog phones front and center in the market. But the electronics stores we've visited jumble inexpensive analog phones next to expensive, full-featured digitals, with no apparent logic as to which phones go where. Tags next to the prices name some features without decoding the jargon. That makes it unnecessarily hard to find the right phone.

What you will see in this thicket are these noteworthy developments:

More multiple-handset models. A growing number of phones can accommodate multiple handsets. The additional handsets don't need a phone jack and come with their own charging cradle, so they can go anywhere there's an electrical outlet.

Many digital multiple-handset phones can also serve as intercoms or walkie-talkies, adding to their versatility. The multiple-handset analog phones don't offer that kind of handset-to-handset talk, so they can't be used like an additional phone you have connected to the same phone line.

Features borrowed from cell phones. Some cordless-phone handsets are smallish, reminiscent of cell phones. Some phones we tested borrow more than looks from the cellular world: They have color displays, let you customize the ringer sound, or have images of frequent callers show up on the caller-ID screen.

More-generous answerers. Some of the phone-answerers give 20 minutes or more of recording time for messages, we found—significantly more than the typical answerer offered a year or two ago.

KEEP A CORDED PHONE

Because most cordless phones draw power from household current, they won't work in a power outage. That's why it's important to keep a corded phone around, if only for emergencies. (Cell phones may not work in an emergency, either, because the circuits could fill up quickly.) If you're shopping for a new corded phone, choose features and price; our tests have found that adequate performance is pretty much a given.

▶▶ For more detailed buying advice on cordless phones, see page 123.

Good news for long-winded callers: Some phone answerers now provide significantly more recording time than earlier models did.

What to do about cordless-phone interference

Many cordless phones on the market share the 2.4-gigahertz (GHz) radio frequency band with other wireless devices. As a result, the devices are likely to interfere with each other. Interference can cause static on the phone, a baby monitor, or wireless speakers; it can disrupt a wireless computer network or the video on a home security monitor.

Here's what you need to know to minimize interference in your household:
• Choose a phone that uses the 900-megahertz (MHz) or 5.8-GHz bands. However, some baby monitors and phones use the 900-MHz band and might interfere with each other. In that case, try switching channels on the phone or the monitor.

• Keep a 2.4-GHz analog phone out of the kitchen, if possible. It can pick up interference from a microwave oven that's running.
• If you want a phone with handset-to-handset talk capability, choose one that uses only the 5.8-GHz band. By contrast, nearly all phones using 2.4-GHz digital spread spectrum technology and those that allow handset-to-handset talk may create interference in other products, many even in standby mode.
• A phone billed as "802.11-friendly" should coexist with a wireless computer network but might interfere with other wireless devices.
• Before you buy a phone, be sure the store will let you exchange it, just in case you can't get rid of interference problems.

09 BUYING ADVICE CELL PHONES

Keys that are arranged in a familiar pattern will make dialing easier.

BUYING ADVICE
Cell phones

▶ Complex pricing schemes and incompatible technologies can make it hard to find the right calling plan and handset.

There are now more than 190 million cell-phone subscribers, more than one per household, on average. A small but steadily growing number of people use a cell phone (a.k.a. a mobile phone) as their only phone. Phone manufacturers and wireless-service providers are promoting new generations of equipment that let users do much more than merely make phone calls.

Despite its popularity, wireless service has a reputation for problems: dead zones, where you can't get service; calls that inexplicably end in midconversation; inadequate capacity, so you can't put a call through when you want; hard-to-fathom calling plans; and errors in bills. Problems like those are why one-third of the cell-phone users we've surveyed say they're seriously considering a switch of carrier.

Switching is now much easier than ever, thanks to the government mandate on local number portability. However, keep in mind that the phones themselves aren't portable. If you switch carriers, expect to buy a new phone.

WHAT'S AVAILABLE
The cell phone itself is only part of what you need. You also have to sign up for service with a wireless provider and choose a calling plan. You can find phones in many outlets, including independent wireless retailers, electronics stores, and Web sites.

The providers. The major national companies are Cingular (which merged with AT&T Wireless), Nextel (which is in the process of merging with Sprint), Sprint PCS, T-Mobile, and Verizon Wireless. There are also numerous local or regional providers.

You'll often find phones described as tri-mode, dual-band, tri-band, or multinetwork. Those terms describe the ways a phone can connect to one or more wireless networks. Here are the specifics:

Tri-mode phones can access a

The dangers in cell-phone batteries, especially counterfeit ones

When Verizon Wireless recalled 50,000 counterfeit LG phone batteries in June 2004, it seemed to be an isolated event. Then Kyocera recalled as many as a million fakes four months later. The Consumer Product Safety Commission has investigated more than 100 incidents involving cell phones, batteries genuine and counterfeit, and chargers since 2002. Most incidents resulted in skin burns and fires. The recalls and investigations highlight three broader problems with the batteries used in cell phones:

Counterfeiting is on the upswing. Worldwide, more than 5 million phony cell-phone batteries and other accessories were destroyed by law-enforcement authorities in 2003. Legitimate lithium-ion batteries cost $40 to $60. But it's easy to make low-quality fakes that look like the originals and sell for a fraction of the price, says Keith Nowak, a spokesman for Nokia, the world's largest cell-phone manufacturer. Counterfeits may lack key safety features to prevent overcharging or to dissipate heat, which can otherwise cause these small, power-packed cells to overheat, expand, explode, and catch fire.

In October, the Office of the U.S. Trade Representative announced a new program to confiscate many types of fake goods, including counterfeit batteries, through international cooperation, heightened criminal prosecution, tougher border patrol, and increased penalties for counterfeiters.

Meanwhile, Nokia is taking its own steps to thwart counterfeiters. In December 2004, the company began branding its batteries with holograms and a 20-digit code hidden under a scratch-off area on the label.

Legitimate batteries can also pose problems. If overcharged, any lithium-ion cell has the potential to erupt, says Jason Howard, chairman of the cell-phone battery working group of the Institute of Electrical and Electronic Engineers, which helps set standards for many electrical products. However, the IEEE also says that safeguards designed into the case of legitimate batteries should minimize hazards if an overcharged cell does erupt.

There are no standards for cell-phone batteries. But that may soon change. The IEEE and the Cellular Telephone and Internet Association, a trade group, with oversight from the CPSC, are meeting to develop voluntary design and performance standards. The group hopes to finish its work by late 2005.

What you can do
Our engineers and the CPSC offer these safety tips for cell-phone batteries:
• If you remove the battery (or if it has exposed terminals when it's in the phone), keep it away from keys, coins, or other metal objects in your pocket, which could cause a short-circuit.
• Buy the battery designed for your particular phone, and buy from your wireless service provider or a reputable retailer. Avoid cheap aftermarket brands. A cheap battery carrying what appears to be a name brand may well be a fake and not properly manufactured.
• Keep the phone and battery away from sources of extreme heat, such as a stove, radiator, or glove compartment.
• Never sit on a battery. Exerting pressure on the battery can crush it, causing it to short-circuit and overheat.
• If you drop a phone with a fully charged battery, it could overheat and explode. Leave it on the ground for a minute to make sure there's no problem.
• Follow the phone manufacturer's instructions for charging.

120 CONSUMER REPORTS ● ELECTRONICS BUYING GUIDE 2006

Expert • Independent • Nonprofit

BUYING ADVICE CELL PHONES

digital network in two frequency bands and older analog wireless networks.

Dual-band phones can connect to a digital network, but in two different frequency bands. GSM providers often use the term 850/1900 MHz instead of dual-band.

Multinetwork phones are compatible with more than one digital network, often in two frequency bands. Some can also access analog networks. Samsung offers a multinetwork world phone. It uses CDMA technology in the U.S. and GSM technology outside the U.S. It's sold by Verizon as the Samsung SCH-A70 and by Sprint as the IP-A790.

Tri-band or "world phones" operate on GSM networks in both the U.S. and abroad. Those with 850/1800/1900 MHz capability can operate on two bands domestically and one internationally. Those with 900/1800/1900 MHz capability operate on one band in the U.S. (1900 MHz) and two bands internationally.

The calling plans. Most providers offer a range of plans based around a "bucket" of calling time minutes. The more minutes in the bucket, the more the plan costs you each month. However, the total number of minutes isn't the most important figure. Some of those minutes may be good anytime, others available only on nights and weekends; if you exceed the allotment of minutes, you'll be charged 20 to 50 cents per minute, depending on the plan. Cingular and Sprint let you avoid wasting unused minutes by either rolling them over to the next month or adjusting your monthly quota. Most plans require you to sign a one- or two-year contract and levy a hefty fee if you want to cancel before the contract expires.

Prepaid plans can be a good alternative if you're averse to a long-term contract. Many wireless providers, as well as Virgin Mobile, Liberty Wireless, Metro PCS, and Tracfone, offer prepaid calling. You pay in advance for airtime minutes, which typically last 45 to 60 days before they expire.

The phones. Some are simple rectangles with a display window and keypad on the front. But most have a flip-open cover to protect the keys. The major phone manufacturers are UTS-Starcom (formerly Audiovox), Kyocera, LG, Motorola, Nokia, Panasonic, Samsung, Sanyo, and Sony-Ericsson. Light weight is pretty much standard. All the newer phones can send and receive text messages of up to 160 characters to or from any other cellphone user, and most phones now come with a full-color display. Phones equipped with cameras allow you to send and receive picture messages from other people, even if they're not on your network. You'll also see phones that can play games, are integrated with a digital camera, offer wireless Internet access, or that are combined with a personal digital assistant (PDA).

FEATURES THAT COUNT

Some cell-phone makers and service providers are offering so-called **3G service**, which enhances the speed of data transfer. 3G services deliver reasonably fast, secure connections to the Internet and allow you to use the cell phone for playing and downloading audio and video, multimedia messages, and e-mail.

Among basic cell-phone features, look for a **display** that is readable in both low- and bright-light conditions. Be sure it's easy to see the battery-life and signal-strength indicators and the number you're dialing. The **keypad** should be clearly marked and easy to use. **Single-key last-number redial** is useful for dropped calls or when you're having trouble connecting. Most phones these days have **voice dial**, which lets you dial someone's phone number by speaking their name. But the number and name have to be in your phone's contact list, and you have to program each voice dial name—a time-consuming process. **Voice command**-enabled phones don't require training. You can dial anyone's number in your contact list, and even dial a number not in the list by speaking the digits.

In addition to ringing, most handsets have a **vibrating alert** or a flashing light-emitting diode to let you know about an incoming call, useful when you're in a meeting or at the movies. Handiest is an **easy-to-mute ringer**, which switches from ring to vibrate when you press and hold one key. **Volume controls** on the side let you change the earpiece volume level without moving the phone too far from your ear. You can't do that if the volume controls are on the keypad. A **speakerphone** boosts the earpiece volume and microphone sensitivity, so you carry on a conversation without having the phone against your ear.

Some cell-phone models include a **headset**. That capability is sometimes demanded by various local laws for drivers using cell phones. A **standard headset connector** (also known

> **If you hate fussing with cords,** and plan to use a headset, consider paying extra for a model that contains Bluetooth wireless technology.

A folding phone's antenna may be susceptible to damage.

09 BUYING ADVICE CELL PHONES

as a 2.5-mm jack) is the most common type of headset connector. Phones with this connector are compatible with a wider variety of wired headsets. If you frequently use a headset but hate fussing with cords, consider a phone with **Bluetooth voice capability**, which allows you to use a cordless headset. Not all phones with Bluetooth are equal. **Bluetooth data** lets you transfer pictures and contacts, etc., to other Bluetooth-enabled devices like printers, PDAs, and computers. Bluetooth data capability is found on GSM phones, but not on CDMA phones.

Many CDMA phones have **analog backup** capability, which may be important if you travel through rural areas, or places where your digital carrier doesn't provide service. Phones with analog capability can sometimes connect in places where digital-only phones cannot.

Phones vary widely in keypad design and readability of screen displays, as well as in the ease of using the function menu or performing such basic tasks as one-button redial and storage of frequently called numbers for speed-dialing later. It's important to handle a phone in the store before you buy, to be sure that its design and your fingers are well-matched.

HOW TO CHOOSE

Begin by selecting a service. Finding good service where you want it can be a challenge. The best way is to ask your local friends and business associates how satisfied they are with their cell-phone service. In addition, keep in mind that Verizon Wireless has consistently come in first in CONSUMER REPORTS' satisfaction surveys and so is worth considering first, if it's offered in your area.

Choose a calling plan. You need to determine when

Cell phones that let you do more than just make and take calls

Wireless carriers have complemented their voice plans with a number of data services, including text messaging, custom ring tones, and Web browsing. The need for some of those services is debatable, but one thing is certain: They represent billions in added revenue to the carriers.

Here's a look at what you'll see—and hear—when you shop for a phone. Pricing is approximate because many services are part of a bundle. Features that keep you on the network, such as Web browsing, may consume plan minutes. When buying phone service, review your contract carefully to be sure the salesperson didn't sign you up for a service you didn't request.

Custom ring tones. If you're tired of reaching for your cell phone every time you hear one ring, you can buy a more distinctive sound. Custom tones, which you download to your phone, include music snippets and sound effects. You can also assign a different ring tone to different callers. **Cost:** $1.99 and up per tone. **Tip:** Read the fine print. In some instances, the fee only entitles you to use the ring tone for a limited amount of time.

Text messaging (also called SMS, for short message service). You tap out a message on the phone's keypad, and it appears on the recipient's screen. Great for sharing private thoughts in public places. Text-message transmissions number in the billions each year. Some providers let you enhance messages with more than text. **Cost:** from 2 cents apiece to $20 a month for several thousand messages, depending on the plan and provider. **Tip:** The meter on the text-messaging toll often runs both ways, although many plans charge less for the messages you receive than for those you send.

Instant messaging. Some providers offer an extension of an instant messaging service for home computers, allowing you to continue trading real-time messages on the phone. **Cost:** from 5 cents apiece to $20 a month for several thousand messages, depending on the plan and provider. **Tip:** The meter often runs both ways on instant messaging, too.

Web browsing. Most phones have Web browsers, which are needed for e-mail or to buy more phone services. **Cost:** $5 per month, plus airtime. Usually bundled with one or more data services. **Tip:** Dealing with limited graphics and slow networks can grate on the nerves.

E-mail. Most providers let you send a message to any e-mail account, as well as access your own e-mail account. **Cost:** 10 cents per transmission or $20 a month. **Tip:** E-mail eats up airtime, and you can't access attachments to e-mail that are sent to cell phones.

Wallpaper and screen savers. These are background pictures for your phone's screen. Now you can bring pictures of your favorite celebrity or cartoon character wherever you go. **Cost:** 99 cents to $1.99. **Tip:** You can use your own photos instead.

Games. You can download any of hundreds directly into your phone. Choices range from relatively tame to high-adrenaline. Selection depends on carrier and phone. **Cost:** 99 cents to $4.99 per game. **Tip:** Some games can only be rented.

Photos. Built-in cameras are now a common cell-phone feature. You can e-mail snapshots or send them like a text message, even print them at a photofinisher. **Cost:** 25 cents per transmission, 50 cents to several dollars for photo prints. **Tip:** Don't expect high-quality images.

Television and video. Some phones can now receive video clips from TV programming. A handful will record and send short video messages to similarly equipped phones. **Cost:** 25 cents per message. **Tip:** Sending videos eats up airtime, and they're low quality.

Text messaging can help you get your point across quietly.

122 CONSUMER REPORTS ● ELECTRONICS BUYING GUIDE 2006   Expert ● Independent ● Nonprofit

BUYING ADVICE CORDLESS PHONES

and where you'll be using a cell phone most in order to select a plan that's right for you. As a rule, a national calling plan (which typically eliminates extra long-distance charges or fees for "roaming" away from your home calling area) is worth considering first, even if you don't travel often. With a regional plan, roaming charges can add up if you make calls too far away from your home.

If two or more family members use cell phones, consider a family plan that lets up to four people share a large monthly pool of minutes for a small additional monthly charge. If you aren't sure how many minutes of phone time you'll use in a month, choose a plan with more minutes than you think you will use. It's often better to let minutes go unused than to have to pay stiff per-minute charges if you exceed your allotment.

Select a phone. You can spend as little as $20 or as much as $600 on a cell phone. You need to begin your selection in the right price tier. Once you've settled on a price range, follow these steps:

First look for practical features. Cameras, games, music players, and the like are appealing, fun, and even useful for some people. However, features such as a folding case, volume controls on the side, and an easy-to-mute ringer will prove useful every day.

Hold the phone. In the store, take the phone in your hand and make sure you can comfortably access most keys with one hand. Try to make a test call and access the menu items on a working demo. We've found that phones with radical shapes can be difficult to use. So are keys that are small, oddly shaped, or arranged in unusual patterns, especially if you're trying to dial a number in dim light.

Check the display. Most color screens perform well in dim light, but some are hard to see in daylight. Try the phone outside or under bright light. In our tests, phones that display incoming and outgoing numbers with large black fonts against a white background were the easiest to read under most conditions. Also make sure indicators such as battery life and signal strength are clearly visible.

Consider insuring pricey phones. All major carriers provide insurance that covers lost, stolen, or damaged phones, typically for about $4 to $5 a month, with a $35 to $50 deductible. At those rates, it wouldn't pay to insure a low-priced phone. But if you paid $200 or more, then insurance may be worth considering. Some insurance plans require a police report. Damaged phones are replaced, often with a refurbished model.

BUYING ADVICE
Cordless phones

▶ Two noteworthy trends: Phones use higher frequency bands, and a growing number can handle multiple handsets from a single base.

It's easier than ever to have a phone where you want one. The newest breed of cordless phones lets you put a handset in any room in the house, even if no phone jack is nearby.

However, manufacturers still offer a bewildering array of phones: inexpensive models that offer the basics; multihandset, full-featured phones with a built-in answering machine; single-line and two-line phones; digital and analog phones, and different frequency bands. In many instances, a phone will have a phone-answerer sibling. Many phone-answerers come in a phone-only version. If you have a cordless phone that's several years old, it's probably a 900-MHz phone. Newer phones use higher frequencies, namely 2.4 or 5.8 GHz. They aren't necessarily better than the older ones, but they may provide more calling security and a wider array of useful capabilities and features.

WHAT'S AVAILABLE

AT&T, Bell South, GE, Panasonic, Uniden, and VTech account for more than 70 percent of the market. VTech owns the AT&T Consumer Products Division and now makes phones under the AT&T brand as well as its own name.

The current trends include phones that support two or more handsets with one base, less expensive 2.4- and 5.8-GHz analog phones, and full-featured 2.4 and 5.8-GHz digital phones. Some of the multiple-handset-capable phones now include an additional handset with a charging cradle. About a third of the cordless phones sold include a digital answering machine.

A main distinction among cordless phones is the way they transmit their signals. Here are some terms you may see while shopping and what they mean for you:

Analog. These phones are the least expensive type available

Multiple-handset cordless models let you station a phone where you need it.

09 BUYING ADVICE CORDLESS PHONES

now. They tend to have better voice quality and enough range to let you chat anywhere in your house and yard, or even a little beyond. They are also unlikely to cause interference to other wireless products. But analog transmission isn't very secure; anyone with an RF scanner or comparable wireless device might be able to listen in. Analog phones are also more likely than digital phones to suffer occasional static and RF interference from other wireless products. **Price range:** $15 to $100.

Digital. These offer about the same range as analog phones, but with better security and less susceptibility to RF interference. And, like analogs, they are unlikely to cause interference to other wireless products. **Price range:** $50 to $130.

Digital spread spectrum (DSS). A DSS phone distributes a call across a number of frequencies, providing an added measure of security and more immunity from RF interference. The range may be slightly better than that of analog or digital phones. Note that some DSS phones—usually the 2.4-GHz or the multiple-handset-capable phones with handset-to-handset talk capabilities—use such a wide swath of the spectrum even in standby mode that they may interfere with baby monitors and other wireless products operating in the same frequency band. **Price range:** $75 to $225 (for multiple handset systems).

Frequency. Cordless phones use one or two of the three available frequency bands:

• **900-MHz.** Some manufacturers still make inexpensive, 900-MHz phones, usually analog. They are fine for many households, and still account for about one-quarter of the market.

• **2.4-GHz.** The band most phones now use. Unfortunately, many other wireless products—baby monitors, wireless computer networks, home security monitors, wireless speakers, microwaves ovens—use the same band. A 2.4-GHz analog phone is inherently susceptible to RF interference from other wireless devices, and a 2.4-GHz DSS phone may cause interference in other products.

• **5.8-GHz.** The band that newer phones use. Its main advantage: less chance of RF interference because few other products currently use this band.

Some phones are dual-band, but that only means they transmit between base and handset in one band and receive in another; you can't switch to or choose one band or another.

FEATURES THAT COUNT

Standard features on most cordless phones include **handset earpiece volume control**, **handset ringer**, **last-number redial**, a **pager** to locate the handset, a **flash button** to answer call waiting, and a **low-battery indicator**.

Some phones let you support two or more handsets with just one base without the need for extra phone jacks. Additional handsets including the charging cradle are usually sold separately, although more phones are being bundled with an additional handset and charging cradle.

An **LCD screen**, found on many handsets and on some bases, can display a personal phone directory and useful information such as the name and/or number dialed, caller ID,

One some phones, a photo you've uploaded is displayed when that person calls.

BUYING ADVICE CORDLESS PHONES

Some answerers have separate, numbered mailboxes.

battery strength, or how long you've been connected. **Caller ID** displays the name and number of a caller and the date and time of the call if you use your phone company's caller ID service. If you have caller ID with call waiting, the phone will display data on a second caller when you're already on the phone.

A phone that **supports two lines** can receive calls for two phone numbers—useful if you have, say, a business line and a personal line that you'd like to use from a single phone. Some of the phones have two ringers, each with a distinctive pitch to let you know which line is ringing. The two-line feature also facilitates conferencing two callers in three-way connections. Some two-line phones have an **auxiliary jack data port** to plug in a fax, modem, or other phone device that can also be useful. A **speakerphone** offers a hands-free way to converse or wait on hold and lets others chime in as well. A base speakerphone lets you answer a call without the handset; a handset speakerphone lets you chat hands-free anywhere in the house as long as you stay within a few feet of the handset.

A **base keypad** supplements the keypad on the handset. It's handy for navigating menu-driven systems, since you don't have to take the phone away from your ear to punch the keys. Some phones have a **lighted keypad** that either glows in the dark or lights up when you press a key, or when the phone rings. This makes the phone easier to use in low-light conditions. All phones have a handset ringer, and many phones have a base ringer. Some let you turn them on or off, adjust the volume, or change the auditory tone.

Many cordless phones have a **headset jack** on the handset and include a **belt clip** for carrying the phone. This allows hands-free conversation anywhere in the house. Some phones have a headset jack on the base, which allows hands-free conversation without any drain on the handset battery. Headsets are usually sold separately for about $20.

Other convenient features include **auto talk**, which lets you lift the handset off the base for an incoming call and start talking without having to press a

A single-handset phone with answerer may be more convenient than two stand-alone units.

Message centers

Answering machines
Digital answering machines come as stand-alone devices or as part of a phone/answerer combo unit. The main advantage of a combo unit—less clutter—has to be weighed against the loss of one part of the combo if the other goes bad. Answerers usually have standard features and capabilities such as a selectable number of rings and a toll-saver, answerer on/off control, call screening, remote access from a touch-tone phone, and a variety of ways to navigate through your messages. Most have a message day/time stamp, can delete all messages or just individual ones, allow you to adjust the speaker volume, and can retain messages and greeting after a momentary power outage.

Other answerer features you may want to consider are the number of mailboxes, advanced playback controls, remote handset access, conversation recording, a message counter display that indicates the number of messages received, and a visual indicator or audible message alert that lets you know when you have new messages.

In CONSUMER REPORTS' tests, many answerers delivered very good voice quality for recorded messages and good quality for the greeting. Phones that let you record your greeting through the handset (i.e., using the remote handset access) usually sound better. Some let you listen to your greeting through the handset, as opposed to listening though the base speaker; that gives you a better indication of how the greeting will sound to the calling party.
Price range: $20 to $80 (stand-alone units); $30 to $240 (combos).

09 BUYING ADVICE CORDLESS PHONES

For maximum talk time, keep the phone in its charging cradle between calls.

button, and **any key answer**. Some phones provide a **battery holder for battery backup**—a compartment in the base to charge a spare handset battery pack or to hold alkaline batteries for base-power backup, either of which can enable the phone to work if you lose household AC power. Still, it's wise to keep a corded phone somewhere in your home.

Some multiple-handset-capable phones allow conversation between handsets in an intercom mode and facilitate **conferencing** handsets with an outside party. In intercom mode, the handsets have to be within range of the base for handset-to-handset use. Others lack this handset-to-handset talk capability; they allow you to transfer calls from handset to handset but not to use several handsets to conference with an outside caller. Still other phones allow direct communication between handsets, so you can take them with you to use like walkie-talkies. Some phones can register up to eight handsets, for instance, but that doesn't mean you can use all eight at once. You might be able to use two for handset-to-handset intercom, while two others conference with an outside party.

HOW TO CHOOSE

Decide how much hardware you need. The basic options are a stand-alone phone, a phone with a built-in answerer, or a phone that supports multiple handsets from one base. A stand-alone phone is best suited for small families or people in a small apartment with little need for more than one phone. The built-in answerer, a common choice, adds a big measure of convenience. A multiple-handset phone is good for active families who need phones throughout the house; this type of phone lets you put handsets in a room that doesn't have a phone jack.

Select the technology and frequency band. A 900-MHz phone should suit most users, but that type may be hard to find because 2.4- and 5.8-GHz models dominate. You're likely to find the widest range of models and prices with 2.4-GHz phones. But if you want to minimize problems of interference with other wireless products, look to a 5.8-GHz or 900-MHz phone. Analog phones, apt to be less expensive than digital, are fine for many people. But if privacy is important, choose a DSS or digital phone.

To be sure you're actually getting a DSS or digital phone for its voice-transmission security, check the packaging carefully. Look for wording such as "digital phone," "digital spread spectrum (DSS)" or "frequency-hopping spread spectrum (FHSS)." Phrases such as "phone with digital security code," "phone with all-digital answerer," or "spread spectrum technology" (not digital spread spectrum) all denote phones that are less secure.

Phones that use dual-band transmission may indicate the higher frequency in a larger print on the packaging. If you want a true 2.4- or 5.8-GHz phone, check the fine print. If only the frequency is shown on the package, it's probably analog.

Settle on the features you want. You can typically expect caller ID, a headset jack, and a base that can be wall-mounted. But the features don't end there for both stand-alone phones and phone-answerers. Check the box or ask to see an instruction manual to be sure you're getting the capabilities and features that matter to you. As a rule, the more feature-laden the phone, the higher its price.

Performance variations. CONSUMER REPORTS' tests show that most new cordless phones have very good overall voice quality. Some are excellent, approaching the voice quality of the best corded phones. In our latest tests, most fully charged nickel-cadmium (Ni-Cd) or nickel-metal hydride (Ni-MH) batteries handled eight hours of continuous conversation before they needed recharging. Most manufacturers claim that a fully charged battery will last at least a week in standby mode. When they can no longer hold a charge, a replacement battery, usually proprietary, costs about $10 to $25. Some phones use less-expensive AA or AAA rechargeable batteries. (To find a store that will recycle a used battery, call 800-822-8837.)

Give the handset a test drive. In the store, hold the handset to your head to see if it feels comfortable. It should fit the contours of your face. The earpiece should have rounded edges and a recessed center that fits nicely over the middle of your ear. Check the buttons and controls to make sure they're reasonably sized and legible.

Don't discard the corded phone. As we've noted before, it's a good idea to keep at least one corded phone in your home, if only for emergencies. A cordless phone may not work if you lose electrical power, and a cell phone won't work if you can't get a signal or the circuits are full. A corded phone draws its power from the phone system and can function without household AC power.

REFERENCE & RATINGS

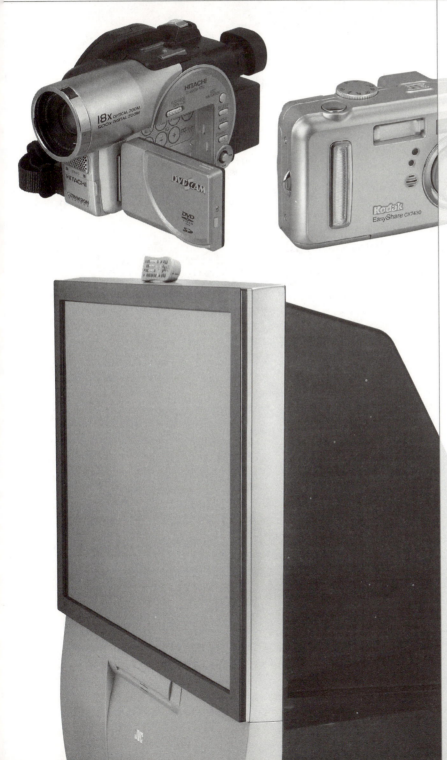

RATINGS

129 Camcorders
132 Computers, desktop
134 Computers, laptop
136 Digital cameras
142 DVD recorders
145 Home theater in a box
146 Monitors
148 MP3 players
152 PDAs
154 Phones, cell
156 Phones, cordless
160 Printers
164 Scanners
166 TVs, LCD
172 TVs, picture-tube
178 TVs, plasma

BRAND LOCATOR
183

GLOSSARY
185

INDEX
206

CAMCORDERS

CR Quick Recommendations

You can expect a digital camcorder to deliver very good video, as our Ratings scores demonstrate. Many of the digital camcorders that record directly onto small DVD discs were ranked at or near the top of the Ratings. However, that doesn't automatically make them the best choice. As the Ratings show, most DVD models were not markedly better than many camcorders that use MiniDV tape. The MiniDV camcorders win on price, making them the type that most people should consider first. The DVD models are for people who want ease of playback above all else.

Most camcorders weigh about a pound, give or take a few ounces. As camcorders get smaller and lighter, image-stabilization features become more important. A lightweight camcorder is harder to hold steady than a heavy one. Fortunately, most did an excellent job of minimizing the shakes.

Nearly all these camcorders turned in fair or poor performance when we tested them in low light. Two Canon models, the Canon Elura 85 (3) and the Canon Elura 60 (17), a Panasonic, the Panasonic PV-GS65 (24) and the Sony DCR-DVD101 (29) were better than the rest.

Analog camcorders are a dying breed. Three models remain in the Ratings, and neither is in the same league as the digitals. Their picture quality is only fair, comparable with that of a rental videotape.

The Ratings rank models strictly on performance. Quick Picks considers other factors such as features, reliability, and value.

Quick Picks

Best values in digital tape:

4, 15 Sony, $335-$380

Sony has been a reliable brand, in contrast with JVC, which also has some high-scoring, low-priced models but has been among the more repair-prone brands of digital camcorders. The Sony DCR-HC21 (4) weighs just a pound and is among the lowest-priced digital camcorders we tested. Although very good overall, its sound quality was only good; that may not matter much for recording speech, but you may notice it with music. The Sony DCR-TRV480 (15), a CR Best Buy, offers more features and better image stabilization—though it, too, has mediocre sound quality.

Best value in a DVD camcorder:

7 Hitachi, $590

This is the least expensive DVD camcorder we tested; its straightforward controls also made it one of the easiest to use. We don't have enough data to judge the reliability of DVD camcorders.

Ratings

In performance order, within categories

Key number	Brand and model	Price	Format	Overall score	Picture quality	Ease of use	Image stabilizer	Audio quality	Weight (oz.)	Optical zoom	LCD size (in.)	Battery life (min.)	Full auto switch	Quick review	Built-in light	AV input	Microphone input	Digital still capable
DIGITAL MODELS																		
1	Panasonic VDR-M70	$695	DVD-RAM, DVD-R		●	○	●	◐	1.2	10x	2.5	105	•			•	•	•
2	JVC Ultra-Compact Series GR-DF450	390	MiniDV		●	○	◐	◐	1.1	15x	2.5	65	•	•		•		•
3	Canon Elura 85	470	MiniDV		◐	◐	●	◐	1.2	18x	2.5	85	•	•		•		•
4	Sony DCR-HC21	380	MiniDV		◐	●	◐	○	1	20x	2.5	80	•	•		•		•
5	Panasonic PV-GS250	780	MiniDV		◐	◐	●	◐	1.3	10x	2.5	115	•	•		•	•	•
6	Panasonic VDR-M50	550	DVD-RAM, DVD-R		◐	◐	●	◐	1.4	18x	2.5	115	•			•		•
7	Hitachi DZ-MV580A	590	DVD-RAM, DVD-R		◐	●	●	◐	1.4	10x	2.5	105	•			•		•
8	Canon ZR200	370	MiniDV		◐	●	●	◐	1.1	20x	2.4	85	•	•		•		•
9	Sony DCR-HC90	785	MiniDV		◐	○	●	◐	1.1	10x	2.7	80	•			•		•

(continued)

Guide to the Ratings

OVERALL SCORE is based mainly on picture quality; ease of use, image stabilizing, and audio quality carried less weight. **PICTURE QUALITY** is based on the judgments of trained panelists who viewed static images shot in good light at standard speed (SP) for tape and fine mode for DVDs. **EASE OF USE** takes into account ergonomics, weight, how accurately the viewfinder frames scenes, and contrast in the LCD viewer. **IMAGE STABILIZER** indicates how well that circuitry worked. **AUDIO QUALITY** represents accuracy using the built-in microphone, plus freedom from noise and flutter. **WEIGHT** includes battery and tape or disk. **OPTICAL ZOOM** range is as stated by the manufacturer. **LCD SIZE** is measured diagonally. **BATTERY LIFE** is as stated by the manufacturer, using the LCD viewer. Turning off the viewer typically extends battery life by 10 to 40 minutes on a charge. NS indicates that the manufacturer did not provide the specification for battery life. **PRICE** is approximate retail.

Expect these camcorders to have: Tape counter, backlight-compensation switch, manual aperture control, high-speed manual shutte, manual white balance, simple switch for manual focus, audio dub, tape-position memory, audio fade, transitional effects, S-video signal out, and video fade. *Based on tests in Consumer Reports in November 2004, with updated prices and availability.*

CAMCORDERS

Ratings (continued)

In performance order, within categories

Excellent ● · Very good ◕ · Good ○ · Fair ◒ · Poor ●

Key number	Brand and model	Price	Format	Overall score	Picture quality	Ease of use	Image stabilizer	Audio quality	Weight (oz.)	Optical zoom	LCD size (in.)	Battery life (min.)	Full auto switch	Quick review	Built-in light	AV input	Microphone input	Digital still capable
	DIGITAL MODELS																	
10	Canon Optura 50	635	MiniDV		●	○	◕	◒	1.3	10x	2.5	75	●		●		●	●
11	Sony DCR-HC20	430	MiniDV		●	○	◕	◒	1	10x	2.5	110	●	●				
12	JVC Everio Series GZ-MC100	900	External Memory		●	◒	◕	◒	0.7	10x	1.8	65						●
13	Sony DCR-IP1	990	MicroMV		●	○	●	◒	0.6	10x	2	90		●				●
14	Sony DCR-PC55	625	MiniDV		●	○	◕	◒	0.8	10x	3	95	●	●				●
15	Sony DCR-TRV480	335	D8		●	○	◕	◒	2	20x	2.5	80	●	●		●		●
16	JVC Compact Series GR-D270	315	MiniDV		●	○	◒	◒	1.1	25x	2.5	65	●	●		●		
17	Canon Elura 60	375	MiniDV		○	◒	●	◒	1.2	14x	2.5	90	●	●				●
18	Panasonic PV-GS31	370	MiniDV		○	○	◒	◒	1	26x	2.5	85	●					●
19	Panasonic PV-GS55	500	MiniDV		●	○	◒	◒	0.8	10x	2.5	NS	●					●
20	Panasonic PV-GS120	640	MiniDV		○	○	◒	●	1.2	10x	2.5	125	●				●	●
21	Sony DCR-DVD201	655	DVD-RAM, DVD-R		○	○	●	◒	1.2	10x	2.5	105	●	●			●	●
22	Sony DCR-PC109	640	MiniDV		●	○	◕	◒	1	10x	2.5	100	●	●			●	●
23	JVC GR-D93US	370	MiniDV		○	○	◒	◒	1.4	10x	2.5	65	●	●	●			
24	Panasonic PV-GS65	520	MiniDV		○	○	◒	◒	1.1	10x	2.5	80	●					●
25	Canon Elura 70	500	MiniDV		○	●	●	◒	1.4	18x	2.5	190	●	●				●
26	Canon ZR85	345	MiniDV		○	○	◒	◒	1.2	20x	2.5	85	●	●				●
27	JVC GR-D230U	390	MiniDV		○	○	◒	◒	1.2	10x	2.5	80	●	●	●	●		
28	Samsung SC-D103	295	MiniDV		○	○	◒	●	1.2	18x	2.5	90	●					●
29	Sony DCR-DVD101	605	DVD-RAM, DVD-R		○	○	●	◒	1.2	10x	2.5	120	●	●				
30	JVC GR-DX77U	350	MiniDV		○	○	●	◒	1.2	12x	2.5	75	●	●				●
31	Panasonic PV-GS9	265	MiniDV		○	○	◒	◒	1	20x	2.5	105	●					
32	Canon ZR80	320	MiniDV		○	◒	○	◒	1.2	18x	2.5	85	●					
	ANALOG MODELS																	
33	Sony CCD-TRV138	235	Hi8		○	○	0	◒	2	20x	2.5	115	●					
34	Sony CCD-TRV128	210	Hi8		◒	○	0	◒	2	20x	2.5	115	●					
35	Panasonic PV-L354D	210	VHS-C		◒	◒	◒	●	2.4	20x	2.5	40	●					

Profiles Model-by-Model

DIGITAL MODELS

1 Panasonic VDR-M70 Very good overall. Excellent picture quality at standard speed. Image stabilizer worked very well. Relatively lightweight. Poor picture quality in low light if simply used in auto mode. Uses proprietary A/V cable. Discontinued, but may still be available.

2 JVC Ultra-Compact Series GR-DF450 Feature-laden model with excellent picture quality and good low-light picture quality. Audio quality was fair. Relatively lightweight, thought it doesn't sit in hand comfortably. JVC in the MiniDV format has been among the more repair-prone brands of digital camcorders. Similar model: Ultra-Compact Series GR-DF430.

3 Canon Elura 85 Very good picture quality, easy to use with an excellent image stabilizer and autofocus. Good low-light picture quality. Relatively lightweight, but hard to hold and operate. Audio quality was only fair, with noticeable background noise. Similar models: Elura 80, Elura 90.

4 Sony DCR-HC21 Very good picture quality. Image stabilizer and autofocus are excellent. Relatively lightweight; sits in the hand well, but record button was in an awkward position. Uses proprietary A/V cable. Lacks: A/V input, still-image digital capture.

5 Panasonic PV-GS250 Easy to use and fits hand well. Very good picture quality. Image stabilizer is excellent. Relatively lightweight. Fair audio quality.

6 Panasonic VDR-M50 Very good overall. Image stabilizer and autofocus worked very well. Poor picture quality in low light if simply used in auto mode. Uses proprietary A/V cable. Discontinued, but may still be available.

7 Hitachi DZ-MV580A Very good over-

CAMCORDERS

Profiles Model-by-Model (continued)

all and easy to use. Image stabilizer worked very well. Poor picture quality in low-light if simply used in auto mode. Uses proprietary A/V cable.

8 Canon ZR200 Easy to use and hold. Very good picture quality. Image stabilizer and autofocus is excellent. Fair audio quality. Similar models: ZR300, ZR100.

9 Sony DCR-HC90 Feature-laden model that has very good picture and audio quality. Uses proprietary A/V cable. Thumb-activated buttons not located well. Does not grip securely.

10 Canon Optura 50 Feature-laden model with very good picture quality. Image stabilizer is excellent, but autofocus failed to work in many situations. Fair audio quality. Sits awkwardly in hand. Similar model: Optura 60.

11 Sony DCR-HC20 Very good overall. Image stabilizer worked very well. Relatively lightweight. Has infrared-sensitive and time-lapse recording modes. Audio had noticeable background noise. Uses proprietary A/V cable. Simple switch for manual focus. Can't capture digital still images. Discontinued, but similar model DCR-HC30 is available.

12 JVC Everio Series GZ-MC100 Very good picture quality. Image stabilizer and autofocus are excellent. Fair audio quality. Somewhat hard to use. Does not fit hand well; fingers can cover flashbulb and lens; strap design does not hold camcorder to hand. Lacks some features found on basic camcorders.

13 Sony DCR-IP1 Very good overall. Relatively lightweight. Image stabilizer and autofocus worked very well. Has time-lapse recording mode. Lacks slow speed, simple switch for manual focus. Uses proprietary A/V cable. Cable connectors are only on docking station, not on the camcorder.

14 Sony DCR-PC55 Very good picture quality. Image stabilizer and autofocus are excellent. Fair audio quality. Uses proprietary A/V cable. Some connectors not on camcorder, only on docking station. Strap design does not hold camcorder to hand.

15 Sony DCR-TRV480 A **CR Best Buy** Feature-laden model with very good picture quality. Image stabilizer and autofocus are excellent. Fair audio quality. Some thumb-activated buttons not located well. Similar model: DCR-TRV280.

16 JVC Compact Series GR-D270 Very good picture quality. VCR controls are very easy to use. Relatively lightweight. Fair audio quality. Angled strap keeps camera comfortably in hand. JVC in the MiniDV format has been among the more repair-prone brands of digital camcorders. Similar models: Compact Series GR-D250, Compact Series GR-D295.

17 Canon Elura 60 Good overall. Relatively lightweight. Image stabilizer and autofocus worked very well. Good picture quality in low light if manual settings are used.

18 Panasonic PV-GS31 Good overall. Autofocus worked very well and menu is very easy to use. Fair audio quality. Fits hand well, but thumb-activated buttons not located well. Similar models: PV-GS35, PV-GS19.

19 Panasonic PV-GS55 Good overall, but somewhat hard to use and had poor picture quality in low light. Relatively lightweight. Battery life under 1 hour.

20 Panasonic PV-GS120 Good overall. Relatively lightweight. Autofocus worked very well. Lacks quick review. Discontinued, but may still be available.

21 Sony DCR-DVD201 Good overall. Image stabilizer worked very well. Relatively lightweight. Poor picture quality in low light if simply used in auto mode. Uses proprietary A/V cable.

22 Sony DCR-PC109 Good overall. Image stabilizer worked very well. Relatively lightweight. Has infrared-sensitive and time-lapse recording modes. It's not obvious how to load the tape or battery. Lacks simple switch for manual focus. Cable connectors are only on docking station, not on the camcorder.

23 JVC GR-D93US Good overall. Very easy-to-use menus, but many drawbacks. Autofocus failed to work in many situations. Audio had noticeable background noise. Lacks quick review. JVC in the MiniDV format has been among the more repair-prone brands of digital camcorders.

24 Panasonic PV-GS65 Very good picture quality in low light if manual settings are used. Menu is very easy to use. Fair audio quality.

25 Canon Elura 70 Good overall. Excellent image stabilizer and autofocus. Good video quality.

26 Canon ZR85 Good overall. Easy to use. Relatively lightweight. Audio had noticeable background noise. Lacks backlight-compensation switch. Similar model: ZR90.

27 JVC GR-D230U Good overall. VCR controls are very easy to use. Relatively lightweight. Fair audio quality. Uses proprietary A/V cable. JVC in the MiniDV format has been among the more repair-prone brands of digital camcorders.

28 Samsung SC-D103 Good overall. Autofocus worked very well. Relatively lightweight. VCR controls are very easy to use. Has infrared-sensitive recording mode. Image stabilizer is only slightly effective. Lacks simple switch for manual focus, A/V input.

29 Sony DCR-DVD101 Good overall. Image stabilizer and autofocus worked very well. Poor video quality in low light.

30 JVC GR-DX77U Good overall, but somewhat hard to use. Excellent image stabilizer. Good video quality. JVC in the MiniDV format has been among the more repair-prone brands of digital camcorders. Similar model: GR-DX97.

31 Panasonic PV-GS9 Good overall. Relatively lightweight. Picture quality was poor in low light or if simply used in auto mode. Audio had noticeable background noise. Lacks quick review, A/V input. Can't capture digital still images.

32 Canon ZR80 Good overall. Relatively lightweight. Easy to use. Audio had noticeable background noise. Lacks backlight-compensation switch, A/V input. Can't capture digital still images.

ANALOG MODELS

33 Sony CCD-TRV138 Good overall. Autofocus is excellent. Good low-light picture quality. Lacks image stabilizer and digital stills. Some-thumb activated buttons not located well.

34 Sony CCD-TRV128 Fair overall. Autofocus worked very well. Has infrared-sensitive recording mode. Lacks image stabilizer, manual white balance, A/V input. Can't capture digital still images. Discontinued, but similar model CCD-TRV328 is available.

35 Panasonic PV-L354D Fair overall. Similar model: PV-L454D

COMPUTERS, DESKTOP

CR Quick Recommendations

Workhorse computers cost more than budget desktops but offer more, especially in expandability, convenience, and multimedia capabilities. Either type can do the job for the most typical uses, including photo editing.

If you're buying a new monitor, consider that LCD screens save desk space and use less power than CRT monitors. Serious photographers, graphic designers, and gamers, however, may prefer the color rendition, response time, and viewing angle of a CRT monitor. Note that the price for both Apples includes a monitor. The iMac (11) has an LCD; the eMac (12), a CRT display.

The Ratings rank desktop computers strictly by performance; brand reliability and tech support may matter more. Quick Picks takes those and other factors into account.

Quick Picks

For the best reliability and support:
- 11 Apple $1,625

As our user surveys continue to indicate, Apple's reliability and tech support have been top-notch. The workhorse Apple (11) performed well and is priced about the same as a similarly equipped Windows system. But it has limited expansion capability. The eMac (12) is more user-friendly than comparable budget Windows models and includes a CRT. But expansion is limited, and extras such as a DVD writer and memory-card slot are lacking.

For a well-rounded budget PC:
- 4 eMachines $500
- 5 Sony $730

Either of these budget models would make a fine computer for home or dorm. The eMachines (4) and the Sony (5) have an attractive mix of features and have been reliable brands. The Sony is better suited to multimedia use, though Sony's tech support has been so-so. (We don't have enough data to report on eMachines.) While no Dells of this type were tested, Dell has done well in prior tests and has been a reliable brand. The Dell Dimension 3000, $605, would be worth a look. We tested a previous version that had a Celeron processor; its successor uses a Pentium 4.

For the best value in a workhorse:
- 7 Dell $1,270
- 9 Sony $1,750

Every workhorse computer we tested would be fine for demanding uses like gaming and video editing. The Dell (7) and Sony (9) scored well, and both brands have been reliable. A chief reason for the Sony's price is its media-center functionality, in the form of a TV tuner and TiVo-like programming storage. It has a memory-card slot, lacking on the Dell, and a larger hard drive. Dell's tech support has been better than Sony's. Since our survey, Sony has added in-home service as standard.

Ratings

In performance order, within categories

Ratings key: Excellent, Very good, Good, Fair, Poor

Key number	Brand & model	Price	Overall score	Convenience	Speed	Multimedia	Expansion	Energy-saving	Warranty	Hard drive (GB)	Video RAM (MB)	USB ports	Free PCI slots	Memory-card slot	FireWire port	DVD writer	Bay for 2nd HD	DVI display port
WINDOWS BUDGET MODELS *Relatively low-cost systems for most general uses, including photo editing.*																		
1	Compaq SR1010Z 1.8-GHz AMD Sempron 3100+	$670		⊖	●	◐	⊖	⊖	○	80	128	7	2	•	•	•		
2	HP Pavilion a1000y 2.93-GHz Celeron D 340	700		⊖	⊖	○	⊖	⊖	⊖	80	64	5	2	•		•		
3	Gateway 3310S 2.93-GHz Celeron D 340	645		⊖	⊖	○	⊖	⊖	○	80	96	6	2		•	•		
4	eMachines T3985 2.93-GHz Celeron D 340	500		⊖	⊖	○	⊖	⊖	○	80	96	7	2	•	•	•		
5	Sony Vaio VGC-RB39C 2.8-GHz Intel Celeron D 335	730		○	⊖	⊖	⊖	⊖	○	80	160	5	2	•	•	•		
WINDOWS WORKHORSE MODELS *Have additional memory and storage for more intensive uses, such as 3D games and video editing.*																		
6	Gateway 9310S 3.4-GHz Pentium 4 650	1,830		⊖	●	⊖	⊖	⊖	○	200	256	6	2	•	•		•	
7	Dell Dimension 8400 3.4-GHz Pentium 4 550	1,270		⊖	●	⊖	⊖	⊖	○	150	256	6	2		•	•		
8	HP Pavilion a1050y 3.4-GHz Pentium 4 550J	1,570		⊖	●	⊖	○	⊖	⊖	200	256	7	1	•	•	•		
9	Sony Vaio VGC-RA930G 3.4-GHz Pentium 4 550	1,750		⊖	●	⊖	⊖	⊖	○	200	256	5	1	•	•	•		
10	Compaq Presario SR1010Z 2.4-GHz Athlon 64 3300+	940		⊖	⊖	⊖	⊖	⊖	○	180	256	6	1	•	•	•		
MACINTOSH MODELS *Include both budget- and workhorse-class models.*																		
11	Apple iMac G5 2-GHz Power PC	1,625		⊖	⊖	⊖	◐	⊖	○	160	128	3	1		•	•		
12	Apple eMac Combo Drive 1.25-GHz Power PC G4	800		⊖	⊖	⊖	◐	⊖	○	80	32	3	1		•			

COMPUTERS, DESKTOP

Guide to the Ratings

OVERALL SCORE covers convenience, speed, and other factors. **CONVENIENCE** covers ergonomics, ports, manuals, audio, and features. **SPEED** measures the quickness of response doing routine office work and content creation. **MULTIMEDIA** measures the ability to render motion smoothly in game-type graphics. **EXPANSION** covers internal and external add-ins and upgrades. **ENERGY-SAVING** rates power consumption in a typical pattern of use, along with power-saving features. **WARRANTY** rates basic provisions for service and support (doesn't affect the model's overall score). **FEATURES** include free expansion slots for internal PCI or PCI Express cards, bay for second hard drive, and DVI display port to connect a flat-panel monitor with a digital input. **PRICE** is approximate retail for the system only (except for the two Macs), to the nearest $5.

All Windows budget computers have 512 megabytes of RAM except the Sony (5) and the Apple (12), which have 256 MB. The Dell (7), Sony (9), and Compaq (10) workhorse Windows computers have 512 MB; the others, including the Apple (11), have 1 GB. *Based on testing in Consumer Reports in September 2005, with updated prices and availability.*

COMPUTERS, LAPTOP

CR Quick Recommendations

As with desktops, we categorize laptops by configuration into budget and workhorse models. But here, the display is more important. Higher resolution allows for finer detail, useful for photos and video, though it also means that objects on the screen are smaller. Of the tested models, all but those with 1,024x768-pixel displays are wide-screen. That comes in handy not only for watching DVDs but also when you're running applications, such as spreadsheets, for which more screen width helps. Such models tend to cost and weigh a bit more than those with the more squarish 4:3 screens.

The Ratings rank laptops strictly by performance. Weight, brand reliability, and tech-support record may matter more. Quick Picks takes those and other factors into account.

Quick Picks

For reliability and the best tech support:
14 Apple $1,300

Apple has been a reliable brand and has the best record for tech support. The iBook (14), roughly a budget machine, scored on a par with the Windows workhorse models and is comparably priced but has a smaller screen and lower display quality than some. The Apple PowerBook (13) also did well, but its battery life was lackluster and it's costly for what it offers—mainly a bigger, higher-resolution wide screen, a slightly faster processor, and a DVD writer.

For good value in a budget laptop:
3 Dell $960
4 IBM $1,105

These basic models are good values if you don't need features such as Wi-Fi (optional, about $50), a memory-card slot, a FireWire port, a DVD writer, or a wide-screen display. The Dell (3) performed well, and its battery life topped 4 hours. The IBM (4) had comparable performance and battery life but more expansion capability. IBM scored well in tech support.

For an easy-to-carry workhorse:
9 Dell $1,520
10 Toshiba $1,500

For very good performance and battery life, the Dell (9) gets our nod. This model also has a wide screen with the highest resolution of the group, at 1680x1050. The Toshiba (10) scored similarly and weighs less but has shorter battery life. Toshiba has been a reliable brand.

For a well-priced workhorse to use at home:
8 HP $1,150

For about what you'd pay for many budget models, the wide-screen HP (8) offers faster speed, more storage, and lots of other features. But its heavier weight and shorter battery life make it more suited for stay-at-home use.

Ratings

In performance order, within categories

Key number	Brand & model	Price	Overall score (0-100)	Convenience	Speed	Multimedia	Display quality	Expansion	Energy-saving	Battery (hr.)	Warranty	Hard drive (GB)	Display resolution	Carry weight (lb.)	Travel weight (lb.)	Memory-card slot	FireWire port	DVD writer	Wi-Fi
	BUDGET LAPTOPS — Relatively low-cost systems for most general uses, including photo editing.																		
1	HP Pavilion dv4000 1.5-GHz Celeron M 370	$1,025		○	◉	◉	◉	◉	●	3½	○	60	1280x800	6.6	8.1	●	●		
2	Compaq M2000 1.5-GHz Celeron M 370	750		◉	◉	○	○	○	●	2½	◉	60	1024x768	6.3	7.8		●		
3	Dell Inspiron 2200 1.5-GHz Celeron M 370	960		○	◉	◉	○	○	●	4¼	◉	60	1024x768	6.3	8.0				
4	IBM ThinkPad R51-2883 1.5-GHz Celeron M 340	1,105		○	◉	○	○	◉	●	4¼	○	30	1024x768	6.4	7.9				
5	Sony VGN-FS500 1.4-GHz Celeron M 360	1,230		○	◉	◉	○	○	●	2½	◉	60	1280x800	6.2	7.9	●	●		
6	Toshiba Satellite M35X-S163 1.4-GHz Celeron M 360	1,000		○	◉	◉	◉	◉	●	1¾	○	60	1280x800	6.0	7.3		●		●
	WORKHORSE LAPTOPS — Have additional memory and storage for more intensive uses, such as 3D games and video editing.																		
7	Gateway M460X 1.86-GHz Pentium M750	1,395		◉	◉	◉	◉	◉	◉	3½	○	80	1280x800	6.4	8.1	●	●		
8	HP Pavilion ZV6000 2.2-GHz Athlon 64 3500+	1,150		◉	●	◉	◉	◉	●	2¼	○	80	1280x800	8.1	10.8	●	●		
9	Dell Inspiron 6000 1.86-GHz Pentium M 750	1,520		◉	◉	○	◉	○	◉	3¼	◉	80	1680x1050	7.0	8.6	●	●		
10	Toshiba Satellite M45-S351 1.73-GHz Pentium M 740	1,500		◉	◉	◉	◉	◉	◉	2¾	○	100	1280x800	6.2	7.9	●	●		
11	IBM ThinkPad G41 1.86-GHz Pentium 4 538	1,840		○	●	◉	◉	◉	◉	3	○	80	1400x1050	8.4	11.3				
12	Sony Vaio VGN-FS500 1.73-GHz Pentium M 740	1,460		○	●	◉	○	○	◉	2	○	60	1280x800	6.4	8.1	●	●		
	MACINTOSH LAPTOP COMPUTERS — Include both budget- and workhorse-class models.																		
13	Apple PowerBook G4 15" 1.5-GHz PowerPC G4	2,000		●	◉	◉	●	◉	●	2	○	80	1280x854	5.6	6.8		●	●	●
14	Apple iBook 14" Combo 1.33-GHz PowerPC G4	1,300		◉	◉	◉	○	○	●	3¼	○	60	1024x768	6	7.5		●		●

All models have 15-inch screen except Apple (14), which has a 14-inch screen.

Ratings key: ● Excellent ◉ Very good ○ Good ◐ Fair ● Poor

COMPUTERS, LAPTOP

Guide to the Ratings

OVERALL SCORE covers convenience, speed, and other factors. **CONVENIENCE** covers ergonomics, ports, manuals, audio, and features. **SPEED** measures the quickness of response doing routine office work and content creation. **MULTIMEDIA** measures the ability to render motion smoothly in game-type graphics. **EXPANSION** covers internal and external add-ins and upgrades. **ENERGY-SAVING** rates power consumption in a typical pattern of use, along with power-saving features. **BATTERY LIFE** is our measurement. **WARRANTY** rates basic provisions for service and support (doesn't affect the model's overall score). **CARRY WEIGHT** is with battery and any removable drives; **TRAVEL WEIGHT** adds the power adapter and a spare battery. **PRICE** is approximate retail.

All budget models, including the Apple (14), have 256 megabytes of RAM except the Toshiba (6), which has 512 MB. The workhorse models all have 512 MB. Most models overall have three or four USB ports, and all but the Apple (14) have a PC-card slot.

Based on testing in Consumer Reports in September 2005, with updated prices and availability.

DIGITAL CAMERAS

CR Quick Recommendations

In our tests, based on judgments of uncropped 8x10-inch prints, all the cameras produced images that were very good or excellent—a quality difference that's subtle. But if we had used a small portion of the original image and enlarged it to 8x10, the higher-megapixel cameras would probably have produced better results than the others.

If you want a camera that's small and light above all else, you'll find several in the Ratings, including the Canon PowerShot SD300 (18) and Casio Exilim EX-Z55 (45). But all make some compromises, such as having a short flash range, shorter battery life, or a nonzoom lens.

Note that battery life, next-shot delay, flash range, size, and other attributes vary widely within each group. So does price.

The Ratings list models by overall performance. Quick Picks considers factors such as features and price, as well as the type of photographer you are. To qualify as a Quick Pick, a camera must have, at a minimum, long battery life and flash range, a short delay between shots, and a design that allows a secure grip.

Quick Picks

Best values overall if you want to get creative:
- 2 Canon, $350
- 31 Fujifilm, $240
- 38 Olympus, $315

These three combine low price with at least a 5x-zoom range and other features that add flexibility. The Canon PowerShot S1IS (2), a 3-megapixel model, has a very long zoom range and an array of useful features that help justify its relatively high price. The other two are 4-megapixel models, giving them a slight edge over the Canon if you regularly crop and enlarge photos. But both have some minor shortcomings: The Olympus C-5500 (38) Sport Zoom has a long next-shot delay, and the Fujifilm FinePix S3100 (31) is rather bulky.

Best values for creative editing, provided a long zoom range isn't critical to you:
- 23, 40 Kodak, $240-$250
- 41 Olympus, $500
- 47 Nikon, $500
- 50 Canon, $290

This large group consists mainly of 4- and 5-megapixel cameras, typically with a 3x or 4x zoom. Look first to the Kodak EasyShare CX7530 (40) for its low price; it's also PictBridge-compatible and uses AA batteries. The other cameras in this group have assets that make them more versatile, but most have one or another minor shortcoming. The Olympus C-Series C-5060 Wide Zoom (41), Nikon Coolpix 5400 (47), and Canon PowerShot A95 (50) have manual controls but are relatively heavy; all but the Canon, a CR Best Buy, use proprietary batteries.

Best choices in point-and-shoots for serious photography:
- 62 Fujifilm, $310
- 65, 68 Olympus, $280-$620
- 67 Canon, $545
- 71 Sony, $365
- 72 Nikon, $640

If you don't want the expense, weight, or complexity of a digital SLR, consider these 6- to 8-megapixel models. They have the manual controls that provide you with a great deal of photographic control, yet can still work with point-and-shoot simplicity. All are much less expensive than an SLR. The Nikon Coolpix 8700 (72) has the longest zoom range in this group. The Canon PowerShot G6 (67) and Olympus C-7070 Wide Zoom (68) are closely matched in many respects; the Canon has a long flash range and better battery life. The Fujifilm FinePix E550 (62) and Olympus C-60 Zoom (65), CR Best Buys, are worth considering if you're on a limited budget and don't need a feature-laden camera. The Fujifilm has slightly lower image quality than others in this group, but that's not a serious drawback. The compact Sony Cyber-shot DSC-P150 (71) has PictBridge capability.

Ratings

In performance order, within categories

Key number	Brand and model	Price	Overall score	Print quality	Weight (oz.)	Flash range (ft.)	Battery life (shots)	Next-shot delay (sec.)	Optical zoom	Manual controls	Secure grip	Movie mode	Charger	AA batteries	Eye glasses
	3-MEGAPIXEL MODELS														
1	Canon PowerShot A510	$180		●	8	11	300	2	4X	●	●		●	●	
2	Canon PowerShot S1IS	350		●	17	14	180	3	10X	●	●		●	●	
3	Olympus Camedia C-740 Ultra Zoom	250		●	13	15	65	3	10X	●			●	●	
4	Fujifilm FinePix F700	360		◐	7	16	180	1	3X			●	●		
5	Canon PowerShot SD110	230		◐	7	10	380	2	2X			●	●		
6	Hewlett-Packard PhotoSmart M307	150		●	6	9	85	4	3X			●	●	●	
7	Olympus Stylus 300 Digital	195		◐	7	12	170	2	3X			●	●		
8	Olympus D-540 Zoom	155		◐	7	11	460	5	3X			●		●	
9	Fujifilm FinePix A330	140		◐	7	11	380	4	3X			●		●	

DIGITAL CAMERAS

Ratings (continued)

In performance order, within categories

Ratings key: ● Excellent ◐ Very good ○ Good ◐ Fair ● Poor

Key number	Brand and model	Price	Overall score	Print quality	Weight (oz.)	Flash range (ft.)	Battery life (shots)	Next-shot delay (sec.)	Optical zoom	Manual controls	Secure grip	Movie mode	Charger	AA batteries	Eye glasses
3-MEGAPIXEL MODELS															
10	Hewlett-Packard PhotoSmart 735	200		◐	10	10	35	3	3X		•	•		•	
11	Sony Cyber-shot DSC-P72	200		◐	9	12	260	3	3X		•	•	•	•	
12	Casio Exilim EX-S100	350		◐	5	8	110	3	2.8X			•	•		
13	Sony CD Mavica MVC-CD350	380		◐	18	8	120	2	3X	•	•	•	•		
14	Kodak EasyShare CX7300	90		◐	7	8	240	2	None			•		•	
4-MEGAPIXEL MODELS															
15	Kodak EasyShare DX6490	380		●	14	16	60	2	10X	•	•	•	•		•
16	Olympus C-765 Ultra Zoom	335		●	11	15	130	2	10X	•	•	•	•		
17	Olympus C-770 Ultra Zoom	435		●	12	15	120	3	10X	•	•	•	•		
18	Canon PowerShot SD300	320		●	5	11	140	1	3X			•	•		
19	Olympus Stylus 410 Digital	265		●	7	12	360	2	3X			•	•		
20	Sony Cyber-shot DSC-L1	245		●	5	7	260	2	3X			•	•		
21	Kodak EasyShare CX7430	185		●	8	12	520	2	3X			•		•	
22	Canon PowerShot S410	280		●	8	11	380	2	3X			•	•		
23	Kodak EasyShare LS743	250		●	6	10	400	2	2.8X			•	•		
24	Konica DiMAGE Z2	320		◐	14	10	280	3	10X	•	•	•		•	
25	Olympus D-580 Zoom	190		●	8	11	600	2	3X			•		•	
26	Panasonic Lumix DMC-LC70	255		●	8	16	320	2	3X			•	•		
27	Pentax Optio S40	210		●	6	19	95	5	3X			•	•		
28	Pentax Optio S4i	280		●	4	11	150	3	3X			•	•		
29	Sony Cyber-shot DSC-P73	205		●	8	11	560	4	3X		•	•		•	
30	Olympus D-425	145		●	6	10	260	2	None			•		•	
31	Fujifilm FinePix S3100	240		◐	14	11	220	3	6X	•	•	•		•	
32	Canon PowerShot SD10	335		●	4	7	110	2	None			•	•		
33	Fujifilm FinePix A340	180		◐	7	11	340	4	3X			•		•	
34	Olympus Stylus Verve	270		◐	5	9	55	2	2X			•	•		
5-MEGAPIXEL MODELS															
35	Panasonic Lumix DMC-FZ20S	495		●	22	23	280	1	12X	•	•	•		•	•
36	Nikon Coolpix 5700	555		●	19	13	100	3	8X	•	•	•	•		•
37	Canon PowerShot S60	395		●	10	14	260	2	3.6X	•		•	•		
38	Olympus C-5500	315		●	12	12	340	5	5X			•		•	
39	Olympus Stylus 500 Digital	280		●	7	14	140	2	3X			•	•		
40	Kodak EasyShare CX7530 [CR BEST BUY]	240		●	9	12	240	2	3X			•		•	
41	Olympus C-Series C-5060 Wide Zoom	500		●	18	12	560	2	4X	•	•	•	•		•
42	Pentax Optio SV	360		●	6	14	100	9	5X			•	•		
43	Epson L-500V	190		●	7	9	140	2	3X			•	•		
44	Hewlett-Packard Photosmart 945	350		●	17	8	60	2	8X	•	•	•		•	
45	Casio Exilim EX-Z55	300		●	6	9	400	2	3X			•	•		
46	Kodak EasyShare LS753	320		●	6	10	400	1	2.8X			•	•		
47	Nikon Coolpix 5400	500		●	14	15	240	2	4X	•	•	•	•		

(continued)

Guide to the Ratings

OVERALL SCORE is based mainly on print quality, weight, and the presence of useful features. **PRINT QUALITY** is based on expert judgments using 8x10-inch prints made with each camera's best resolution and compression settings and printed on a high-rated inkjet printer. **WEIGHT**, in ounces, includes battery and memory card. **FLASH RANGE**, in feet, is the maximum claimed range for a well-lighted subject. **BATTERY LIFE** is the number of high-resolution photos taken with the batteries supplied, if the camera uses a proprietary size, or with rechargeable nickel-metal hydrides for those using AAs; half the shots used flash, and the zoom lens was racked in and out. **NEXT-SHOT DELAY** is the time, in seconds, the camera needs to ready itself for the next photo. **OPTICAL ZOOM** refers to the range of focal lengths. **MANUAL CONTROLS** refers to settings that let you adjust shutter speed and lens opening. **SECURE GRIP** refers to a design that makes it easy to hold the camera. **MOVIE MODE** allows you to record short video clips. Some models record with sound, others do not. **CHARGER** is for the batteries. **AA BATTERIES** denotes cameras that use that size, which are much more widely available than proprietary batteries. **EYE GLASSES** denotes cameras with viewfinder diopter adjustment, which allows some eyeglass wearers to take off their glasses when using the camera. **PRICE** is approximate retail. *Based on testing in Consumer Reports in July 2005, with updated prices and availability.*

DIGITAL CAMERAS

Ratings (continued)

Excellent ● | Very good ◕ | Good ○ | Fair ◐ | Poor ⬤

In performance order, within categories

Key number	Brand and model	Price	Overall score (P F G VG E)	Print quality	Weight (oz.)	Flash range (ft.)	Battery life (shots)	Next-shot delay (sec.)	Optical zoom	Manual controls	Secure grip	Movie mode	Charger	AA batteries	Eye glasses
5-MEGAPIXEL MODELS															
48	Sony Cyber-shot DSC-M1	520		●	8	6	160	4	3X			●	●		
49	Sony Cyber-shot DSC-P100	320		●	7	11	460	3	3X	●		●	●		
BEST BUY 50	Canon PowerShot A95	290		●	12	14	650	2	3X	●	●	●		●	
51	Fujifilm FinePix F450	315		●	6	12	150	4	3.4X			●	●		
52	Hewlett-Packard Photosmart R707	250		●	7	9	320	3	3X	●		●	●		
53	Canon PowerShot S500	330		●	8	11	320	3	3X			●	●		
54	Olympus C-5000 Zoom	285		◐	10	12	40	3	3X	●	●	●		●	
55	Sony Cyber-shot DSC-T1	365		●	6	5	120	4	3X			●	●		
56	Sony Cyber-shot DSC-W1	300		◐	9	11	240	4	3X	●		●	●		
57	Konica Minolta DiMAGE X50	280		◐	5	6	240	3	2.8X			●			
58	Nikon Coolpix 5200	335		●	6	15	120	3	3X		●				
59	Sony CD Mavica MVC-CD500	555		◐	21	16	55	2	3X	●		●			
60	Pentax Optio X	295		◐	5	12	90	9	3X			●			
61	Panasonic Lumix DMC-FX7	345		◐	5	13	45	7	3X			●			
6-MEGAPIXEL MODELS															
BEST BUY 62	Fujifilm FinePix E550	310		◐	9	15	300	1	4X	●		●	●	●	
63	Fujifilm FinePix S7000	515		●	21	28	60	2	6X	●	●	●		●	●
64	Kodak EasyShare DX7630	295		●	10	14	400	3	3X			●	●		
BEST BUY 65	Olympus C-60 Zoom	280		●	8	11	400	3	3X	●		●	●		
66	Casio Exilim EX-P600	430		◐	9	10	260	4	4X	●		●	●		
7-MEGAPIXEL MODELS															
67	Canon PowerShot G6	545		●	17	16	850	2	4X	●	●	●	●		●
68	Olympus C-7070 Wide Zoom	620		●	18	12	750	2	4X	●	●	●	●		
69	Sony Cyber-shot DSC-V3	530		●	14	10	300	1	4X	●		●	●		
70	Pentax Optio 750Z	460		●	9	17	170	4	5X	●		●		●	
71	Sony Cyber-shot DSC-P150	365		●	6	11	420	2	3X	●		●	●		
8-MEGAPIXEL MODELS															
72	Nikon Coolpix 8700	640		●	19	13	140	3	8X	●	●	●	●		●
73	Nikon Coolpix 8400	700		●	17	20	180	5	3.5X	●	●	●	●		●
74	Canon PowerShot Pro1	640		●	23	16	110	3	7x	●	●	●	●		
75	Olympus C-8080 Wide Zoom	715		●	27	19	120	3	5X	●	●	●	●		●
76	Konica Minolta DiMAGE A2	795		●	24	8	160	1	7X	●	●	●	●		●
77	Sony Cyber-shot DSC-F828	830		●	33	15	110	4	7X	●	●	●	●		●

DIGITAL CAMERAS

Profiles Model-by-Model

1 Canon PowerShot A510 Very good overall. Excellent battery life. Has special scene modes (foliage, snow, beach, fireworks, underwater, indoor, and kids and pets).

2 Canon PowerShot S1IS Very good overall. Excellent battery life. Supports PictBridge direct print system. Has 10x optical zoom, image-stabilization system, full manual control, swing-out LCD display. Can edit movies.

3 Olympus Camedia C-740 Ultra Zoom Very good overall. Has 10x zoom, electronic viewfinder, diopter adjustment for eyeglass wearers, and print image matching. Amount of light emitted by flash is adjustable.

4 Fujifilm FinePix F700 Very good overall. Has Super CCD SR sensor and interpolated 6-megapixel image resolution setting.

5 Canon PowerShot SD110 Very good overall. Supports PictBridge direct print system. Can edit movies.

6 Hewlett-Packard PhotoSmart M307 Good overall, compact, has internal descriptive help menu, has fair battery life, has 16 MB internal memory, has undelete feature.

7 Olympus Stylus 300 Digital Very good overall. Compact. Weatherproof.

8 Olympus D-540 Zoom Very good overall. Has print image matching and supports PictBridge direct print system. Lacks manual controls.

9 Fujifilm FinePix A330 Very good overall. Very good battery life. Supports PictBridge direct print system. Discontinued, but may still be available.

10 Hewlett-Packard PhotoSmart 735 Very good overall. Compact and very easy to use. Discontinued, but may still be available.

11 Sony Cyber-shot DSC-P72 Very good overall. Has resizing/cropping in camera, video cutting in camera, and e-mail format. Movie records in MPEG. Lacks manual controls. Discontinued, but may still be available.

12 Casio Exilim EX-S100 Good overall, subcompact, ultrathin, no viewfinder, large LCD, requires included dock for downloading images and for charging, has automatic noise reduction at slow shutter speeds.

13 Sony CD Mavica MVC-CD350 Very good overall. Large, with large LCD display. Storage medium is compact CD-R/RW and movie file is in MPEG1 format. Lacks viewfinder.

14 Kodak EasyShare CX7300 Good overall. No optical zoom or manual controls. Very good battery life.

4-MEGAPIXEL MODELS

15 Kodak EasyShare DX6490 Excellent overall, with superb picture quality. Has 10X optical zoom, 16 megabytes of internal memory, large LCD screen, external flash socket. Comes with docking station. Discontinued, but model may still be available.

16 Olympus C-765 Ultra Zoom Very good overall. Has 10X zoom, electronic viewfinder, diopter adjustment for eyeglass wearers. Supports PictBridge direct print system. Amount of light emitted by flash is adjustable.

17 Olympus C-770 Ultra Zoom Very good overall. Has super zoom mode to extend the optical zoom to up to 14X at the 1600x1200 pixel setting. Can edit movies. Has flash intensity control and two flashes; camera automatically decides which one to use depending on zoom setting. Has hot shoe for accessory flash and histogram showing image characteristics.

18 Canon PowerShot SD300 Very good overall. Has special scene modes (kids and pets, indoor, and underwater).

19 Olympus Stylus 410 Digital Very good overall. Weatherproof case. Has print image matching and supports PictBridge direct print system. Lacks manual controls.

20 Sony Cyber-shot DSC-L1 Very good overall. Small LCD monitor. Has special scene modes (soft snap, snow, beach, and candle). Uses new MemoryStick Duo Pro to store images and will not accept regular MemoryStick. Tripod socket via adapter.

21 Kodak EasyShare CX7430 A **CR Best Buy.** Very good overall. Has 16 megabytes of internal memory, excellent battery life. Lacks manual controls.

22 Canon PowerShot S410 Very good overall. Very good battery life. Supports PictBridge direct print system. Has Quick Shots mode to reduce shutter lag time, long shutter mode with a variety of shutter speeds from 1 second to 15 seconds available. Can edit movies.

23 Kodak EasyShare LS743 Very good overall. Has 16 megabytes of internal memory, excellent battery life. Lacks manual controls.

24 Konica DiMAGE Z2 Very good overall. Has 10X optical zoom, night movie mode. Can edit movies.

25 Olympus D-580 Zoom Very good overall. Has print image matching and supports PictBridge direct print system. Lacks manual controls.

26 Panasonic Lumix DMC-LC70 Very good overall. Very good battery life. Supports PictBridge direct print system. Has real-time histogram to show image characteristics.

27 Pentax Optio S40 Very good overall. Supports PictBridge direct print system. Has multiple program settings. Long next-shot delay.

28 Pentax Optio S4I Very good overall. Supports PictBridge direct print system. Has multiple program settings. Discontinued, but model may still be available.

29 Sony Cyber-shot DSC-P73 Very good overall. Excellent battery life. Supports PictBridge direct print system. Long next-shot delay. Can edit movies.

30 Olympus D-425 Very good overall. No zoom lens. Small LCD monitor. Has special scene modes (sports, self-portrait, and beach and snow).

31 Fujifilm FinePix S3100 Very good overall, 6X optical zoom, SLR-like body style.

32 Canon PowerShot SD10 Very good overall. Small, stylized design. Supports PictBridge direct-print system. Can edit movies. Discontinued, but model may still be available.

33 Fujifilm FinePix A340 Very good overall. Very good battery life. Supports PictBridge direct print system.

34 Olympus Stylus Verve Very good overall, subcompact, no viewfinder, fashionable body style.

(continued)

DIGITAL CAMERAS

Profiles Model-by-Model (continued)

5-MEGAPIXEL MODELS

35 Panasonic Lumix DMC-FZ20S Excellent overall Has special scene modes (sports, scenery, panning, fireworks, party, and snow). Comes with large lens hood, hot shoe for add-on flash. Image stabilizer. Noise reduction.

36 Nikon Coolpix 5700 Very good overall, but expensive. Has 8x optical zoom, swing-and-flip LCD, SLR-type body, advanced menu system, and hot shoe for accessory flash.

37 Canon PowerShot S60 Very good overall, ultra wide angle, has RAW Image file format, has underwater white balance setting for use with optional waterproof case, does not support Print Image Matching.

38 Olympus C-5500 Very good overall. Excellent battery life. Has special scene modes (sport, beach & snow, fireworks, sunset, candle, and available light portrait). Can fix red-eye in flash photos in the camera.

39 Olympus Stylus 500 Digital Very good overall. Large LCD monitor. All-weather construction. Has special scene modes (indoor, sport, beach and snow, behind glass, sunset, cuisine, documents, candle, underwater wide, underwater macro, and shoot and select).

40 Kodak EasyShare CX7530 A **CR Best Buy.** Very good overall, has 32 MB internal memory.

41 Olympus C-Series C-5060 Wide Zoom Very good overall. Supports PictBridge direct print system. Has full manual controls, 4X optical zoom, extra wide angle lens, hot shoe for accessory flash, swing-out LCD, dual memory slots, very good battery life.

42 Pentax Optio SV Very good overall. Has live histogram that graphically displays image information on LCD. Has special scene modes (flower, sports, surf and snow, autumn colors, sunset, museum, food, and 3D).

43 Epson L-500V Very good overall. Large LCD monitor. Print image framer feature allows users to combine photos with decorative frames to create greeting cards and keepsakes.

44 Hewlett-Packard Photosmart 945 Very good overall. Has manual controls, 8X optical zoom. Short battery life.

45 Casio Exilim EX-Z55 Very good overall. Excellent battery life. Has docking station for charging and all connections. Large LCD monitor. Has 19 special scene modes, with detailed in-camera explanation of each.

46 Kodak EasyShare LS753 Very good overall. Has 32 MB of internal memory, excellent battery life, lacks manual controls.

47 Nikon Coolpix 5400 Very good overall. Has 4X optical zoom, swivel LCD display, hot shoe for accessory flash, multiple scene modes, and 28-116 35mm equivalent zoom lens.

48 Sony Cyber-shot DSC-M1 Very good overall. Swivel LCD monitor and body. Has MPEG4 full-motion video capability with stereo sound. Comes with dock for connections other than battery-charging. Stores images on new MemoryStick Duo Pro and will not accept regular MemoryStick.

49 Sony Cyber-shot DSC-P100 Very good overall. Excellent battery life. Supports PictBridge direct print system. Can edit movies.

50 Canon PowerShot A95 A **CR Best Buy.** Very good overall. Has LCD that flips and swivels, automatic noise reduction at slow shutter speeds, excellent battery life.

51 Fujifilm FinePix F450 Very good overall.

52 Hewlett-Packard Photosmart R707 Very good overall. Has red-eye removal tool in playback menu. Has beach/snow, sunset, document settings. Very good battery life.

53 Canon PowerShot S500 Very good overall. Very good battery life. Supports PictBridge direct print system. Has Quick Shots mode to reduce shutter lag time, long shutter mode with a variety of shutter speeds from 1 second to 15 second available. Can edit movies.

54 Olympus C-5000 Zoom Very good overall. Short battery life. Has full manual controls, hot shoe for accessory flash.

55 Sony Cyber-shot DSC-T1 Very good overall. Supports PictBridge direct print system. Has large LCD screen, internal telephoto lens. Lacks viewfinder, tripod socket. Can edit movies.

56 Sony Cyber-shot DSC-W1 Very good overall. Has manual controls. Supports PictBridge direct print system. Can edit movies.

57 Konica Minolta DiMAGE X50 Very good overall. Subcompact, large LCD.

58 Nikon Coolpix 5200 Very good overall. Compact. Has multiple scene modes, movie mode, and records in QuickTime. Very good battery life.

59 Sony CD Mavica MVC-CD500 Very good overall. Storage medium is CD-R/CD-RW. Has adjustable flash level and hot shoe for accessory flash. Lacks viewfinder.

60 Pentax Optio X Very good overall. Compact, no viewfinder, large LCD. Has fashionable twist design, 14 MB internal memory, requires included dock for downloading images and for charging, only fair battery life.

61 Panasonic Lumix DMC-FX7 Good overall. Subcompact, has image stabilizer, no viewfinder, has large LCD.

6-MEGAPIXEL MODELS

62 Fujifilm FinePix E550 A **CR Best Buy** Very good overall. 4X optical zoom, RAW image file format, has Super CCD HR sensor.

63 Fujifilm FinePix S7000 Very good overall. Excellent picture quality. Has 6X optical zoom, hot shoe, full manual control, dual memory slots, true 6 megapixel Super CCD that is capable of 12-megapixel output. Supports PictBridge direct print system.

64 Kodak EasyShare DX7630 Very good overall. Has multiple program modes. Very good battery life.

65 Olympus C-60 Zoom A **CR Best Buy** Very good overall. A CR Best Buy. Very good battery life. Supports PictBridge direct print system.

66 Casio Exilim EX-P600 Very good overall. Has 4X optical zoom, print image matching. Good battery life. Supports PictBridge direct print system.

DIGITAL CAMERAS

Profiles Model-by-Model (continued)

7-MEGAPIXEL MODELS

67 Canon PowerShot G6 Very good overall, 4X optical zoom, RAW image file format, SLR-style body, large LCD that flips and swivels, excellent battery life.

68 Olympus C-7070 Wide Zoom Very good overall. Excellent battery life. Extended wide-angle zoom from 28mm equivalent. Swivel LCD monitor. Uses CompactFlash I/II and xD-Picture Card memory cards. Can fix red-eye in flash photos in the camera. Has hot shoe for add-on flash. Noise reduction. Supports RAW image file format.

69 Sony Cyber-shot DSC-V3 Very good overall. Excellent battery life. Large LCD monitor. Can shoot close-up (macro) movies. Has hot shoe for add-on flash. Supports RAW image-file format. Has infrared night-shot mode. Has special scene modes (snow, beach, and candle).

70 Pentax Optio 750Z Very good overall, 5X optical zoom, large LCD that flips and swivels, automatic noise reduction at slow shutter speeds.

71 Sony Cyber-shot DSC-P150 Very good overall, compact, automatic noise reduction at slow shutter speeds, excellent battery life.

8-MEGAPIXEL MODELS

72 Nikon Coolpix 8700 Very good overall. Supports PictBridge direct print system. Has time-lapse movie option and interval timer photography option for time-lapse photography. Has option to create copy of RAW image in the TIFF format. Has 12 scene modes: portrait, party/indoor, night portrait, beach/snow, landscape, sunset, night landscape, fireworks show, close up, copy (for pictures of text or drawings), back light, and panorama assist. The included software may have problems modifying RAW images created by the camera.

73 Nikon Coolpix 8400 Very good overall. Ultra-wide-angle lens, noise reduction, has RAW Image file format, has hot shoe. Does not come with card, does not support PictBridge, does not support Print Image Matching.

74 Canon PowerShot Pro1 Very good overall. Has Interval shooting feature with intervals of 1 to 60 minute in 1-minute increments. Supports Canon Direct Print, Bubble Jet Direct, and PictBridge for printing directly from camera. Has wireless control, with wireless controller included in the camera kit. Can save images shot in JPEG format to the RAW format right after shooting, but the JPEG will not be saved. Can do rudimentary editing of video clips, deleting unwanted portions.

75 Olympus C-8080 Wide Zoom Very good overall. Supports PictBridge direct print system. Has shortest zoom ratio of 8-megapixel models tested, but longest normal focus (80 centimeters). Has USB 2.0 connectivity, streaming movie clips, 5X optical zoom.

76 Konica Minolta DiMAGE A2 Very good overall. Has anti-shake feature, depth-of-field preview, night movie mode to record under low light levels, and an auto select mode to automatically switch between standard and night movie depending on the lighting conditions. Supports PictBridge direct print system.

77 Sony Cyber-shot DSC-F828 Very good overall. Supports PictBridge direct print system. Can edit movies. Has two compression settings for the highest movie resolution setting. RAW file creates two formats, JPEG and SRF.

DVD RECORDERS

CR Quick Recommendations

Used at their highest-quality (one-hour-capacity fine) settings to record a clean TV signal to a DVD, most recorders produced excellent images. Recordings at the next-to-fine (SP) setting were very nearly as good and allow you to fit a two-hour movie on one DVD. But at the lowest (extended-play) setting, images had considerably less detail and a greater tendency to occasionally display fleeting little squares. (With combo DVD/hard-drive units, hard-drive recordings were identical in quality to content recorded on DVD at the same quality settings.)

In fact, overall quality at the extended settings differed little from what you'd get from VCR recordings–including those from the tested DVD/VCR units, which all yielded good-quality images at their best (SP) VCR setting and fair quality at their extended-play (EP) setting.

Like DVD players, DVD recorders varied in ease of use (remote, menus, etc.). But while all models except the JVC DR-MV1S (17) can provide a smoother picture when playing film-based commercial DVDs (for example, movies) on digital TVs, only the Pioneer DVR-320-S (3), JVC DR-M10S (4), and Pioneer DVR-520-H (14) provided similar performance with video-based commercial DVDs (say, TV series and concerts) played on a digital TV.

The Ratings rank models by overall performance. The Quick Picks consider other factors, such as price or capabilities.

Quick Picks

Best choices to record only to DVD:
1, 2 Panasonic, $280-$310
3 Pioneer, $295

The Panasonic DMR-E55K (1), Panasonic DMR-E65S (2), and Pioneer DVR-320-S (3) use VCR Plus+ to ease setup of future recordings. The Panasonic (2), a CR Best Buy, adds an electronic program guide and a memory-card reader (for JPEG image files) to what the Panasonic (1) offers, though the program guide isn't compatible with satellite-TV broadcasts. The Pioneer can automatically record from timer-controlled cable and satellite boxes.

If you want a built-in hard drive:
12, 13 Panasonic, $450-$500
14 Pioneer, $450

All three of these are exceptional choices. The Panasonic DMR-E85HS (12) can control a cable box and comes with TV Guide Onscreen, a free program guide that further simplifies TV recording (though it isn't compatible with satellite-TV broadcasts). For $50 more, the Panasonic DMR-E95HS (13) adds a bigger hard drive, a memory-card reader, and digital-video input from a camcorder. The Pioneer DVR-520-H (14) can automatically record from timer-controlled cable and satellite boxes.

Best choice for DVD and tape:
16 Panasonic, $350
17 JVC, $350

The Panasonic DMR-E75VS (16) is the best for extended-play recording. The JVC DR-MV1S (17) has two tuners, which allows you to record two off-air programs simultaneously; it's a good choice for use with a standard TV set.

Ratings

In performance order, within categories

Key number	Brand and model	Price	Overall score	Prerecorded DVDs	Recording (fine)	Recording (extended play)	Playback ease of use	Recording ease of use	Records to DVD-R	Records to DVD+R	Records to DVD+RW	Records to DVD-RW (VR)	Records to DVD-RW (video)	Records to DVD RAM	VCR Plus+	Cable box control	Satellite box control	Coaxial digital audio out	Optical digital audio out	Digital camcorder DVD in
DVD-ONLY RECORDERS																				
1	Panasonic DMR-E55K	$290		●	●	○	●	●	•					•	•				•	
2 CR BEST BUY	Panasonic DMR-E65S	220		●	●	○	●	●	•					•	•				•	
3	Pioneer DVR-320-S	260		●	●	◐	◐	◐	•	•	•	•	•		•			•	•	
4	JVC DR-M10S	290		●	●	◑	●	◐	•	•	•	•	•						•	
5	Sony RDR-GX300	300		●	●	◐	◑	◐	•	•	•		•						•	
6	Aspire Digital AD-8091	160		●	●	◐	●	◐	•	•	•		•						•	
7	Go-Video R6740	160		●	◐	◐	●	◐	•	•	•		•						•	
8	Samsung DVD-R100	300		●	●	◐	●	◐	•	•	•		•						•	
9	Toshiba D-R2	235		●	●	◐	●	◐	•										•	
10	Philips DVDR615	195		●	◐	◐	○	○		•	•								•	
11	RCA DRC8005N	285		●	◐	◐	◐	○		•	•								•	
DVD/HARD-DRIVE RECORDERS																				
12	Panasonic DMR-E85HS	455		●	●	○	●	●	•					•		•			•	
13	Panasonic DMR-E95HS	410		●	●	○	●	●	•					•					•	•
14	Pioneer DVR-520-H	415		●	●	◐	●	◐	•	•	•	•	•				•		•	
15	Toshiba RD-XS32	425		●	●	◐	●	●	•					•					•	•

DVD RECORDERS

Ratings (continued)

In performance order, within categories

Excellent ● | Very good ◐ | Good ○ | Fair ◐ | Poor ●

Key number	Brand and model	Price	Overall score (0-100, P/F/G/VG/E)	Prerecorded DVDs	Recording (fine)	Recording (extended play)	Playback ease of use	Recording ease of use	Records to DVD-R	Records to DVD+R	Records to DVD+RW	Records to DVD-RW (VR)	Records to DVD-RW (video)	Records to DVD RAM	VCR Plus+	Cable box control	Satellite box control	Coaxial digital audio out	Optical digital audio out	Digital camcorder DV in
DVD RECORDERS WITH BUILT-IN VCR																				
16	Panasonic DMR-E75VS	360	━━━	●	●	○	◐	●	●			●		●	●	●	●		●	
17	JVC DR-MV1S	320	━━━	●	●	◐	◐	●	●						●	●	●		●	
18	Toshiba D-VR3	325	━━━	●	◐	◐	◐	○	●					●	●	●	●		●	
19	RCA DRC8300N	330	━━━	●	●	◐	◐	○	●	●	●				●	●	●		●	

Guide to the Ratings

OVERALL SCORE is based mainly on picture quality and ease of use. **PRERECORDED DVDS** indicates the sharpness and detail of images when playing prerecorded discs. **PICTURE QUALITY** for Fine recording and Extended recording indicates the sharpness and detail of recordings made in those modes to both blank DVDs (at the minimum one-hour setting for fine and a six-hour setting for extended-play) and, when applicable, the unit's hard-drive. (Recordings made at quality setting immediately below fine scored only slightly below fine-mode quality.) **EASE OF USE** assesses user-friendliness of the remote control, console front panel, and menus, for basic Playback and basic Recording and set-up functions. **RECORDING DISC TYPES** indicates the types of discs on which each player can record and play back from other machines. **VCR PLUS+** is a capability that simplifies time-shift recording by letting you punch in a program's code (from TV listings) rather than the program's date, time, and channel. **CABLE BOX CONTROL** and **SATELLITE BOX CONTROL** indicate a recording device's ability to change channels automatically on a cable or satellite box—needed to record programs from several channels when time-shift recording. **COAXIAL** and **OPTICAL DIGITAL AUDIO OUT** are important if you plan to pipe the signal from the DVD recorder into a home-theater system that has a digital receiver. All DVD recorders have digital audio outputs—coaxial, optical, or both. **DIGITAL CAMCORDER DV IN** is the ability to accept audio/video input (for recording) from a digital camcorder's DV (digital video) output.

Based on testing in Consumer Reports in March 2005, with updated prices and availability.

Profiles Model-by-Model

DVD-ONLY RECORDERS

1 Panasonic DMR-E55K Excellent. Simultaneous record/playback when using DVD-RAM discs. Depending on the recording media used, editing capability ranges from limited to full. Plays DVD-Audio in stereo only.

2 Panasonic DMR-E65S A **CR Best Buy.** Excellent. Simultaneous record/playback when using DVD-RAM discs. Depending on the recording media used, editing capability ranges from limited to full. Reads JPEG image files from DVD-RAM (but not CD-R/RW) discs and memory cards and can copy JPEG files between the two. Plays DVD-Audio in stereo only. Interactive electronic programming guide does not work with satellite-TV systems.

3 Pioneer DVR-320-S Very good. Progressive-scan video is smoother than that of most other units tested when playing back video-based, pre-recorded DVDs. Simultaneous record/playback when using DVD-RW discs in VR mode. Time-shift recording can be controlled by timer-controlled cable or satellite box. Depending on the recording media used, editing capability ranges from very limited to full.

4 JVC DR-M10S Very good. Progressive-scan video is smoother than that of other units tested when playing back video-based, pre-recorded DVDs. Simultaneous record/playback when using DVD-RAM discs. Depending on the recording media used, editing capability ranges from very limited to full.

5 Sony RDR-GX300 Very good. Simultaneous record/playback when using DVD-RW discs in VR mode. Depending on the recording media used, editing capability ranges from limited to full.

6 Aspire Digital AD-8091 Very good overall, but has limited editing capability with any recording media. Progressive-scan playback of video-based, pre-recorded DVDs is no smoother than that of standard players. Has Dolby Digital decoder. Lacks auto clock-set. Worse performance, in our tests, at playing damaged CDs than most other models tested. Failed to play CD-audio portion of hybrid SACD discs.

7 Go-Video R6740 Very good overall, but has limited editing capability with any recording media. Lacks auto clock-set.

8 Samsung DVD-R100 Very good overall, but progressive-scan video is much worse than that of other units tested when playing back video-based, pre-recorded DVDs; during scenes with panning camera, images becomes blurry. Simultaneous record/playback when using DVD-RAM discs. Depending on the recording media used, editing capability ranges from limited to full.

9 Toshiba D-R2 Very good. Simultaneous record/playback when using DVD-RAM discs. Depending on the recording media used, editing capability ranges from limited to full. Worse performance, in our tests, at playing damaged CDs than most other models tested.

(continued)

DVD RECORDERS

Profiles Model-by-Model (continued)

10 Philips DVDR615 Very good overall, but progressive-scan playback of video-based, pre-recorded DVDs is no smoother than that of standard players. Depending on the recording media used, editing capability ranges from limited to moderate.

11 RCA DRC8005N Very Good. Depending on the recording media used, editing capability ranges from very limited to moderate. Has USB port to connect optional external-media reader for reading or copying MP3 or JPEG files. Worse performance, in our tests, at playing damaged DVDs and CDs than most other models tested.

DVD/HARD-DRIVE RECORDERS

12 Panasonic DMR-E85HS Excellent. Simultaneous record/playback when using hard drive or DVD-RAM discs, and can record to one type of media while playing back another. Depending on the recording media used, editing capability ranges from limited to full. Plays DVD-Audio in stereo only. Interactive electronic programming guide does not work with satellite-TV systems.

13 Panasonic DMR-E95HS Excellent. Simultaneous record/playback when using hard drive or DVD-RAM discs, and can record to one type of media while playing back another. Reads JPEG image files from DVD-RAM (but not CD-R/RW) discs and memory cards and can copy JPEG files between the two. Depending on the recording media used, editing capability ranges from limited to full. Plays DVD-Audio in stereo only. Interactive electronic programming guide does not work with satellite-TV systems.

14 Pioneer DVR-520-H Very good. Progressive-scan video is smoother than that of most other units tested when playing back video-based, pre-recorded DVDs. Simultaneous record/playback when using hard drive or DVD-RW discs in VR mode, and can record to one type of media while playing back another. Time-shift recording can be controlled by timer-controlled cable or satellite box. Depending on the recording media used, editing capability ranges from very limited to full.

15 Toshiba RD-XS32 Very good. Simultaneous record/playback when using hard drive or DVD-RAM discs, and can record to one type of media while playing back another. Depending on the recording media used, editing capability ranges from limited to full. Worse performance, in our tests, at playing damaged CDs than most other models tested.

DVD RECORDERS WITH BUILT-IN VCR

16 Panasonic DMR-E75VS Excellent. Simultaneous record/playback when using DVD-RAM discs, and can record to one type of media while playing back another. Depending on the recording media used, editing capability ranges from limited to full. Plays DVD-Audio in stereo only.

17 JVC DR-MV1S Very good overall, but progressive-scan playback of most movies on pre-recorded DVDs is no smoother than that of standard players. Has two TV tuners; allows DVD recorder and VCR to independently record two different TV channels at once. Time-shift recording (onto DVD only) can be controlled by timer-controlled cable or satellite box. Simultaneous record/playback when using DVD-RAM discs, and can record to one type of media while playing back another. Depending on the recording media used, editing capability ranges from very limited to full. Can provide progressive-scan video output when playing VHS tapes; improvement over standard VHS, while not equivalent to DVD, is noticeable when viewing certain motion scenes. Can output DVD video and audio to antenna/cable input of older TVs.

18 Toshiba D-VR3 Very good. Simultaneous record/playback when using DVD-RAM discs, and can record to one type of media while playing back another. Depending on the recording media used, editing capability ranges from limited to full. Can output DVD video and audio to antenna/cable input of older TVs.

19 RCA DRC8300N Very good. Depending on the recording media used, editing capability ranges from very limited to moderate. Can output DVD video and audio to antenna/cable input of older TVs. Worse performance, in our tests, at playing damaged DVDs and CDs than most other models tested.

HOME THEATER IN A BOX

CR Quick Recommendations

Many of the systems in the Ratings—even some toward the bottom of the list—were solid performers. Models judged excellent for sound had the crispest, smoothest, fullest audio without excessive bass. Those scoring very good should suit all but the pickiest. Paying more may get you more features and inputs but won't necessarily get you better performance.

Quick Picks

For the best sound and simple design:
1 Yamaha $500
2 Yamaha $700

The two Yamahas produced excellent sound and were easy to use, with lots of convenience features. Both support Dolby 6.1 and have a third rear speaker. Yamaha (1) has no DVD player and has midsized speakers; (2) has a player that's separate from the receiver and has small speakers.

For excellent sound plus sleek styling:
3 Kenwood $900
5 Sony $800
7 Sony $700

The Kenwood (3) has two slim towers, three small rear speakers, and a separate DVD player. The Sony (5) has four slim towers; (7) has two towers and two small cubes. Both have a combo receiver/DVD player. All three systems support Dolby 6.1 surround.

For excellent sound at the lowest price:
9 Panasonic $400
14 Sony $350

You won't get all the bells and whistles, but you will get great performance. The Sony (14) has a receiver/DVD player. Its style is functional; speakers are small cubes. The Panasonic (9) has a sleeker design and adds a VCR to the receiver/DVD player. Its speakers are small cubes. Both lack front-panel input and volume control on the subwoofer.

If you want fewer wires:
12 Samsung $500

The Samsung has very good sound, a sleek design, and wireless rear speakers. The DVD player and receiver are combined.

For decent sound, sleek styling, low cost:
17 JVC $300

The JVC has a very slim console and tiny silver speakers. Sound was very good. The DVD player and receiver are combined.

Ratings

In performance order

Key number	Brand & model	Price	Overall score	Sound quality	Ease of use	Features	Separate	Integrated	No. of discs	VCR	6.1 surround	Front input	Onscreen display	Composite-video in/out	Component-video in/out
	DVD PLAYERS														
1	Yamaha YHT-450	$500		●	●	●			N/A		●	●		4/1	2/0
2	Yamaha YHT-750	700		●	●	●	●		5		●	●		4/1	2/0
3	Kenwood HTB-S715DV	900		●	○	○	●		1		●	●		5/2	2/0
4	Onkyo HT-S777C	700		●	●	●	●		6		●	●		4/1	2/0
5	Sony DAV-FR9	800		●	○	○		●	5		●		●	0/0	0/0
6	Panasonic SC-HT920	500		●	○	○		●	5				●	0/0	0/0
7	Sony DAV-FR8	700		●	○	○		●	5		●		●	0/0	0/0
8	Sony HT-V2000DP	400		●	●	○		●	1	●				0/0	0/0
9	Panasonic SC-HT820V	400		●	○	○		●	5	●			●	1/1	0/0
10	Philips MX5600D	500		●	○	○		●	5				●	0/0	0/0
11	Cambridge Soundworks MegaTheater 505	500		●	○	○		●	1			●	●	3/1	0/0
12	Samsung HT-DB390	500		●	○	○		●	1				●	2/0	0/0
13	Pioneer HTZ-940DV	1,200		●	○	○		●	1					0/0	0/0
14	Sony DAV-BC150	350		●	○	◐		●	5					0/0	0/0
15	Toshiba SD-V55HT	300		●	○	○		●	1	●			●	2/1	0/0
16	JVC TH-M505	400		●	○	○		●	5				●	1/0	0/0
17	JVC TH-M303	300		●	○	○		●	5				●	1/0	0/0
18	Samsung HT-DS660T	600		○	○	○		●	5					2/0	1/0

Guide to the Ratings

OVERALL SCORE is based mostly on sound quality. **SOUND QUALITY** represents accuracy of the front speakers, subwoofer, center-channel speaker, and surround speakers, with tone controls adjusted for best sound. **EASE OF USE** reflects the design of the front panel and the remote control, legibility of controls, and ease of setup. **FEATURES SCORE** is based on the presence or absence of useful features. The inputs and outputs shown are on the receiver. (Does not include outputs on the DVD player, if that is separate.) **PRICE** is approximate retail.
Based on testing in Consumer Reports in November 2004, with updated prices and availability.

MONITORS

CR Quick Recommendations

Most LCDs offer very good display quality. Models differ in the features they provide and how well-designed their controls are. A 17-inch model will meet most people's needs. Look to a 19-inch or larger model only if you have poor vision and prefer a larger screen, routinely edit photos, run multiple applications, or play games often.

The Ratings rank monitors strictly according to performance. Quick Picks considers other factors, such as price.

Quick Picks

For Macintosh users:
9 Apple $1,000

Designed for use with a Power Mac, this 20-inch display is the smallest and cheapest Apple LCD. Its very wide viewing angle and wide shape make it ideal for editing photos, running programs simultaneously, playing games, or watching videos. But you pay a premium. Any of the LCD monitors that are Quick Picks will work with Macintoshes.

For a full-featured 17-inch LCD:
1 Dell, $350
2 Samsung, $420

Both are very good performers and easy to use, with displays that can be rotated (to portrait orientation) and adjusted for height. The Dell, a CR Best Buy, was one of the lowest-priced LCDs we tested.

If convenience doesn't matter:
5 Envision $280

This is a good performer, can be adjusted for height, and is the lowest-priced LCD we tested. But control buttons and on-screen menus are harder to use than on most monitors.

For a full-featured 19- to 20-inch monitor:
11 Samsung $465
12 Dell $500
13 Dell $750

All are very good and can be rotated and height-adjusted. The Samsung, a CR Best Buy, has a 19-inch image. The 20-inch Dell has a very wide viewing angle, USB 2.0 hub, and composite- and S-video inputs to connect a DVD player or camcorder.

Ratings

In performance order

Ratings scale: Excellent ● | Very good ◕ | Good ◐ | Fair ◔ | Poor ○

Key number	Brand and model	Price	Overall score (P F G VG E)	Viewable image (in.)	Display quality	Ease of use	Wide viewing angle	Detachable video cable	DVI input	DVI cable included	Display rotates	Adjustable height	Warranty is 3 years
17-INCH LCD MONITORS													
1 (CR Best Buy)	Dell UltraSharp 1704FPV	$350		17	●	◕	●		●	●	●	●	●
2	Samsung SyncMaster 711t	420		17	●	◕	●	●	●		●	●	●
3	IBM ThinkVision L170P	445		17	●	◕			●		●	●	●
4	KDS Radius Rad-7c	450		17	●	◕		●				●	
5	Envision EN-7220	280		17	●	○						●	
6	ViewSonic Professional Series VP171s	400		17	○	○			●				●
7	NEC MultiSync LCD1770NX	365		17	○	○			●			●	●
19- TO 21-INCH LCD MONITORS													
8	Samsung SyncMaster 213t	900		21	●	◕	●	●	●	●	●	●	●
9	Apple 20" Cinema Display	1000		20	●	○	●		●	●			●
10	NEC AccuSync LCD200VX	725		20	●	○							●
11 (CR Best Buy)	Samsung SyncMaster 910t	465		19	●	◕			●		●	●	●
12	Dell UltraSharp 1905FP	500		19	●	○			●		●	●	●
13	Dell UltraSharp 2005FPW	750		20	●	◕			●		●	●	●
14	Gateway FPD1950	450		19	●	◕	●		●				●
15	KDS Radius Rad-9gs	390		19	●	○							●
16	NEC MultiSync LCD1935NXM	475		19	●	○	●	●	●				●
17	Sony SDM-HS95P	700		19	●	○			●				●
18	ViewSonic Professional Series VP912b	580		19	○	○			●		●	●	●

MONITORS

Guide to the Ratings

OVERALL SCORE is based on display quality, ease of use, and features. **VIEWABLE IMAGE** is our measurement of the viewable image size, in inches. **DISPLAY QUALITY** covers image clarity, color accuracy, and contrast. It's based on the judgments of a panel of trained viewers who looked at text and photographs on each monitor, as well as laboratory measurements. **EASE OF USE** includes readability of buttons and other controls, the clarity of onscreen control menus, and the ability to tilt the monitor on its base. **FEATURES** columns list **WIDE VIEWING ANGLE**, indicating which models our tests showed can be viewed clearly from positions far off the centerline (most models are fine for most viewers); monitors with a **DETACHABLE VIDEO CABLE** (more convenient to repair if the cable breaks or malfunctions); a **DVI INPUT**, which requires a digital output from the PC, making it easier than with analog VGA to configure your monitor for the best picture quality; a display that **ROTATES** from landscape to portrait orientation and that adjusts for **HEIGHT**; and a **THREE-YEAR WARRANTY. PRICE** is approximate retail.

Based on testing in Consumer Reports in June 2005, with updated prices and availability.

MP3 PLAYERS

CR Quick Recommendations

Like most digital devices, MP3 players perform very well at their key task. As the Ratings show, the audio output from the headphone jack of the best MP3 players we tested produced near-CD-quality sound, and the others were nearly as good. The headphones supplied with the players were a bit better on some models than others, though even the worst performed respectably.

Flash-memory players offer the smallest, lightest, and most affordable way to enjoy MP3 music on the go, and are less likely to break if accidentally dropped than are their hard-disk cousins. But hard-disk players have larger LCD displays, better controls, and much greater storage capacity. The microdrive 4 gigabyte or 5 GB models offer an appealing compromise between price and capacity.

All players accept music you already own on CD, which you convert into digital music files and transfer to the player using supplied software and a computer. Only one Sony we tested, the Sony Psyc Network Walkman NW-E105PS (512 MB) (3) can play MP3 files. With the Sony Network Walkman NW-E75 (256 MB) (5) and Sony Network Walkman NW-HD1 (20 GB) (12), you have to convert MP3 files to ATRAC—Sony's own format—a slow extra step. Avoid those two unless you're prepared to do extra work to load MP3 files. Also, be aware that the two iRiver models and the Archos player can't play any copyright-protected MP3 music—which precludes shopping from any of the growing number of online music stores. The remaining players work with the many online stores that use WMA format—except the Sony models, which can only play music downloaded from Sony's own Connect online store, and the three Apple models, which only work with Apple's iTunes site. As always, check to make sure the player will work with your computer and operating system before purchasing it.

The Ratings rank models within types in performance order. The Quick Picks list models you might consider based on such factors, as value and capabilities.

Quick Picks

If low price, light weight, and small size are paramount:
1 iRiver, $130
2 Creative, $85
3 Sony, $100

This category, comprising flash-memory players, is the only one in which we do not recommend an Apple iPod; the Apple iPod Shuffle M9724LL/A (512 MB), while the smallest and lightest player in our tests, lacks a display screen, cannot handle more than one playlist at a time, and has relatively short playback time. The iRiver iFP-790 (256 MB) (1) and Creative MuVo TX FM (256 MB) (2) are almost as small—about the size of a pack of gum—and have better controls and more features, including an LCD display, an FM radio, and a built-in microphone. Only the iRiver iFP-790 (256 MB) (1) lets you scroll within a playlist to find songs easily and, along with the Apple iPod Shuffle M9724LL/A (512 MB), works with Macintosh computers. But choose the iRiver only if you already have a large CD collection, because it does not play music bought from online stores. The pocket-watch-sized Sony Psyc Network Walkman NW-E105PS (512 MB) (3) couples very good overall performance with long playback time. However, some controls are awkwardly located on the back of the unit.

For the best combination of huge capacity and a fairly low price:
11 Apple, $290
13 Creative, $230
14 Dell, $250
16 Rio, $200

Like the microdrive players we tested, these hard-drive models have simple controls for managing your music collection. Their differences: They can hold about 5,000 songs and are slightly larger and heavier. Choose the Apple iPod M9282LL/A (20 GB) (11) if you value ease of use over a wide range of choices in online music. If you want access to a variety of online music stores—or do not own a Macintosh computer—consider the Creative Zen Touch (20 GB) (13), Dell DJ (20 GB) (14), or Rio Karma (20 GB) (17). The Creative Zen Touch (20 GB) (13) offers exceptionally long playing time on a single charge; the Dell DJ (20 GB) (14) features intuitive, iPod-simple controls and menus. The Rio Karma (20 GB) (16) offers premium-player features, including a line output for connecting to a home audio system, at a bargain-basement price.

For fairly high capacity in a compact size:
7 Apple, $195
8 Dell, $180

Both the Apple iPod Mini (4 GB) (7) and Dell DJ (5 GB) (8)—holding about 1,000 and 1,250 songs respectively—fit comfortably in most palms and have very good controls and displays for finding songs on the fly or editing playlists. The Apple iPod Mini (4 GB) (7) provides a seamless link between computer, player, and Apple's iTunes online music store, though you would not be able to shop for music anywhere else. The Dell gives you more options for purchasing music online and, unlike the Apple, allows you to delete songs. But it would not work with a Mac.

If you need a hard-drive player with an FM radio:
15 Samsung, $250

These very good performers provide new channels of entertainment when your playlists get played out. The Samsung YH-920 GS (20 GB) (15) lacks a microphone but allows you to record FM broadcasts directly from its onboard tuner.

MP3 PLAYERS

Ratings

In performance order, within categories

Legend: ● Excellent | ◖ Very good | ○ Good | ◐ Fair | ● Poor

Key number	Brand and model	Price	Overall score (0-100)	Signal quality	Ease of use	Headphone quality	Playback time (hr.)	Dimensions (WxHxD in.)	Weight (oz.)	Audio playback formats	Mac-compatible	FM radio	Built-in microphone	Firmware upgradeable	Plays online music
FLASH-MEMORY PLAYERS															
1	iRiver iFP-790 (256 MB)	$130		◖	◖	◖	32	3.4x1.3x1.1	2.2	MP3, WMA, OGG, ASF		•	•	•	
2	Creative MuVo TX FM (256 MB)	85		●	○	○	18	3.0x1.4x0.6	1.6	MP3, WMA		•	•	•	
3	Sony Psyc Network Walkman NW-E105PS (512 MB)	100		●	○	◖	45	2.3x2.2x0.7	1.4	MP3, ATRAC3, ATRAC3 Plus					•
4	Rio Forge Sport (256 MB)	145		◖	○	○	14	2.6x2.5x0.8	2.2	MP3, WMA, AA	•	•			•
5	Sony Network Walkman NW-E75 (256 MB)	155		●	○	○	63	2.3x1.6x0.6	1.8	ATRAC3, ATRAC3 Plus					•
6	Apple iPod Shuffle M9724LL/A (512 MB)	100		◖	○	◖	10	1.0x3.4x0.3	.8	MP3, AAC, WAV, AA	•				
MICRODRIVE HARD-DISK PLAYERS (4 TO 5 GB)															
7	Apple iPod Mini (4 GB)	195		◖	◖	◖	10	2.0x3.6x0.5	3.6	MP3, AAC, WAV, AA, AIFF, Apple Lossless	•			•	
8	Dell DJ (5 GB)	180		●	◖	○	10	2.1x3.6x0.5	3.8	MP3, WMA, WAV					•
9	Rio Carbon (5 GB)	190		◖	◖	○	16	2.4x3.2x0.5	3.1	MP3, WMA, AA	•		•		•
10	Creative Nomad MuVo2 (4 GB)	200		●	○	○	17	2.8x2.6x0.8	3.5	MP3, WMA, WAV					•
HARD-DISK PLAYERS (20 TO 30 GB)															
11	Apple iPod M9282LL/A (20 GB)	290		◖	◖	◖	14	2.4x4.1x0.6	5.6	MP3, AAC, WAV, AA, AIFF, Apple Lossless	•			•	
12	Sony Network Walkman NW-HD1 (20 GB)	350		●	○	○	30	2.5x3.5x0.5	4	ATRAC3, ATRAC3 Plus					•
13	Creative Zen Touch (20 GB)	230		●	◖	○	26	2.7x4.1x0.9	7.2	MP3, WMA, WAV				•	•
14	Dell DJ (20 GB)	250		●	◖	○	13	2.4x4.0x0.7	6.5	MP3, WMA, WAV					•
15	Samsung YH-920 GS (20 GB)	250		●	◖	◖	10	2.4x4.2x0.6	5.4	MP3, WMA, AA				•	•
16	Rio Karma (20 GB)	200		◖	◖	○	16	3.1x3.1x1.1	6	MP3, WMA, OGG, FLAC					•
17	RCA Lyra RD 2850 (20 GB)	215		●	○	○	9	2.9x3.4x1.0	5.2	MP3, WMA, MP3Pro	•	•		•	
18	Archos Gmini 220 (20 GB)	270		●	◖	○	7	2.7x3.1x0.8	6	MP3, WMA, WAV				•	

Guide to the Ratings

OVERALL SCORE is within types, in performance order. There are two types; a **STANDARD-CAPACITY** player is a solid-state device, with no moving parts, typically small and lightweight with storage capacity measured in megabytes. A **HIGH-CAPACITY** player has a hard drive with storage capacity measured in gigabytes and is typically larger and heavier. **OVERALL SCORE** is based primarily on signal quality, ease of use, and playback time, with headphone quality also considered. For signal quality and playback time, all uncompressed (WAV or audio CD files) music and test sources were ripped (encoded) to the manufacturer's recommended CD-quality setting (e.g., 128 Kbps rate) using the music-management software application provided with the player. If the player was not bundled with ripping software, MusicMatch was used. **SIGNAL QUALITY** mainly reflects judgments from an expert listening panel comparing the player with a test audio CD, using high-fidelity headphones, and includes lab measurements of the player's frequency-response flatness accuracy and any noise or distortion. **EASE OF USE** mainly covers player characteristics that aid in convenience and versatility. These primarily include the accessibility, readability, and tactile feedback of the controls, and the readability and breadth of the information in the display (such as music-track data and battery-life indicator). **HEADPHONE QUALITY** mainly reflects judgments from an expert listening panel of the headphone compared to a high-fidelity headphone using a test audio CD, and includes lab measurements of the headphone-frequency response accuracy. **PLAYBACK TIME** (hr.) reflects lab measurements of continuous playback time, to the nearest hour, using new alkaline or fully charged rechargeable batteries, at maximum volume without clipping and display backlight at minimum. **DIMENSIONS** are measured to the nearest tenth of an inch. **WEIGHT** is how much the player weighs in ounces including batteries, but not including accessories; for models with no internal memory, the memory card is included. **AUDIO PLAYBACK FORMATS** are the audio format(s) the player will recognize and be able to play. Even when a format isn't supported, most players come with music-management software that can convert or "rip" the file into a format the player can play. Some formats supported for voice are ADPCM and ACELP.
Based on testing for Consumer Reports online in July 2005, with updated prices and availability.

MP3 PLAYERS

Profiles Model-by-Model

FLASH-MEMORY PLAYERS (128 MB to 1 GB)

1 iRiver iFP-790 (256 MB) Among the best choices in flash-memory players. Lets you scroll within a playlist, but doesn't play files purchased from online music stores. Has line input, FM radio recording capability, custom and presets equalizer, A-B repeat, and alarm clock. On player, can delete files, but can't edit playlist or rename files. Includes earbud-type headphone. Uses one AA battery. USB2 interface. Similar moels: iFP-795 (512 MB), $145 iFP-799 (1 GB), $190.

2 Creative MuVo TX FM (256 MB) Among the best and least-expensive flash-memory players. Can play WMA-format files purchased from online music stores. Has FM-radio recording capability, custom and presets equalizer, and A-B repeat. Doesn't list tracks. On player, can delete files, but can't edit playlist or rename files. Includes earbud-type headphone. Uses one AAA battery. USB2 interface. Similar models: TX FM (128 MB) $70, MuVo TX FM (512 MB) $115.

3 Sony Psyc Network Walkman NW-E105PS (512 MB) Among the best choices in flash-memory players, with long playback time. Pocket-watch size and shape. Can play ATRAC-format files purchased from Sony Connect online music store. Has custom equalizer, and A-B repeat. Doesn't list tracks. On player can't edit playlist, rename or delete files. Includes earbud-type headphone. Uses one AAA battery. USB2 Interface. Similar models: Network Walkman NW-E107 (1 GB), $150 Psyc Network Walkman NW-E103PS (256 MB), $90.

4 Rio Forge Sport (256 MB) A fine, if somewhat pricey, player. Can play WMA-format files purchased from online music stores. Can accept a MultiMedia or Secure Digital memory card. Has FM radio recording capability, stopwatch, clock, and custom and presets equalizer. Doesn't list tracks. On player can't edit playlist, rename or delete files. Includes over-the-ear, earbud-type headphone. Uses one AAA battery. USB2 Interface. Similar models: Forge Sport (128 MB), $115 Forge Sport (512 MB), $180.

5 Sony Network Walkman NW-E75 (256 MB) A fine, if somewhat pricey performer. Plays only ATRAC-format files, and can only download songs from Sony Connect online music store. MP3, WMA, or WAV files have to be converted to ATRAC during transfer to player. This increases transfer time and amount of disk space used on computer since multiple file formats will reside on the computer. Doesn't list tracks. On player, can edit playlist, but can't rename or delete files. No custom or presets equalizer. Includes earbud-type headphone. Uses one AAA battery. USB2 interface.

6 Apple iPod Shuffle M9724LL/A (512 MB) Fine player, but lacks a display screen, can't handle more than one playlist at a time, and has relatively short playback time. Can play Apple AAC-format files purchased from iTunes online music store. Includes earbud-type headphone. Has nonremoveable battery that charges via USB2 interface. Similar model: iPod Shuffle M9725LL/A (1 GB), $150.

MICRODRIVE HARD-DISK PLAYERS (4 TO 5 GB)

7 Apple iPod Mini (4 GB) Among the best microdrive players. Can play Apple AAC-format files purchased from iTunes online music store. Has presets equalizer, contact and calendar appointment application, alarm clock, games, and can display text files. On player, can edit playlist, but can't rename or delete files. Includes earbud-type headphone. Has non-removeable battery. USB2 and FireWire interface.

8 Dell DJ (5 GB) Among the best microdrive players. Can play WMA-format files purchased from online music stores. Has custom and presets equalizer, calendar and clock. On player, can edit playlist and delete files, but can't rename files. Includes earbud-type headphone. Has nonremoveable battery. USB2 Interface.

9 Rio Carbon (5 GB) A fine player. Can play WMA-format files purchased from online music stores. Has stopwatch, clock, and custom and presets equalizer. Doesn't list tracks. On player, can't edit playlist, rename or delete files. Includes earbud-type headphone. Has nonremoveable battery. USB2 interface.

10 Creative Nomad MuVo2 (4 GB) A fine player. Can play WMA-format files purchased from online music stores. Has custom and presets equalizer. Doesn't list tracks. On player, can delete files, but can't edit playlist or rename files. Includes earbud-type headphone. Removeable rechargable replacement battery costs about $50. USB2 interface.

HARD-DISK PLAYERS (20 TO 30 GB)

11 Apple iPod M9282LL/A (20 GB) Among the best hard-disk players. Can play Apple AAC-format files purchased from iTunes online music store. Has presets equalizer, contact and calendar appointment application, alarm clock, games, and can display text files. On player, can edit playlist, but can't rename or delete files. Includes earbud-type headphone. Has nonremoveable battery. USB2 and FireWire interface.

MP3 PLAYERS

Profiles Model-by-Model (continued)

12 Sony Network Walkman NW-HD1 (20 GB) A fine, if somewhat pricey, performer. Plays only ATRAC-format files, and can only download songs from Sony Connect online music store. MP3, WMA, or WAV files have to be converted to ATRAC during transfer to player. This increases transfer time and amount of disk spaced used on computer since multiple file formats will reside on the computer. Has A-B repeat. Has line output, custom and presets equalizer, and clock. On player, can't edit playlist, rename or delete files. Needs docking station to transfer music or charge. Includes earbud-type headphone. Has nonremoveable battery. USB2 interface.

13 Creative Zen Touch (20 GB) A fine player. Can play WMA-format files purchased from online music stores. Has custom and presets equalizer. On player, can edit playlist and delete files, but can't rename files. Includes earbud-type headphone. Has non-emoveable battery. USB2 interface.

14 Dell DJ (20 GB) A fine player. Can play WMA-format files purchased from online music stores. Has custom and presets equalizer, calendar and clock. On player, can edit playlist and delete files, but can't rename files. Includes earbud-type headphone. Has nonremoveable battery. USB2 interface. Similar model: DJ (30 GB) $300.

15 Samsung YH-920 GS (20 GB) A fine player. Can play WMA-format files purchased from online music stores. Has line input, FM radio recording capability, and presets equalizer. On player, can't edit playlist, rename or delete files. Includes earbud-type headphone, and wired remote control. Has nonremoveable battery. USB2 interface.

16 Rio Karma (20 GB) A fine player. Can play WMA-format files purchased from online music stores. Has line output using included docking station, stopwatch, clock, custom and presets equalizer, and A-B repeat. On player, can edit playlist and delete files, but can't rename files. Includes earbud-type headphone. Has nonremoveable battery. USB2 interface. Has an ethernet port to connect to a network.

17 RCA Lyra RD 2850 (20 GB) There are better choices. Can play WMA-format files purchased from online music stores. Includes cassette adapter and player charger for car. Has FM radio recording capability, and custom and presets equalizer. On player, can't edit playlist, rename or delete files. Includes clip-on, on-the-ear type headphone. Has nonremoveable battery. USB2 interface.

18 Archos Gmini 220 (20 GB) There are better choices. Doesn't play files purchased from online music stores. Can copy files directly from a CompactFlash card, though can't play music files from the card. Has line input, custom and presets equalizer, clock, and can display images. On player, can edit playlist, rename, and delete files. Includes earbud-type headphone with volume control. Has nonremoveable battery. USB2 interface.

PDAs

CR Quick Recommendations

The Ratings tell you which models were easiest to use, had the longest battery life, and performed best overall. The table also indicates the models' major features. Quick Picks highlights good values that our experts consider full-featured or especially well designed.

Quick Picks

For a basic organizer at a good price:
- **3** palmOne, $250
- **17** Dell, $300

The palmOne Tungsten E2 (3) and the Dell Axim X50 416 MHZ (17) are well priced yet offer plenty. Both have Bluetooth capability and let you view pictures, listen to music, and see daily tasks at a glance. The Tungsten E2 retains all of your data automatically in its non-volatile memory, even when the battery has drained completely. The Dell Axim X50 series includes a task-switcher program that lets you manage multiple tasks better than other Pocket PCs, and it supports multiple memory cards. Another unit, the palmOne Zire 21 (11), is the only monochrome unit tested. It's low-priced and fine for to-do lists and contacts.

For a full-featured Palm OS unit:
- **1, 2** palmOne, $360-$500

The palmOne LifeDrive (1) is the closest thing we've seen to a "laptop replacement" in a PDA. It has an internal 3.7GB hard drive and lets you view and store photos, listen to music, manage email, and edit documents and spreadsheets. You can access the hard drive via a desktop computer. Like the LifeDrive, the palmOne Tungsten T5 (2) combines the versatility of typical Palm OS models with the drag-and-drop convenience of the Pocket PC. It has 64 MB of user memory, plus another 161 MB that a connected Windows computer can recognize as an external drive. Both models have Bluetooth capability, and the LifeDrive has Wi-Fi as well.

For a Windows look and feel in a PDA:
- **13** Hewlett-Packard, $395
- **15** Dell, $500

The Hewlett-Packard iPAQ h4355 (13) is well designed and has Wi-Fi and Bluetooth capability. It squeezes a usable keyboard and easily readable display into a slim case. The Dell Axim X50v (15) is similar to the Dell Axim X50 416 MHZ (17) but has a faster processor, more non-volatile memory, and a larger display that is very readable, even in bright sunlight. It also has both Wi-Fi and Bluetooth capability.

For a portable navigation system:
- **9** Garmin, $465

The Garmin iQUE 3600 (9) is the only unit tested to include a GPS-equipped navigation system. It was easy to use, though its battery life was lacking.

Ratings

In performance order, within categories.

Key	Brand and model	Price	Ease of use	Battery life	Display	Convenience	InSync	Pocket size	Memory (MB)	Expansion card	Replaceable battery	Wireless connectivity	Display size (in.)	Office software	MP3 player
PALM OS MODELS															
1	palmOne LifeDrive	$500	◐	○	◐	●	●		65	●				3.8	●	●
2	palmOne Tungsten T5	360	◐	○	○	●	●		64	●				3.7	●	●
3	palmOne Tungsten E2	250	◐	◐	○	○	◐		30	●				3	●	●
4	palmOne Tungsten C	360	○	◐	◐	○	◐		51	●				3	●	
5	palmOne Zire 72	290	◐	◐	◐	○	◐		25	●				3	●	●
6	palmOne TungstenE	200	◐	◐	○	○	◐		29	●				3	●	●
7	Garmin iQUE 3600	465	◐	◑	◐	○	○		23	●				3.7	●	●
8	palmOne Zire 31	150	○	◐	◑	○	◐		14	●				2.6		●
9	palmOne Zire 21	100	○	○	○	○	◐		7.3					2.7		
POCKET PC MODELS															
10	ASUS MyPal A716	395	◐	◐	◐	●	◐		56	●			●	3.5	●	●
11	Hewlett-Packard iPAQ h4355 (iPAQ h4350 440)	395	◐	◐	◐	●	◐		57	●			●	3.5	●	●
12	Hewlett-Packard iPAQ rx3715 (iPAQ rx3115 315)	445	○	◐	○	●	◐		57	●			●	3.5	●	●
13	Dell Axim X50v	500	○	◐	○	●	◐		62	●			●	3.7	●	●
14	ASUS MyPal A620BT (MyPal A620 285)	310	○	◐	◐	●	◐		55	●			●	3.5	●	●
15	Dell Axim X50 416 MHZ (Axim X50 520 MHZ 400)	300	○	◐	●	●	◐		63	●			●	3.5	●	●
16	Hewlett-Packard iPAQ hx2415 (iPAQ hx2410 315)	435	○	◐	○	●	◐		60	●			●	3.5	●	●
17	Dell Axim X30 312 MHZ (non-wireless) (Axim X30 312 MHZ (WiFi) 240, Axim X30 624 MHz 300)	170	○	◐	◐	●	◐		31	●				3.5	●	●
18	Hewlett-Packard iPAQ h2215	350	○	◐	◐	●	◐		57	●				3.6	●	●
19	Hewlett-Packard iPAQ rz1715	225	○	○	○	○	◐		27	●				3.5	●	

Ratings key: ● Excellent, ◐ Very good, ○ Good, ◑ Fair, ● Poor

Guide to the Ratings

OVERALL SCORE is based primarily on ease of use, battery life, and display. **EASE OF USE** considers overall design, navigation, and built-in software. **BATTERY LIFE** is how long fully charged models lasted with continuous use. (For battery life and display, we scored monochrome and color models differently.) For color units: 5 15 hours or more; 4 8 to 15 hours; 3 4 to 8 hours; 2 less than 4 hours. **DISPLAY** is readability in low and normal room light and in sunlight. **CONVENIENCE** considers battery type, expansion capability, and software. **EXPANSION SLOT** indicates the type of removable media you can add: CompactFlash (CF), MultiMedia/SecureDigital Card (M), or Memory Stick (MS). **WIRELESS CONNECTIVITY** indicates connection type: Bluetooth (B) or Wi-Fi (W). Price is approximate retail.

Based on testing in Consumer Reports in March 2005, with updated prices and availability.

PDAs

Profiles Model-by-Model

PALM OS MODELS

1 palmOne LifeDrive Very good. A worthy laptop replacement for travelers. Combines the ease of use of Palm OS with the drag-and-drop convenience of Pocket PC. Easily readable display. Overall design better than most, and basic organizer functions easy to use. Has picture viewer, expense tracker, eBook Reader, and LED alarm. Can record voice memos. But too bulky to fit in a shirt pocket. Doesn't include backup program. New e-mail program is less reliable than previous versions. 3.7GB hard drive for storage. 6.8 oz.

2 palmOne Tungsten T5 Very good. Combines the ease of use of Palm OS with the drag-and-drop convenience of Pocket PC. Overall design better than most, and basic organizer functions easy to use. Has picture viewer, expense tracker, and eBook Reader. Office software installed in ROM. But too bulky to fit in a shirt pocket. Doesn't include backup program. 161 MB flash memory for storage. 5.2 oz.

3 palmOne Tungsten E2 Very good. Overall design better than most, and basic organizer functions easy to use. All memory is nonvolatile, which prevents data loss even if battery dies. Fits easily in a shirt pocket. Has picture viewer, expense tracker, and eBook Reader. Doesn't include backup program. 26 MB flash memory for storage. 4.7 oz.

4 palmOne Tungsten C Very good; a fine choice for viewing and editing documents, accessing e-mail, and wireless web surfing. Has one of the most readable screens we've seen, plus picture viewer, expense tracker, eBook reader, and LED and vibrating alarms. Basic organizer functions easy to use. But too bulky to fit in a shirt pocket. Doesn't include backup program. 6.3 oz.

5 palmOne Zire 72 Good. Overall design better than most, and basic organizer functions easy to use. Fits easily in a shirt pocket. Has picture viewer, expense tracker, eBook Reader, and LED alarm. Can record voice memos. Doesn't include backup program. 4.8 oz.

6 palmOne TungstenE A fine choice for Palm users looking to upgrade. Easily readable display. Improved datebook software lets you see daily tasks at a glance. Basic organizer functions easy to use. Has expense-tracker software, picture viewer, and eBook reader. Fits easily in a shirt pocket. But doesn't include backup program. Battery life not as good as most others tested. 4.6 oz.

7 Garmin iQUE 3600 A good organizer with GPS capability. Well-conceived design, with large, easily readable display. Basic organizer functions easy to use, and user interface better than most. Has handy jog dial, eBook reader, and LED and vibrating alarms. Can record voice memos. But lacks e-mail and backup software. Not much battery life for GPS functionality. Too bulky to fit in a shirt pocket. 5.8 oz.

8 palmOne Zire 31 Good overall, though display is difficult to read. Basic organizer functions easy to use. Fits easily in a shirt pocket. Has picture viewer, expense tracker, and eBook Reader. But doesn't include backup program or email program. 4.1 oz.

9 palmOne Zire 21 Good, but there are better choices. Basic organizer functions easy to use. Fits easily in a shirt pocket. Has expense tracker and eBook reader. But doesn't include e-mail or backup programs. Disappointing battery life for a monochrome-display PDA. Display lacks backlight and is difficult to read. No external memory card. 3.9 oz.

POCKET PC MODELS

10 ASUS MyPal A716 Very good; a fine choice if you want to add peripherals. Overall design better than most, with easily readable display. User interface better than most. Has picture viewer, eBook reader, printed manual, and LED alarm. Can record voice memos. But too bulky to fit in a shirt pocket. 25 MB flash memory for storage. 7.2 oz.

11 Hewlett-Packard iPAQ h4355 Very good; a fine organizer with laptop-like functionality and an easily readable display. Slim case design incorporates many features. User interface better than most. Has built-in keyboard, picture viewer, eBook reader, and LED alarm. Can record voice memos. But too bulky to fit in a shirt pocket. 3 MB memory for storage. 5.9 oz. Similar model: iPAQ h4350

12 Hewlett-Packard iPAQ rx3715 Very good. Overall design and user interface better than most, and basic organizer functions easy to use. Has picture viewer and LED alarm. Can record voice memos. Fits easily in a shirt pocket. 96 MB flash memory for storage. 5.7 oz. Similar model: iPAQ rx3115

13 Dell Axim X50v Very good, with a display that's easily readable even in bright sunlight. User interface better than most. Has picture viewer, printed manual, and LED alarm. Can record voice memos. 91 MB flash memory for storage. 6 oz.

14 ASUS MyPal A620BT Very good, with easily readable display. User interface better than most. Fits easily in a shirt pocket. Has picture viewer, eBook reader, printed manual, and LED alarm. Can record voice memos. 31 MB flash memory for storage. 5.2 oz. Similar model: ASUS MyPal A620

15 Dell Axim X50 416 MHZ Very good. User interface better than most. Has picture viewer, printed manual, and LED alarm. Can record voice memos. 31 MB flash memory for storage. 5.7 oz. Similar model: Dell Axim X50 520 MHZ

16 Hewlett-Packard iPAQ hx2415 Very good. Overall design better than most, and basic organizer functions easy to use. Has picture viewer and LED alarm. Can record voice memos. But too bulky to fit in a shirt pocket. 22 MB flash memory for storage. 6.1 oz. Similar model: Hewlett-Packard iPAQ hx2410.

17 Dell Axim X30 312 MHZ (nonwireless) Very good, with a better user interface than most. Fits easily in a shirt pocket. Has LED alarm, printed manual, and picture viewer. Can record voice memos. 3 MB flash memory for storage. 4.7 oz. Similar models: Dell Axim X30 624 MHz, Dell Axim X30 312 MHZ (Wi-Fi)

18 Hewlett-Packard iPAQ h2215 Good, with a lot of capability in a small case; a fine choice if you want to add peripherals. User interface better than most. Basic organizer functions easy to use. Fits easily in a shirt pocket. Has picture viewer and eBook reader. Can record voice memos. 4 MB flash memory for storage. 5.1 oz.

19 Hewlett Packard iPAQ rz1715 Good, with a better user interface than most. Fits easily in a shirt pocket. Has LED alarm and picture viewer. Can record voice memos. But doesn't include backup program. 10 MB flash memory for storage. 4.4 oz.

PHONES, CELL

CR Quick Recommendations

We've grouped the tested phones by carriers to make it easier for you to find a phone once you've settled on a company for service. Overall, the phones are closely matched in voice quality and sensitivity. We found GSM phones have better talk time compared with CDMA phones, except for the Sharp TM-150. GSM phones also tend to offer more advanced features, like Bluetooth, for the money, but they lack analog backup.

The phones' weights range from 3.1 ounces, for the Siemens CF62T, to 6.3 ounces for the PalmOne Treo 650. All measure about 4 inches long.

The Ratings rank phones strictly on performance. Quick Picks considers other factors, such as coverage and value.

Quick Picks

Best for Verizon (CDMA):
1 LG VX8000, $150
6 Samsung SCH-a650, $20

The LG is a good choice for a multimedia phone. It features a high resolution camera, speakerphone, one of the easiest-to-read keypads we've seen in all lighting conditions, and a display that's easily readable except in bright light. It's also compatible with Verizon's high speed EV-DO network, which allows access to Verizon's VCast TV service. Its main drawback is the lack of analog backup.

The Samsung is a good choice for an inexpensive phone. It has good battery life for a CDMA phone, plus analog backup. Its keypad is a bit hard to read in dim light and its display is hard to read in bright light. It lacks a second display you can read with the case closed.

Best for Sprint (CDMA):
8 Samsung MM-A700, $200
10 LG PM-325, $40

The Samsung is a good choice for a high-end phone. It has an easy-to-use keypad viewable in all lighting conditions. The display is bright and easy to see in low and normal lighting, but somewhat difficult in bright light. It also features a high-resolution camera that lets you record short videos. A voice command feature lets you call anyone in your phone book without having to program the voice dialing function; you can dial a number simply by speaking the digits. Its four-way jog dial can be programmed with shortcuts to frequently used functions. The phone is compatible with Sprint's TV service.

The LG is a good choice for an inexpensive phone. Its keypad is easy to use and readable in all lighting conditions, and the display is viewable everywhere except in bright light. It has a compact sliding case: The keypad slides down while on a call, extending the microphone and putting it closer to your mouth when you're speaking. The result is very good voice quality when listening, and good voice quality when talking, comparable to some folding case phone designs. It also has a built-in VGA-resolution camera and is Bluetooth compatible. But the Bluetooth connection only supports headsets and handsfree devices; you can't use it to transfer pictures or other digital data. The average talk-time battery life of 3¼ hours is less than with other CDMA phones.

Both phones are tri-mode; they can connect digitally in both the cellular and PCS bands and have analog backup. This allows users to make calls on roaming networks when outside Sprint's network.

Ratings

Excellent · Very good · Good · Fair · Poor

In performance order, within categories

Key number	Brand and model	Price	Overall score (0–100; P F G VG E)	Performance: Listening	Talking	Talk time (hr.)	Sensitivity	Ease of use	Features: Easy-to-mute ringer	Speakerphone	Std. headset connector	Voice command	Bluetooth voice	Bluetooth data	Camera	Analog backup
	VERIZON PHONES *These work on Verizon's CDMA digital network.*															
1	**LG** VX8000	$150		Good	Very good	4¼	Very good	Very good	•	•	•				M	
2	**LG** VX7000	100		Good	Very good	4	Good	Very good	•		•				S	
3	**Samsung** SCH-a790	430		Good	Very good	3¼	Very good	Very good	•		•	•			S	
4	**Kyocera** SE47	40		Fair	Good	3¾	Excellent	Good	•	•	•					
5	**LG** VX3200	40		Good	Very good	3¼	Good	Very good	•	•	•					•
6	**Samsung** SCH-a650	20		Good	Very good	3½	Good	Good	•		•					•
7	**Motorola** V710	100		Fair	Very good	3¼	Very good	Very good			•	•	•		M	•
	SPRINT PCS PHONES *These work on Sprint's CDMA digital network.*															
8	**Samsung** MM-A700	200		Good	Very good	4¼	Very good	Very good			•	•			M	•
9	**PalmOne** Treo 650	420		Good	Good	4¼	Very good	Very good	•	•	•		•		S	
10	**LG** PM-325	40		Good	Good	3¼	Very good	Good			•		•		S	•
11	**Sanyo** PM-8200	50		Good	Very good	2¾	Very good	Very good		•	•				S	•
12	**Nokia** 6016i	0		Good	Good	3¼	Very good	Good		•	•					•
13	**Motorola** V60v	70		Good	Very good	2½	Good	Good			•					•

PHONES, CELL

Ratings (continued)

In performance order, within categories

Excellent ● | Very good ◐ | Good ○ | Fair ◔ | Poor ●

Key number	Brand and model	Price	Overall score (P F G VG E)	Listening	Talking	Talk time (hr.)	Sensitivity	Ease of use	Easy-to-mute ringer	Speakerphone	Std. headset connector	Voice command	Bluetooth voice	Bluetooth data	Camera	Analog backup
CINGULAR AND T-MOBILE PHONES These work on GSM digital networks.																
14	**Samsung** SGH p735 (T-Mobile)	$500		○	○	6¼	◐	◐	•						M	
15	**Motorola** Razr V3 GSM (Cingular)	200		○	○	5¼	◐	◐		•			•	•	S	
16	**Nokia** 6010 (Cingular, T-Mobile)	20		○	○	6¾	◐	3								
17	**Siemens** CF62T (T-Mobile)	0		○	◐	4¾	●	○	•	•						
18	**Nokia** 6620 (Cingular)	200		○	○	4½	●	○		•			•	•	S	
19	**Nokia** 6820 (Cingular)	100		○	○	5¼	●	◓			•		•	•	S	
20	**Siemens** C61 (Cingular)	10		○	◐	4½	●	○	•	•						
21	**Nokia** 6230 (Cingular)	0		○	○	5½	●	○		•			•	•	S	
22	**Sony** Ericsson Z500a (Cingular)	50		○	◐	5	◐	○	•	•					S	
23	**Sharp** TM150 (T-Mobile)	100		○	○	3¼	●	◐	•		•				M	

Guide to the Ratings

OVERALL SCORE is based mainly on voice quality and talk time. **LISTENING** rates voice quality for those calling you; **TALKING** rates voice quality for your speech. Listening and talking tests were conducted in noisy and quiet environments using live phone calls. **TALK TIME** is the average time for calls you should expect, based on our tests with strong and weak signals. **SENSITIVITY** is a measure of a phone's voice quality when a call is placed using a weak signal. The scores are applicable only within a Ratings group, not between groups. **EASE OF USE** takes in the design of the display and keypad and the ease with which we could program and access speed-dial numbers, redial, send or receive text messages, and the like. **FEATURES COLUMNS** show which have a folding case, which can enhance voice quality; an **EASY-TO-MUTE RINGER** (lets you mute the ringer and vibrate with the press of one key); volume control on the side; a built-in **CAMERA** (S denotes a resolution of less than 1 megapixel; M denotes 1 megapixel); **BLUETOOTH** wireless capability; and **ANALOG** backup. **PRICE** is the approximate price for a phone purchased from the carrier in the fall of 2004. Prices don't include rebates or special offers.

Based on tests in Consumer Reports in February 2005, with updated prices and availability.

PHONES, CORDLESS

CR Quick Recommendations

Phones and answerers that use analog transmission are the only ones with excellent scores in voice quality. But phones with very good voice quality should be just fine, too. As the Ratings show, multiple-handset models generally have more features.

With similar phones and phone-answerers, the phone performance should be like that of the tested model. Phone-answerer versions of tested phones should perform like the answerer of the same brand. Consider a similar model if you can't find a product we've tested.

The Ratings list products strictly on performance. Quick Picks considers factors such as features and value.

Quick Picks

Good choices in single-handset phones. All are CR Best Buys:
- 14 Panasonic, $30
- 16 GE, $25
- 17 Uniden, $20
- 18 Bell South, $30

They offer excellent voice quality and plenty of talk time.

Good choices for a multiple-handset phone. Both are CR Best Buys:
- 24, 25 Uniden, $40-$50

Both have excellent voice quality and come with an additional handset and a charging cradle.

A good, basic choice, a CR Best Buy:
- 1 AT&T, $45

Very good voice quality and an answerer that is very easy to use.

Good choices for a phone-answerer with multiple handsets:
- 4, 6 AT&T, $160-$180
- 5 VTech, $110

The AT&T E2600B (4) and the AT&T E5965C (6) come loaded with features and offer long recording times. The VTech i5867 (5) is less expensive but has fewer features. All three can coexist with a wireless computer network, use rechargeable AA batteries, and can work during a power outage.

Ratings

In performance order, within categories

Key number	Brand and model	Type	Price	Overall score	Voice quality	Phone ease of use	Talk time (hrs.)	Message	Answerer ease of use	Greeting	Recording time (min.)	Two phone lines	Multiple handset support	Handset to handset support	Caller ID	Base speakerphone	Base keypad	Handset speakerphone	Lighted keypad	Wall mountable	Mailboxes	Advanced playback controls
SINGLE-HANDSET PHONES WITH ANSWERER																						
1 (CR Best Buy)	AT&T 1465	2.4 GHz/900 MHz Analog	$45		●	●	8	●	◉	●	20	NA			•					•	1	•
2	GE 25898GE3	5.8 GHz/900 MHz Analog	70		●	●	10	○	●	○	15	NA			•					•	1	
3	GE 27958GE1	2.4 GHz Analog	80		●	●	11	○	●	◐	16	NA			•	•	•			•	1	
MULTIPLE-HANDSET PHONES WITH ANSWERER																						
4	AT&T E2600B	2.4 GHz DSS	160		●	●	12	●	●	●	30		8 (1)	•	•			•		•	1	•
5	VTech i5867	5.8 GHz/2.4 GHz DSS	110		●	●	10	●	●	●	31		8	•				•			3	
6	AT&T E5965C	5.8 GHz/2.4 GHz DSS	180		●	●	7	●	●	●	30		8	•	•			•		•	1	•
7	Motorola MD681	5.8 GHz DSS	110		●	●	7	●	●	●	30		6	•				•			3	
8	Panasonic KX-TG5240M	5.8 GHz DSS	130		●	●	5	●	●	○	15		4	•				•			3	
9	AT&T 2256	2.4 GHz DSS	85		●	●	17	●	●	●	20		2 (1)	•	•			•			3	
10	Panasonic KX-TG2770S	2.4 GHz DSS	115		●	●	7	●	●	○	15		8	•	•			•			3	
11	Uniden TRU 8885-2	5.8 GHz DSS	170		●	●	7	●	●	●	14		10 (1)	•	•			•		•	1	•
12	Panasonic KX-TG2344B	2.4 GHz DSS	90		●	●	8	●	●	○	14		2 (1)	•	•			•		•	1	
13	Uniden DCT 6485-2	2.4 GHz DSS	110		●	●	9	○	○	○	12		4 (1)	•	•			•		•	1	

Excellent ● Very good ◉ Good ○ Fair ◐ Poor ●

PHONES, CORDLESS

Ratings (continued)

In performance order, within categories

Excellent ● | Very good ◓ | Good ○ | Fair ◐ | Poor ●

Key number	Brand and model	Type	Price	Overall score (0-100, P F G VG E)	Voice quality	Phone ease of use	Talk time (hrs.)	Message	Answerer ease of use	Greeting	Recording time (min.)	Two phone lines	Multiple handset support	Handset to handset support	Caller ID	Base speakerphone	Base keypad	Handset speakerphone	Lighted keypad	Wall mountable	Mailboxes	Advanced playback controls
SINGLE-HANDSET PHONES																						
CR BEST BUY 14	Panasonic KX-TC1486B	900 MHz Analog	30		●	◓	12	0	0	0	NA		NA			•				•		NA
15	Uniden EXI 5160	5.8 GHz/900 MHz Analog	45		●	◓	10	0	0	0	NA		NA			•				•		NA
CR CR BEST BUY 16	GE 26938GE1	900 MHz Analog	25		●	◓	11	0	0	0	NA		NA			•				•		NA
CR BEST BUY 17	Uniden EXI 976	900 MHz Analog	20		●	◓	12	0	0	0	NA		NA			•				•		NA
CR BEST BUY 18	Bell South MH9111SL	900 MHz Analog	30		●	◓	10	0	0	0	NA		NA			•				•		NA
19	Uniden EZI 996	900 MHz Analog	45		◓	●	10	0	0	0	NA		NA			•			•	•		NA
20	GE 27938GE6	2.4 GHz Analog	30		◓	○	8	0	0	0	NA		NA			•				•		NA
21	Panasonic KX-TG2313W	2.4 GHz DSS	50		◓	◓	8	0	0	0	NA		NA			•			•	•		NA
22	Panasonic KX-TG5050W	5.8 GHz DSS	75		◓	◓	5	0	0	0	NA		NA			•			•	•		NA
23	Bell South GH9457BK	2.4 GHz Analog	30		◓	○	8	0	0	0	NA		NA			•				•		NA
MULTIPLE-HANDSET PHONES																						
CR BEST BUY 24	Uniden DXI 986-2	900 MHz Analog	40		●	◓	12	0	0	0	NA		2 (1)			•				•		NA
CR BEST BUY 25	Uniden DXI 7286-2	2.4 GHz/900 MHz Analog	50		●	◓	9	0	0	0	NA		2 (1)			•				•		NA
26	VTech ev 2625	2.4 GHz DSS	65		●	◓	11	0	0	0	NA		2 (1)	•		•			•	•		NA
27	Radio Shack ET-3570	2.4 GHz DSS	60		●	◓	10	0	0	0	NA		4	•		•			•	•		NA
28	Panasonic KX-TG2700S	2.4 GHz DSS	80		●	◓	7	0	0	0	NA		8	•		•	•	•	•	•		NA
29	Uniden DCT 646-2	2.4 GHz DSS	65		●	◓	9	0	0	0	NA		4 (1)	•		•			•	•		NA
30	VTech VT20-2431	2.4 GHz DSS	150		●	◓	10	0	0	0	NA	•	8	•		•	•	•	•	•		NA
31	Bell South GH9702BKEX	2.4 GHz DSS	80		○	○	6	0	0	0	NA		9 (1)	•		•				•		NA
32	Motorola MD451	2.4 GHz DSS	60		○	◓	6	0	0	0	NA		4	•		•			•	•		NA

Guide to the Ratings

OVERALL SCORE mainly covers voice quality, ease of use, unobstructed range, electrical surge protection, and privacy. **VOICE QUALITY** covers listening and talking, as judged by trained panelists. **EASE OF USE** includes handset comfort and weight, talk time, setup and control accessibility, clarity of labels and the presence of useful features. **TALK TIME** is based on continuous-use tests with fully charged batteries. **MESSAGE** reflects the judgment of a trained panel listening to playback of a message recorded from a corded phone of high-quality voice recordings in a quiet, acoustic environment. **ANSWERER EASE OF USE** covers ease of setup and use; adequate labeling, size and location of buttons and controls; and other convenience factors, such as the ability to play new messages first, to not erase unplayed messages, and the presence of advanced playback features such as slow, fast, and rewind. **GREETING** reflects the judgments of a trained panel listening on a corded phone to the greeting on a cordless phone-answerer. The greeting was recorded in a quiet acoustic environment, following directions in the user's manual using high-quality voice recordings. Also referred to as outgoing message (OGM). **RECORDING TIME** Our measurements, to the nearest minute, of total recording time using continuous speech. Cordless phones of all types are available with a built-in answering machine that has digital message storage, typically 15 to 20 minutes. In many cases, recording time may include not only incoming messages, but greetings, memos, and saved messages, so the total may be misleading. Most answerers maximize capacity by detecting pauses in a message and not storing them in memory to increase recording time. **FEATURES COLUMNS** list features that enhance versatility, such as a base speakerphone and a lighted keypad. We also list the **TOTAL NUMBER** of handsets that multiple-handset models can support, along with the number of extra handsets supplied with the base unit. **PRICE** is the approximate retail.

All tested phones have: 1-year warranty; flash to answer call-waiting, handset earpiece volume control, handset ringer, at least 10 memory-dial slots, last-number redial, and low-battery indicator. Most phones have caller ID and are wall-mountable.

Based on testing in Consumer Reports in October 2004, with updated prices and availability.

PHONES, CORDLESS

Profiles Model-by-Model

1 AT&T 1465 A **CR Best Buy.** Very good combo. Has any-key answer and multilingual menus. Answerer has audible new message alert. Similar model: 1445

2 GE 25898GE3 Very good combo. Has multilingual menus. But answerer lacks announce-only mode. Discontinued, but similar model 25838GE3 is available.

3 GE 27958GE1 Very good phone with good answerer. Cordless handset has own charging cradle that is seperate from base. Corded phone on base can work during household AC power loss. Has multilingual menus, and conferencing capable. But answerer message had noticeable background noise, does not play new messages first, and lacks toll saver and announce-only modes.

MULTIPLE-HANDSET PHONES WITH ANSWERER

4 AT&T E2600B Excellent phone with very good answerer. Can work during household AC power loss with optional batteries. Handset-to-handset talk within range to base. Uses two AA rechargeable batteries. Has side volume control for handset earpiece, sound select button, any-key answer, conferencing capable, and multilingual menus. 2.4-GHz wireless LAN friendly but still may cause interference to other 2.4-GHz wireless products. Answerer has audible new message alert. Extra handsets with charging cradle (AT&T E250 $80). Similar models: E2525, E2555.

5 VTech i5867 Very good combo. Can work during household AC power loss with optional batteries. Handset-to-handset talk within range to base. Custom picture caller ID and recordable ringer. Uses two AA rechargeable batteries. Has side volume control for handset earpiece, sound select button, any-key answer, conferencing capable, and multilingual menus. Answerer has audible new message alert. 2.4-GHz wireless LAN friendly. Does not cause interference to other 2.4-GHz wireless products in standby mode, but may in 5.8-GHz wireless products and in talk mode for 2.4-GHz and 5.8-GHz. Extra handsets with charging cradle (VTech i5807 (color display) $80, i5803 (monochrome display) $60). Similar models: i5853, i5857, i5866.

6 AT&T E5965C Very good combo. Can work during household AC power loss with optional batteries. Handset-to-handset talk within range to base. 2.4-GHz wireless LAN friendly. Uses two AA rechargeable batteries. Has side volume control for handset earpiece, sound select button, talking caller ID, any-key answer, conferencing capable, and multilingual menus. Answerer has audible new message alert. Does not cause interference to other 2.4-GHz wireless products in standby mode, but may in 5.8-GHz wireless products and in talk mode for 2.4-GHz and 5.8-GHz. Extra handsets with charging cradle (AT&T E580-2 (color display) $90, E580-1 (monochrome display) $70). Similar models: E5860, E5865.

7 Motorola MD681 Very good combo. Can work during household AC power loss with optional battery. Handset-to-handset talk within range to base. Has audio settings of normal or hearing aid compatible. Has side volume control for handset earpiece, any-key answer, conferencing capable, and multilingual menus. Answerer has audible new message alert. But may cause interference to other 5.8-GHz wireless products. Extra handsets with charging cradle (Motorola MD61 $80). Similar model: MD671.

8 Panasonic KX-TG5240M Very good combo. Handset-to-handset talk within range to base. Has talking caller ID, auto talk, any-key answer, conferencing capable, multilingual menus, Energy Star label, and caller ID. But phone had noticeable background noise, may cause interference to other 5.8-GHz wireless products, and shorter talk time than most, about 5 hours. Answerer setup judged more complicated than most, and easy to accidentally erase unplayed messages. Extra handsets with charging cradle (Panasonic KX-TGA520M $80, KX-TGA523M $100). The KX-TGA523M base has an AM/FM radio and alarm clock. Similar models: KX-TG5202M, KX-TG5230M, KX-TG5200M, KX-TG5210M, KX-TG5212M.

9 AT&T 2256 Very good combo. Longer talk time than most, about 17 hours. Handset-to-handset talk within range to base. Has any-key answer, voice-mail indicator, conferencing capable, and multilingual menus. Answerer has audible new message alert. But phone had noticeable background noise, and may cause interference to other 2.4-GHz wireless products.

10 Panasonic KX-TG2770S Very good cordless/corded combo. Cordless handset has own charging cradle that is seperate from base. Corded phone on base can work during household AC power loss. Handset-to-handset talk within range to base, and a walkie-talkie like mode. Has auto talk, any-key answer, conferencing capable, and Energy Star label. But may cause interference to other 2.4-GHz wireless products. Easy on answerer to accidentally erase unplayed messages. Extra handsets with charging cradle (Panasonic KX-TGA270S $80, KX-TGA273S $100). The KX-TGA273S base has an AM/FM radio and alarm clock.

11 Uniden TRU 8885-2 Very good phone with good answerer. Small, lightweight handset. Handset-to-handset talk within range to base, and a walkie-talkie like mode. Shouldn't cause interference like other DSS phones. Has auto talk, any-key answer, conferencing capable, multilingual menus, Energy Star label, and call waiting deluxe. Answerer has audible new message alert, and can record greeting using handset. But line-of-site range measured shorter than most. Extra handsets with charging cradle (Uniden TCX 800 $60). Similar models: TRU 8860-2, TRU 8865-2, TRU 8885.

12 Panasonic KX-TG2344B Very good combo. Handset-to-handset talk within range to base. Has auto talk, any-key answer, conferencing capable, multilingual menus, Energy Star label, and caller ID. But may cause interference to other 2.4-GHz wireless products. Answerer setup judged more complicated than most, and easy to accidentally erase unplayed messages. Similar model: KX-TG2314W.

13 Uniden DCT 6485-2 Very good phone with good answerer. Small, lightweight handset. Handset-to-handset talk within range to base, and a walkie-talkie like mode. Has auto talk, any-key answer, conferencing capable, multilingual menus, Energy Star label, and call waiting deluxe. Answerer has audible new message alert, and can record greeting using handset. But phone and answerer message had noticeable background noise, and may cause interference to other 2.4-GHz wireless products. Extra handsets with charging cradle (Uniden DCX 640 $40). Similar models: DCT 6465-2, DCT 648-2, DCT 6485.

SINGLE-HANDSET PHONES

14 Panasonic KX-TC1486B A **CR Best Buy.** Very good overall. Has any-key answer, and multilingual menus. But line-of-site range measured shorter than most.

15 Uniden EXI 5160 Very good overall. Has auto talk, any-key answer, voice-mail indicator, multilingual menus, and energy star label. Similar model: EXAI 5180.

PHONES, CORDLESS

Profiles Model-by-Model (continued)

16 GE 26938GE1 A **CR Best Buy.** Very good overall. Has multilingual menus. Similar models: 26998GE1, 26928GE1.

17 Uniden EXI 976 A **CR Best Buy.** Very good overall. Has auto talk, any-key answer, voice-mail indicator, multilingual menus, and energy star label. But line-of-site range measured shorter than most. Similar model: EXAI 978i.

18 Bell South MH9111SL A **CR Best Buy.** Very good overall. Small, lightweight handset. Has side volume control for handset earpiece, voice-mail indicator, and multilingual menus.

19 Uniden EZI 996 Very good overall. Marketed for the visually or hearing impaired. Has big keypad buttons on handset, side volume control for handset earpiece, auto talk, any-key answer, voice-mail indicator, multilingual menus, and Energy Star label.

20 GE 27938GE6 Very good overall. Has voice-mail indicator, and multilingual menus. Similar model: 27928GE6.

21 Panasonic KX-TG2313W Very good overall. Has auto talk, any-key answer, voice-mail indicator, multilingual menus, Energy Star label, and caller ID. But may cause interference to other 2.4-GHz wireless products. Similar model: KX-TG2312W.

22 Panasonic KX-TG5050W Very good overall. Has auto talk, any-key answer, voice-mail indicator, multilingual menus, Energy Star label, and caller ID. But phone had noticeable background noise, may cause interference to other 5.8-GHz wireless products, and shorter talk time than most, about 5 hours. Similar model: KX-TG5055W.

23 Bell South GH9457BK Very good overall. Small, lightweight handset. Has side volume control for handset earpiece, voice-mail indicator, and multilingual menus. We tested the 50 channel version.

MULTIPLE-HANDSET PHONES

24 Uniden DXI 986-2 A **CR Best Buy.** Very good overall. Shouldn't cause interference like other multiple handset capable phones. Has auto talk, any-key answer, voice-mail indicator, multilingual menus, and Energy Star label. But lacks handset-to-handset talk capability so can't conference handsets with an outside party, and line-of-site range measured shorter than most.

25 Uniden DXI 7286-2 A **CR Best Buy.** Very good overall. Shouldn't cause interference like other multiple handset capable phones. Has auto talk, any-key answer, voice-mail indicator, and multilingual menus. But lacks handset-to-handset talk capability so can't conference handsets with an outside party. Similar model: DXAI 7288-2.

26 VTech ev 2625 Very good overall. Handset-to-handset talk within range to base. Uses three AAA rechargeable batteries. Has side volume control for handset earpiece, any-key answer, voice-mail indicator, conferencing capable, and multilingual menus. 2.4 GHz wireless LAN friendly but still may cause interference to other 2.4-GHz wireless products. Phone had noticeable background noise. Similar model: ev 2650.

27 Radio Shack ET-3570 Very good overall. Small, lightweight handset. Handset-to-handset talk within range to base, and a walkie-talkielike mode. Has auto talk, any-key answer, voice-mail indicator, conferencing capable, multilingual menus, Energy Star label, and call waiting deluxe. But phone had noticeable background noise, and may cause interference to other 2.4-GHz wireless products. Extra handsets with charging cradle (Radio Shack ET-3571 $35). Similar model: TAD-3871.

28 Panasonic KX-TG2700S Very good overall. Handset-to-handset talk within range to base, and a walkie-talkie like mode. Has auto talk, any-key answer, conferencing capable, and Energy Star label. But may cause interference to other 2.4-GHz wireless products. Extra handsets with charging cradle (Panasonic KX-TGA270S $80, KX-TGA273S $100). The KX-TGA273S base has an AM/FM radio and alarm clock. Discontinued, but similar model KX-TG2740S is available.

29 Uniden DCT 646-2 Very good overall. Small, lightweight handset. Handset-to-handset talk within range to base, and a walkie-talkielike mode. Has auto talk, any-key answer, voice-mail indicator, conferencing capable, multilingual menus, Energy Star label, and call waiting deluxe. But phone had noticeable background noise, and may cause interference to other 2.4-GHz wireless products. Extra handsets with charging cradle (Uniden DCX 640 $40). Similar model: DCT 646.

30 VTech VT20-2431 Very good overall. Small, lightweight handset. Can work during household AC power loss with optional battery. Handset-to-handset talk within range to base. Has voice-mail indicator, and conferencing capable. But may cause interference to other 2.4-GHz wireless products. Extra handsets with charging cradle (VTech VT20-2420 $80). Similar model: VT20-2481.

31 Bell South GH9702BKEX Good overall. Small, lightweight handset. Handset-to-handset walkie-talkielike mode. Shouldn't cause interference like other DSS phones. Has voice-mail indicator, and multilingual menus. But phone had noticeable background noise, and lacks handset-to-handset intercom capability so can't conference handsets with an outside party. Extra handsets with charging cradle (Bell South HCB702BK $35). Similar model: GH9762BKEX.

32 Motorola MD451 Good overall. Can work during household AC power loss with optional battery. Handset-to-handset talk within range to base, and a walkie-talkie like mode. Has side volume control for handset earpiece, voice-mail indicator, conferencing capable, and multilingual menus. But phone had noticeable background noise, and may cause interference to other 2.4-GHz wireless products. Extra handsets with charging cradle (Motorola MD41 $50). Discontinued, but similar models MD481, MD481sys, and MD471 are available.

PRINTERS

CR Quick Recommendations

A standard inkjet remains the best all-purpose printer, and one model, the Canon Pixma iP8500 (8), has even outpaced the inkjet-based 4x6 photo printers for snapshot speed. Multifunction inkjets are worth a look if you need to fit multiple functions into a small space. And 4x6 printers are best for the casual digital-camera user who cares more for convenience and speed than for print quality and flexibility.

There's no connection between price and print quality. The CR Best Buy has low per-page costs. Supplies can make even low-priced units costly to own over time.

The Ratings rank models by performance. Quick Picks highlights models you might consider first based on how they scored and on other factors, such as price and features.

Quick Picks

Top choices if you frequently print text and photos:
1 Hewlett-Packard, $130
2 Canon, $140

Consider the Hewlett-Packard Deskjet 6540 (1) and the Canon Pixma iP4000 (2), a CR Best Buy, for fast, first-rate photos and text. The Canon's low cost per page makes it a good value if you print lots of text. Neither supports memory cards, but the Canon accepts images via cable from cameras supporting the PictBridge standard.

Smart choices for photographers:
3, 6 Hewlett-Packard, $130-$230
8 Canon, $335

Excellent photos, memory-card support, PictBridge, and an LCD for previewing and cropping make the Hewlett-Packard PhotoSmart 7760 (3) and the Hewlett-Packard PhotoSmart 8450 (6) good choices for camera buffs. None of the tested inkjets, including 4x6-inch models, could match the speed of the Canon Pixma iP8500 (8), which produced excellent photos. The Canon holds eight ink cartridges. The HP 8450 holds three multicolor cartridges; the 7760, two. For the best-quality photos from both models, HP recommends swapping out the black-ink cartridge for photo ink. Some users may find this inconvenient.

For printing limited to 4x6 photos:
28, 29 Hewlett-Packard, $190

Overall, standard-sized inkjets produced better photos and cost less to buy and use than printers limited to 4x6 snapshots. The Hewlett-Packard PhotoSmart 245 (28) and Hewlett-Packard PhotoSmart 375 (29) were the only 4x6 printers to receive an excellent score for photo quality. Photo quality for the 245 was slightly better, but the newer 375 offers PictBridge support, a trimmer package, and faster printing. Another inkjet, the Epson PictureMate (35), costs only 20 cents per photo but scored lower in photo quality. If print speed is paramount, consider the Sony Picturestation DPP-EX50 (31), among the highest-rated dye-sublimation models.

For a multifunction printer:
17 Hewlett-Packard, $390
18 Canon, $300

While relatively pricey, the Hewlett-Packard PhotoSmart 2710 (17) and Canon Pixma All in One MP780 (18) were the best all-around performers among multifunction models, with fine text and photo printing at high speeds. Both feature a built-in fax modem, as does the Dell Photo All in One 962 (22). But the Canon offers the best text and 8x10-inch photo costs of its category. Both the 1,200-dot-per-inch HP and the 2,400-dpi Canon were judged very good for scan quality and speed.

Ratings

In performance order, within categories

Excellent ●   Very good ◕   Good ○   Fair ◐   Poor ●

Key number	Brand and model	Price	Overall Score	Photo quality	8x10 photo time (min.)	8x10 photo cost ($)	4x6 photo time (min.)	4x6 photo cost ($)	Text quality	Text speed (ppm)	Text cost (cents)	Graphics quality	LCD viewer	Individual color tanks	Swap black for photo ink	Memory-card support	PictBridge support	Borderless photos
REGULAR INKJET MODELS
1	Hewlett-Packard Deskjet 6540	$130		●	5.5	1.15	3	0.45	●	11	5.5	◐		•			•	•
2	Canon Pixma iP4000 (CR BEST BUY)	140		●	5.5	0.80	3	0.35	●	10	3	○		•			•	•
3	Hewlett-Packard PhotoSmart 7760	130		●	7.5	1.00	4	0.40	●	6	6	◐	•		•	•	•	•
4	Hewlett-Packard Deskjet 5850	215		●	7.5	1.00	4	0.40	●	6	6	○				•		•
5	Hewlett-Packard PhotoSmart 7960	230		●	9.5	1.30	5.5	0.50	●	6	6	◐	•		•	•	•	•
6	Hewlett-Packard PhotoSmart 8450	230		●	9	1.50	3.5	0.55	●	7	5.5	◐	•		•	•	•	•
7	Canon Pixma iP5000	190		●	9	0.80	4.5	0.35	●	9	3	◐		•			•	•
8	Canon Pixma iP8500	335		●	1.5	0.95	1	0.40	●	4.5	3.5	○		•			•	•
9	Hewlett-Packard Deskjet 6127	250		●	11.5	0.80	NA	NA	●	7	4.5	●						•
10	Lexmark P915 Photo	130		●	4.5	1.00	3	0.40	●	9	7.5	◐	•			•	•	•
11	Epson Stylus Photo R800	390		●	7	1.35	5.5	0.50	●	2.5	4	◐		•				•
12	Lexmark Color Jetprinter Z816	95		◐	8.5	1.00	5	0.40	●	9.5	7.5	○						•
13	Epson Stylus Photo R320	180		◐	11	1.00	7	0.40	●		4.5	◐	•	•		•	•	•
14	Epson Stylus 86	100		◐	17	0.90	14	0.40	○	6.5	6	○		•				•

PRINTERS

Ratings (continued)

In performance order, within categories

Excellent ● | Very good ◐ | Good ○ | Fair ◑ | Poor ●

Key number	Brand and model	Price	Overall Score (P F G VG E)	Photo quality	8x10 photo time (min.)	8x10 photo cost ($)	4x6 photo time (min.)	4x6 photo cost ($)	Text quality	Text speed (ppm)	Text cost (cents)	Graphics quality	LCD viewer	Individual color tanks	Swap black for photo ink	Memory-card support	PictBridge support	Borderless photos
REGULAR INKJET MODELS
15	Epson Stylus Photo R200	100		●	11	1.00	7	0.40	○	2.5	4.5	○		●				●
16	Epson Stylus Photo R300M	150		●	11	1.00	7.5	0.40	○	2.5	4.5	○	●	●			●	●
MULTIFUNCTION INKJET MODELS
17	Hewlett-Packard PhotoSmart 2710	390		◑	5.5	1.15	3	0.45	●	9	5.5	●	●	●		●	●	●
18	Canon Pixma All in One MP780 Pixma All in One MP750 $240	300		●	6	0.80	3	0.35	●	10	3	○	●	●		●	●	●
19	Hewlett-Packard PSC 1350	120		●	20.5	1.00	10.5	0.40	●	5.5	6	●				●		●
20	Canon MultiPASS MP370	150		◑	6.5	0.85	4	0.35	●	8	6.5	●				●		●
21	Hewlett-Packard PSC 1315	100		●	20	1.00	10.5	0.40	●	6	6	●						●
22	Dell Photo All in One 962	130		●	8.5	1.00	4.5	0.40	●	10.5	8	●	●			●		●
23	Epson Stylus Photo RX500	235		●	10	1.00	7	0.40	◑	3	4.5	○		●		●		●
24	Lexmark X5270	100		●	8.5	1.00	5	0.40	◑	9	7.5	◐				●	●	●
25	Epson Stylus All in One CX6600	195		◑	17.5	0.90	7.5	0.35	●	6.5	4	○		●		●		●
26	Lexmark P6250 Photo	160		●	4.5	1.00	3	0.40	●	3	7.5	●	●			●	●	●
27	Epson Stylus CX4600	110		○	20	0.85	14.5	0.35	●	3	7.5	○		●				●
4X6 PHOTO MODELS
28	Hewlett-Packard PhotoSmart 245	190		●	NA	NA	2.5	0.35	0	NA	NA	0	●			●		●
29	Hewlett-Packard PhotoSmart 375	190		●	NA	NA	1.5	0.35	0	NA	NA	0	●			●	●	●
30	Canon Selphy CP400	150		◑	NA	NA	1.5	0.50	0	NA	NA	0				●	●	●
31	Sony Picturestation DPP-EX50	175		◑	NA	NA	1	0.45	0	NA	NA	0	●			●		●
32	Sony DPP-FP30	150		◑	NA	NA	1.5	0.40	0	NA	NA	0	●			●	●	●
33	Olympus P-10 Digital Photo Printer	140		◑	NA	NA	1	0.60	0	NA	NA	0						●
34	Canon Selphy DS700	185		○	NA	NA	1.5	0.55	0	NA	NA	0				●	●	●
35	Epson PictureMate	200		○	NA	NA	2.5	0.20	0	NA	NA	0				●	●	●
36	Dell Photo Printer 540	130		○	NA	NA	1	0.50	0	NA	NA	0	●			●		●
37	Lexmark P315	130		○	NA	NA	3	0.30	0	NA	NA	0				●	●	●
38	Polaroid PP46d Digital Photo Printer	210		◑	NA	NA	3	0.60	0	NA	NA	0						●
39	Kodak EasyShare Printer Dock Plus	185		○	NA	NA	1	0.55	0	NA	NA	0				●	●	●
40	Kodak EasyShare Printer Dock	140		○	NA	NA	2	0.55	0	NA	NA	0				●		●
41	Olympus P-S100	200		○	NA	NA	1.5	0.60	0	NA	NA	0					●	●
42	Canon CP-330	255		○	NA	NA	1.5	0.50	0	NA	NA	0					●	●

Guide to the Ratings

OVERALL SCORE is based mainly on speed and text/photo quality. For multifunction models, only printing is scored; see CR Quick Picks for results of tests on recommended models' scanning function. **PHOTO QUALITY** reflects a color snapshot's appearance. 8x10 time measures, to the nearest half-minute, the time to print an 8x10-inch color photo at the best-quality setting. 4x6 time measures the time to print a borderless 4x6-inch color photo. **TEXT QUALITY** is for clarity and crispness of black text. **TEXT SPEED** measures pages per minute (ppm) for a 10-page document at default settings. **GRAPHICS QUALITY** assesses output such as greeting cards and charts. **COST** is estimated for one black text page (for ink and plain paper), one 8x10-inch color photo (ink and glossy 8½x11-inch paper), or one 4x6-inch color photo (ink or, for dye-sublimation 4x6 printers, ribbon and glossy 4x6-inch paper). Under features for inkjet and multifunction printers, swap black for photo ink means you have to change cartridges for optimum photo quality, which some may find a nuisance. **PRICE** is approximate retail.

All tested models work with Windows XP and 2000; all but the Dell (22, 36) support Windows ME and 98; most support Mac OS. All standard-size printers can hold at least 100 sheets or 10 envelopes; the 4x6 photo printers hold at least 20 ready-cut, 4x6-inch photo sheets. *Based on testing in Consumer Reports May 2005, with updated prices and availability.*

PRINTERS

Profiles Model-by-Model

REGULAR INKJET MODELS

1 Hewlett-Packard Deskjet 6540 Excellent, with fast text printing. Can print from a shared Windows network. Space required (HWD): 6x18x21 inches.

2 Canon Pixma iP4000 A **CR Best Buy.** Very good and fast, with low cost per text page. PictBridge support permits direct cable connection from compatible cameras. Black-and-white photos judged more neutral than most. Cannot print banners. Space required (HWD): 13x17x22 inches.

3 Hewlett-Packard PhotoSmart 7760 Excellent. Connects to compatible HP cameras via USB port. Has separate paper tray for 4x6-inch photo paper. Supports automatic two-sided printing. Can print from a shared Windows network. Black-and-white photos judged more neutral than most. Black cartridge not included. Space required (HWD): 8x18x20 inches. Similar model: PhotoSmart 7660 $130.

4 Hewlett-Packard Deskjet 5850 Very good, with excellent text and photos. Supports wireless and Ethernet connectivity. Can print from a shared Windows network. Space required (HWD): 6x18x18 inches.
Similar model: Deskjet 5650 $130.

5 Hewlett-Packard PhotoSmart 7960 Very good. Connects to compatible HP cameras via USB port. Has separate paper tray for 4x6-inch photo paper. Supports automatic two-sided printing. Can print from a shared Windows network. Black-and-white photos judged more neutral than most. Space required (HWD): 8x21x21 inches.

6 Hewlett-Packard PhotoSmart 8450 Very good, but slow for text. Has separate paper tray for 4x6-inch photo paper. Supports automatic two-sided printing. Can print from a shared Windows network. Black-and-white photos judged more neutral than most. Black cartridge not included. Space required (HWD): 8x22x22 inches.

7 Canon Pixma iP5000 Very good, with low-cost text printing. Black-and-white photos judged more neutral than most. Cannot print banners. Space required (HWD): 14x17x24 inches.

8 Canon Pixma iP8500 Very good. Black-and-white photos judged more neutral than most. Cannot print banners. Space required (HWD): 14x18x24 inches.

9 Hewlett-Packard Deskjet 6127 Very good. Supports automatic two-sided printing. Can print from a shared Windows network. Space required (HWD): 8x18x17 inches.

10 Lexmark P915 Photo Very good, but text speed is much slower if color added. Can print from a shared Windows network. Noisy. Black cartridge not included. Space required (HWD): 12x18x21 in

11 Epson Stylus Photo R800 Very good. Excellent text and photos, but slow for text and only fair graphics quality. Includes accessory for printing directly onto printable CDs and DVDs and attachment for printing photos on roll paper. Pigment-based color and black inks water-resistant on plain or photo paper. Can print from a shared Windows network. Black-and-white photos judged more neutral than most. Stops printing when cartridge runs low. Space required (HWD): 13x20x25 inches.

12 Lexmark Color Jetprinter Z816 Good. Fast for text, but text speed is much slower if color added. Can print from a shared Windows network. Space required (HWD): 13x18x21 inches.

13 Epson Stylus Photo R320 Good. Includes accessory for printing directly onto printable CDs and DVDs. Can print from a shared Windows network. Stops printing when cartridge runs low. Space required (HWD): 14x20x21 inches.

14 Epson Stylus 86 Good, but slow for photos. Text speed is much slower if color added. Pigment-based color and black inks water-resistant on plain but not photo paper. Can print from a shared Windows network. Stops printing when cartridge runs low. Space required (HWD): 14x18x20 inches.

15 Epson Stylus Photo R200 Good. Excellent for photos, but slow for text. Includes accessory for printing directly onto printable CDs and DVDs. Can print from a shared Windows network. Stops printing when cartridge runs low. Space required (HWD): 13x19x22 inches.

16 Epson Stylus Photo R300M Good but slow for text. PictBridge support permits direct cable connection from compatible cameras. Includes accessory for printing directly onto printable CDs and DVDs. Can print from a shared Windows network. Stops printing when cartridge runs low. Space required (HWD): 13x20x22 in. Discontinued, but similar model Stylus Photo R300 is available.

MULTIFUNCTION INKJET MODELS

17 Hewlett-Packard PhotoSmart 2710 Very good. Flatbed design for scanning and copying. Supports wireless and Ethernet connectivity, and can print from a shared Windows network. Supports automatic two-sided printing. USB cable included. Cannot print banners. Space required (HWD): 11x19x21 in.

18 Canon Pixma All in One MP780 Very good, with fast, low-cost text printing. Flatbed design for scanning and copying. Supports automatic two-sided printing. Black-and-white photos judged more neutral than most. Cannot print banners. Space required (HWD): 15x20x23 in. Similar model: Canon Pixma All in One MP750.

19 Hewlett-Packard PSC 1350 Very good, with excellent text and photos, but slow for photos. Compact for a multifunction printer. Flatbed design for scanning and copying. Can be set for no more than 9 copies at a time. Cannot print banners. Space required (HWD): 7x17x19 in.

20 Canon MultiPASS MP370 Very good, with both excellent and fast text printing. Text speed is much slower if color added. Flatbed design for scanning and copying. Allows direct printing from compatible Canon cameras via cable; PictBridge support also permits direct cable connection from compatible non-Canon cameras. Noisy. Cannot print banners. Space required (HWD): 13x18x23 in. Discontinued, but similar model Canon MultiPASS MP390 still available.

21 Hewlett-Packard PSC 1315 Very good, and compact for a multifunction printer, but slow for photos. Flatbed design for scanning and copying. PictBridge support permits direct cable connection from compatible cameras. Can be set for no more than 9 copies at a time. Cannot print banners. Space required (HWD): 7x17x18 in.

22 Dell Photo All in One 962 Very good, with fast text printing, but text speed is much slower if color added. Supports only Windows XP and 2000. Flatbed

PRINTERS

Profiles Model-by-Model (continued)

design for scanning and copying. Can print from a shared Windows network. Noisy. Space required (HWD): 13x20x24 in. Similar model: Dell Photo All in One 942.

23 Epson Stylus Photo RX500 Very good, with low-cost but slow text printing. Flatbed design for scanning and copying. USB cable included. Stops printing when cartridge runs low. Space required (HWD): 14x18x20 in.

24 Lexmark X5270 Good. Fast for text, but text speed is much slower if color added. Flatbed design for scanning and copying. Can print from a shared Windows network. Noisy. Space required (HWD): 12x18x20 in.

25 Epson Stylus All in One CX6600 Good overall, but slow photo printing; text speed is much slower if color added. Flatbed design for scanning and copying. Pigment-based color and black inks water-resistant on plain but not photo paper. Stops printing when cartridge runs low. Space required (HWD): 13x18x24 in.

26 Lexmark P6250 Photo Good overall, but slow for text—and much slower if color added. Flatbed design for scanning and copying. Can print from a shared Windows network. Noisy. Black cartridge not included. Space required (HWD): 13x18x21 in.

27 Epson Stylus CX4600 Good, but slow text and photo printing. Flatbed design for scanning and copying. Pigment-based color and black inks water-resistant on plain but not photo paper. Stops printing when cartridge runs low. Space required (HWD): 12x17x22 in.

4X6 PHOTO MODELS

28 Hewlett-Packard PhotoSmart 245 Excellent inkjet model. Black-and-white photos judged more neutral than most. Space required (HWD): 6x9x16 in. Similar model: Hewlett-Packard PhotoSmart 145.

29 Hewlett-Packard PhotoSmart 375 Excellent inkjet model. PictBridge support permits direct cable connection from compatible cameras. Black-and-white photos judged more neutral than most. Space required (HWD): 7x9x9 in. Similar model: Hewlett-Packard PhotoSmart 325, $150

30 Canon Selphy CP400 Very good dye-sublimation model. PictBridge support permits direct cable connection from compatible cameras. Noisy. Space required (HWD): 3x7x16 in.

31 Sony Picturestation DPP-EX50 Very good dye-sublimation model. PictBridge support permits direct cable connection from compatible cameras. Composite-video output permits use of TV as image viewer. Noisy. Does not come with a ribbon cartridge or paper. Space required (HWD): 8x3x16 in.

32 Sony DPP-FP30 Very good dye-sublimation model. PictBridge support permits direct cable connection from compatible cameras. Noisy. Lacks low cartridge warning. Space required (HWD): 3x7x17 in.

33 Olympus P-10 Digital Photo Printer Very good dye-sublimation model, but clips away outer 20 percent of image when printing from computer. PictBridge support permits direct cable connection from compatible cameras. Noisy. Space required (HWD): 7x8x9 in.

34 Canon Selphy DS700 Very good inkjet model. PictBridge support permits direct cable connection from compatible cameras. Space required (HWD): 3x9x16 in.

35 Epson PictureMate Very good inkjet model. PictBridge support permits direct cable connection from compatible cameras. Pigment-based color and black inks water-resistant on plain or photo paper. Stops printing when cartridge runs low. Space required (HWD): 8x11x14 in.

36 Dell Photo Printer 540 Very good dye-sublimation model, but supports only Windows XP and 2000. PictBridge support permits direct cable connection from compatible cameras. Noisy. Space required (HWD): 5x8x17 inches.

37 Lexmark P315 Very good inkjet model overall. LCD screen indicates approximate time left to finish printing photo. PictBridge support permits direct cable connection from compatible cameras. Lacks USB support; can print only from PictBridge cable or removable media. Space required (HWD): 8x11x14 inches.

38 Polaroid PP46d Digital Photo Printer Very good dye-sublimation model. Noisy. Space required (HWD): 8x5x17 inches.

39 Kodak EasyShare Printer Dock Plus Very good dye-sublimation model. PictBridge support permits direct cable connection from compatible cameras. Black-and-white photos judged more neutral than most. Can print from devices that use IrDA wireless technology. Noisy. Space required (HWD): 4x8x17 inches.

40 Kodak EasyShare Printer Dock Very good dye-sublimation model. PictBridge support permits direct cable connection from compatible cameras. Black-and-white photos judged more neutral than most. Noisy. Space required (HWD): 4x8x17 inches.

41 Olympus P-S100 Good dye-sublimation model. PictBridge support permits direct cable connection from compatible cameras. Noisy. Space required (HWD): 3x7x16 inches.

42 Canon CP-330 Good dye-sublimation model. PictBridge support permits direct cable connection from compatible cameras. Noisy. Space required (HWD): 3x7x17 inches.

SCANNERS

CR Quick Recommendations

Any scanner judged very good for quality should be fine for typical photos, text, and artwork. You'll generally pay more for higher resolution. As a rule, you'll want 2,400 dpi or more only for scanning film; most other scanning can be done at much lower dpi settings. And while none of these models is slow, consider the speed scores if you expect to use a scanner heavily. Most will work with Windows and Macintosh computers, but there are a few exceptions; the Microtek (13), for example, works only with Windows.

The Ratings rank models strictly by performance. Quick Picks highlights models you might consider first based on how they scored and on factors such as price.

Quick Picks

Fine, economical choices for photos and text:
- **1** Canon $130
- **6** Canon, $100
- **7** Epson, $100

Not all of these models would do full justice to film or slide scanning, but all three produce fast, very good scans of printed originals and would suffice for everyday tasks. The 3,200-dpi Canon (6), a CR Best Buy, is the best choice if you expect to do enlargements. The Canon (1) and Epson (7), also a CR Best Buy, have a lower resolution of 2,400 dpi.

Fine choices for enlargements, negatives, slides, and line art:
- **8** Epson, $200
- **16** Microtek, $145

Both the Epson (8) and Microtek (16) have 4,800-dpi scanning with the 48-bit-color depth that captures ample detail from negatives and slides. For the higher price, the Epson consistently offers very good performance and a host of features. The Microtek, also full-featured, costs much less but is particularly slow.

Ratings

In performance order

Key number	Brand & model	Price	Overall score	Quality	Speed	Features	Resolution (dpi)	Color-bit depth	Slide/negative adapter	Supports Macintosh
1	**Canon** CanoScan LiDE 80	$130		⊖	⊖	⊖	2,400	48	•	•
2	**Canon** CanoScan 8400F	150		⊖	⊖	⊖	3,200	48	•	•
3	**Epson** Perfection 2580 Photo	180		⊖	⊖	⊖	2,400	48	•	•
4	**Epson** Perfection 3170 Photo	180		⊖	⊖	⊖	3,200	48	•	•
5	**HP** ScanJet 4670	180		⊖	⊖	●	2,400	48		•
6	**Canon** CanoScan 4200F (CR Best Buy)	100		⊖	⊖	○	3,200	48	•	
7	**Epson** Perfection 2480 Photo (CR Best Buy)	100		⊖	⊖	⊖	2,400	48	•	•
8	**Epson** Perfection 4180 Photo	200		⊖	⊖	●	4,800	48	•	•
9	**Visioneer** One Touch 9320 USB	125		⊖	○	⊖	3,200	24	•	
10	**HP** ScanJet 4070 PhotoSmart	130		○	⊖	⊖	2,400	48	•	•
11	**Microtek** ScanMaker i320	120		○	○	●	3,200	48	•	•
12	**HP** ScanJet 3670	80		⊖	○	⊖	1,200	48	•	•
13	**Microtek** ScanMaker 5900	180		⊖	⊙	●	2,400	48	•	
14	**Canon** CanoScan LiDE 35	80		○	⊖	○	1,200	48		•
15	**HP** ScanJet 3970	100		○	⊖	⊖	2,400	48	•	•
16	**Microtek** ScanMaker s400	145		⊖	⊙	●	4,800	48	•	•
17	**Microtek** ScanMaker 5800	80		○	⊙	⊖	2,400	48	•	•

Ratings key: ● Excellent · ⊖ Very good · ○ Good · ⊙ Fair · ● Poor

SCANNERS

Guide to the Ratings

OVERALL SCORE is based on color and black-and-white photo-scan quality, scanning speed, and features. **QUALITY** received the greatest weight in the Ratings. It measures how faithfully the scanner reproduced a color photo and black-and-white images. Using the software included with each unit, we scanned images at the highest optical resolution and printed them on a high-rated inkjet printer. **SPEED** received slightly less weight. It measures how quickly each model scanned 8x10-inch color and black-and-white photos at both 150- and 300-dpi resolution. **FEATURES**, our assessment of helpful features, received the least weight in the Ratings. **RESOLUTION**, in dots per inch (dpi), lists the scanner's maximum optical resolution. Figures higher than 1,200 dpi are of use primarily for scanning slides and negatives. **COLOR-BIT DEPTH** refers to the scanner's ability to differentiate among gradations of light and dark; it matters only if you scan slides and negatives. **PRICE** is approximate retail. All tested models have support for Windows 98, ME, XP, and 2000; USB transmission (USB 1.0 with Windows 98); TWAIN compliance for scanning directly into third-party software; ability to scan full area of an 8½x11-inch or larger page; buttons that automate routine tasks. Scanning and image-editing program and USB cable. Most tested models support Macintosh, include quick-start guide but not printed owner's manual, have photocopy function and 1-year warranty, are AC-powered.

Based on testing in Consumer Reports in May 2005, with updated pricing and availability.

TVs, LCD

CR Quick Recommendations

The best LCD TVs, all HD models, can display a very good picture from a high-quality source such as a satellite receiver or a digital-cable box. On the best of the tested models, picture quality was clear, crisp, and detailed, especially with HD programming and progressive-scan DVD signals. But none of the LCD models in the Ratings had picture quality equaling that of the best conventional TVs and plasma sets. However, in bright lighting, the LCD TV's antireflective surface helps it maintain better contrast than you'll see with a plasma TV.

Lower-priced sets with good picture quality could be fine if the image quality isn't critical. (Scores for HD programming and DVD playback are held to higher standards than scores for regular TV.)

An enhanced-definition (ED) set may cost a bit less than an HD model, but the picture quality probably won't be as good. Unlike the plasma ED sets we've tested, most of these ED sets were unable to display a down-converted version of HD signals. Stick with an HD set for a primary TV you'll be watching often. We'd consider an ED set or a smaller-screen standard-definition LCD TV only for uses such as casual viewing in the kitchen, where you might not want the cable or satellite box you generally need for an HD model.

The Ratings list models by performance. Quick Picks highlights models that you might want to consider based on how they scored and on factors such as price.

Quick Picks

Best choices among bigger screens:
1, 2 Sony, $2,640-$3,860

These two 32-inch wide-screen Sony TVs had very good picture quality across the board. The higher price of the Sony Wega KDL-32XBR950 (2) gets you an integrated digital tuner, a Memory Stick slot for viewing digital images, and two component-video inputs (its sibling has one) on a separate control unit.

Best choices for a smaller primary set:
3   Sony, $1,760
4   Sharp, $2,050
13 Philips, $1,360

The digital-cable-ready 26-inch Sharp LC-26GD4U had very good picture quality with all types of signals and was easy to use. Both the 26-inch Sony Wega KLV-26HG2 (3) and Philips 26PF9966 (13) were very good for HD. The Sony Wega KLV-26HG2 (3) was better for regular TV, the Philips 26PF9966 (13) for DVDs. The Philips 26PF9966 (13) is a good value, but note that its remote control and onscreen menu were harder to use than most. All three of these sets are wide-screen models.

If you want bang for the buck in a smaller HD set:
17 Philips, $600

The 17-inch wide-screen Philips 17PF8946 (17) was very good for both HD and DVDs and good for standard-definition programming via the S-video input.

Ratings

In performance order, within categories

HIGH-DEFINITION MODELS

Key	Brand and model	Price	Size	HD pic	DVD pic	S-video pic	Antenna/cable pic	Sound	Ease of use	Aspect	Rear S-video	Rear component	Computer monitor	Uses control set-top box
1	Sony Wega KLV-32M1	$2690	32	●	●	●	◐	◉	○	16:9	2	1		
2	Sony Wega KDL-32XBR950	4000	32	●	●	●	◐	◉	○	15:9	2	2		●
3	Sony Wega KLV-26HG2	1900	26	●	●	○	◐	◉	○	15:9	2	1		
4	Sharp Aquos LC-26GD4U	2750	26	●	●	●	◐	◉	◉	16:9	1	2		
5	Mitsubishi LT-3050	3100	30	●	●	○	◐	◉	○	15:9	2	2	●	
6	Mitsubishi LT-3040	3200	30	●	●	○	◐	◉	◐	15:9	2	2	●	
7	Toshiba 26HL84	1450	26	○	●	◐	◐	◉	○	16:9	3	2		
8	Panasonic Viera TC-32LX20	2000	32	●	●	◐	◐	◉	○	15:9	1	2		
9	JVC LT-26X575	1400	26	●	○	◐	◐	◉	○	16:9	2	1		
10	Toshiba 32HL84	2050	32	○	●	◐	◐	◉	○	16:9	2	2		
11	Sharp Aquos LC-37GD4U	3800	37	○	●	◐	◐	◉	◐	16:9	1	2		
12	Zenith L17W36	500	17	○	●	◐	◐	◉	○	15:9	1	1	●	
13	Philips 26PF9966	1350	26	●	●	○	◐	◉	◐	15:9	2	2	●	
14	Samsung LT-P326W	2220	32	○	●	◐	◐	◉	○	15:9	1	2	●	
15	Samsung LT-P266W	1400	26	○	●	◐	◉	◉	○	15:9	1	2	●	
16	Sharp Aquos LC-32GD4U	2750	32	○	◐	◐	◐	◉	◐	16:9	1	2		
17	Philips 17PF8946	600	17	●	●	◐	◐	◉	○	15:9	2	2	●	
18	LG DU-30LZ30	2270	30	○	○	◐	◐	◉	○	15:9	2	2		
19	Samsung LT-P227W	1030	22	◐	○	○	◐	◉	○	15:9	1	2		
20	Westinghouse W33001	1200	30	◐	○	◐	●	◐	○	15:9	1	2	●	

TVs, LCD

Ratings (continued)

In performance order, within categories

Excellent ● | Very good ◕ | Good ○ | Fair ◔ | Poor ●

Key number	Brand and model	Price	Size	Overall score	HD picture quality	DVD picture quality	S-video picture quality	Antenna/cable picture quality	Sound quality	Ease of use	Aspect ratio	Rear S-video inputs	Rear component inputs	Computer monitor option	Uses control set-top box
HIGH-DEFINITION MODELS
21	LG RU-23LZ21	1200	23		◔	○	○	◔	●	○	15:9	1	1	•	
22	Panasonic Viera TC-26LX20	1480	26		◔	○	◔	◔	●	◔	15:9	1	2		
23	BenQ DV-2680	1100	26		◔	◔	◔	◔	●	◔	15:9	2	1	•	
24	Gateway GTW-L26M103	1000	26		●	◔	◔	◔	●	○	15:9	2	1		
25	RCA Scenium LCDX3022W	2400	30		●	○	○	◔	●	◔	15:9	1	1	•	
ENHANCED-DEFINITION MODELS
26	Panasonic TC-20LA2	700	20		NA	◔	◔	◔	●	◔	4:3	2	1		
27	JVC LT-17X475	650	17		NA	○	◔	●	◔	◔	15:9	1	1	•	
28	JVC LT-23X475	1000	23		NA	○	◔	●	◔	◔	15:9	1	1	•	
29	Sharp Aquos S2 series LC-20S2US	820	20		NA	◔	◔	◔	●	◔	4:3	2	1		
30	Sharp Aquos LC-20B4U-S	650	20		NA	●	◔	◔	●	◔	4:3	1	1		
STANDARD-DEFINITION MODELS
31	Panasonic TC-17LA2	650	17		NA	NA	●	◔	◔	○	4:3	2	1		
32	Samsung LT-P2035	680	20		NA	NA	○	◔	●	○	4:3	1	1		
33	Toshiba 20DL74	720	20		NA	NA	◔	●	●	◔	4:3	2	1		

Guide to the Ratings

OVERALL SCORE is based primarily on picture quality; sound quality and ease of use are also figured in. Expert panelists evaluated picture quality for clarity and color accuracy. HD programming reflects display of a 1080i signal. **DVD PLAYBACK** indicates how a set displayed a 480p signal, such as the output from a progressive-scan DVD player. Regular TV scores are for a 480i signal, such as that of a regular TV program, received via high-quality (S-video) and basic (antenna/cable) inputs. Since HD and DVD images can look much better than regular TV programming, we used higher standards when judging HD and DVD content; thus, a very good score for HD indicates a better picture than a very good score for regular TV signals. **SOUND QUALITY** is for the set's built-in speakers. **EASE OF USE** is our assessment of the remote control, onscreen menus, labeling of inputs, and useful features. **SIZE** indicates diagonal screen size, in inches. **PRICE** is approximate retail. Based on testing in Consumer Reports in March 2005, with updated price and availability.

Profiles | Model-by-Model

HIGH-DEFINITION MODELS

1 Sony Wega KLV-32M1 Very good, with excellent sound, but picture via basic connection only fair. Has auto volume leveler and customizable channel labels. Front A/V inputs include S-video. Excellent sensitivity. Very good remote, but hard to use in low light. Lacks virtual surround sound, automatic display of active program's rating, and channel block-out. Single component-video input limits connection options. Cannot receive Extended Data Services (XDS) program information. Panel dimensions (HWD): 24x33x5 inches, 44 lbs. Base-stand depth: 12 inches.

2 Sony Wega KDL-32XBR950 Very good, with excellent sound. Has integrated tuner for decoding off-air digital signals, virtual surround sound, slot for viewing digital photos stored on Memory Stick media, auto volume leveler, and customizable channel labels. Front A/V inputs include S-video. Very good remote, but hard to use in low light. Lacks automatic display of active program's rating and channel block-out. Cannot receive Extended Data Services (XDS) program information. Panel dimensions (HWD): 25x42x4 inches, 64 lbs. Control-unit dimensions (HWD): 4x17x16 inches. Base-stand depth: 10 inches.

3 Sony Wega KLV-26HG2 Very good, with excellent sound. Has virtual surround sound, slot for viewing digital photos stored on Memory Stick media, customizable channel labels, and automatic display of active program's rating. Very good remote, but hard to use in low light. Lacks auto volume leveler and channel block-out. Single component-video input limits connection options. Cannot receive Extended Data Services (XDS) program information. Front A/V inputs located on side. Panel dimensions (HWD): 17x32x5 inches, 34 lbs. Base-stand depth: 10 inches.

(continued)

TVs, LCD

Profiles Model-by-Model (continued)

4 Sharp Aquos LC-26GD4U Very good, with excellent sound from detachable speakers, but picture via basic connection only fair. Has integrated tuner for decoding off-air digital and digital-cable signals, optical digital-audio output to receiver, tilt/swivel base, virtual surround sound, slot for viewing digital photos stored on PC Card media, automatic display of active program's rating. Lacks auto volume leveler, customizable channel labels, and channel block-out. Cannot receive Extended Data Services (XDS) program information. Panel dimensions (HWD): 20x34x4 inches, 42 lbs. Base-stand depth: 12 inches.

5 Mitsubishi LT-3050 Very good, with excellent sound, but picture via basic connection only fair. Has tilt base, virtual surround sound, auto volume leveler, and customizable channel labels. Excellent sensitivity. Lacks automatic display of active program's rating and channel block-out. Remote control hard to use in low light. Cannot receive Extended Data Services (XDS) program information. Panel dimensions (HWD): 24x30x5 inches, 53 lbs. Base-stand depth: 12 inches.

6 Mitsubishi LT-3040 Good, with very good HD and DVD pictures and excellent sound, but picture via basic connection only fair. Has tilt base, virtual surround sound, auto volume leveler, and customizable channel labels. Excellent sensitivity. Lacks automatic display of active program's rating and channel block-out. Remote control hard to use in low light. Cannot receive Extended Data Services (XDS) program information. Panel dimensions (HWD): 24x30x5 inches, 53 lbs. Base-stand depth: 12 inches.

7 Toshiba 26HL84 Good, with excellent sound and very good S-video picture, but picture via basic connection only fair. Has virtual surround sound, swivel base, scrolling channel preview, auto volume leveler, automatic display of active program's rating, and channel block-out. Excellent remote. Front A/V inputs, located on side, include S-video. Can receive Extended Data Services (XDS) program information, if available. Lacks customizable channel labels and channel block-out. Panel dimensions (HWD): 20x28x5 inches, 52 lbs. Base-stand depth: 13 inches.

8 Panasonic Viera TC-32LX20 Good, with very good DVD and S-video picture and excellent sound, but picture via basic connection only fair. Has slot for viewing digital photos stored on PC Card and SD media. Has swivel base. Very good remote. Front A/V inputs include S-video. Excellent sensitivity. Lacks virtual surround sound, auto volume leveler, automatic display of active program's rating, customizable channel labels, and channel block-out. Single S-video input limits connection options. Cannot receive Extended Data Services (XDS) program information. Panel dimensions (HWD): 22x40x5 inches, 61 lbs. Base-stand depth: 13 inches.

9 JVC LT-26X575 Good, with very good HD picture and excellent sound, but picture via basic connection only fair. Motion compensation feature worked well. Has scrolling channel preview, tilt/swivel base, auto volume leveler, and channel block-out. Can receive Extended Data Services (XDS) program information, if available. Lacks virtual surround sound, customizable channel labels, and automatic display of active program's rating. Panel dimensions (HWD): 22x28x5 inches, 42 lbs. Base-stand depth: 12 inches.

10 Toshiba 32HL84 Good, with very good S-video picture and excellent sound, but picture via basic connection only fair. Has scrolling channel preview, auto volume leveler, customizable channel labels, channel block-out, and swivel base. Very good remote. Front A/V inputs, located on side, include S-video. Excellent sensitivity. Lacks virtual surround sound and automatic display of active program's rating. Rear jacks' labels hard to read. Cannot receive Extended Data Services (XDS) program information. Panel dimensions (HWD): 23x33x5 inches, 63 lbs. Base-stand depth: 13 inches.

11 Sharp Aquos LC-37GD4U Good, with very good DVD picture and excellent sound, but picture via basic connection only fair. Has integrated tuner for decoding off-air digital and digital-cable signals, optical digital-audio output to receiver, slot for viewing digital photos stored on PC Card media, automatic display of active program's rating, and swivel base. Very good remote. Excellent sensitivity. Lacks virtual surround sound, auto volume leveler, customizable channel labels, and channel block-out. Cannot receive Extended Data Services (XDS) program information. Panel dimensions (HWD): 22x44x4 inches, 61 lbs. Base-stand depth: 13 inches.

TVs, LCD

Profiles Model-by-Model (continued)

12 Zenith L17W36 Good, with very good S-video picture and sound. Has virtual surround sound. Lacks auto volume leveler, customizable channel labels, automatic display of active program's rating, and channel block-out. Single S-video and component-video inputs limit connection options. Cannot receive Extended Data Services (XDS) program information. Front A/V inputs located on side. Panel dimensions (HWD): 14x19x4 inches, 15 lbs. Base-stand depth: 8 inches.

13 Philips 26PF9966 Good, with very good HD and DVD pictures and excellent sound, but picture via basic connection only fair. Has virtual surround sound, auto volume leveler, and channel block-out. Excellent sensitivity. Lacks automatic display of active program's rating and customizable channel labels. Single component-video input limits connection options. Onscreen menu relatively hard to use, and remote control hard to use in low light. Cannot receive Extended Data Services (XDS) program information. Panel dimensions (HWD): 18x32x5 inches, 42 lbs. Base-stand depth: 11 inches.

14 Samsung LT-P326W Good, with very good DVD picture and excellent sound, but picture via basic connection only fair. Has virtual surround sound, auto volume leveler, and customizable channel labels. Excellent sensitivity. Lacks automatic display of active program's rating and channel block-out. Remote control hard to use in low light. Cannot receive Extended Data Services (XDS) program information. Panel dimensions (HWD): 23x34x5 inches, 51 lbs. Base-stand depth: 13 inches.

15 Samsung LT-P266W Good, with very good DVD picture and excellent sound, but picture via basic connection only fair. Has virtual surround sound, auto volume leveler, and customizable channel labels. Excellent sensitivity. Lacks automatic display of active program's rating and channel block-out. Remote control hard to use in low light. Rear jacks' labels hard to read. Cannot receive Extended Data Services (XDS) program information. Panel dimensions (HWD): 20x30x5 inches, 34 lbs. Base-stand depth: 11 inches.

16 Sharp Aquos LC-32GD4U Good, with excellent sound, but regular-TV pictures only fair. Has integrated tuner for decoding off-air digital and digital-cable signals, optical digital-audio output to receiver, swivel base, slot for viewing digital photos stored on PC Card media, and automatic display of active program's rating. Very good remote. Excellent sensitivity. Lacks virtual surround sound, auto volume leveler, customizable channel labels, and channel block-out. Cannot receive Extended Data Services (XDS) program information. Panel dimensions (HWD): 19x39x4 inches, 56 lbs. Base-stand depth: 13 inches.

17 Philips 17PF8946 Good, with very good HD and DVD pictures and very good sound, but picture via basic connection only fair. Has virtual surround sound, built-in FM radio tuner, auto volume leveler, customizable channel labels, automatic display of active program's rating, and channel block-out. Remote control hard to use in low light. Rear jacks' labels hard to read. Cannot receive Extended Data Services (XDS) program information. Panel dimensions (HWD): 12x21x3 inches, 13 lbs. Base-stand depth: 7 inches.

18 LG DU-30LZ30 Good, with excellent sound, but S-video and antenna/cable pictures only fair. Motion compensation feature worked well. Has integrated tuner for decoding off-air digital signals, optical digital-audio output to receiver, DVI input, scrolling channel preview, virtual surround sound, auto volume leveler, automatic display of active program's rating, customizable channel labels, and channel block-out. Wider viewing angle than for most others tested. Excellent remote, but onscreen menu relatively hard to use. Lacks front A/V inputs and headphone jack. Rear jacks' labels hard to read. Vertical viewing angle cannot be adjusted while unit attached to stand. Cannot receive Extended Data Services (XDS) program information. Panel dimensions (HWD): 21x35x4 inches, 74 lb. Base-stand depth: 8 inches. Discontinued, but may still be available.

19 Samsung LT-P227W Good, with excellent sound, but HD and basic-connection pictures only fair. Has virtual surround sound, auto volume leveler, and automatic display of active program's rating. Excellent remote, but hard to use in low light. Lacks customizable channel labels and channel block-out. Cannot receive Extended Data Services (XDS) program information. Panel dimensions (HWD): 17x24x5 inches, 20 lbs. Base-stand depth: 9 inches.

(continued)

TVs, LCD

Profiles Model-by-Model (continued)

20 Westinghouse W33001 Good, with excellent sound, but HD and antenna/cable pictures only fair. Has DVI input, scrolling channel preview, and virtual surround sound. Wider viewing angle than for most others tested. Very good remote. Lacks front A/V inputs, auto volume leveler, automatic display of active program's rating, customizable channel labels, channel block-out, and headphone jack. Single S-video input limits connection options. Vertical viewing angle cannot be adjusted while unit attached to stand. Cannot receive Extended Data Services (XDS) program information. Panel dimensions (HWD): 19x35x4 inches, 42 lb. Base-stand depth: 9 inches.

21 LG RU-23LZ21 Good, with very good sound, but HD and antenna/cable pictures only fair. Has swivel base, auto volume leveler, channel block-out, and headphone jack. Very good remote, but hard to use in low light. Lacks audio output, virtual surround sound, auto volume leveler, and customizable channel labels. Single S-video and component-video inputs limit connection options. Cannot receive Extended Data Services (XDS) program information. Front A/V inputs located on side. Panel dimensions (HWD): 20x24x9 inches, 24 lb. Base-stand depth: 9 inches. Discontinued, but may still be available.

22 Panasonic Viera TC-26LX20 Good, with excellent sound, but HD and basic-connection pictures only fair. Has virtual surround sound, swivel base, slot for viewing digital photos stored on Secure Digital and PC Card media, auto volume leveler, and automatic display of active program's rating. Front A/V inputs include S-video. Lacks customizable channel labels and channel block-out. Onscreen menu relatively hard to use. Cannot receive Extended Data Services (XDS) program information. Panel dimensions (HWD): 19x34x6 inches, 50 lbs. Base-stand depth: 13 inches.

23 BenQ DV-2680 Fair, with good S-video picture and excellent sound. Has auto volume leveler. Very good remote, but hard to use in low light. Lacks virtual surround sound, audio output, customizable channel labels, channel block-out, and headphone jack. Single component-video input limits connection options. Onscreen menu relatively hard to use. Vertical viewing angle cannot be adjusted while unit attached to stand. Cannot receive Extended Data Services (XDS) program information. Panel dimensions (HWD): 18x34x4 inches, 34 lb. Base-stand depth: 8 inches. Discontinued, but may still be available.

24 Gateway GTW-L26M103 Fair, with excellent sound but poor HD picture; there are better choices. Has swivel base. Very good remote. Lacks virtual surround sound, auto volume leveler, customizable channel labels, automatic display of active program's rating, and channel block-out. Single component-video input limits connection options. Cannot receive Extended Data Services (XDS) program information. Panel dimensions (HWD): 17x33x4 inches, 31 lbs. Base-stand depth: 9 inches.

25 RCA Scenium LCDX3022W Poor overall, with good DVD and S-video pictures and excellent sound; there are better choices. Has tilt base, virtual surround sound, auto volume leveler, and channel block-out. Lacks customizable channel labels and automatic display of active program's rating. Single component-video and S-video inputs limit connection options. Cannot receive Extended Data Services (XDS) program information. Panel dimensions (HWD): 20x36x4 inches, 44 lbs. Base-stand depth: 9 inches.

ENHANCED-DEFINITION MODELS

26 Panasonic TC-20LA2 Good, with excellent sound, but picture via basic connection only fair; cannot accept an HD signal for down-converted display. Has automatic display of active program's rating. Very good remote, but hard to use in low light. Lacks virtual surround sound, auto volume leveler, customizable channel labels, and channel block-out. Single component-video input limits connection options. Onscreen menu relatively hard to use. Cannot receive Extended Data Services (XDS) program information. Panel dimensions (HWD): 18x20x4 inches, 17 lbs. Base-stand depth: 11 inches.

27 JVC LT-17X475 Good, with very good sound, but picture via basic connection poor; cannot accept an HD signal for down-converted display. Has virtual surround sound, swivel base, automatic display of active program's rating, and channel block-out. Very good remote, but hard to use in low light.

TVs, LCD

Profiles Model-by-Model (continued)

Lacks auto volume leveler and customizable channel labels. Single S-video and component-video inputs limit connection options. Single-tuner PIP works for computer-monitor use only. Cannot receive Extended Data Services (XDS) program information. Panel dimensions (HWD): 13x19x4 inches, 16 lbs. Base-stand depth: 8 inches.

28 JVC LT-23X475 Good, with very good sound, but S-video picture fair and picture via basic connection poor; cannot accept an HD signal for down-converted display. Has virtual surround sound, swivel base, automatic display of active program's rating, and channel block-out. Very good remote, but hard to use in low light. Lacks auto volume leveler and customizable channel labels. Single S-video and component-video inputs limit connection options. Single-tuner PIP works for computer-monitor use only. Cannot receive Extended Data Services (XDS) program information. Panel dimensions (HWD): 18x25x4 inches, 22 lbs. Base-stand depth: 9 inches.

29 Sharp Aquos S2 series LC-20S2U Fair overall, with excellent sound; cannot accept an HD signal for down-converted display. Has swivel base and automatic display of active program's rating. Can receive Extended Data Services (XDS) program information, if available. Lacks virtual surround sound, customizable channel labels, and channel block-out. Single component-video input limits connection options. Onscreen menu relatively hard to use, and remote control hard to use in low light. Panel dimensions (HWD): 16x19x3 inches, 16 lbs. Base-stand depth: 9 inches.

30 Sharp Aquos LC-20B4U-S Fair overall, with excellent sound but poor DVD picture; cannot accept an HD signal for down-converted display. Has automatic display of active program's rating. Lacks audio tone controls, virtual surround sound, auto volume leveler, customizable channel labels, and channel block-out. Single S-video and component-video inputs limit connection options. Cannot receive Extended Data Services (XDS) program information. Panel dimensions (HWD): 16x25x3 inches, 18 lbs. Base-stand depth: 10 inches.

STANDARD-DEFINITION MODELS

31 Panasonic TC-17LA2 Good, with very good S-video picture and sound, picture via basic connection only fair. Excellent sensitivity. Has swivel base. Excellent remote, but hard to use in low light. Lacks virtual surround sound, auto volume leveler, customizable channel labels, automatic display of active program's rating, and channel block-out. Single component-video input limits connection options. Cannot receive Extended Data Services (XDS) program information. Panel dimensions (HWD): 16x18x4 inches, 15 lbs. Base-stand depth: 11 inches.

32 Samsung LT-P2035 Fair overall, with very good sound and good S-video picture. Has automatic display of active program's rating. Excellent remote, but hard to use in low light. Lacks audio tone controls, virtual surround sound, auto volume leveler, customizable channel labels, and channel block-out. Single S-video and component-video inputs limit connection options. Cannot receive Extended Data Services (XDS) program information. Panel dimensions (HWD): 17x24x5 inches, 22 lbs. Base-stand depth: 10 inches.

33 Toshiba 20DL74 Fair overall, with excellent sound, but picture via basic connection poor; there are better choices. Narrow viewing angle. Has tilt/swivel base. Lacks virtual surround sound, auto volume leveler, customizable channel labels, automatic display of active program's rating, and channel block-out. Remote control hard to use in low light. Cannot receive Extended Data Services (XDS) program information. Panel dimensions (HWD): 18x20x4 inches, 20 lbs. Base-stand depth: 11 inches.

REFERENCE & RATINGS

TVs, PICTURE-TUBE, 26- TO 27-INCH

CR Quick Recommendations

Quick Picks

For a conventional analog set:
1. Sony, $360
2. Toshiba, $240

The Sony FD Trinitron Wega KV-27FS120 (1), a flat-screen set, had good picture quality and front-panel A/V input. The Toshiba 27A44 (2), which has a curved screen, displayed very good S-video picture quality and also accepts connections through its front panel. Both, however, have only a 3-mo. labor warranty.

For an HD set:
7. Sony, $640

The Sony FD Trinitron Wega Hi-Scan KV-27HS420 (7) had very good picture quality across the board, though it lacks special aspect-ratio settings such as zoom or stretch, has only one S-video input, and comes with a short (3-mo.) labor warranty. Like many HD sets tested, it has HDMI input, which may provide enhanced picture quality from newer devices with a matching digital output.

Ratings

In performance order, within categories

Ratings key: Excellent ● | Very good ◕ | Good ○ | Fair ◐ | Poor ●

Key no.	Brand and model	Price	Overall score	HD picture quality	DVD picture quality	S-video picture quality	Ant/cable picture quality	Sound quality	Ease of use	Flat screen	PIP (no. of tuners)	Rear S-video inputs	Rear component inputs	Front panel A/V inputs
27-INCH STANDARD-DEFINITION MODELS														
1	Sony FD Trinitron Wega KV-27FS120	$360		NA	NA	○	○	●	○	●	No	2	1	1
2	Toshiba 27A44	240		NA	NA	◕	○	●	◐		No	2	1	1
3	JVC l'Art AV-27F475	300		NA	NA	○	◐	●	○	●	No	1	1	1
4	Panasonic Tau PureFlat Series CT-27SL14	345		NA	NA	○	◐	◐	○	●	No	2	1	1
5	JVC D-Series AV-27D305	215		NA	NA	○	◐	●	○		No	1	1	1
6	Philips 27PT6441	290		NA	NA	○	◐	●	◐		No	2	1	1
26- AND 27-INCH HIGH-DEFINITION MODELS														
7	Sony FD Trinitron Wega Hi-Scan KV-27HS420	700		◕	●	◕	◕	●	○	●	No	2	1	2
8	Samsung DynaFlat TX-P2775H	630		○	◕	○	○	●	○	●	No	1	1	2
9	Panasonic Tau PureFlat Series CT-27HL14	515		○	◐	●	●	●	◐	●	No	3	1	1

Guide to the Ratings

OVERALL SCORE is based primarily on picture quality; sound quality and ease of use are also figured in. Expert panelists evaluated picture quality for clarity and color accuracy. **HD PICTURE QUALITY** is based on an expert viewing panel's judgment of an HD TV's picture clarity and color accuracy, relative to these attributes in other HD sets, when displaying a 1080i HD signal. The signal is received through the component-video input, which can be used to connect a digital-cable box, satellite receiver, or off-air digital receiver/tuner to the TV. **DVD PICTURE QUALITY** is based on an expert viewing panel's judgment of an HD or ED TV's picture clarity and color accuracy, relative to these attributes in similar sets, when displaying a 480p signal, such as the output from a progressive-scan DVD player. The signal is received through the component-video input, which can be used to connect a digital-cable box, satellite receiver, or off-air digital receiver/tuner to the TV. **S-VIDEO PICTURE QUALITY** is based on an expert viewing panel's judgment of a TV's picture clarity and color accuracy, relative to these attributes in other sets, when displaying a standard 480i signal received through the set's S-video input. This input offers a better connection to the set than that of an antenna/cable input. DVD players, digital-cable boxes, and satellite receivers are among products with S-video output. **ANT/CABLE PICTURE QUALITY** is based on an expert viewing panel's judgment of a TV's picture clarity and color accuracy, relative to these attributes in other sets, when displaying a standard 480i signal such as that of a typical TV program. The signal is received through the set's antenna/cable (UHF/VHF) input, which is often used to connect a conventional cable box, VCR, or antenna to the TV. **SOUND QUALITY** is measured from the set's built-in speakers using computer-driven test equipment. You can get a wider range of frequencies or deeper bass if you route the TV's sound to external speakers–say, through a home-theater system. **EASE OF USE** is a usability assessment of the set's remote control, onscreen menus, labeling of inputs, and useful features. **PRICE** is approximate retail.

Based on testing in Consumer Reports in March 2005, updated for price and availability.

TVs, PICTURE-TUBE, 26- TO 27-INCH

Profiles Model-by-Model (continued)

27-INCH STANDARD DEFINITION

1 Sony FD Trinitron Wega KV-27FS120 Good, with excellent sound. Has virtual surround sound, auto volume leveler, and customizable channel labels. Can receive Extended Data Services (XDS) program information, if available. Very good remote, but hard to use in low light. Lacks automatic display of active program's rating and channel block-out. Short (3-mo.) labor warranty. Rear jacks' labels hard to read. Dimensions (HWD): 24x31x20 inches, 100 lbs.

2 Toshiba 27A44 Good, with very good S-video picture and excellent sound. Has virtual surround sound, auto volume leveler, customizable channel labels, and channel block-out. Cannot receive Extended Data Services (XDS) program information. Short (3-mo.) labor warranty. Rear jacks' labels hard to read. To see program ratings, must push a button on remote. Dimensions (HWD): 23x30x20 inches, 82 lbs.

3 JVC I'Art AV-27F475 Good, with excellent sound, but picture via basic connection only fair. Has virtual surround sound, auto volume leveler, and channel block-out. Can receive Extended Data Services (XDS) program information, if available. Lacks customizable channel labels and automatic display of active program's rating. Remote control hard to use in low light. Rear jacks' labels hard to read. Dimensions (HWD): 24x33x21 inches, 95 lbs. Discontinued, but may still be available.

4 Panasonic Tau PureFlat Series CT-27SL14 Good, with very good sound, but picture via basic connection only fair. Has virtual surround sound, auto volume leveler, customizable channel labels, automatic display of active program's rating, and channel block-out. Very good remote, but hard to use in low light. Short (3-mo.) labor warranty. Cannot receive Extended Data Services (XDS) program information. Dimensions (HWD): 24x31x20 inches, 95 lbs.

5 JVC D-Series AV-27D305 Good, with very good sound, but picture via basic connection only fair. Has virtual surround sound, auto volume leveler, and channel block-out. Can receive Extended Data Services (XDS) program information, if available. Lacks customizable channel labels and automatic display of active program's rating. Remote control hard to use in low light. Rear jacks' labels hard to read. Dimensions (HWD): 24x30x23 inches, 71 lbs. Discontinued, but may still be available.

6 Philips 27PT6441 Good, with excellent sound, but picture via basic connection only fair. Has auto volume leveler and channel block-out. Front A/V inputs located on side. Lacks virtual surround sound, customizable channel labels, and automatic display of active program's rating. Remote control only so-so, and hard to use in low light. Short (3-mo.) labor warranty. Rear jacks' labels hard to read. Cannot receive Extended Data Services (XDS) program information. Dimensions (HWD): 20x30x20 inches, 108 lbs. Discontinued, but may still be available.

26- AND 27-INCH HIGH-DEFINITION

7 Sony FD Trinitron Wega Hi-Scan KV-27HS420 Very good, with excellent sound. Has virtual surround sound, auto volume leveler, and customizable channel labels. Front A/V inputs include S-video. Can receive Extended Data Services (XDS) program information, if available. Very good remote, but hard to use in low light. Lacks special aspect-ratio settings (such as zoom or stretch), automatic display of active program's rating, and channel block-out. Short (3-mo.) labor warranty. Dimensions (HWD): 24x31x21 inches, 111 lbs.

8 Samsung DynaFlat TX-P2775H Good, with very good DVD picture and excellent sound, but had intermittent HD-decoding problem. Has integrated tuner for decoding off-air digital signals, optical digital-audio output to receiver, auto volume leveler, and customizable channel labels. Motion compensation feature worked very well. Front A/V inputs, located on side, include S-video. Excellent sensitivity. Very good remote, but hard to use in low light. Lacks virtual surround sound and channel block-out. To see program ratings, must push a button on remote. Cannot receive Extended Data Services (XDS) program information. Dimensions (HWD): 24x30x21 inches, 105 lbs.

9 Panasonic Tau PureFlat Series CT-27HL14 Good, with very good regular-TV pictures and excellent sound, but DVD picture only fair. Can't display an image from a 720p HD signal. Has virtual surround sound, auto volume leveler, automatic display of active program's rating, customizable channel labels, and channel block-out. Excellent selectivity. Very good remote control, but hard to use in low light. Lacks special aspect-ratio settings (such as zoom or stretch). Single S-video and component-video inputs limit connection options. Onscreen menu hard to use. Short (3-mo.) labor warranty. Cannot receive Extended Data Services (XDS) program information. Dimensions (HWD): 23x28x20 in., 100 lbs. Discontinued, but may still be available.

TVs, PICTURE-TUBE, 30- TO 36-INCH

CR Quick Recommendations

Quick Picks

For a 32-inch, conventional analog set:
- 1 Toshiba, $350
- 4 JVC, $450

The Toshiba FST Black 32A43 (1), a CR Best Buy, offers good picture quality and very good ease of use at a low price. It has a curved screen. Among the flat-screen sets, we'd recommend the JVC l'Art AV-32F475 (4), which had a better S-video picture than the Toshiba, though its remote control was hard to use in low light.

For a 36-inch, conventional analog set:
- 9 Sony, $800

The Sony FD Trinitron Wega KV-36FS320 (9), a flat-screen set, had a very good S-video picture and includes ample inputs plus a Memory Stick slot for viewing photos taken with a compatible digital camera. Shortcomings are 30-day labor and on-site warranties and a remote control that was difficult to use in low light.

For a wide-screen HD set that will provide the best viewing experience:
- 13, 18, 19, 20 Sony, $855-$1,800

All four of these Sony TVs were excellent with HD and very good or excellent for DVD and regular TV. The Sony FD Trinitron Wega HDTV KD-34XBR960 (18) and Sony FD Trinitron Wega Hi-Scan KD-34XS955 (19) are 34-inch digital-cable-ready sets with built-in tuners and CableCard slots, plus features such as a Memory Stick slot for viewing digital images. The Sony FD Trinitron Wega HDTV KD-34XBR960 (18) has a longer warranty than its brand-mates. The Sony FD Trinitron Wega Hi-Scan KV-34HS420 (20) and Sony FD Trinitron Wega Hi-Scan KV-30HS420 (13) are HD-ready models with 34-inch and 30-inch screens, respectively.

If you want to spend less for HD and are happy with the familiar squarish screen:
- 8, 23 Sony, $845-$1,130
- 24 Panasonic, $1,030

The 36-inch Panasonic Tau PureFlat Series CT-36HL44 (24) was excellent for picture quality nearly across the board and is well-priced for this size. The 36-inch Sony FD Trinitron Wega Hi-Scan KV-36HS420 (23) and 32-inch Sony FD Trinitron Wega Hi-Scan KV-32HS420 (8) were judged excellent for HD and very good or better for other content. Both have a front-panel S-video input.

Ratings

In performance order, within categories.

Ratings key: Excellent ● | Very good ◖ | Good ○ | Fair ◐ | Poor ●

Key numbers	Brand and model	Price	Overall score (P F G VG E)	HD picture quality	DVD picture quality	S-video picture quality	Ant/cable picture quality	Sound quality	Ease of use	Flat screen	PIP (no. of tuners)	Rear S-video inputs	Rear component inputs	Front panel A/V inputs
32-INCH STANDARD-DEFINITION MODELS														
1 (CR BEST BUY)	Toshiba FST Black 32A43	350		NA	NA	○	○	●	◖		No	1	1	●
2	RCA 32V430T	400		NA	NA	◖	○	●	◐		No	1	1	●
3	Sony FD Trinitron Wega KV-32FS120	550		NA	NA	○	◐	○	◐	●	No	1	1	●
4	JVC l'Art AV-32F475	450		NA	NA	◖	○	◐	○	●	No	1	1	●
5	JVC D-Series AV-32D305	355		NA	NA	○	○	●	○		No	1	1	●
6	Toshiba FST Pure 32AF44	495		NA	NA	○	◐	●	◐	●	No	1	1	●
7	Panasonic Tau PureFlat Series CT-32SL14	500		NA	NA	○	●	●	◐	●	No	1	1	●
32-INCH HIGH-DEFINITION MODELS														
8	Sony FD Trinitron Wega Hi-Scan KV-32HS420	845		●	◖	◖	●	●	○	●	No	2	2	●
9	Sony FD Trinitron Wega KV-36FS320	800		NA	NA	◖	◐	●	◐	●	No	1	2	●
10	JVC l'Art AV-36F475	700		NA	NA	◖	◐	●	○	●	No	1	1	●
11	Sony FD Trinitron Wega KV-36FS120	820		NA	NA	○	◐	●	◐	●	No	1	1	●
12	Toshiba Cinema Series 35AF44	690		NA	NA	○	◐	●	◐	●	No	1	1	●
30-INCH WIDE-SCREEN HIGH-DEFINITION MODELS														
13	Sony FD Trinitron Wega Hi-Scan KV-30HS420	855		●	◖	◖	●	●	○	●	No	2	2	●
14	Sony FD Trinitron Wega Hi-Scan KD-30XS955	1070		●	◖	◖	●	●	○	●	No	2	2	●
15	Panasonic Tau PureFlat Series CT-30WX54	750		○	◖	○	◐	●	○	●	2	2	2	●
16	Toshiba TheaterWide HD 30HF84	720		○	◖	●	◐	●	○	●	No	2	2	●
17	Philips 30PW8402	775		○	◖	○	◐	●	◐	●	No	1	2	●

TVs, PICTURE-TUBE, 30- TO 36-INCH

Ratings (continued)

In performance order, within categories

Ratings key: Excellent ● | Very good ◉ | Good ◐ | Fair ◑ | Poor ○

Key numbers	Brand and model	Price	Overall score (P F G VG E, 0–100)	HD picture quality	DVD picture quality	S-video picture quality	Ant/cable picture quality	Sound quality	Ease of use	Flat screen	PIP (no. of tuners)	Rear S-video inputs	Rear component inputs	Front panel A/V inputs
34-INCH WIDE-SCREEN HIGH-DEFINITION MODELS														
18	Sony FD Trinitron Wega HDTV KD-34XBR960	1895		●	●	◉	◉	●	◐	●	2	2	2	●
19	Sony FD Trinitron Wega Hi-Scan KD-34XS955	1800		●	●	◉	◉	●	◐	●	No	2	2	●
20	Sony FD Trinitron Wega Hi-Scan KV-34HS420	1340		●	◉	◉	◉	●	◐	●	No	2	2	●
21	Toshiba TheaterWide 34HF84	1170		◉	◐	◐	◐	●	◑	●	2	2	2	●
22	Panasonic Tau PureFlat Series CT-34WX54	1070		◐	◐	◐	◐	●	◐	●	2	2	2	●
36-INCH HIGH-DEFINITION MODELS														
23	Sony FD Trinitron Wega Hi-Scan KV-36HS420	1230		●	●	◉	◉	●	◐	●	No	2	2	●
24	Panasonic Tau PureFlat Series CT-36HL44	1400		●	●	●	◉	●	◑	●	2	2	2	●

Guide to the Ratings

OVERALL SCORE is based primarily on picture quality; sound quality and ease of use are also figured in. Expert panelists evaluated picture quality for clarity and color accuracy. HD programming reflects display of a 1080i signal. **DVD PLAYBACK** indicates how a set displayed a 480p signal, such as the output from a progressive-scan DVD player. Regular TV scores are for a 480i signal, such as that of a regular TV program, received via high-quality (S-video) and basic (antenna/cable) inputs. Since HD and DVD images can look much better than regular TV programming, we used higher standards when judging HD and DVD content; thus, a very good score for HD indicates a better picture than a very good score for regular TV signals. **SOUND QUALITY** is for the set's built-in speakers. **EASE OF USE** is our assessment of the remote control, onscreen menus, labeling of inputs, and useful features. **SIZE** indicates diagonal screen size, in inches. **PRICE** is approximate retail. Based on testing in Consumer Reports in March 2005, updated for price and availability.

Profiles Model-by-Model

32-INCH STANDARD DEFINITION

1 Toshiba FST Black 32A43 A **CR Best Buy.** Very good, with excellent sound. Has virtual surround sound and channel block-out. Very good remote control and excellent onscreen menu. Lacks auto volume leveler, customizable channel labels, and automatic display of active program's rating. Rear jacks' labels hard to read. Cannot receive Extended Data Services (XDS) program information. Dimensions (HWD): 28x34x22 in., 111 lbs.

2 RCA 32V430T Good, with very good S-video picture and excellent sound, but RCA has been among the most repair-prone brands of 30-32-in. sets. Has virtual surround sound, auto volume leveler, and customizable channel labels. Excellent sensitivity. Lacks automatic display of active program's rating and channel block-out. Remote control hard to use in low light. Short (3-mo.) labor warranty. Cannot receive Extended Data Services (XDS) program information. Dimensions (HWD): 29x31x23 in., 120 lbs.

3 Sony FD Trinitron Wega KV-32FS120 Good, with excellent sound, but picture via basic connection only fair. Has virtual surround sound, auto volume leveler, and customizable channel labels. Can receive Extended Data Services (XDS) program information, if available. Very good remote, but hard to use in low light. Lacks automatic display of active program's rating and channel block-out. Short (3-mo.) labor warranty. Rear jacks' labels hard to read. Dimensions (HWD): 28x36x23 in., 166 lbs.

4 JVC l'Art AV-32F475 Good, with very good S-video picture and excellent sound. Has virtual surround sound, auto volume leveler, and channel block-out. Can receive Extended Data Services (XDS) program information, if available. Lacks customizable channel labels and automatic display of active program's rating. Remote control hard to use in low light. Dimensions (HWD): 27x37x23 in., 141 lbs.

5 JVC D-Series AV-32D305 Good, with excellent sound. Has virtual surround sound, auto volume leveler, and channel block-out. Can receive Extended Data Services (XDS) program information, if available. Lacks customizable channel labels and automatic display of active program's rating. Remote control hard to use in low light. Dimensions (HWD): 27x34x22 in., 115 lbs.

6 Toshiba FST Pure 32AF44 Good, with excellent sound, but picture via basic

(continued)

TVs, PICTURE-TUBE, 30- TO 36-INCH

Profiles Model-by-Model (continued)

connection only fair. Has virtual surround sound, customizable channel labels, and channel block-out. Front A/V inputs include S-video. Very good remote control. Lacks auto volume leveler. Rear jacks' labels hard to read. Cannot receive Extended Data Services (XDS) program information. To see program ratings, must push a button on remote. Dimensions (HWD): 27x35x23 in., 144 lbs. Discontinued, but may still be available.

7 Panasonic Tau PureFlat Series CT-32SL14 Good, with excellent sound, but antenna/cable picture only fair. Has virtual surround sound, auto volume leveler, automatic display of active program's rating, customizable channel labels, channel block-out, and headphone jack. Front A/V inputs include S-video. Very good remote, but hard to use in low light. Rear jacks' labels hard to read. Cannot receive Extended Data Services (XDS) program information. Dimensions (HWD): 27x35x23 in.

32-INCH HIGH-DEFINITION

8 Sony FD Trinitron Wega Hi-Scan KV-32HS420 Very good, with excellent sound and HD picture. Motion compensation feature worked well. Has virtual surround sound, auto volume leveler, and customizable channel labels. Front A/V inputs include S-video. Can receive Extended Data Services (XDS) program information, if available. Excellent sensitivity. Very good remote, but hard to use in low light. Lacks special aspect-ratio settings (such as zoom or stretch), automatic display of active program's rating, and channel block-out. Short (3-mo.) labor and in-home warranties. Dimensions (HWD): 28x36x24 in., 165 lbs.

35- AND 36-INCH STANDARD DEFINITION

9 Sony FD Trinitron Wega KV-36FS320 Good, with very good S-video picture and excellent sound, but picture via basic connection only fair. Has virtual surround sound, slot for viewing digital photos stored on Memory Stick media, auto volume leveler, and customizable channel labels. Can receive Extended Data Services (XDS) program information, if available. Excellent sensitivity. Lacks automatic display of active program's rating and channel block-out. Short (3-mo.) labor and in-home warranties. Remote control hard to use in low light. Rear jacks' labels hard to read. Dimensions (HWD): 30x40x26 in., 223 lbs.

10 JVC I'Art AV-36F475 Good, with excellent sound, but picture via basic connection only fair. Has virtual surround sound, auto volume leveler, and channel block-out. Can receive Extended Data Services (XDS) program information, if available. Lacks customizable channel labels and automatic display of active program's rating. Remote control hard to use in low light. Dimensions (HWD): 30x41x25 in., 187 lbs

11 Sony FD Trinitron Wega KV-36FS120 Good, with very good S-video picture and excellent sound, but picture via basic connection only fair. Has virtual surround sound, auto volume leveler, and customizable channel labels. Can receive Extended Data Services (XDS) program information, if available. Very good remote, but hard to use in low light. Lacks automatic display of active program's rating and channel block-out. Short (3-mo.) labor warranty. Rear jacks' labels hard to read. Dimensions (HWD): 31x39x25 in., 217 lbs.

12 Toshiba Cinema Series 35AF44 Good 35-inch set, with excellent sound, but picture via basic connection only fair. Has virtual surround sound, auto volume leveler, customizable channel labels, and channel block-out. Front A/V inputs include S-video. Excellent sensitivity. Remote control only so-so. Rear jacks' labels hard to read. Cannot receive Extended Data Services (XDS) program information. To see program ratings, must push a button on remote. Dimensions (HWD): 30x39x25 in., 154 lbs.

30-INCH WIDE-SCREEN HIGH-DEFINITION

13 Sony FD Trinitron Wega Hi-Scan KV-30HS420 Very good, with excellent sound and HD picture. Motion compensation feature worked well. Has virtual surround sound, auto volume leveler, and customizable channel labels. Front A/V inputs include S-video. Excellent sensitivity. Can receive Extended Data Services (XDS) program information, if available. Very good remote control, but difficult to use in low light. Lacks automatic display of active program's rating and channel block-out. Short (3-mo.) labor and in-home warranties. Dimensions (HWD): 24x36x23 in., 150 lbs.

14 Sony FD Trinitron Wega Hi-Scan KD-30XS955 Very good, with excellent HD and DVD pictures and excellent sound. Motion compensation feature worked well. Has integrated tuner for decoding off-air digital and digital-cable signals, optical digital-audio output to receiver, slot for viewing digital photos stored on Memory Stick media, virtual surround sound, auto volume leveler, customizable channel labels, and automatic display of active program's rating. Front A/V inputs include S-video. Can receive Extended Data Services (XDS) program information, if available. Lacks channel block-out. Remote control hard to use in low light. Short (3-mo.) labor and in-home warranties. Dimensions (HWD): 24x36x22 in., 154 lbs.

15 Panasonic Tau PureFlat Series CT-30WX54 Good, with very good DVD picture and excellent sound, but can't display an image from a 720p HD signal. Has scrolling channel preview, virtual surround sound, auto volume leveler, customizable channel labels, automatic display of active program's rating, and channel block-out. Excellent remote control. Front A/V inputs include S-video. Can receive Extended Data Services (XDS) program information, if available. Dimensions (HWD): 23x36x23 in., 140 lbs. Discontinued, but may still be available.

16 Toshiba TheaterWide HD 30HF84 Good, with very good DVD picture and excellent sound, but picture via basic connection only fair. Has virtual surround sound, auto volume leveler, customizable channel labels, and channel block-out. Front A/V inputs include S-video. Very good remote control, but onscreen menu hard to use. Cannot receive Extended Data Services (XDS) program information. To see program ratings, must push a button on remote. Dimensions (HWD): 22x32x23 in., 88 lbs.

17 Philips 30PW8402 Good, with very good DVD picture and excellent sound, but picture via basic connection only fair. Can't display an image from a 720p HD signal. Has virtual surround sound, auto volume leveler, customizable channel labels, and channel block-out. Front A/V inputs, located on side, include S-video. Lacks automatic display of active program's rating. Remote control hard to use in low light. Short (3-mo.) labor warranty. Rear jacks' labels hard to read. Cannot receive Extended Data Services (XDS) program information. Dimensions (HWD): 22x36x22 in., 117 lbs. Discontinued, but may still be available.

TVs, PICTURE-TUBE, 30- TO 36-INCH

Profiles Model-by-Model (continued)

34-INCH WIDE-SCREEN HIGH-DEFINITION

18 Sony FD Trinitron Wega HDTV KD-34XBR960 Very good, with excellent HD and DVD pictures and excellent sound. Has integrated tuner for decoding off-air digital and digital-cable signals, optical digital-audio output to receiver, scrolling channel preview, slot for viewing digital photos stored on Memory Stick media, virtual surround sound, and auto volume leveler. Long (2-yr.) parts and labor warranty. Front A/V inputs include S-video and FireWire. Can receive Extended Data Services (XDS) program information, if available. Very good remote, but hard to use in low light. Lacks customizable channel labels, automatic display of active program's rating, and channel block-out. Dimensions (HWD): 26x40x24 in., 196 lbs.

19 Sony FD Trinitron Wega Hi-Scan KD-34XS955 Very good, with excellent DVD picture and sound. Has integrated tuner for decoding off-air digital and digital-cable signals, optical digital-audio output to receiver, slot for viewing digital photos stored on Memory Stick media, virtual surround sound, and auto volume leveler. Front A/V inputs include S-video. Can receive Extended Data Services (XDS) program information, if available. Very good remote, but hard to use in low light. Lacks customizable channel labels, automatic display of active program's rating, and channel block-out. Short (3-mo.) labor warranty. Dimensions (HWD): 26x40x24 in., 205 lbs.

20 Sony FD Trinitron Wega Hi-Scan KV-34HS420 Very good, with excellent sound and HD picture. Motion compensation feature worked well. Has virtual surround sound, auto volume leveler, and customizable channel labels. Front A/V inputs include S-video. Excellent sensitivity. Can receive Extended Data Services (XDS) program information, if available. Very good remote control, but difficult to use in low light. Lacks automatic display of active program's rating and channel block-out. Short (3-mo.) labor and in-home warranties. Dimensions (HWD): 26x40x24 in., 194 lbs.

21 Toshiba TheaterWide 34HF84 Good, with very good HD and S-video pictures and excellent sound. Motion compensation feature worked very well. Has scrolling channel preview, virtual surround sound, auto volume leveler, customizable channel labels, and channel block-out. Front A/V inputs include S-video. Excellent sensitivity and selectivity. Remote control only so-so, and hard to use in low light. Cannot receive Extended Data Services (XDS) program information. To see program ratings, must push a button on remote. Dimensions (HWD): 25x34x24 in., 119 lbs.

22 Panasonic Tau PureFlat Series CT-34WX54 Good, with very good S-video picture and excellent sound, but can't display an image from a 720p HD signal. Has virtual surround sound, scrolling channel preview, auto volume leveler, automatic display of active program's rating, customizable channel labels, and channel block-out. Front A/V inputs include S-video. Excellent selectivity. Lacks headphone jack. Remote control hard to use in low light. Cannot receive Extended Data Services (XDS) program information. Dimensions (HWD): 25x40x24 in.

36-INCH HIGH-DEFINITION

23 Sony FD Trinitron Wega Hi-Scan KV-36HS420 Very good, with excellent HD and DVD pictures and excellent sound. Has virtual surround sound, auto volume leveler, and customizable channel labels. Motion compensation feature worked well. Front A/V inputs include S-video. Can receive Extended Data Services (XDS) program information, if available. Excellent sensitivity. Lacks special aspect-ratio settings (such as zoom or stretch), automatic display of active program's rating, and channel block-out. Remote control hard to use in low light. Short (3-mo.) labor and in-home warranties. Dimensions (HWD): 31x40x25 in., 230 lbs.

24 Panasonic Tau PureFlat Series CT-36HL44 Very good overall, with excellent HD, DVD, and S-video pictures and excellent sound, but can't display an image from a 720p HD signal. Has scrolling channel preview, auto volume leveler, and customizable channel labels, automatic display of active program's rating, and channel block-out. Front A/V inputs include S-video. Excellent selectivity. Lacks special aspect-ratio settings (such as zoom or stretch), virtual surround sound, Remote control only so-so, and hard to use in low light. Cannot receive Extended Data Services (XDS) program information. Dimensions (HWD): 30x39x24 in., 217 lbs.

TVs, PLASMA

CR Quick Recommendations

Of the plasma sets we tested, all of which are 42-inch wide-screen, the best can display an excellent picture when connected to a high-quality source, such as an HD-capable satellite receiver or digital-cable box. They had clearer, crisper images than lower-rated models, which had pictures that often looked soft or did not accurately display colors. All looked best in low light. The picture quality of the best ED set, the Sony KE-42M1 (11), matched that of the best HD models when it was viewed from the appropriate distance, about 8 feet.

Sound quality was excellent for all but the ViewSonic CinemaWall VPW-425, which has rear-facing speakers. The Marantz PD4220V (12), Fujitsu Plasmavision P42HHA30 (9), and Daewoo DP-42SM (21) don't come with speakers; for those, we tested optional speakers sold by the manufacturer.

If you watch a lot of DVDs, check out the DVD-playback scores, which indicate picture quality from a progressive-scan DVD player. Note that scores for HD and DVD images are judged on a higher scale than are scores for regular TV signals.

Most tested HD models are HD-ready. Five digital-cable-ready sets that accept CableCards–the Sony KDE-42XS955 (1), Panasonic TH-42PX25U/P (3), Panasonic TH-42PD25U/P (16), and Pioneer PDP-4345 (7)–and the Dell W4200HD (6), all have a built-in digital tuner.

The Ratings list models by performance. Quick Picks highlights models that you might want to consider based on how they scored and on factors such as price.

Quick Picks

For a fine picture at a great price:
11 Sony, $2,650

This ED set, a CR Best Buy, scored as well as the best HD sets for picture quality with content of all types, despite a native resolution of only 852x480 pixels. Sit closer than about 8 feet away, however, and you may see the pixels forming the images. The onscreen menu was also hard to navigate.

If you want a true HD model:
1 Sony, $4,390
2 Toshiba, $3,000
4 Philips, $3,100

True HD sets will look better than ED models when viewed up close. The Sony's built-in tuner can receive off-air digital signals, and it can accept digital-cable signals via a CableCard. Picture quality was excellent for HD and DVDs and very good for regular TV via the S-video input, but its onscreen menu was fairly hard to use. The Toshiba 42HP84 (2), a CR Best Buy, had an excellent HD picture and was very good with DVDs and regular TV. The Philips 42PF9956 (4) was excellent with HD and DVD content. At these prices, the Toshiba and the Philips are good values.

Ratings

In performance order, within categories

HIGH-DEFINITION MODELS

Key number	Brand and model	Price	Overall score	HD picture quality	DVD picture quality	S-video picture quality	Ant/cable picture quality	Sound quality	Ease of use	Rear S-video inputs	Rear component inputs	PIP (no. of tuners)	Parts/labor warranty
1	Sony KDE-42XS955	$4390		●	●	◐	○	●	◐	2	2	1	12/12
2	Toshiba 42HP84	3000		●	◐	◐	◑	●	○	2	2	2	12/12
3	Panasonic TH-42PX25U/P	3300		◐	◐	◐	●	●	◐	2	2	2	12/12
4	Philips 42PF9956	3100		●	●	○	◑	●	○	2	2	2	12/12
5	Philips 42PF9966	3300		●	◐	◐	◑	◑	◐	2	2	2	12/12
6	Dell W4200HD	2800		◐	◐	○	◑	●	○	2	2	2	12/12
7	Pioneer PDP-4345	3100		◐	◐	○	◑	●	○	2	2	2	12/12
8	Philips 42PF9976	3500		◐	◐	◐	◑	●	◑	2	2	2	12/12
9	Fujitsu Plasmavision P42HHA30	5385		◐	○	○	NA	●	◐	1	2	No	36/36
10	Samsung HP-P4261	2900		◐	◐	○	◑	●	○	1	2	2	24/24

 CR BEST BUY (applies to row 2)

TVs, PLASMA

Ratings
In performance order, within categories

Excellent ● | Very good ◉ | Good ○ | Fair ◐ | Poor ⬤

ENHANCED-DEFINITION MODELS

Key	Brand and model	Price	HD picture quality	DVD picture quality	S-video picture quality	Ant/cable picture quality	Sound quality	Ease of use	Rear S-video inputs	Rear component inputs	PIP (no. of tuners)	Parts/labor warranty
11	Sony KE-42M1 **CR Best Buy**	2650	●	●	◉	○	●	◐	2	1	No	12/12
12	Marantz PD4220V	4900	●	●	○	NA	●	◐	1	2	No	12/12
13	Fujitsu P42VHA30	4255	●	●	○	NA	●	◐	1	2	No	36/36
14	JVC PD-42V475	2700	●	●	◐	◉	●	○	2	2	1	12/12
15	Mitsubishi PD-4225S	3800	●	○	○	○	●	○	No	1	1	12/12
16	Panasonic TH-42PD25U/P	2500	○	○	○	○	●	●	2	2	2	12/12
17	Samsung SP-P4251	1900	○	●	○	○	●	○	1	2	2	24/24
18	Samsung SP-P4231	2000	○	●	○	○	●	○	1	1	1	24/24
19	Zenith P42W46X	2190	●	○	○	○	●	○	2	2	2	12/12
20	Philips 42PF9936	2200	○	○	○	○	●	◐	2	1	No	12/12
21	Daewoo DP-42SM	2000	◐	○	○	NA	●	◐	2	2	No	12/12
22	ViewSonic VPW-425	2600	○	○	◐	◐	●	○	1	2	1	12/12

Guide to the Ratings

OVERALL SCORE is based primarily on picture quality; sound quality and ease of use are also figured in. Expert panelists evaluated **PICTURE QUALITY** for clarity and color accuracy. HD programming reflects display of a 1080i signal. **DVD PLAYBACK** indicates how a set displayed a 480p signal, such as the output from a progressive-scan DVD player. Regular TV scores are for a 480i signal, such as that of a regular TV program, received via high-quality (S-video) and basic (antenna/cable) inputs. Since HD and DVD images can look much better than regular TV programming, we used higher standards when judging HD and DVD content; thus, a very good score for HD indicates a better picture than a very good score for regular TV signals. **SOUND QUALITY** is for the set's built-in speakers. **EASE OF USE** is our assessment of the remote control, onscreen menus, labeling of inputs, and useful features. **SIZE** indicates diagonal screen size, in inches. For microdisplay TVs, type indicates the technology the set uses. **PRICE** is approximate retail. *Based on testing in Consumer Reports in March 2005, updated for price and availability.*

Profiles Model-by-Model

HIGH-DEFINITION MODELS

1 Sony KDE-42XS955 A Very good, with excellent HD and DVD picture and sound. Motion compensation feature worked well. Has integrated tuner for decoding off-air digital and digital-cable signals, optical digital-audio output to receiver, virtual surround sound, swivel base, slot for viewing digital photos stored on Memory Stick media, auto volume leveler, customizable channel labels, and automatic display of active program's rating. Front A/V inputs, located on side, include S-video. Can receive Extended Data Services (XDS) program information, if available. Lacks auto power-off and channel block-out. Remote control hard to use in low light, and onscreen menu generally hard to use. Panel dimensions (HWD): 27x45x4 in., 125 lbs.

2 Toshiba 42HP84 A **CR Best Buy** Very good, with excellent HD picture and sound, but picture via basic connection only fair. Has auto power-off, virtual surround sound, auto volume leveler, customizable channel labels, and channel block-out. Front A/V inputs, located on side, include S-video. Can receive Extended Data Services (XDS) program information, if available. To see program ratings, must push button on remote. Panel dimensions (HWD): 28x51x5 in., 113 lbs.

3 Panasonic TH-42PX25U/P Very good, with excellent sound. Can't display an image from a 720p HD signal. Has integrated tuner for decoding off-air digital and digital-cable signals, optical digital-audio output to receiver, virtual surround sound, slot for viewing digital photos stored on Secure Digital (SD) or PC Card media, auto volume leveler, customizable channel labels, and channel block-out. Can receive Extended Data Services (XDS) program

(continued)

TVs, PLASMA

Profiles Model-by-Model (continued)

information, if available. Lacks auto power-off and automatic display of active program's rating. Panel dimensions (HWD): 30x45x6 in., 93 lbs.

4 Philips 42PF9956 Very good, with excellent HD and DVD picture and sound, but picture via basic connection only fair. Can't display an image from a 720p HD signal. Has virtual surround sound, auto volume leveler, automatic display of active program's rating, and channel block-out. Front A/V inputs, located on side, include S-video. Can receive Extended Data Services (XDS) program information, if available. Excellent sensitivity. Remote control very good but hard to use in low light. Lacks customizable channel labels. Onscreen menu hard to use. Panel dimensions (HWD): 31x44x5 in., 96 lbs.

5 Philips 42PF9966 Very good, with excellent HD and DVD picture and sound. Has HDMI input, virtual surround sound, auto volume leveler, automatic display of active program's rating, channel block-out, and headphone jack. Front A/V inputs, located on side, include S-video. Can receive Extended Data Services (XDS) program information, if available. Remote control very good but hard to use in low light. Lacks customizable channel labels. Onscreen menu harder to use than for most others tested. Panel dimensions (HWD): 31x44x5 in., 96 lb.

6 Dell W4200HD Very good, with excellent DVD picture and sound. Motion compensation feature worked well. Has integrated tuner for decoding off-air digital signals, optical digital-audio output to receiver, detachable speakers, scrolling channel preview, virtual surround sound, and channel block-out. Front A/V inputs, located on side, include S-video. Lacks auto power-off, auto volume leveler, customizable channel labels, and automatic display of active program's rating. Remote control hard to use in low light. Cannot receive Extended Data Services (XDS) program information. Panel dimensions (HWD): 25x48x4 in., 101 lbs.

7 Pioneer PDP-4345 Very good, with excellent HD picture and sound, and very good DVD picture, but picture via basic connection only fair. Has integrated tuner for decoding off-air digital and digital-cable signals, optical digital-audio output to receiver, detachable speakers, auto power-off, virtual surround sound, swivel base, and customizable channel labels. Front A/V inputs, located on control unit, include S-video. Lacks auto volume leveler, automatic display of active program's rating, and channel block-out. Cannot receive Extended Data Services (XDS) program information. Panel dimensions (HWD): 26x51x4 in., 84 lbs. Control-unit dimensions (HWD): 4x17x13 in.

8 Philips 42PF9976 Very good, with excellent sound. Has scrolling channel preview, virtual surround sound, auto volume leveler, and channel block-out. Front A/V inputs, located on side, include S-video. Can receive Extended Data Services (XDS) program information, if available. To see program ratings, must push button on remote. Lacks auto power-off and customizable channel labels. Remote control hard to use in low light, and onscreen menu generally hard to use. Rear jacks' labels hard to read. Panel dimensions (HWD): 31x44x4 in., 98 lbs.

9 Fujitsu Plasmavision P42HHA30 Good, with very good HD picture and excellent sound, but requires external tuner to receive standard-definition channels. Relatively fewer features than most other sets tested. Detachable speakers ($900) and stand ($500) must be purchased separately. Has auto power-off. Lacks antenna/cable input, virtual surround sound, auto volume leveler, customizable channel labels, automatic display of active program's rating, and channel block-out. Single S-video input limits connection options. Remote control hard to use in low light. Cannot receive Extended Data Services (XDS) program information. Display warranty, 12-mo. Panel dimensions (HWD): 26x41x5 in., 66 lbs. Discontinued, but may still be available.

10 Samsung HP-P4261 Good, with very good HD and DVD picture and excellent sound, but picture via basic connection only fair. Has virtual surround sound and auto volume leveler. Front A/V inputs, located on side, include S-video. Excellent sensitivity. Lacks customizable channel labels, automatic display of active program's rating, and channel block-out. Single S-video input limits connection options. Remote control hard to use in low light. Cannot receive Extended Data Services (XDS) program information. Panel dimensions (HWD): 30x42x4 in., 79 lbs.

ENHANCED-DEFINITION MODELS

11 Sony KE-42M1 A **CR Best Buy** Very good, with excellent display of down-converted HD programming, DVD picture, and sound. Motion compensation feature worked well. Has virtual surround sound, auto volume leveler, customizable channel labels, and channel block-out. Front A/V inputs, located on side, include S-video. Excellent sensitivity. Remote control very good but hard to use in low light. Lacks automatic display of active program's rating. Single component-video input limits connection options. Onscreen menu hard to use. Cannot receive Extended Data Services (XDS) program information. Panel dimensions (HWD): 30x43x5 in., 100 lbs.

12 Marantz PD4220V Very good, with excellent sound, but requires external tuner to receive standard-definition channels. Side-mounted, detachable speakers ($290 for tested pair from set manufacturer NEC) must be purchased separately. Lacks antenna/cable input, auto power-off, virtual surround sound, auto volume leveler, customizable channel labels, automatic display of active program's rating, and channel block-out. Remote control hard to use in low light. Cannot receive Extended Data Services (XDS) program information. Panel dimensions (HWD): 24x40x4 in., 65 lbs. Discontinued, but may still be available.

13 Fujitsu P42VHA30 Very good, with excellent sound, but requires external tuner to receive standard-definition channels. Motion compensation feature worked well. Relatively fewer features than most other sets tested. Detachable speakers ($900 for tested pair) and stand ($500) must be purchased separately. Has auto power-off. Lacks antenna/cable input, virtual surround sound, auto volume leveler, customizable channel labels, automatic display of active program's rating, and channel block-out. Single S-video input limits connection options. Remote control hard to use in low light. Cannot receive Extended Data Services (XDS) program information. Display warranty, 12-mo. Panel dimensions (HWD): 26x41x5 in., 66 lbs. Discontinued, but may still be available.

14 JVC PD-42V475 Very good, with excellent sound, but regular-TV pictures only fair. Has auto power-off, scrolling channel preview, and channel block-out. Front A/V inputs include S-video. Can receive Extended Data Services (XDS) program information, if available. Lacks virtual surround sound, auto volume leveler, customizable channel labels, and automatic display of active program's rating. Panel dimensions (HWD): 29x42x5 in., 107 lbs.

15 Mitsubishi PD-4225S Very good, with excellent sound from detachable

TVs, PLASMA

Profiles Model-by-Model (continued)

speakers. Motion compensation feature worked very well. Lack of rear S-video input and single component-video input limit connection options. Has auto power-off and auto volume leveler. Front A/V inputs include S-video. Lacks virtual surround sound, customizable channel labels, automatic display of active program's rating, and channel block-out. Cannot receive Extended Data Services (XDS) program information. Panel dimensions (HWD): 26x50x5 in., 82 lbs. Discontinued, but may still be available.

16 Panasonic TH-42PD25U/P Very good, with excellent sound, but picture via basic connection only fair. Can't display an image from a 720p HD signal. Has integrated tuner for decoding off-air digital and digital-cable signals, optical digital-audio output to receiver, virtual surround sound, slot for viewing digital photos stored on Secure Digital (SD) media, auto volume leveler, customizable channel labels, and channel block-out. Can receive Extended Data Services (XDS) program information, if available. Lacks auto power-off and automatic display of active program's rating. Panel dimensions (HWD): 26x46x4 in., 80 lbs.

17 Samsung SP-P4251 Good, with excellent sound. Has virtual surround sound and auto volume leveler. Lacks auto power-off, customizable channel labels, automatic display of active program's rating, and channel block-out. Remote control hard to use in low light. Cannot receive Extended Data Services (XDS) program information. Panel dimensions (HWD): 30x42x4 in., 79 lbs.

18 Samsung SP-P4231 Good, with very good HD and DVD pictures and excellent sound from detachable speakers. Motion compensation feature worked well. Has virtual surround sound and auto volume leveler. Lacks auto power-off, customizable channel labels, automatic display of active program's rating, and channel block-out. Remote control hard to use in low light. Cannot receive Extended Data Services (XDS) program information. Panel dimensions (HWD): 25x50x4 in., 73 lbs.

19 Zenith P42W46X Good, with very good display of down-converted HD programming and DVD picture, and excellent sound, but picture via basic connection only fair. Motion compensation feature worked well. Has virtual surround sound, and auto volume leveler. Front A/V inputs, located on side, include S-video. Lacks customizable channel labels, automatic display of active program's rating, and channel block-out. Single S-video input limits connection options. Remote control hard to use in low light, and onscreen menu generally hard to use. Rear jacks' labels hard to read. Cannot receive Extended Data Services (XDS) program information. Panel dimensions (HWD): 26x48x4 in., 66 lbs.

20 Philips 42PF9936 Good, with very good DVD picture and excellent sound, but can't display an image from a 720p HD signal. Has virtual surround sound, auto volume leveler, automatic display of active program's rating, and channel block-out. Lacks auto power-off and customizable channel labels. Remote control hard to use in low light, and onscreen menu generally hard to use. Panel dimensions (HWD): 26x48x6 in., 95 lbs.

21 Daewoo DP-42SM Good, with excellent sound, but requires external tuner to receive standard-definition channels. Motion compensation feature worked well. Relatively fewer features than most other sets tested. Side-mounted, detachable speakers ($150) must be purchased separately. Has virtual surround sound. Lacks closed-caption display, auto power-off, auto volume leveler, customizable channel labels, automatic display of active program's rating, and channel block-out. Cannot receive Extended Data Services (XDS) program information. Panel dimensions (HWD): 25x41x4 in., 67 lbs. Discontinued, but may still be available.

22 ViewSonic VPW-425 There are better choices. Relatively fewer features than most other sets tested. Rear-firing speakers. Has auto power-off and virtual surround sound. Lacks auto volume leveler, customizable channel labels, and automatic display of active program's rating. Single S-video input limits connection options. Remote control hard to use. Cannot receive Extended Data Services (XDS) program information. Panel dimensions (HWD): 28x41x4 in., 77 lbs.

BRAND LOCATOR

Manufacturer contacts

Name	Phone number	Web address
ACD systems	866-244-2237	www.acdsystems.com
Adobe	800-833-6687	www.adobe.com
Akai	888-697-2247	www.akaiusa.com
AMD	800-222-9323	www.amd.com
America Online	800-827-6364	www.aol.com
Apex Digital	909-930-1239	www.apexdigitalinc.com
Apple	800-538-9696	www.apple.com
Asus	510-739-3777	usa.asus.com
ArcSoft	510-440-9901	www.arcsoft.com
AT&T	800-222-3111	www.att.com
Audiovox	800-229-1235	www.audiovox.com
Brother	800-276-7746	www.brotherusa.com
Canon	800-652-2666	www.usa.canon.com
Casio	800-706-2534	www.casio.com
Cingular	800-331-0500	www.cingular.com
Compaq	800-345-1518	www.compaq.com
CompuServ	800-336-6823	www.compuserve.com
Corel	800-772-6735	www.corel.com
CTX	877-688-3288	www.ctxintl.com
Dell	800-879-3355	www.dell.com
Disney Interactive	800-900-9234	disney.go.com/disneyinteractive
DirectTV	888-777-7454	www.directv.com
DirecWay	866-347-3292	www.direcway.com
Dish Network	800-333-3474	www.dishnetwork.com
EarthLink	800-327-8454	www.earthlink.net
Emachines	877-566-3463	www.E4me.com
Envision	888-838-6388	www.envisionmonitor.com
Epson	800-463-7766	www.epson.com
Ericsson	800-374-2776	www.ericsson.com
Fisher	818-998-7322	www.fisherav.com
Franklin	800-266-5626	www.franklin.com
Fujifilm	800-800-3854	www.fujifilm.com
Fujitsu	800-838-5487	www.fujitsupc.com
Gateway	800-846-2000	www.gateway.com
Garmin	800-800-1020	www.garmin.com
Handspring	888-565-9393	www.handspring.com
Hewlett-Packard	800-724-6631	www.hp.com
Hitachi	800-448-2244	www.hitachi.com
IBM	800-426-7235	www.ibm.com

Manufacturer contacts (continued)

Name	Phone number	Web address
Inkjetsinc	800-275-2410	www.inkjetsinc.com
Intel	800-628-8686	www.intel.com
Iomega	800-697-8833	www.iomega.com
GE	800-626-2000	www.geappliances.com
Jasc	800-622-2793	www.jasc.com
JVC	800-252-5722	www.jvc.com
KDS	800-283-1311	www.kdsusa.com
Kodak	800-235-6325	www.kodak.com
Konica	800-695-6642	www.konicaminolta.us
Kyocera	800-349-4188	www.kyocera.com
LearningCo.com	800-395-0277	www.learningco.com
Lexmark	888-539-6275	www.lexmark.com
LG	800-243-0000	www.lgeus.com
Lotus	800-465-6887	www.lotus.com
Lucent	888-458-2368	www.lucent.com
Microsoft	800-426-9400	www.microsoft.com
Microtek	800-654-4160	www.microtekusa.com
Minolta	877-462-4464	www.minoltausa.com
Mintek	866-709-9500	www.mintekdigital.com
Motorola	800-353-2729	www.motorola.com
Network Associates (McAfee VirusScan)	800-338-8754	www.mcafee.com
NEC	888-632-6487	www.necmitsubishi.com
Nextel	800-639-6111	www.nextel.com
Nikon	800-645-6689	www.nikonusa.com
Nintendo	800-255-3700	www.nintendo.com
Nokia	888-665-4228	www.nokiausa.com
Olympus	888-553-4448	www.olympusamerica.com
PalmOne	800-881-7256	www.palmone.com/us
Panasonic	800-742-8086	www.panasonic.com
Pentax	800-877-0155	www.pentaxusa.com
Philips	800-531-0039	www.philipsusa.com
SBC Prodigy	866-722-9246	myhome.prodigy.net
RadioShack	800-843-7422	www.radioshack.com
RCA	800-336-1900	www.rca.com
ReplayTV	866-286-3662	www.replaytv.com
Riverdeep	319-247-3333	www.riverdeep.net
Samsung	800-726-7864	www.samsungusa.com
Sanyo	818-998-7322	www.sanyousa.com
Sega	800-872-7342	www.sega.com
Sharp	800-237-4277	www.sharpusa.com
Siemens	888-777-0211	www.icm.siemens.com
Sierra	310-649-8033	www.sierra.com
Sony	800-222-7669	www.sonystyle.com
Sprint PCS	888-253-1315	www.sprintpcs.com
Symantec (Norton AntiVirus)	800-441-7234	www.symantec.com
TiVo	877-289-8486	www.tivo.com
T-Mobile	800-866-2453	www.t-mobile.com
Toshiba	800-631-3811	www.toshiba.com
Ulead	800-858-5323	www.ulead.com
Uniden	800-297-1023	www.uniden.com
Verizon Wireless	800-922-0204	www.verizonwireless.com
ViewSonic	800-888-8583	www.viewsonic.com
Visioneer	925-251-6398	www.visioneer.com
Vtech	800-595-9511	www.vtech.com
WinBook	800-254-7806	www.winbook.com
Zone Labs	415-633-4500	www.zonealarm.com

GLOSSARY

With advice on choosing and using electronics products.

A

Access The ability to connect to the Internet. Also, to store or retrieve data from a storage device such as a disk or from a database. Sometimes access is restricted by an authentication scheme, such as a password.

Accessibility The degree to which hardware or software is designed to allow persons with disabilities to use a computer. Windowed operating systems have many accessibility features, such as the ability to enlarge fonts, icons, and menus, and to use alternate Human Interface Devices (HIDs).

Additional disc formats In addition to playing DVD-video discs, DVD players can handle audio CDs. (Some can also play video CDs, a format that's popular overseas.) Other disc formats that some players support include CD-R and CD-RW (the audio discs you record yourself, using other equipment); MP3 on CDs; HDCD; DVD-Audio and Super Audio CD (SACD), two audio-centric formats intended to succeed CD audio; and the DVD-RAM, DVD+R, DVD-R, DVD-RW, and DVD+RW writable formats.

Active-matrix display A high-quality, flat-panel display in which a separate transistor switch is used for each pixel, allowing viewing from wider angles.

Additional connectors, camcorders All camcorders have audio and composite-video output jacks, which let you monitor during recording or playback. Other connectors include stereo-audio, headphone, and S-video outputs and a microphone input. Edit-control signal inputs (including LANC, JLIP, and Control-L) are for use with editing equipment or a suitable VCR. A FireWire (IEEE-1394) port lets you connect to a computer or digital camcorder. And for camcorders that let you capture still images, a USB or FireWire port lets you transfer saved images to the computer.

Add-on (or add-in) A computer component that can be attached to a larger device by a simple process such as plugging it in.

Add-on lens A digital-camera lens that attaches to the one built into the unit. Though not as versatile as an interchangeable lens, an add-on does extend your options for composing a shot by providing an extended telephoto or wide-angle view. To date, few models offer this feature.

Adjustable color temperature Also known as "color warmth adjustment" or "white balance," the adjustable color temperature lets you vary the overall color tone of the picture between cooler (bluish) and warmer (reddish).

Advanced playback controls Most phone answerers can skip to the next message, back to a previous one, or repeat a message. Some also have more advanced conveniences such as fast playback, slow playback (say, to slow down a part of the message to understand a phone number), and rewind (to go back to a certain part of a message).

Ad-ware software that displays advertising when it is being used.

Alarm timer On TVs equipped with a clock, a feature that will turn on the set at a preset time.

All-in-one A computer design with all parts built in—display, hard drive, optical drive and speakers. Apple's iMac is one example. Multifunction printers—which scan, copy, and sometimes fax as well as print—are also called all-in-ones.

Analog A representation of a continuous measurement of some function. A common example is the telephone, where sound is converted to a varying voltage that is transmitted via wires and converted from voltage to sound on the other end.

Analog input Lets a camcorder record analog audio and video from other devices, such as a VCR or another camcorder. This feature can drive up the price of a digital camcorder, since a unit would require additional circuitry to convert analog signals to digital.

Announce-only mode For phones with an answerer, this mode lets you set the unit to play a greeting without giving callers the option to leave a message.

Answerer mailboxes Some answering machines have mailboxes that let you separate business from personal calls or set up boxes for different members of the household.

Answering machine Cordless phones of all types are available with a built-in answering machine that has digital message storage, typically 15 to 20 minutes. Desirable features include a digital message-counter display, the ability to repeat or skip the message, and, for large households or for separating personal and business, several mailboxes. May be referred to as ITAD (integrated telephone answering device).

Antenna/cable input Also called RF or VHF/UHF, the most basic connection through which the TV can receive the signal it displays. It's the easiest to use because it's the only connection available on every TV that carries both sound and picture. A newer connection available on many digital (HD/ED/SD) sets, HDMI (see "HDMI") also carries both signals. The other video inputs—chiefly composite-video, S-video, and component-video—accept only the picture, requiring the use of a separate pair of audio inputs to receive the sound. These other inputs, however, offer incremental improvements in quality.

Antivirus program A program designed to detect, remove, and protect against computer viruses, worms, and Trojan horses. Antivirus programs must be updated regularly to maintain protection against new threats.

Any-key answerer The ability to answer an incoming phone call by pressing any key (except "off").

Aperture modes The number or range of settings for a digital camera's aperture, which is the opening in the lens that controls how much light hits the camera's image sensor. Apertures are stated as f-stops or f-numbers (for example, f/8). The smallest number in this range is the most important: The smaller that number, the larger the maximum aperture, and the less light the camera requires to take a picture.

Aperture range The minimum and maximum aperture (lens opening) range for wide and telephoto shots.

Applications programs with a particular function. Typical examples are word processors, spreadsheets, and games. For a PDA (as with personal computers), these are the software programs included. Contacts/address book, calendar/date book, to-do list/tasks, and memo pad/notes are standard on every unit.

Aspect ratio The aspect ratio is the proportion of a TV screen's width to its height. Standard TV screens have an aspect ratio of 4:3, giving them a squarish shape that is 4 units wide for every 3 units high. Wide-screen TVs typically have a 16:9 aspect ratio, giving them a wider screen that better resembles the screen in a movie theater. (Some LCD TVs have a 15:9 aspect ratio that differs slightly, but they're often not identified as such.) Wide-screen TVs can use the full screen to display HDTV broadcasts and prerecorded movies. When displayed on a standard screen, such images must be framed at the top and bottom with black bars in order to maintain the wide-screen aspect ratio. Conversely, regular TV programming displayed on a wide screen has black bars on both sides. (Note that much programming actually differs from 4:3 or 16:9, often necessitating bars of some width.) Many sets have stretch and zoom modes to eliminate the bars and fit the image to the screen, albeit with some distortion.

Athlon A family of microprocessors from AMD that competes with Intel's Pentium series and has similar performance.

ATSC Advanced Television Systems Committee, an international, nonprofit organization developing voluntary standards for digital television. In the United States, digital off-air tuners such as those in HDTVs receive content transmitted in ATSC formats. These formats include 480p, 720p and 1080i. An ATSC tuner refers to one capable of accepting HD (720p or 1080i) and 480p signals.

Audible message alert An answerer alert, typically in the form of a beep, that proves handy if you often forget to look at the answerer to see if you have new messages.

Audio dynamic range control This DVD-player feature, useful for late-night viewing, keeps explosions and other loud sound effects from sounding too loud, while it makes whispers loud enough to be heard.

Audio outputs Audio outputs, found on many sets, let you relay the TV's audio signal to a receiver or external, powered speakers, a must if you desire top-quality sound. Fixed-audio outputs, true to their name, have a fixed output level; you might prefer them if you will use a receiver to control the TV's volume. With variable-audio outputs, the sound level you'll hear from your sound system or external speakers rises and falls with any adjustment of the TV's volume control.

Audio playback formats The audio formats an MP3 player will recognize and be able to play. Formats include AAC, ATRAC, ADPCM, AIFF, ACELP, MP3, MPEG, Real G2, WAV, and WMA. Formats such as MP3, WMA, and WAV may be supported using the music-management software application bundled with the player; this allows the music to be recorded to a format the player supports.

Audio recording With digital cameras, this feature lets you record a short sound bite with each image, say, to make notes for future reference. May also permit the recording of sound with any mini-movie feature.

Audio tone controls Found on nearly all TVs equipped with built-in speakers, a control for adjusting treble and bass.

Auto channel setup Useful when you connect your TV set for the first time, this common feature scans all the channels you receive and sets up the TV to access only the ones with programming, so you don't have to program the channels yourself. Once they're set up, your remote will skip the blank channels when you scroll up or down channels.

Auto-clock set The ability of some TVs equipped with a clock to set the time automatically using a signal transmitted along with a certain channel's audio/video content.

Auto convergence On CRT-based projection sets, it provides a one-touch adjustment to automatically align the three CRTs for a sharp, accurate image. It's much more convenient than manual convergence alone, which can require many time-consuming adjustments.

Auto fleshtone correction A feature you can set to automatically adjust color balance to make flesh tones look more natural.

Autofocus Automatically brings the subject into sharp focus. Some cameras offer manual focus in addition to auto focus.

Auto power-off Shuts off a TV after a preset (and often adjustable) period during which the screen image is stationary, intended to prevent screen burn-in.

Auto volume leveler Found on some TV sets, the auto volume leveler compensates for changes in the audio signal that you'd hear as a jump in volume. With this somewhat-helpful feature, there are fewer fluctuations in sound level as you switch between channels and view commercials, which are frequently louder than regular programming.

Autofocus Automatically brings the subject into sharp focus. Some digital cameras offer manual focus in addition to auto focus.

Auto talk Also referred to as auto answer, this cordless-phone feature allows you to lift the handset off its base for an incoming call and start talking without having to press a button. On some phones this is automatic; for others, it is a selectable feature.

AV input These let you record sound or images from another camcorder or VCR.

Available memory, PDAs The amount of usable internal memory in a PDA that is available for new uses—such as appointments, addresses and applications—when the model is new. For memory-intensive applications, such as MP3 playing and picture taking, most new PDAs support the use of external memory cards to store the music and video files.

B

Back up To copy data or other content onto a computer's removable disk, a second hard drive, or other storage medium, to prevent loss if the original is damaged.

Backlight A PDA feature, found in units with a monochrome screen, that lets you view the display better under low-light conditions. Using the backlight, however, will cause the unit's battery to run down more rapidly.

Backlight compensation Ordinarily, when the light behind your camcorder's subject is brighter than the light on your subject, the subject will appear silhouetted. Backlight compensation increases the exposure slightly to make the subject more visible.

Backlit keypad A cordless-phone keypad that glows in the dark or when you press a key.

Backward compatibility The ability of a new computer product to work properly with other products that use older technology.

Bandwidth The maximum speed of a data link in bits per second (bps), thousands of bps (kbps), or million of bits per second (megabits per second, or Mbps). Ethernet has a bandwidth of 10 to 1000 Mbps, typical consumer-grade DSL has a download bandwidth of 384 to 768 kbps, and a V.90 or V.92 modem connection has a theoretical bandwidth of 53.3 kbps.

Base keypad Also referred to as a cordless phone's dual or second keypad, a keypad on the base that supplements the one on the handset. It can be handy for navigating menu-driven systems, because you don't have to take the phone away from your ear to punch the keys. When it's used with the speakerphone, you can make a call from the base hands-free.

Base speakerphone A base speakerphone offers a hands-free way to converse or wait on hold and lets others chime in as well, and allows you to answer a call without the handset. When used with a base keypad, you can make a call from the base and have a hands-free conversation.

Bass boost Akin to a receiver's loudness switch, the bass boost amplifies low frequencies, supposedly to enhance the overall sound. An inessential feature, it's found on only a small number of sets.

Battery backup Protects cordless-phone memory (stored phone numbers) during power outages or when the phone is unplugged. On an answerer, this feature can save greetings and messages.

Battery holder A compartment in a cordless phone's base to charge a spare handset battery pack. The spare battery is usually not included; most batteries cost about $10 to $20. The pack sometimes doubles as a power backup, enabling the phone to operate during a power outage.

Battery life (min.), camcorder The manufacturer's statement of how long the camcorder can continuously record images with the LCD viewer in use. "Not stated" indicates the manufacturer's specification for battery life was not available.

Battery life, cordless phones Talk time represents how long you can converse on a handset when the battery is fully charged; most phones we tested lasted 8 hours or longer. Standby time represents how long a battery will last when the handset is left off the charging cradle. Most phones last a week or more, based on manufacturer's specifications.

Battery type, camcorders All models come with a rechargeable battery and an AC adapter. The adapter can recharge the battery or power the camcorder if an outlet is nearby (but generally not at the same time). Most models let you install a more powerful battery than the original. Commonly used battery types are lithium-ion, nickel-cadmium, and nickel-metal hydride.

Battery type, cordless phones Nickel-cadmium is the most common; nickel-metal hydride batteries are less prevalent.

Battery type, digital cameras Many digital cameras use two or four AA batteries. Nonrechargeable batteries, such as alkaline and lithium, or rechargeable batteries, such as nickel-metal hydride or lithium-ion, may be used. Some cameras that use rechargeable batteries come with a charger and a set of rechargeable batteries.

Battery type, PDAs Single-use batteries (most convenient, but vanishing from the market) are the AA, AAA, or coin-cell types–you replace them when they are spent. Rechargeable batteries can be replaceable and easily removed from the unit, or non-replaceable–requiring the dealer or manufacturer to replace.

Bay A position in a computer case to mount a device, such as a drive.

BBE audio processing A feature in some TVs, from BBE Sound, that boosts bass and treble to enhance sound from the set's built-in speakers.

Bidirectional With computers, capable of transferring information in both directions.

BIOS Basic Input/Output System, the fundamental instructions by which a computer communicates with various peripheral devices. The BIOS usually resides in a firmware chip on the motherboard, allowing the computer to boot. A "flash" BIOS can be updated by overwriting its contents with new instructions from a file.

Bit Short for binary digit, it's the smallest piece of data recognized by a computer. Abbreviated as b.

Black level adjustment This feature lets you make adjustments to the intensity of black in the picture from a DVD. When the black is too deep, details in dark areas of images may be obscured; when black isn't deep enough, dark areas of images will be too bright.

Bluetooth A short-range (35 feet) wireless-data protocol that can link compatible devices in a secure connection, using the 2.5-GHz radio-frequency band, with transfer speeds of up to 720 kbps. Examples are computer-to-printer, PDA-to-computer, and headset-to-telephone.

Board A thin, usually rectangular unit on which various electronic components are mounted.

Bookmark An easy way to access frequently visited Web sites, the user saves Web-page URLs to a list (called either Bookmarks or Favorites) through a drop-down menu in the browser.

Boot To bring a system into operation. This normally includes loading part or all of the operating system into main memory from a storage device.

bps Bits per second, a measure of data-transfer throughput. Rates are usually expressed with the prefixes k- for kilo-, M- for mega-, or G for giga-.

Broadband As commonly used, a connection to the Internet that has a receiving bandwidth greater than that of dial-up modem or ISDN service, about 128 kbps. (The FCC specifies 256 kbps in at least one direction.) Common broadband connections are cable modem, DSL, and satellite. Broadband makes streaming audio and video practical.

Buffer A computer memory area used to hold data temporarily while it is being transferred from one location or device to another or waiting to be processed. Buffers are essential for the efficient operation of the CPU and are often used in graphics processors, CD-ROM drives, printer drivers, and other input/output devices to compensate for differences in processing speed.

Bug An error in a computer program that prevents proper operation.

Built-in digital tuner Includes a tuner that can decode digital TV signals received off-air (ATSC broadcasts) or via cable or satellite. An HD set with such a tuner may be referred to as an "integrated HDTV." A TV that requires you to connect an external tuner (in a cable box, satellite receiver, or set-top box) is called a TV "monitor"–as in "HDTV monitor"–or labeled with the word "ready," as in "HD-ready."

Built-in fax modem Comes with a modem that lets you send and receive faxes without using the computer's own faxing capability.

Built-in light On a camcorder, it provides illumination for close-ups when the image would otherwise be too dark, but it's no substitute for a well-lit room.

Built-in microphone Useful for recording interviews, lectures, etc., onto an MP3 player.

Built-in multichannel audio decoder output For a DVD player with built-in decoding of Dolby Digital or DTS multichannel audio (necessary for full enjoyment of multichannel audio soundtracks if your receiver lacks this capability), the ability to connect speakers and a subwoofer directly to the DVD player.

Bundle The software that comes preloaded with many personal computers. This typically includes a word processor, financial program, encyclopedia, productivity suite, and assorted games. Also, the combination of a PC and peripheral devices such as a monitor, printer, scanner, or accessories, usually as a sales incentive.

Burner A computer disk drive, also called a CD-writer, that can save data or program content.

Burst mode Allows you to take multiple, rapid-fire shots with one touch of a camcorder's shutter button; useful when you're shooting a subject in motion. The number of shots that can be taken in burst mode varies from camera to camera. Burst mode may not be available in a camera's highest-resolution mode. Also called "continuous shooting" or "rapid-fire shots."

Bus A pathway that connects devices inside a computer, usually the CPU and memory, or a peripheral such as an adapter card. Common bus designs include PCI and CardBus.

Byte The basic computer-storage unit needed to store a single character, nominally 8 bits. Abbreviated as B.

CableCard For digital-cable-ready (DCR) TVs, this credit-card-sized card must be inserted into a slot on the set in order for you to receive digital-cable programming without the need for a cable box. (You typically rent the card from your cable operator for a few dollars a month.) Current (2004-2005) DCR TVs are one-way, so they don't provide an interactive program guide, video on demand, or pay-per-view ordering via the remote control. For those features, you'll still need a cable box. Two-way DCR TVs are expected to be out soon, but it's uncertain if they'll need an updated CableCard.

Cable modem A means of providing high-speed Internet service through a TV cable.

Cable/sat. box control A recording device's ability to change channels automatically on a cable box or satellite receiver–needed to record programs from several channels when time-shift recording from either satellite or cable systems that use cable boxes.

Cache Memory that is dedicated specifically to improve the performance of a computer. This is accomplished by either setting aside part of main memory, using driver software, or employing special high-speed memory.

Calendar and contact applications Some MP3 players have applications that let you schedule calendar appointments and/or store contact information such as names and phone numbers.

Caller ID Caller ID with a three-line display shows the name and phone number of a caller and the date and time of the call, provided you subscribe to Caller ID services. Some models have an additional display line that shows on which line–say, line 1 or line 2–the call came in, or indicators such as battery strength or voice mail. If you have Caller ID with Call Waiting, the phone displays the name and number of the second caller if you're already on the phone.

Caller ID memory locations Provided you subscribe to Caller ID services, the maximum number of Caller ID memory locations the phone can store for the most recent incoming phone numbers, along with associated names and information such as date and time of call.

Caller IQ Also referred to as Viewer IQ, or Info IQ, this cordless-phone feature is compatible with a free service provided by openLCR (*www.openlcr.com*). The service claims to offer low-cost routing for reducing your phone bills. It also handles date and time settings, and information updates shown on your phone's display such as weather forecasts and stock quotes. You can also save your directory and setups on the site.

GLOSSARY

Call screening An answering-machine feature. It allows you to listen to the caller over the speaker while the caller's message is being recorded, so you can decide whether to answer the call.

Camera connections Input or output connections for data transfer, power, display of images on a video monitor, and/or addition of an external flash unit.

Capacity provided The total memory that comes with an MP3 player, combining memory built into the unit plus any external media supplied with the unit.

Card An electronic circuit board that serves a particular function, such as memory or graphics; in a PC, cards are usually plugged into a bus connector on the motherboard.

Carpal Tunnel Syndrome A painful, potentially debilitating injury that can arise from very heavy or non-ergonomic keyboard use. Symptoms may include weakness, numbness, tingling, and burning in the hands and fingers.

CCD pixels Light from a camcorder's subject is focused by the lens onto a charge-coupled device (CCD), a sensor that converts light into minute blocks of information, called pixels. A CCD's light-sensitive area is typically composed of 250,000 pixels or more. A higher number of active pixels generally means a sharper picture but less sensitivity to light.

CCD size A charge-coupled device (CCD) converts light into minute blocks of information, called pixels, to form the images stored on a camcorder. Almost all CCDs measure ¼-inch diagonally. A few are larger; the additional size generally produces more light sensitivity. Some high-end camcorders have more than one CCD.

CD, or Compact disc A 5-inch, aluminum-coated polycarbonate plastic disc with embedded digital data, read by focusing a laser beam on the data tracks and sensing its reflection. CDs can carry about 650 megabytes (MB) of digital information, which can be entertainment like music and motion video or computer data.

CD-R CD-Recordable, a disc that can be recorded, once only, in a CD-writer.

CD-R and CD-RW, digital cameras A few cameras use small-size versions of these optical discs to store images. The discs are about 3 inches in diameter, hold 165 MB of data, and can be read in a computer's CD-ROM drive.

CD-ROM Compact Disc-Read Only Memory, a 5-inch disc holding data or software; also, the drive that retrieves digital data from the disc.

CD-RW CD-Rewritable, a disc that can be recorded repeatedly, and used like a high-capacity floppy disk, in a CD-writer.

CD-writer A drive that lets you record to or copy CD-ROM discs. With the right software, you can also record to or copy audio and video CDs. CD-writers and blank media have dropped in price significantly over the past few years, and are now virtually standard in PCs.

Celeron A processor series from Intel that is slower and less costly than its Pentium counterpart, used in lower-priced PCs.

Center-channel audio input An input, found in some TVs, that accepts the center-channel portion (mostly comprising dialog) of a multichannel audio soundtrack for output through the set's built-in speakers, as opposed to an external center-channel speaker.

Channel block-out A TV parental-control feature that can block specific channels altogether, as opposed to the program-specific V-chip, and may also prevent or otherwise limit use of the audio/video inputs to which video games are connected.

Channel labels With this common TV feature, you can enter a channel's name into an onscreen display. As you surf, you can then quickly identify the channel.

Channel-guide menu A feature, such as Guide Plus, that displays program listings. The set receives program information while off but still in "standby."

Chapter preview Movies on DVD are divided into "chapters." This feature helps you find the scene you are looking for by playing the first few seconds of each chapter–or, with the related chapter gallery, showing the first scene of each chapter. This, in effect, allows you to visually scan the disc.

Chip An integrated circuit such as those commonly used for a PC's microprocessor and memory systems. It is composed of a small, rectangular "chip" of semiconductor material, encased in a larger rectangular carrier with electrical connections.

Clock A TV's internal time-keeper, primarily for use with the set's alarm ("on") timer.

Clock speed The rate at which the CPU clock operates, measured in megahertz (MHz) or gigahertz (GHz). In theory, the faster the clock speed, the faster the CPU will perform its operations. Most new PCs now work at clock speeds ranging from 900 MHz to over 3 GHz.

Closed caption on mute. With this feature, your TV's screen will automatically display captions whenever you mute the sound. Otherwise, you typically would have to press several buttons to mute the sound and view closed captions.

Closed captioning Closed captioning displays the dialog and other sounds in text across the bottom of the screen. It is particularly useful for the hearing-impaired.

Coaxial cable A type of telecommunications link that carries more data than conventional phone lines. It is also used for cable TV.

Coaxial digital audio out Digital-audio output is important only if you plan to pipe the signal from the DVD player into a home-theater system that has a digital receiver. When choosing your DVD player, consider the models that have the outputs to match the inputs on your digital receiver or external, digital decoder. All DVD players have digital audio outputs–coaxial, optical, or both.

Code (1) A set of instructions, written by a programmer, that tells the computer what to do; (2) to write a program; or (3) one or more characters that perform a specific function, such as a control code.

Cold boot To start or restart a computer from the power-off condition, or via a reset button.

Color display PDA screens have either a color display capable of as many as 64,000 colors or a black-and-white display capable of multiple shades of gray. While a color screen offers rich detail, it will drain the batteries faster than a monochrome one. The quality of a color display (for example, detail and sharpness) is most affected by its contrast ratio; the greater the ratio, the better the display.

Comb filter Found on most TV sets with a fine picture and virtually all sets with a screen 27 inches or larger, a comb filter minimizes extraneous colors within the image and increases picture detail. It comes into play only when you receive your TV signals through the antenna/cable or composite-video input. CONSUMER REPORTS, however, has found that the presence of a comb filter, of any type, does not alone ensure a fine picture.

Command An instruction, usually entered directly from a computer's keyboard or a pointing device, that is designed to bring about an action.

Commercial skip Useful to channel surfers and anyone averse to commercials, the commercial skip function lets you jump temporarily to another channel, in 30-second increments, for a duration you select.

CompactFlash CompactFlash (CF) memory cards are about the size of a matchbook. Most digital cameras equipped with a type-II CF slot can also accept the high-capacity IBM Microdrives.

Compatible operating system An operating system is the underlying program that manages a computer's applications. Most computers use a version of the Windows or Macintosh operating system. The type of computer a printer can serve also depends on its interfaces, or ports. All printers have a universal serial bus (USB) port, which makes them compatible with newer Windows or Macintosh computers. Some have USB2, a higher-speed port found on the latest computers. Some have an IEEE 1284-compliant parallel port, which lets them work with older Windows machines. (IEEE 1284 refers to the timing specifications of the electronics and the design properties of the cable used.) All of these printers lack a serial port, which means they won't work with older Macs.

Component-video inputs Component-video inputs use three jacks that separate the video signal into three parts: two for color and one for luminance. This provides slightly better quality than an S-video connection, most evident in color fidelity. They can be used only with a DVD player, digital-cable box, or other equipment that has component-video output.

Component-video output Some newer (and mostly expensive) TVs accept a component-video input. Superior even to an S-video connection, a component-video connection can provide a picture with better color accuracy.

Composite-video inputs Composite-video inputs are the most common type of video inputs found on TVs. These carry only the video signal, providing better picture quality than RF (often labeled as "VHF/UHF" on your TV). These are often used to connect a VCR or cable box. Many sets have front-panel composite-video inputs, which let you make temporary connections to camcorders, game consoles, digital cameras, and other devices with composite-video output.

Composite-video output All DVD players offer composite-video output at a minimum. A composite-video connection between the DVD player and the TV provides a picture with less detail and more color artifacts than you're likely to get using an S-video connection. (See "S-video output.") A component-video connection (see "Component-video output") is necessary for optimal picture quality from a progressive-scan player used with a digital TV.

Computer link for stills For camcorders that have still-image-capture capability, a USB or serial port is used to transfer saved still images to a computer.

Computer monitor option The ability of some flat-panel TVs, notably LCD models, to double as a computer monitor, having the required inputs for a computer connection. Some models, notably HD sets, may accept computer signals through their Digital Visual Interface (DVI) input if compatible. A standard VGA connection, however, is the surest guarantee of dual-use potential.

Conferencing Also referred to as three-way conferencing. For some single-line phones, allows conversation among an outside party, the handset, and base speakerphone. For some two-line phones, you can conference two callers in a three-way conversation. Some two-line phones with a base speakerphone can support four-way conferencing. For multiple-handset-capable phones, conferencing can take place among the handsets and an outside party.

Configuration The way various components of a system (such as a computer) are linked. This refers not only to the way the hardware is physically connected but also to how the software is set up to govern the system and its parts; also, the setup and operating parameters of a software program.

Conversation recording A feature that, in some phones with answerers, allows you to record a two-way conversation.

CPU Central Processing Unit, the part of the computer that controls and performs all processing activities. It consists of the ALU (arithmetic logic unit), control unit, and main memory.

Crash An uncontrolled shutdown of one task or the entire computer.

CRT For cathode-ray tube, the familiar picture tube used to create a TV picture since the advent of television. Despite the growing popularity of other technologies such as LCD, plasma, and DLP, CRT TVs represent a mature technology with proven reliability and long life. The best sets have top-notch picture quality, with excellent detail, color, and contrast, plus no limit on viewing angle. CRTs are also used in many rear-projection TVs, in which case the TV contains three CRTs—one each for red, green, and blue—making the cabinet relatively big and heavy. Three beams converge on the inside of the screen to form an image. You must periodically align the CRTs, using the TV's controls, to ensure a sharp image.

Cursor A symbol that marks the current position on the screen and moves as the position changes. It is most often a single underline, a vertical line, or a block the size of one character. It may be either steady or blinking.

Cursor-control keys A special group of keys on a keyboard or keypad (designated by arrows pointing up, down, left, and right) that perform cursor movement functions.

Custom bookmark Should you want to view a DVD scene again later, this feature lets you mark a spot on the disc to which you can later return.

Cyber- Relating to the rapidly growing interactive world between humans and computers.

Cyberspace First used by William Gibson in the novel "Neuromancer" to refer to a futuristic computer network into which people plugged their brains and interacted with it. It has come to refer to the interconnection of computers known as the Internet.

D/A converter sampling rate With respect to video, most standard DVD players use a 10-bit/27-MHz digital-to-analog converter. Progressive-scan DVD players use a 10- or 12-bit/54-MHz digital-to-analog converter.

Data An item or collection of items of information to be processed, displayed, or stored. Data can be text, numbers, binary code, images, sounds, or any combination.

Data file A collection of information to be used as input to a program for processing, display, or any other useful purpose.

Data storage The ability of an MP3 player to store files other than digital-audio files, including text, image, and video files.

Database A collection of data, organized for retrieval, on a specific topic or for a designated purpose.

DCR See "Digital-cable-ready."

Decoder A circuit that converts the TV signal's information into another set of information. In video, it usually decompresses the information to convert it into a playable form.

Dedicated line A telephone line used solely for data or fax services.

Default A value that is automatically assigned to a setting when no other value is entered. A default password, such as "secret," should be changed to ensure security.

Delay between shots The time, in seconds, it takes a digital camera to ready itself for another picture when shooting in normal mode (non-burst), at the camera's highest-resolution, lowest-compression, JPEG setting. Also called lag time or maximum-recycle time.

Desktop In a window-based user interface, the bottom-level window you see when no program window is open. The desktop can be set up as a user prefers, with icons allowing easy launching of often-used programs and documents.

Desktop computer A PC featuring the traditional full-size case, monitor, and keyboard designed to be used in a stationary, "desk-centered" environment.

Dialog box A window that appears onscreen on-computer to convey a message (such as a warning or error) or to request input (such as a choice of alternatives or a confirmation of some action).

Dialog enhancer If you're having trouble hearing dialog in a movie, this feature makes dialog stand out from other noises in the soundtrack.

Dial-up line A communications line that connects through the telephone system, usually by dialing touch-tones.

Digital Characterized by the representation of data as numbers; computers, for example, are digital.

Digital-cable-ready Digital-cable-ready (DCR, or plug-and-play) TVs are a new type of integrated HDTV. They not only get broadcast HD by antenna but they also receive digital-cable programming without using a box. For digital-cable programming, including HD fare, you insert a CableCard into a slot on the set. Many of the integrated HDTVs coming out now are DCR models, and they typically cost more than other HDTVs. In addition, while the first-generation of DCR TVs can receive digital-cable signals without a cable box, they're only one-way—you'll lose the two-way features: interactive program guide, video on demand, and scheduling of pay-per-view events via the remote control. Two-way DCR TVs are expected to be out soon, but it's uncertain if they'll need an updated CableCard.

Digital camcorder DV in For DVD recorders, the ability to accept audio/video input (for recording) from a digital camcorder's DV (digital video) output.

Digital camera or **digicam** A photographic still-image recording device that uses an electronic sensor and memory system instead of film to record and store images as data files. The images can be subsequently transferred to a computer for long-term storage, editing, inclusion in documents, or sent to others over the Internet. Some digicams can take short, low-resolution motion-video clips.

Digital effects Permits special camcorder effects beyond the usual, analog effects such as fading. Examples include cross-fades, wipes, overlaps, bounces, and cross-dissolves. Found on both analog and digital camcorders.

Digital output type Important only if you plan to pipe the signal from a DVD player into a home-theater system that has a digital receiver. When choosing your DVD player, consider the models that have the outputs to match the inputs on your digital receiver or external, digital decoder. All DVD players have digital audio outputs–coaxial, optical, or both.

Digital security A built-in cordless-phone security feature in which digital verification between the base and handset prevents your dial tone from being intercepted and used to make calls.

Digital still capable Some camcorders can take snapshots, much like a digital camera (though not necessarily of the same quality). The camcorder can then be plugged into a computer and the images downloaded from the memory. Using a removable memory card (such as MemoryStick, Compact Flash, MultiMedia Card, or SmartMedia), you can transfer stills to a computer without having to connect the camcorder, but you need proper card-reader hardware.

Digital video input This input is found on some computers and increasingly on digital (HD/ED/SD) TVs. Found in the form of DVI or HDMI (See "DVI" and "HDMI"), it provides a high-quality digital connection for video while potentially allowing the content providers to control your ability to record the content.

Digital video recorder (DVR). Another name for a hard-drive recorder, the term originated years ago with TiVo and ReplayTV models.

Digital Visual Interface See "DVI."

Digital zoom Magnifies the central portion of a digital camera's or camcorder's image by interspersing additional pixels among those captured by the image sensor. This makes the image larger but does not add detail or improve sharpness. You could get the same effect by trimming or cropping the full image later, on the computer. Always use the maximum optical zoom before resorting to digital zoom.

Digital8 (D8) A camcorder format that uses 8mm or Hi8 tape to record images digitally. Many models can also read 8mm and Hi8 recordings. Tapes generally offer a shorter recording time than most other formats.

Digitize To convert an analog signal to digital format.

Digitizer A device that converts an analog signal (such as video or sound) into a series of digital values.

Disc capacity DVD changers range in capacity from two discs to several hundred. (The larger, "jukebox" changers may suit you if you'd like to store your entire CD collection in the player.)

Disc formats: CD The disc format of commercial audio CDs. All DVD players can play commercial audio CDs, though not all will play CD-R or CD-RW audio discs burned on a PC or a CD recorder.

Disc formats: CD-R Allows you to play CD-Recordable (CD-R) audio discs burned on a PC or a CD recorder. Some discs may not play on a particular player for one reason or another.

Disc formats: DVD In addition to playing DVD-video discs, DVD players can handle audio CDs. (Some can also play video CDs, a format that's popular overseas.) Other disc formats that some players support include CD-R and CD-RW (the audio discs you record yourself, using other equipment); MP3 on CDs; HDCD; DVD-Audio and Super Audio CD (SACD), two audio-centric formats intended to succeed audio CDs; and the emerging writable formats, such as DVD-R, DVD-RW, and DVD+RW.

Diskette A small, portable plastic-encased flexible (floppy) disk used as a magnetic data storage medium. Data is recorded as magnetic signals that are arranged in a series of circular tracks. Most diskettes hold 1.44 megabytes of data, a small capacity by today's standards.

Display Any electronic device that visually conveys information or images, usually graphically.

Display size A PDA-screen measurement that, as with computer monitors, is made diagonally, in inches.

Display type, MP3 Most players have a liquid crystal display (LCD) screen lets you view the song title, track number, amount of memory remaining, the battery life indicator, and other functions. Many are backlit. Display size and shape vary, including shapes such as square, rectangular, or oval. Some new players have a color LCD display.

Display type, PDA Screens come with either color or monochrome screen displays. Color screens offer more detail but also tend to drain the batteries more quickly than monochrome.

DLP Digital Light Processing, a form of projection-TV technology that creates images using a chip with millions of tiny swiveling mirrors. Most rear-projection DLP sets currently employ one chip and a rotating color wheel, which may cause occasional annoying flashes of color visible to some viewers–what's called the rainbow effect. Some front projectors have three chips, which alleviates the problem.

Dock on Apple's Mac OS X desktop, an icon-filled bar for launching and switching between applications.

Docking station A rectangular platform with a connector and a power supply for a laptop or handheld computer. It connects with a CRT monitor, printer, and other peripherals to, essentially, turn a laptop computer into a desktop computer.

Document Any human-readable file containing information entered by the user. Examples are word-processing files, spreadsheets, and databases.

Documentation Material that comes with a software package or a computer system and offers directions for setup and operation, features, capabilities, and troubleshooting advice. More and more often, paper documentation is being replaced by "online" help, files installed on the PC's hard disk, a CD-ROM, or the Internet.

Dolby Digital (AC-3) All DVD players can extract the typically six-channel Dolby Digital soundtrack from a DVD-video disc. To hear all the channels discretely, however, requires that either the player or a digital receiver to which it's connected have a built-in multichannel audio decoder–or that you have a separate decoder connected between the DVD player and the receiver. It also demands a full multi-speaker home-theater system. If you don't have all that equipment, the soundtrack can be "down-mixed" to two channels with no loss of key audio information.

Dolby Pro Logic An analog audio-encoding format that, when output by the DVD player and decoded by a sound system, splits the signal into four: left and right front, center channel (for dialog), and one limited-range surround channel carried by two rear speakers. Audio encoded in this way is found on most prerecorded VHS movies, all DVDs, many movies on TV, and some TV-show soundtracks.

Domain name A structured, alphabetic name, such as consumerreports.org, for a location on the Internet. These names are aliases for numeric IP addresses and are leased from an Internet naming authority by the domain-name owner.

Dongle Any small peripheral device connected to a computer by a short cord and plug.

DOS Disk Operating System, a set of programs that activates the computer and allows the user or other programs to perform simple functions; the term is used synonymously with MS- or PC-DOS, early operating systems used in personal computers in the 1970s and 1980s. A simple command-line DOS was built into Windows 95 and 98 and can be invoked, if needed, in later versions of Windows.

Double-click A quick double-press of the left button on a computer mouse (or the typical Mac mouse's single button) to activate a file or icon.

Download To transfer a copy of a file from a host (server) computer to a client computer, a term frequently used to describe the process of transferring a file or data from the Internet to a computer's hard drive. In the other direction, it's an upload.

dpi Dots per inch, a common measure of the resolution of a printer, scanner, or display. In theory, the higher the dpi, the better the image quality. But the unaided human eye cannot distinguish differences beyond about 200 dpi.

DPOF With digital cameras, digital print-order format lets you store information on the camera's memory card that indicates how many prints to make of each image. It's intended for use when having prints made at a digital photo kiosk or when printing images on certain inkjet printers.

Draft mode A faster, ink-saving printing mode for inkjet printers, and a toner-saving mode for laser printers.

Drag and drop Using a computer's mouse, this refers to the way you move objects onscreen, and by reference, among the storage devices, in a graphical operating system such as Windows or Mac OS. You click on an item, which represents a folder or file, and drag it while holding the mouse

button; you then release the button wherever you want to place the item.

Drive A unit that writes data to or reads it from a storage medium such as a tape or disk.

Driver A program that controls some component of a computer system, such as a monitor, disk drive, or printer.

DRM Digital rights management, any scheme used to prevent the unauthorized use or dissemination of copyrighted, file-based content, such as music, video, or software. DRM often makes use of data encryption in combination with a software or hardware decoder that performs user authentication at the point of content use. Hackers, however, are often able to "crack" DRM schemes and provide programs over the Internet to allow other users to circumvent DRM protections.

DSL Digital Subscriber Line, which provides high-speed Internet access through existing phone lines without affecting normal phone operation.

DTS Audio Digital Theater Systems, a multichannel sound format used in some movies. It's a useful extra that ensures you can hear multichannel sound from virtually any movie–provided you have the necessary speakers and that the DVD player or connected digital receiver has a multichannel DTS decoder; a separate DTS decoder can also be connected between the player and the receiver. While all DVD players support Dolby Digital surround sound, many models also support DTS.

Dual antenna inputs With two antenna inputs, you can easily switch between two antenna signals using your remote control. This capability can be handy if you use, for example, both a roof antenna and a cable hookup, or in order to take full advantage of dual-tuner picture-in-picture (PIP).

Dual-band Some cordless-phone models have dual-band transmission, which–between the base and handset–wirelessly transmit within one frequency band and receive on the other. Some 2.4-GHz models are dual-band (2.4-GHz/900-MHz) transmission, and some 5.8-GHz models are dual-band (5.8-GHz/2.4-GHz) transmission.

Dual-sided printing This capability is also known as double-sided or two-sided printing. Some printer models can print on both sides of a page automatically, typically more slowly than when printing on one side of a page. With most others, you can print the odd-numbered pages first, then manually flip the document over to print the even-numbered pages.

Duron A processor family from AMD that is generally slower and less costly than its Athlon counterpart. It is used in lower-priced PCs.

Duty cycle For printers, the monthly volume, in number of pages, that the manufacturer recommends for optimal use.

DVD Digital Versatile Disk or Digital Video Disk, an optical digital-storage medium the same size as a CD, but with at least 4 times the capacity. DVDs were originally used for consumer distribution of movies and were adapted for computer use. There are now drives with write-once (DVD-R) and rewrite (DVD-RW, DVD+RW and DVD-RAM) capabilities.

DVD-Audio This is one of two new, competing music formats. DVD-Audio discs encode the music so that it can be output in either two or up to six channels. Both this and the other competing format, Super Audio CD (SACD), claim to offer better sound quality than CDs can deliver. Note that while program material formatted in DVD-Audio will only play on DVD players that specify DVD-Audio capability, DVD-Audio discs may also contain a Dolby Digital or DTS version of the program material that will play on any DVD player.

DVD-R A write-once DVD format. Certain camcorders record in this format onto a disc measuring a little over 3 inches (8cm) in diameter. Discs can be played on most DVD players.

DVD-RAM A rewritable DVD format supported by some DVD recorders. Certain DVD-RAM camcorders record onto discs measuring a little over 3 inches (8cm) in diameter, in MPEG-2 format, the same technology used for commercial DVD. However, discs cannot be played on most DVD players.

DVD recorder. A device that records video to a DVD. It may be a stand-alone recorder or integrated with a DVR or VCR in a combination model.

DVI Digital Visual Interface, a relatively new form of digital video input in some high-definition TVs; it matches a corresponding output in some DVD players and digital TV tuners. Like HDMI (See "HDMI"), it potentially allows content providers to control your ability to record the content. Unlike HDMI, DVI requires a separate audio cable to carry the audio signals.

DV input. An interface found on many DVD recorders, it allows direct transfer of digital video and audio from a digital camcorder.

DVI output, DVD players Has Digital Visual Interface (DVI) output for direct digital video connection to digital TVs with DVI input. Can output 480p, 720p, and 1080i video signals, although signals upconverted from 480i or 480p to 720p or 1080i do not produce a true HD picture.

Ease of download How the camera transfers images to your computer or printer. Most digital cameras offer more than one means of transferring images. Some require that you purchase special accessories. **Via removable memory** Many digital cameras store images on removable memory cards that go in and out of the camera like a roll of film (Compact Flash and SmartMedia are two common types). These can then be used with a variety of memory card readers sold as computer accessories. A few models store images on CD-R or CD-RW optical disks that can be read in a computer's CD-ROM drive. **Via USB port** A USB (Universal Serial Bus) cable transfers image files from your digital camera to the computer.

EBook reader PDA software that, when installed, lets you read electronic books. Generally, you have to purchase the eBooks separately and download them onto your PDA.

ED-ready Also referred to as an EDTV monitor, a TV (typically flat-panel) that requires you to connect an external tuner that can decode digital signals for display. The category EDTV (for enhanced-definition TV) lies between high-definition and standard-definition in terms of resolution and, generally, picture quality. Overall, ED sets can display smooth, pleasing images such as those from a progressive-scan DVD player. When connected to an HD tuner, some ED sets down-convert HD signals to display a less-detailed version of HD images.

EDTV A TV (typically flat-panel) that includes a built-in tuner for digital signals for display (see "Built-in digital tuner"). The category EDTV (for enhanced-definition TV) lies between high-definition and standard-definition in terms of resolution and, generally, picture quality. Overall, ED sets can display smooth, pleasing images such as those from a progressive-scan DVD player. When receiving an HD signal, some ED sets down-convert it to display a less-detailed version of HD images.

Edit search Allows you to search for specific footage on a camcorder's recording; it can be very helpful when editing.

Editor A program that lets you create or make changes in a document. A word processor is an advanced type of editor, with special features such as word wrap, headers and footers, and print attributes (boldface, underline, italics).

EFT Electronic funds transfer, a system commonly used by banks and other money handlers that involves secure, computer-controlled money transfers between accounts.

Electronic commerce Shopping through electronic catalogs and making purchases using the Internet.

E-mail or email Electronic mail lets you send and receive personal messages, including those with attached files such as text or graphics, through the Internet, an online service, a BBS, a network, or other system.

Encryption A process applied to a data file to render its contents unreadable to a non-authorized user or computer system. Reading an encrypted file requires a software "key" that is available only to an authenticated user.

End user The final person or business to make use of a product or service. This is generally you, the consumer.

Energy Star A label on many kinds of appliances that designates compliance with energy-efficiency goals developed by the U.S. Environmental Protection Agency. In order to qualify for certification, a typical computer or monitor must power down to no more than about 10 percent of normal power consumption after a period of inactivity.

Envelope capacity The number of standard-weight, business-size (#10) envelopes that a printer with an envelope-input tray can accommodate.

Envelope input This can be an input tray or slot that holds a small stack of envelopes in a printer, though it doesn't have to be dedicated to envelopes. It can also be a manual, single-feed envelope slot.

Equalizer Most MP3 players have an equalizer, which allows the listener to adjust the sound in various ways. A custom setting via separate bass and treble controls or adjustable equalizers give you the most control over the sound. Some players simply have a bass boost control, not considered an equalizer.

Ergonomic Designed with the needs and comfort of the user in mind.

Ethernet The most common type of local area network (see "LAN") used to connect personal computers to each other, or to a router or other devices on a network.

EULA End-User License Agreement. A legal instrument, accompanying most software, that states the terms under which the company is allowing its use by the consumer. An EULA is typically written in virtually incomprehensible legal jargon, but must often be agreed with by clicking an on-screen "I Agree" button before one can use the software.

Expansion card Most PDAs come with expansion slots for flash memory, a modem, or another device. The most common expansion option for PDAs is through a connector that accommodates either a MultiMedia Card (or Secure Digital card), Memory Stick, or CompactFlash card. A few models offer more than one type of expansion.

Expansion capability The handheld PDA includes expansion slots for flash memory, a pager card, or other device.

Expansion memory format The format for the removable-memory medium used in a standard-capacity MP3 player: Most are external cards (some the size of a matchbook) that install into the player. Among the most common are CompactFlash, MultiMedia Card, Secure Digital, and SmartMedia. In addition, some players use a proprietary memory format, such as Sony's MagicGate Memory Stick (a copy-protected version of Sony's existing Memory Stick media) or SONICblue Rio Memory Backpacks.

Expansion slot A position in a computer for adding an expansion board or card. Desktop PCs usually have at least two free PCI expansion slots. Laptops use PC cards for expansion.

Exposure compensation Allows for minor adjustments to the automatic-exposure settings. When a scene has high contrast, as in a backlit scene, automatic exposure may not achieve the effect you want. It helps to be able to alter the settings so that the subject of the photo does not appear too dark or too light.

Export To transfer from the file format currently in use to another one.

External bay In a desktop computer, a front-mounted drive bay that allows physical access.

External drive A storage device that is physically separate from the computer. Such drives often have their own power supply and attach to the computer through a FireWire port, SCSI port, or a laptop computer's PC card.

F connector A type of coaxial connector, most frequently used to connect cable or satellite television signals to components such as TVs, VCRs, and PC tuner cards. Receivers and minisystems may also have F connectors to connect to FM antennas.

FAQ A list of frequently asked questions and their answers, meant to help users of a product or service understand its features and operation, and perform simple troubleshooting.

Fatal error The cause of premature termination of processing, often as a crash. Fatal errors can occur as a result of read/write errors, program bugs, system conflicts, and hardware defects. Some errors crash only one application; others require that you restart the computer.

File A collection of related records. Computer data and documents are normally stored as files.

File extension An identifier of the type or purpose of a file, usually written as one to three letters following the filename and separated from it by a period. For example, the file My Letter.doc might be a text document, while Numbers.dat could be a data file. File extensions are used by Windows to determine what program to use to open a file, and are hidden by default if Windows has registered a program for the extension.

Filename The unique identification given to a program or data file for storage. Filenames were once limited to eight characters (plus a three-character extension) in older operating systems like DOS. Newer operating systems such as Windows and Mac OS allow much longer filenames.

File-sharing One of the common uses for a network. Files can be designated as shared by their owners on one PC, and accessed by other authorized users in the same network workgroup, or over the Internet through peer-to-peer protocols.

File-swapping An Internet activity, popularized by free, peer-to-peer services such as KaZaA and Gnutella, with which users can search for files of interest and download them from designated shared folders on a network of thousands of other users' computers. File-swapping has been criticized because users often trade files containing copyrighted material.

Film mode See "3:2-pulldown compensation."

Firewall A network gateway (software or hardware) that "filters" data requests, rejecting those that lack the necessary security clearance. Firewalls were originally used to protect corporate, government, or institutional networks from unauthorized access; they now also help keep individuals' home computers safe from intruders on the Internet.

FireWire input Also known as IEEE-1394 and iLink, an all-digital means of relating audio as well as video digitally from, say, a digital camcorder to a computer or DVD recorder. It's found on some computers, DVD recorders, D-VHS decks, digital set-top boxes, and high-definition TVs. Among TVs, it is less common than HDMI and DVI inputs. Like both of those inputs, it supports copy-protection schemes.

FireWire port, camcorders A FireWire (IEEE-1394) port is used to connect the camcorder to a computer, or to another digital camcorder for monitoring or video editing.

Firmware-upgradable The firmware—the player's built-in operating instructions—can be upgraded so the player does not become obsolete. Upgrades can add or enhance features, fix "bugs," and add support for other audio formats and operating systems. Check the manufacturer's and music-management software application Web sites for upgrades.

Flash animation A programming platform commonly used for embedding animation in Web pages. Flash "movies" are relatively small, allowing them to download quickly on slow dialup connections. Playing a Flash movie requires a plug-in for your browser.

Flash, cameras Like film cameras, most digital cameras have a built-in flash for shooting indoors or in other low-light conditions. Many cameras have an automatic-flash mode, which automatically fires the flash when more light is needed. The flashes built into most digital cameras have fairly limited range (up to 10 to 13 feet on most models), compared with external flash units, which can be much more powerful. A camera with an external "flash sync" or "hot shoe" will usually have a built-in flash as well.

Flash, cordless phones A button to answer call waiting.

Flash memory A low-cost, high-density, erasable memory chip that holds its data without power. It's used in computers and peripheral devices to hold settings and allow easy BIOS updating, and packaged in plug-in cards to act as data storage in small portable devices such as digital cameras.

Flat-panel display A thin display screen employing one of several technologies, usually LCD or plasma. Flat-panel displays are commonly used on portable devices to reduce size and weight, and are increasing in popularity as desktop monitor replacements. They're also used in costly but lightweight TVs.

Flat screen Indicates whether the set has a flat screen. (It refers to flat-front picture tubes on conventional TVs, not to be confused with flat-panel LCD or plasma models.) While a flat screen looks sleek and shows fewer reflections than a curved screen, it doesn't guarantee better picture quality.

Flexible LCD angle A camcorder's LCD monitor with this feature is adjustable so you can angle it, making it easy to view while you record.

Floppy disk See diskette.

Folder The Windows and Mac OS name for a disk directory.

Font In word processing, a typeface enhancement such as bold or script. The term also is often used to refer to a typeface style such as Arial, Times Roman, or Courier.

Footer A special message or identification placed at the bottom of a document page.

Footprint The space on a floor or table occupied by a piece of hardware.

Format (1) To initialize a data-storage medium; (2) to lay out in a specific pattern, such as a screen or report format; or (3) the layout or pattern itself.

Format, camcorders Format is based on the type of recording tape or disc that a camcorder uses and whether the model records in analog or digital mode. Currently, there are at least nine formats: Hi8, MiniDV, MicroMV, Digital8 (D8), VHS, VHS-C, S-VHS-C, DVD-RAM, and DVD-R. Key differences among these formats include picture quality, size of camcorder, and compatibility with a VCR.

Formats supported, MP3 players The formats (such as MP3, WMA, and AAC) that the bundled music-management software can convert to a format compatible with the player.

Forum An information exchange, usually found on the Internet, that is confined to a single topic or area of interest.

FPS See "frame rate."

Frame advance Allows you to advance DVD playback frame-by-frame, instead of at normal play speed.

Frame rate Expressed in FPS (frames-per-second), the rate at which a display of moving graphical images is updated. Motion-picture film runs at 24 FPS, the minimum considered to be essentially jitter-free. Computer-generated graphics, such as from games, can run at much higher rates, limited by the graphics processor. Avid gamers look for rates of 50 FPS or higher, producing more-realistic motion.

Freeware Software that is distributed, mostly via the Internet, essentially without charge to all interested users.

Freeze frame A DVD-player feature that allows you to pause playback on your screen.

Frequency Cordless phones transmit their signals between the base and handset wirelessly in the 900-MHz, 2.4-GHz, and/or 5.8-GHz frequency bands.

Front-panel A/V inputs These are handy if you want to connect a camcorder or video game to the TV without having to reach around to the rear of the set.

Front-firing speakers Front-firing speakers, found on most sets, are built into the front of the TV set. Such speakers provide direct sound to the viewer, desirable if you plan to put the TV in a wall unit—a placement that can make side-firing speakers sound muffled.

Front-projection A display system where the image is beamed from a projector onto the front of a projection screen. You view the same side of the screen that faces the projector.

FTP File Transfer Protocol, an Internet protocol that lets you transfer files between your computer and an FTP site. "Anonymous" FTP allows a user to retrieve files without having to establish a user ID and password.

Full auto switch A camcorder feature that essentially lets you point and shoot. The camcorder automatically adjusts the color balance, shutter speed, focus, and aperture (also called the "iris" or f-stop with camcorders).

G4 The newest family of PowerPC microprocessors from Motorola, available in Apple Macintosh computers ranging in speed from 800 to 1420 MHz.

Game controller Originally limited to knobs and joysticks, such devices now include driving simulators, cockpit simulators, movement sensors, and the entire class of human interface devices (HIDs).

Game port A 15-pin serial port used for attaching joysticks or other game controllers, along with MIDI music devices, to a computer. Game ports can handle a pair of controllers and may come as part of an original system or be supplied on sound boards. They are becoming less common on new PCs, supplanted by newer interfaces like USB.

Game timer A parental-control feature that limits the number of minutes an input will accept signals from a gaming system such as Xbox or PlayStation.

GB See gigabyte.

GIF (jiff) Graphics Interchange Format, a lossless, compressed file format for image bitmaps created by the CompuServe online service to reduce download time.

Gigabyte 1,024 megabytes, which is 1,073,741,824 bytes. Sometimes manufacturers will misrepresent hard-drive capacities by defining a GB as a billion bytes, but this is not strictly accurate.

Glitch A nonreproducible problem in a system. Glitches often result from voltage fluctuations, static discharges, and data-transmission errors.

Graphics board or adapter In a computer, an expansion card or built-in circuitry that provides the memory and graphics coprocessor necessary to produce text and graphics displays; along with the monitor, it determines the resolution and colors that can be displayed.

Graphics processor or GPU On a computer's graphics adapter, a set of chips that has built-in firmware, processing capabilities, and adequate memory (usually 32 to 128 MB) to relieve the CPU of much of the burden of processing graphics.

Graphics Special characters or drawings such as graphs, charts, and picture-like renderings of various objects or entire scenes.

Guide Plus Found on a limited number of sets, TV Guide Plus+ receives on-screen program information. Versions such as Guide Plus+ Gold offer additional features, such as VCR recording control.

Hacker A nonprofessional computer whiz; usually one who tries to gain unlawful access to a computer system, or alters programs to allow unlicensed usage.

Handheld Short for any computing device that is operated while held in the hand.

Handset memory dialing locations The number of phone numbers and names, for phones with an LCD display, that you can program into the handset's memory to make calls with only a few button presses.

Handset speakerphone A handset speakerphone offers a hands-free way to converse or wait on hold and lets others chime in as well, conveniently, anywhere in the house as long as you stay within a few feet of the handset.

Handset to handset talk Most multiple-handset-capable phones allow conversation handset to handset, or among handsets for conferencing. For some phones the handsets have to be within range of the base, while others allow a direct link among handsets so you can take them with you to use like a walkie-talkie. Also referred to as Handset to Handset Intercom.

Handset volume control Found on all cordless-phone handsets, this lets you adjust the volume of the voice in the handset's earpiece.

Hard copy Printed text.

Hard disk or hard drive A magnetic data storage system using one or more rigid platters sealed in a dustproof housing and spun at several thousand RPM. Data are recorded as magnetic signals arranged in a pattern of concentric circles on the surfaces. Typical storage capacities range from about 20 to 200 gigabytes. With IBM-brand computers, they're referred to as fixed disks.

Hard-drive recognition Computers with newer operating systems, such as Windows XP, can recognize an MP3 player as a hard or removable drive when you plug it in. Some players require you to install software before they can be recognized as hard drives. You may also have to upgrade software if your computer has an older or less-common operating system. These situations make the MP3 player less convenient for shuttling files from one PC to another.

Hard-drive recorder. A video recorder that stores recordings on a computer-style hard drive. Variations include stand-alone models designed to work with an onscreen programming service and combination models that include a DVD recorder.

Hard-drive recording times (min./max., hrs.) For a DVD recorder with a built-in hard drive, the minimum and maximum hours of content that may be recorded onto the drive using, respectively, the least and most compression.

Hardware The electronic equipment that makes up

GLOSSARY

a system. In a computer system, hardware includes the CPU, monitor, printer, circuit boards, drives, cables, etc. It does not include data or computer programs, which are software.

Hard-wired Connected with a non-detachable cable; permanently wired.

HDMI A relatively new form of digital audio/video input in some high-definition TVs, it matches a corresponding output in some DVD players and digital TV tuners. Like DVI, it potentially allows content providers to control your ability to record the content. Unlike DVI, HDMI carries audio and video signals on the same cable.

HDMI output Has High-Definition Multimedia Interface (HDMI) output for direct digital audio and video connection to digital TVs with HDMI input. Can output 480p, 720p, and 1080i video signals, although signals upconverted from 480i or 480p to 720p or 1080i do not produce a true HD picture.

HD-ready HD-ready TVs, also known as HDTV monitors, lack a high-definition receiver (tuner) and require an external device to decode the HD signals displayed on the TV. Sources for HD signals include HD-capable satellite receivers, over-the-air digital TV (DTV) receivers, and HD-capable digital-cable boxes. These devices connect to the TV's HD component-video, HDMI, DVI, or FireWire input. An integrated "HDTV" has a built-in DTV receiver/decoder and typically costs more.

HDTV An HDTV is capable of displaying high-definition TV signals and has a built-in receiver (tuner) to decode the HD signals displayed on the TV (see "Built-in digital tuner"). Note that the included tuner will decode digital TV (DTV) signals from specific sources, such as off-air (broadcast) signals, cable, or satellite. HDTVs that can decode digital-cable signals are called Digital-cable-ready. Some HD-capable cable boxes and satellite receivers also include a tuner to decode off-air DTV.

Header A special message or identification that is placed at the top of a document page; also, the information, sometimes hidden at the top of an e-mail message, that lists each computer the message passed from sender to recipient, along with the date and time.

Headphone out, camcorders An output for connecting a pair of headphones to a camcorder.

Headphone type The type of headphone or earphone included with an MP3 player. Some can fold up or permit volume control.

Headset jack Allows you to plug a headset into the phone. Many cordless phones have a handset headset jack plus a belt clip (headset usually sold separately), allowing hands-free conversation anywhere in the house. Useful for, say, a home office, some have a base headset jack, allowing long or many hands-free conversations without needing to be concerned about the handset's battery life.

Hertz or **Hz** A measure of frequency, being the number of cycles per second.

Hi8 A camcorder format that uses a specific tape about the size of an audiocassette. Most Hi8 models can also operate in 8mm format.

Hibernation A shutdown mode in many PCs and most laptops that saves the current state of the machine and all its running processes on the hard drive for quick restoration on demand. It's also called suspend-to-disk.

High image capacity A relatively high number of pictures you can take on a digital camera before you run out of storage space. Capacity varies depending on what the memory card can store and on the resolution and file-compression settings in use. The more storage available, the more pictures you can take before having to transfer images to a computer or erase them.

High recycle time A relatively high period of time, in seconds, it takes a digital camera to ready itself to take another picture when shooting in normal mode (non-burst), at the camera's highest-resolution, lowest-compression, JPEG setting.

High-resolution Showing great detail; the higher the resolution of a television, computer monitor or printer, the greater the detail of a drawing or image it is able to reproduce.

Home page The page in a Web site usually visited first; it contains links to other pages in the site or to other sites. The home page is automatically selected when you type a Web address ending in ".com," ".org," or another common domain suffix.

Horizontal resolution, TVs This indicates the maximum number of displayed vertical lines that can be counted horizontally across the screen. Most analog sets 27 inches and larger have roughly the same horizontal resolution. Higher horizontal resolution (a higher line count) is said to provide a better picture, but this claim is not necessarily true. Some TVs with a lower line count but higher contrast, for example, can actually provide a picture that looks sharper.

Horizontal resolution, camcorders A technical specification that offers a rough guide to picture quality. Essentially, it represents how many of the vertical lines that create the video image can fit in a picture before they blur together. The closer they can get before blurring, the more lines of horizontal resolution there are.

Host computer A computer that serves as a source for data and information retrieval for client computers, usually networked PCs.

Hotkey A key or combination of keys that, when pressed, take priority in causing an action to take place. Typical uses for hotkeys include initiating menu options or interrupting an ongoing process.

HTML HyperText Markup Language, the standard language for creating pages on the World Wide Web. Even if you do not understand HTML, you can create it with Web-page authoring programs, popular word-processors, or basic step-by-step instructions at certain Web sites to build pages.

http HyperText Transfer Protocol, a protocol developed for exchange of hypertext documents across the Internet. All Web addresses begin with http://, which a browser will automatically insert for you.

Hub A multiport device that connects several computers together into a wired network, without performing any data-management functions. A "switched" hub adds the ability to prevent data "collisions," increasing overall speed.

Hyperlink Within a hypertext document, a clickable object that retrieves another location within the document or anywhere else on the Web. These can be either graphics or text; text links are usually blue and underlined.

Hypertext A method of linking information within and between text or other files. The linked data may be almost anything from text to graphics to programs. The Internet's World Wide Web is an ad-hoc collection of linked hypertext documents.

I

I/O Input/output, referring to an electronic device's transfer of digital data or analog signals.

Icon A small graphical image that appears on a graphical user interface such as a computer's desktop in a Windows or Mac system. These normally represent a specific file or program or cause a desired action to occur when clicked with a mouse.

IDE Integrated Drive Electronics, a hard-disk interface technology.

IEEE A standards organization that publishes computer-industry-defined standards for hardware, software, and data communications. IEEE 1394 is the standard for the FireWire interface, and IEEE 802.11 is the standard for Wi-Fi wireless networking.

IEEE-1394 port Now found on virtually all digital camcorders, this feature (also known as a FireWire or iLink connection) lets you transfer video data to a computer or another digital camcorder with little or no loss of quality. The other device, however, must also have an IEEE-1394 connection, and only some new computers are so equipped.

Illuminated remote Some remote controls offer illuminated buttons for easier operation in a dimly lit room.

Image stabilization A feature that automatically reduces the shakes in a scene caused by holding the camcorder. It's also called digital image stabilization (DIS), electronic image stabilization (EIS), picture stabilizer, or steady shot. Using a tripod is the surest way to get a steady image.

Import To transfer data from another file into the one currently in use.

In-camera editing All but universal, this digital-camera feature allows you to decide to keep or erase pictures you've taken. You can review the pictures on the LCD display and delete those you don't want, which will free up memory for more pictures.

In-home warranty A warranty under which a technician comes to your home to either retrieve or diagnose and service the set when you have a problem—of particular importance with heavy (especially projection) or wall-mounted sets.

Incompatible Unable to work with, usually referring to a program that can't be run under a different operating system than that for which it was created, or a device not supported by a computer's hardware or BIOS.

Individual color tanks Some printers use a separate tank for each color. Others have tri-color cartridges with three colors in one. Individual tanks allow you to replace only the color that runs out rather than tossing out a tri-color cartridge that may have some ink left.

Initialize To set up, prepare, or start from the beginning. Initializing a disk deletes any data on it and makes it ready for use by a system.

Inkjet printer A printer that uses tiny jets or droplets of charged ink particles, projected from a set of nozzles, to create images, usually of high quality. Inkjet printers are currently the most popular printers for home use and are the most economical means of producing high-quality full-color printouts.

Instant messaging An online system, usually proprietary, that lets you hold a private, real-time text-based conversation among two or more users.

Installed memory Measured in megabytes (MB), this is the amount of memory installed in a printer—not an important consideration for most home users. While inkjet printers themselves contain varying amounts of installed memory, they mainly use a computer's microprocessor and memory to process data.

Instruction In the computer world, a command to the CPU to carry out an operation.

Interactive electronic program guide An on-screen guide to upcoming TV programming. Using your remote, you can switch channels, select programs to record (on models with recording capability), and—depending on the guide—search for upcoming material.

Integrated amplifier A few DVD players have built-in amplifiers; connected to speakers, such models can amplify signals from the player and any other components of a home-theater system.

Integrated receiver A few DVD players have a built-in audio receiver; connected to speakers, such models can amplify signals from the player and any other components of a home-theater system. They also include an AM/FM radio tuner.

Interactive Able to respond to a user's wishes. Interactive software usually refers to a multimedia presentation that the user controls, moving at a speed and in a direction the user wishes.

Interchangeable lens Allows you to physically change the lens being used on a camera. Rarely found on digital cameras; when it is, you can expect a hefty price tag.

Interface The connection between two components such as the PC and a printer; also, to connect two components together.

Interface type The connection type required on your computer to interface (usually via a cable and/or interface module) with an MP3 player, or its memory card adapter. Most players use Universal Serial Bus (USB).

Interlaced A video display (can be a TV as well as a computer monitor) in which odd and even scan lines are displayed on alternate cycles. Interlaced signals require less processing and tend to be faster but can produce flicker. Standard-definition televisions use an interlaced display.

Internal bay A drive bay inside a computer that does not permit physical access from the outside; these often hold a hard drive.

Internal drive A drive housed within the computer's case. Such drives normally derive power from the computer's power supply.

Internal dubbing For DVD recorders that include a built-in hard drive or VCR, the ability to copy recorded content internally from one medium to another.

Internal memory, MP3 players Also called onboard or built-in memory, the amount of internal memory that comes with the player for storing music. Standard-capacity players typically have 64 or 128 MB. Some players have no internal memory to store music but instead include a memory card. Many MP3 players have additional memory slots in which removable media such as the CompactFlash, MultiMedia Card, Secure Digital, or SmartMedia can be inserted. Hard-drive high-capacity players currently have internal memory storage capacities of 5 to 40 GB.

Internet A "super" network consisting of a collection of many commercial, academic, and governmental networks throughout the world. Public access to the Internet, now used by millions of people, is obtained through a contract with an Internet Service Provider (ISP).

Internet gateway A device or computer that provides the connection and protocols to link a single computer or network to the Internet.

Intranet An "Internet-like" hyperlinked information-exchange system established within an organization or institution, for its own purposes, protected from unauthorized public access.

IP or IP address Internet Protocol address, a means of referring to locations on the Internet. Composed of a series of four numbers from 0 through 255, separated by decimal points. All machines on the Internet have one, often assigned by the ISP at connection time.

IP telephony The use of IP protocols to establish two-way voice communications between users.

IRC For Internet Relay Chat, Internet communication where anyone can carry on real-time conversation by typing messages back and forth.

ISDN Integrated Services Digital Network, a high-speed telephone line that is a faster but expensive alternative to traditional dial-up modems.

ISO equivalent Conventional camera film speed is rated using a standard from the International Standards Organization (ISO). The higher the ISO film speed, the more sensitive, or "faster," the film—meaning that less light is needed to take a picture. Although digital cameras don't use traditional film, the industry uses an ISO equivalency rating to describe their light sensitivity.

Java or JavaScript A programming language that brings animation and interactivity to Web pages by embedding program code that is run on the client PC.

Jog/shuttle on unit A DVD player's jog control lets you advance or rewind just one frame at a time to find the exact spot you want, while a shuttle control lets you scan video segments at speeds from slow to fast.

Joystick A device used with computer games and other interactive programs to manually control the cursor, an object, or the action by moving a stick back and forth, right and left, or by the push of a "fire" button.

JPEG Joint Photographic Experts Group, an image-file format that allows for several levels of file compression from "lossless" (high quality, large file) to quite "lossy" (lower quality, small file), to suit different needs. Commonly used on Web pages or digital-camera files.

Justification The alignment of text or images in a document, usually to the left and/or right margins, or centered.

K or KB Kilobyte, which is exactly 1,024 bytes but is usually thought of as 1,000 bytes. Sometimes incorrectly represented by a small k, which just represents the prefix kilo.

Karaoke available On some DVD players, this feature lets you sing along with special karaoke DVDs. These discs provide backing music as the lyrics appear on the screen, often along with a bouncing ball to help you stay in time with the music.

kb Kilobit.

Key A button on a computer's keyboard. Also, in a database, an item—usually a field within a record—that is used to uniquely identify the record.

Keyboard The typewriter-like panel used to enter and manipulate text or other data and enter instructions to direct the computer's operations.

Keypad A set of keys grouped together and performing a particular function. The most common keypads on a computer are the numeric and cursor control.

Kilo- A prefix meaning 1,000. Because of the binary nature of computers, kilo is also used to refer to 1,024.

Kilobit 1,024 bits (2 to the 8th power), usually thought of as 1,000 bits.

Kilobyte 1,024 bytes (2 to the 8th power), usually thought of as 1,000 bytes.

L

LAN Local Area Network, a system of two or more computers within an area (typically a building) that share some of the same facilities, such as files, disks, printers, and software.

Landscape A page or screen orientation in which information is printed or displayed across the longer dimension.

Laptop computer A portable, battery-equipped computer with a flat-panel display screen, small enough to be used on a lap or small table. Also called notebook computers, some are complete systems offering advanced features nearly the equal of desktop PCs, along with wireless-networking capability.

Laser printer A fast, economical page printer that produces high-quality print and graphics. Color laser printers have been too expensive for most consumers, though prices are starting to decrease.

Last channel recall Found on many sets, this feature lets you return to the previous channel you were watching with just a single button push on the remote. It will also let you switch back and forth easily between two channels.

Launch To load and run a program.

Layer indicator Certain DVDs have two layers of data for additional capacity; a dual-layer disc can typically hold about four hours of video. All DVD players are designed to play these discs, but not all have an indicator showing which layer of a dual-layer disc is playing.

LCD, TV Liquid Crystal Display. Like plasma TVs, LCD sets are renowned for their slimness and light weight, making small models good candidates for wall-mounting or hanging below a cabinet. On a stand, they have a compact footprint that fits neatly on a kitchen counter or desk. Picture quality of the best LCD sets, usually high-definition (HD) models, is very good. But LCD panels still aren't as good as picture-tube TVs at displaying fast motion and deep black levels. LCD technology is also used in some microdisplay projection TVs, which are slimmer than CRT-based models.

LCD size, camcorders A camcorder's LCD typically ranges from 2 to 4 inches, measured diagonally.

LCD size, digital cameras Most digital cameras have a small LCD screen on the back so you can view images and decide which to keep. (You can use the LCD to help frame photos, but that's a sure way to run down the battery in a hurry.) Most LCD screens are too dim for viewing clearly in sunlight.

LCoS Liquid Crystal on Silicon, a form of projection-TV technology that shares some attributes with DLP and LCD in its use of both tiny mirrors and liquid-crystal technology. The technology's rollout has been hampered by production problems and costs, prompting some companies to abandon their plans.

LED Light-emitting diode, a small electrical component that produces light when a current is passed through it. LEDs are very efficient and can now produce virtually any color of light.

Lighted keypad Also referred to as backlit keypad. A cordless-phone keypad that either glows in the dark or lights up when you press a key; it makes the phone easier to use in low-light conditions.

Line input A digital, optical, or analog line input allows you to record from an external audio system to the player.

Line output A line output is intended to work best when the player is connected to an external audio system, with a fixed-level output and no effect when using the player's volume control.

Link See "hyperlink."

Linux A freely downloadable, user-supported open-source computer operating system, based on Unix. Linux is touted as an alternative to Windows but is more suited to certain business applications, such as Web servers.

Lists tracks On the MP3 player's display, the songs can be shown in the form of a list.

Lock control A button, switch, or set through the player's menu system that lets you lock the controls of the player. Also referred to as Hold.

Low recycle time A relatively low period of time that it takes a digital camera to process and store an image when shooting in normal (non-burst) mode, at the camera's lowest-resolution, highest-compression setting.

Low-battery indicator A visual or auditory signal that indicates a cordless phone's handset battery needs to be recharged.

Lux rating Supposedly the minimum amount of light needed for a camcorder to produce a usable picture (the lower, the better). Because there is no agreed-upon standard, however, it's an imprecise way to compare light sensitivity.

M

Mac Short for Apple's Macintosh computer.

Mac OS The windowed operating system of the Apple Macintosh computer family. Mac OS X (version 10) departs radically from earlier versions—it's Unix-based and has its user-interface modernized with an equivalent to the Windows taskbar called the "dock."

Macintosh A computer from Apple that was the first to use a mouse and icon-based operating system to make it user-friendly.

Macro A series of commands that can be easily initiated, often by a solitary keystroke or simple combination of keys; also, a sequence of instructions embedded in a spreadsheet or other document that can be easily executed at will.

Macro, digital cameras A lens feature that lets you take close-up shots, usually within a foot or less; good for taking pictures of small objects such as a stamp or an insect.

Macro focus This camcorder feature allows you to focus on small objects from a close distance (say, less than 3 feet).

Mailboxes For cordless phones with an answerer, some models let you assign individual voice mailboxes for business and personal calls, or for each person who uses the phone.

Mailing list A list of subscribers to a topical information exchange that operates through e-mail. Most mailing list users refer to their group as "the list." The list server is the host software, residing on a server computer that manages the traffic for the list. A directory of more than 50,000 public lists is available at www.lsoft.com/catalist.html.

Main memory The data storage locations inside a computer and directly accessible by the CPU; memory can range from as little as 1 MB to more than 8 GB.

Manual aperture Gives the digital-camera user more control over how much light hits the lens. Manual exposure compensation can serve the same function.

Manual controls, camcorders These let you override automatic settings and allow more control over your recording. May include aperture, color (white) balance, focus, and shutter speed. They're useful for nonideal situations.

Manual controls, digital cameras Some cameras allow the user to set the aperture (f-stop) and/or shutter speed; used to override the automatic exposure settings when more control is needed.

Manual convergence On CRT-based projection TV sets, the need to manually align the three cathode-ray tubes that together form the image. This must be performed upon delivery and must be repeated periodically—especially if you move the set.

Manual exposure Allows the user to control both the shutter speed and the aperture settings. Most digital cameras offer fully automatic exposure, often with an exposure-compensation option. While these options cover most situations, direct control of the shutter-speed setting is desirable when going for more specialized effects, such as a blurred image.

Manual exposure compensation Not to be confused with manual exposure, this allows for minor adjustments to a digital camera's automatic-exposure settings. When a scene has high contrast, automatic exposure may not achieve the effect you want. Being able to lighten or darken the scene is an important option.

Manual focus Digital cameras provide greater depth of field than cameras with longer focal-length lenses, such as 35mm or APS cameras; therefore, manual focusing will rarely be needed. Manual focus options vary; a few cameras provide a continuously adjustable manual focus ring, others only a limited number of discrete focus distance settings.

Manual plus auto convergence On CRT-based projection sets, the ability to further fine-tune the one-touch convergence setting provided by the set's auto-convergence capability.

Manual shutter The camera's shutter opens and closes when you take a shot, allowing light to hit the image sensor. Being able to control the speed of the shutter allows for more creative control over how motion is expressed in your pictures.

Manual white balance In a digital camera, this feature corrects for differences in lighting so white objects remain white and colors appear the same as they do by eye. Most cameras have automatic white balance, which works well for most scenes. A manual white balance control lets the user set the proper lighting type when the automatic system errs.

Matrix An array or an ordered arrangement. For example, 63 dots might be arranged into a rectangular matrix, an array of nine rows and seven columns.

Maximum aperture The aperture is the opening in the lens that controls how much light hits a camera's image sensor; maximum aperture refers to the widest it will open. Apertures are stated in f-stops or f-numbers (for example, f/2). The smaller the f-stop number, the larger the aperture, and the less light the camera requires to take a picture. A maximum aperture of f/2.8 is typical for a digital camera.

Maximum focal length (35mm) When set to its maximum (longest) focal length, a digital-camera lens gives its narrowest, most telephoto-like angle of view. For comparison purposes, it is often given in terms of the 35mm camera lens focal length that would cover the same angle of view.

Maximum horizontal pixels The number of pixels along the longer (horizontal) dimension of the image when a digital camera is set to its highest resolution.

Maximum image quality An indication of the color intensity of a digital camera's images. The more bits a camera uses to indicate the intensity of the three colors for each pixel, the more precisely the pixel's color can be specified. Almost all digital cameras have 24-bit color depth (8 bits each for red, green, and blue, within each pixel) and are capable of reproducing millions of different colors.

Maximum number of still pictures The maximum number of still images that can fit on a tape, for a camcorder that can record still images.

Maximum shutter speed, camcorders Camcorders electronically adjust their light sensitivity in a way that models a film camera's shutter. All camcorders do this automatically; some also have a manual override capability. Shutter speed is measured in fractions of a second.

Maximum shutter speed, digital cameras The fastest shutter speed provided, often 1/1000th of a second or less. Being able to control shutter speed lets you decide if a moving object will appear sharp or blurred in the image. A faster shutter speed lets you freeze faster action.

Maximum vertical pixels The number of pixels along the shorter (vertical) dimension of the image when a digital camera is set to its highest resolution.

Mb Megabit.

MB Megabyte.

Media The physical object, usually a disk or tape, upon which digital data is stored.

Media-card slot On some printers, it's where you can insert a memory card from a digital camera. Once you've inserted the card into the slot, you can either print the card's files directly or download them to your computer.

Media player Generically, a program that decodes file- or Internet-based multimedia material into an audible and/or visual presentation. Examples are Windows Media Player, RealOne Player, and MusicMatch Jukebox.

Meg Short for megabyte or megahertz.

Mega- A prefix usually meaning one million but, because of computers' binary nature, is used to refer to 1,048,576 (or 2 to the twentieth power).

Megabit 1,024 kilobits, yielding 1,048,576 bits, usually considered a million.

Megabyte 1,024 kilobytes, yielding 1,048,576 bytes, usually considered a million.

Megahertz 1 million hertz.

Megapixels (MB) This shows how many million pixels a digital camera's image sensor has. As a rule, with more megapixels, you can make larger prints or enlarge parts of an image without losing detail or image quality.

Memory The amount of usable internal memory, available for new uses—such as appointments, addresses, and applications—when the handheld PDA model is new.

Memory-card slot Found in a few TVs, a slot that accepts memory cards for viewing still images from digital cameras. Inserting the camera's card typically results in better image quality than if you connect the camera to the TV's composite-video input. Some memory cards are specific to one or more specific manufacturers—such as Memory Stick slots in some Sony TVs. Other slots may accept CompactFlash, SmartMedia, MultiMedia Card, Secure Digital, and/or other media.

Memory-card support Indicates whether the printer has a built-in memory-card reader. If so, this feature lets you print image files from a digital camera's memory card without using a computer. You can also download the files to a computer. Some printers have a slot for a PC-card adapter. You can then purchase the adapter for the type of memory card your camera uses.

Memory Stick A type of digital data storage card, introduced by Sony, that is smaller than a stick of chewing gum. A diskette-shaped adapter is also available for using Memory Stick cards in a computer or in some Sony cameras that use diskette storage. Memory Stick Pro has the same form factor as the original Memory Stick but with twice the number of connectors as the original.

Memory Stick with select function On a digital camera, this card provides higher capacity for other Memory Stick devices by providing two banks of 128 MB on a standard Memory Stick, which can be selected with a manually operated switch.

Menu A list of available options, often in a "drop-down" or "pull-down" list, that is typically hidden until activated via a mouse click.

Menu-access lock A parental-control feature that requires password access to call up a TV's menu, using which other restrictions could potentially be disabled.

Menu bar A bar across the top of a computer screen that presents the first level of options for a drop-down menu system.

Menu-driven A program or computer system that uses a series of menus to make it easier to use. The user selects the desired option by clicking on an entry with the mouse, typing the corresponding letter or number, or moving the cursor to the proper selection and hitting the Enter key. The program will then perform the chosen function.

MHz Megahertz.

Microdisplay An industry term sometimes used to describe rear-projection sets using LCD (liquid-crystal display), DLP (digital light-processing), or LCoS (liquid-crystal on silicon) chips and a bright lamp to create images. This space-saving "light-engine" technology makes microdisplays slimmer and lighter than CRT-based sets.

MicroMV Sony's relatively new camcorder-tape format, which uses cassettes smaller than MiniDVs.

Micron One-millionth of a meter, or one-thousandth of a millimeter.

Microphone input A jack for an external microphone to improve sound quality and prevent picking up noise from the camcorder. It's an alternative to using the built-in mike.

Microprocessor The CPU of a personal computer, such as the Pentium 4 or Athlon XP. Microprocessors have an arithmetic logic unit to perform calculations and a control unit with limited memory to hold instructions.

Microsecond One-millionth of a second.

MIDI Musical Instrument Digital Interface, standard for the exchange of information among various musical devices, including instruments, synthesizers, and computers that are MIDI-capable.

MiniDV Refers to a camcorder that uses a MiniDV tape (a little larger than a matchbox) to record images digitally. Some models produce exceedingly high picture quality. Tapes generally offer a shorter recording time than most other formats.

Mini-movie With digital cameras, lets you create a short, low-frame-rate, low-resolution movie (with sound on some models).

Minimum focal length (35mm) When set to its minimum (shortest) focal length, a digital-camera lens gives its widest angle of view. For comparison purposes, it is often given in terms of the 35mm

GLOSSARY

camera lens focal length that would cover the same angle of view.

Minimum shutter speed The slowest shutter speed provided in a digital camera, often ½ or ¼ of a second or less. Being able to control shutter speed lets you decide if a moving object will appear sharp or blurred in the image.

Minitower case and microtower case Smaller versions of the tower case of some computers.

Memory cards Indicates whether the printer has a built-in memory-card reader. If so, this feature lets you print image files from a digital camera's memory card without using a computer. You can also download the files to a computer. Some printers have a slot for a PCMCIA memory card adapter. You can then purchase the adapter for the type of memory card your camera uses.

Mode A condition or set of conditions for operation. A printer may have modes for different print qualities, or a different port for different transmission speeds or protocols.

Modem modulator/demodulator Used to connect a digital device (computer) to a data communications channel (telephone line, cable or radio link). A modem is used to send a fax, to access e-mail, and to get online to the Internet. A modem intended to work with normal dial-up telephone lines has a top speed of nominally 56 kilobits per second (kbps). (DSL and cable models permit much higher speeds.) A connection between 34 kbps and 53 kbps (the U.S. limit) can be established only if both the local telephone line and the Internet Service Provider are properly equipped.

Modular bay In a modular laptop computer, a device bay that accepts a device such as an optical disk drive, a diskette drive, a second battery, a back-up hard drive, or a memory-card reader.

Modular laptop A laptop PC that contains one or more modular bays allowing various drives or a battery to be inserted as desired, or removed to save travel weight.

Monitor The "face" of the computer, most often a CRT screen. Monitors are similar to TVs but usually do not have a tuner and so cannot directly receive television broadcast signals.

Monochrome One color, usually referring to a monitor or printer.

Motherboard The main board inside a PC into which a computer's memory, microprocessor, and other components are plugged.

Motion compensation HD TVs often internally convert an interlaced video signal to progressive scan signal, or up-convert it—adapt a low-resolution image signal to a high-definition display. The circuitry uses an advanced mathematical process to reduce motion blur in moving scenes. Also see "Native resolution."

Movie mode This feature allows you to record short video clips using your digital camera; some models record with sound, while others do not.

Mouse A palm-size device that controls the cursor, an object on the screen, or other screen action by moving the device around on a flat surface. A small ball or optical sensor on the bottom of the mouse senses direction of the motion, transferring this action to the screen. One or more buttons are also used for additional control, such as clicking and dragging.

Mouse pad A thin, resilient pad used as a surface to support a computer mouse, providing a better "grip" for the ball than some desk surfaces, along with a cushion for the wrist.

Mouse pointer A type of cursor used by a computer mouse or other pointing device to indicate a specific screen location. The pointer may be any number of different shapes, but the most common types are the arrow and crosshair.

MP3 An encoding format (it stands for Moving Pictures Expert Group 1 Audio Layer 3) for compressed digital music files. It offers high quality with less than one-tenth the data rate of an uncompressed CD-music bitstream. The small files required for typical songs allow for fairly fast transfer over consumer-grade Internet connections, and have spawned a hobby of sharing music over the Internet, both within and in violation of copyright laws.

MPEG Motion Picture Experts Group, a modern-standard format for compression and storage of video files. MPEG-1 allows a full-length movie to be stored on a standard CD-ROM disc with a moderate amount of visual artifacts; MPEG-2 allows a full-length movie to be stored on a DVD-ROM with few visual artifacts.

MSRP The manufacturer's suggested retail price is generally higher than the price you will pay at the store for a given product.

Multi-angle Enables you to see DVD scenes from different camera angles, provided that the scenes are recorded that way on the disc.

Multifunction keyboard A computer keyboard that has additional keys to launch e-mail, the Internet, and selected applications, and to control computer functions such as the CD or DVD drive, sound volume, and sleep mode.

Multifunction printer An inkjet, laser, or thermal printer that, in addition to printing, may serve as a fax machine, scanner, copier, or other device.

Multihandset capability Multiple-handset-capable phones support more than one handset with one base, so you can have several handsets around the house, each charging in a base, without the need for extra phone jacks. Additional handsets, including the charging cradle, are usually sold separately.

Multilingual menu A multilingual menu that presents the onscreen TV menu in a choice of languages, usually English, Spanish, and French.

Multilingual support With this DVD-player feature, you can choose from among various audio or subtitle languages from compatible DVDs.

Multimedia Generally, any computer system or application that incorporates two or more of graphics, text, audio, and video into an integrated presentation.

Multiple-disc player Most DVD players still hold only a single disc at a time. While that suffices for movies, a multiple-disc (or multidisc) player may be useful if you'll also use the unit as your primary CD player. These units accommodate discs using either a carousel- or drawer-type changer.

Multitasking A computer's ability to run more than one program or process at the same time—for example, printing a document while you're surfing the Web. The increasing power of 32-bit and 64-bit processors has made multitasking more efficient and popular.

N

Native resolution Applies to "fixed-pixel" display types such as LCD, DLP, plasma, and LCoS. It's expressed in horizontal by vertical pixels (for the picture elements making up a displayed image). Incoming signals of higher or lower resolution must be down- or up-converted as necessary to match the set's native resolution.

Network Any system of two or more connected computers, along with their peripherals, organized to share files and other resources.

Network ready Some printers can be used in a local-area network (LAN), a link of computers within a building; a home network is one example. You may have to follow special instructions to install.

Newsgroup One of the informal information-sharing message boards on the part of the Internet known as Usenet. It is accessed through a newsreader such as Outlook Express.

NIC Network Interface Card, an expansion card used to connect a computer to a local-area network (LAN).

Night vision This feature allows you to record in very dim or dark situations, using invisible infrared light that is emitted from the camcorder. The picture is grainy and monochrome. It's also called zero lux, nightshot, IR filter, or infrared sensitive recording mode.

Noise Unwanted electrical or communication signals; interference.

Noise filter An electric device designed to reduce electrical noise on a data or AC line.

Noise level Measured in decibels one meter away (dBA), this tells you how noisy a printer is when in use. A typical noise level for an inkjet printer is 50 dBA. As a frame of reference, a soft whisper is about 20 dBA; a normal conversation, about 60 dBA.

Noninterlaced Video display mode used in computer monitors and HDTV in which every scan line is displayed progressively. Noninterlaced images are more stable to view but place more demands on the monitor.

Notebook computer Another name for a laptop computer.

Numeric keypad A group of keys set aside for the entry of numeric data and the performance of simple arithmetic operations.

OCR Optical Character Recognition, a text-recognition program that converts scanned paper documents into a word-processing file format for storage, editing, and inclusion into other documents.

Off-air broadcast TV, a.k.a. Analogue Terrestrial Television (ATT), the way the nation invariably received television signals before the debuts of cable and satellite service. In addition to the standard analog TV signals transmitted via antenna for decades, digital broadcast TV signals (typically high-definition) are increasingly available as well. Off-air digital TV is also referred to as Digital Terrestrial Television (DTT) or Digital Video Broadcasting–Terrestrial (DVB-T).

Office suite A collection of office-oriented programs, sold as a single product. Examples are Microsoft Office, Corel WordPerfect Office, Lotus SmartSuite, and Sun StarOffice.

Offline Not currently accessible by the PC; a PC that is not networked.

One-touch dial A dedicated button or buttons on a cordless phone's handset or base that let you dial a phone number with the press of a single key. It's useful for, say, an emergency number or a number called frequently.

Online Connected to the Internet or to another computer via modem, cable, or satellite. Going online refers to using the Internet.

Online help A feature of many software programs that provides assistance in how to operate the program. You normally access it by hitting a key such as F1 or selecting a menu option.

Online music store If you plan to download copyright-protected music from an online music store, check to see that it supports the player you plan to buy. Some popular sites are iTunes, which supports Apple iPods, and Sony Connect, which supports Sony MP3 players. BuyMusic, Napster, Musicmatch, and Walmart Music Downloads offer copyright-protected songs in the WMA format; players supported by these sites can be found on the Microsoft Web site.

Operating system and configuration requirements The minimum recommended operating system and configuration requirements for the MP3 player and its software package. If your computer has less than the minimum requirements, it may still work with the player, but make sure you can return the player in case it doesn't. Check the manufacturer's and music-management software application Web sites for availability of previously unsupported operating systems.

Operating system type For a PDA, the control program that runs it. PDAs use either Pocket PC (formerly known as Windows CE), Palm OS, or a proprietary operating system.

Optical cable Cable that contains very thin, flexible glass or plastic fibers through which information is carried using a modulated light beam. It's used in cable TV systems, some home-theater gear, and in high-speed data-communication links.

Optical digital audio out Digital-audio output is important only if you plan to pipe the signal from a DVD player into a home-theater system that has a digital receiver. When choosing your DVD player, consider the models that have the outputs to match the inputs on your digital receiver or external, digital decoder. All DVD players have digital audio outputs–coaxial, optical, or both.

Optical disk Generally refers to any disk read or written to by a laser or other light-emitting/sensing device.

Optical zoom, camcorders Allows a camcorder to fill the frame with far-away objects at the touch of a button. An optical zoom rated at 16x means the camcorder can magnify the image up to 16 times the normal size.

Optical zoom, digital cameras Magnifies the image using a real multifocal-length lens, whereas a digital zoom uses electronics to enlarge the center portion of the image using interpolation. Some cameras have both optical and digital zoom. The optical-zoom range is what really matters; image quality decreases the further one goes into the digital-zoom range.

OS Operating System, the software that is necessary to control the basic operation of the computer. Examples are DOS, Windows, Mac OS, and Linux. A computer's OS determines, to a large extent, the "look and feel" of the machine.

Outputs TVs may have one or more of several outputs. Many models have audio outputs, which enable you to pipe the set's sound to a sound system (to drive unpowered speakers) or directly to powered speakers. (See "Audio outputs.") A few models also have a headphone jack in front. Higher-end models may additionally have various video outputs (of the antenna/cable, composite-video, or S-video types). These are useful if you want to route the set's video signal to another device, say, for recording.

Page/handset locator In cordless phones (also called one-way paging) a button on the base set sends a beep tone from the base to the handset so that a missing handset can be located.

Paint program An application that lets a user draw a graphical "bitmap" image directly by moving the pointing device.

PAL/SECAM-compatible In the U.S., TVs use the NTSC television format signal; however, PAL- or SECAM-format signals are used in most other countries. Sets equipped to handle PAL and SECAM signals in addition to NTSC may be useful if you want to receive or view foreign programming, or if you're using a VCR or camcorder of a different standard.

Palette The range of colors and shades that are displayable on a certain TV or monitor, or that are printable with a certain printer.

Parallel port A type of connection that transmits data one byte or data word at a time. Parallel ports were most frequently used for printers on IBM-compatible systems but are being supplanted by the faster USB port.

Parental control With such frequently available features, you may keep a child from watching one or more channels that you select. On some sets it can also block the use of audio/video inputs, to which video games could be connected, or limit the time a game can be played. The V-chip (included in all TVs with screens 13 in. or larger) is also a parental-control feature.

Parental security A feature that allows parents to "lock out" DVD content based on various criteria, such as a movie's title or rating.

Parts/labor warranty The length of time, expressed in months, that the television is covered by its manufacturer for defects or repairs. Most warranty coverage is divided into parts and labor, typically 12 months for each and, for CRT-based TVs, 24 months for the picture tube. Labor is occasionally covered for only 90 days.

Passive-matrix display An early flat-panel LCD display in which all transistors are outside the display area. Passive matrix displays lose brightness when not viewed from straight on, and they blur moving images.

Password A series of characters used as a code to access a system, program, or file. A password should be chosen that is hard to guess, and not a common word.

PC Personal computer; sometimes used to denote any IBM-compatible personal computer; also, a printed circuit.

PC card A credit card-size, Plug and Play module commonly used to attach expansion devices (such as memory, modems, and drives) to portable computers.

PC-compatible Used to indicate compatibility with Windows or IBM PCs, not Apple Macintosh.

PCI Peripheral Component Interconnect, a local bus design, popular on Pentium-based computers, that provides high-speed communications between various components and the processor.

PDA Personal Digital Assistant, a small handheld computer that functions as a personal organizer, with a calendar/reminder, to-do list, notepad, and address/phone directory. Usually uses a stylus for input, though some have small keyboards. Some PDAs offer optional wireless access to such services as e-mail, Internet, or cellular phone service.

Peer-to-peer A network architecture in which data can flow directly among any of the nodes without the need for a computer to act as a server.

Pentium An Intel microprocessor employing a fast, 32-bit architecture (with a 64-bit internal bus) that makes extensive use of RISC technology, employs internal memory caches, and can execute multiple independent instructions in the same clock cycle, giving it higher performance than its predecessors. The most recent series is the Pentium 4, which is available in clock speeds up to 3 GHz.

Peripheral Any hardware attachment to a computer, such as a keyboard, monitor, disk, or printer.

PictBridge support This feature allows direct printing (without the use of a computer) from any brand of digital camera to any brand of printer.

Picture presets Some TVs offer different picture settings, each designed to complement different programming, such as movies or sporting events.

Picture zoom One of the effects DVD players offer: the ability to zoom in on details in the picture.

PIM Personal Information Manager, a software application that organizes information on a day-to-day basis. PIMs routinely include features such as a reminder calendar, notepad, address book, phone dialer, calculator, and alarm clock.

Pincushion effect A bowing-in on each side of the image on a CRT monitor screen, usually correctable with the monitor's controls. Flat-panel monitors do not have this effect.

PIP Many TV sets offer PIP (picture-in-picture), a feature that lets you watch two images at the same time on one screen: the first, full-size; the second, in a small box within the larger picture. A variant of this is POP (picture-outside-of-picture), with which the screen image is split evenly in two. TVs with dual-tuner PIP or POP can tune into two channels simultaneously without the contribution of additional equipment. Those with only one tuner require a second, external tuner, such as a VCR, in order to use PIP. Some TVs can send the second channel's audio to a separate audio output.

Pixel Short for picture element, the smallest individually controllable unit of a visible image on a display. Often erroneously used to refer to the triad of dots on a CRT screen. On flat-panel (LCD) displays, there is always one pixel per triad of stripes, but there is no such mapping on a CRT monitor.

Plasma A plasma screen is made up of thousands of pixels containing gas that's converted into "plasma" by an electrical charge. The plasma causes phosphors to glow red, green, or blue, as dictated by a video signal. The result: a colorful display with high brightness and a wider viewing angle than most rear-projection sets and LCD (see "LCD") TVs. Image quality may not be quite the equal of a very good picture-tube TV, especially with quickly moving images or dark scenes, but plasma technology is gradually narrowing the gap. Like CRT-based TVs, plasma sets are vulnerable to screen burn-in. Plasma sets run hot and consume more power than any other type of TV.

Platform The hardware architecture on which software applications are intended to run; the operating system or user interface under which the software application is intended to be used. Also, with digital cameras, the provided camera software's compatibility with a Windows-based PC, a Macintosh, or both.

Platform, MP3 players This refers to whether an MP3 player and its software are compatible with a Windows-based PC, a Macintosh computer, or both. Check the manufacturer and music-management software application Web sites for upgrades or new platforms supported.

Playback time Also referred to as battery life. This reflects our lab measurements of continuous playback time, to the nearest hour, using new alkaline or fully charged rechargeable battery (or batteries). Playback time with an asterisk (*) is the manufacturer's specifications.

Play exchange For multidisc CD or DVD players, this feature (also called Disc Exchange) lets you remove or swap out one disc while another is playing.

Play modes Many MP3 players let you set a play mode so you can repeat one or all music tracks, or in a random order, also referred to as "shuffle" mode. Some players have A-B repeat, a way to set bookmarks, to repeat a section of the music track.

Plug and play A standard for managing the installation of expansion cards and peripherals in modern PCs and operating systems. If both a PC and a device are Plug and Play compatible, the computer should handle the installation automatically.

Pointing device A hand-operated device used to move a pointer on the screen of a graphical user interface, selecting program objects, activating controls, or manipulating objects. A mouse is one type of pointing device.

POP or POP3 Post Office Protocol, an e-mail system that communicates between your primary mailbox in your own computer and the one at your access provider's site. POP mail is the usual protocol for incoming mail, while SMTP is used for outgoing.

POP, TVs See "PIP."

Pop-up A message or window that appears on a computer screen, often in response to a user or program action. Pop-ups are also a common way to present advertising associated with Web sites. Pop-up ads that appear when you close a browser window are called "pop-under" ads.

Port A socket on a computer that's used to connect a peripheral such as a printer or modem.

Port expander A small plastic box or bracket with connectors for attaching peripheral devices to laptop computers.

Portrait A page or screen orientation in which information is displayed or printed across the shorter dimension.

Power strip An AC electrical device that provides multiple outlets, usually having an on/off switch, a circuit breaker, and surge protection.

PowerMac A desktop Apple Macintosh computer that employs the PowerPC microprocessor.

PowerPC A fast, 32-bit chip that employs advanced RISC technology. It is made by Motorola and used in Apple computers.

ppm Pages per minute, a measure of the speed of a printer.

Print server A small device that connects a printer directly to a network for shared use.

Printhead The part of a character printer (such as an inkjet) that moves across the paper to produce the characters or images.

Prints from camera This feature allows the printer to receive images directly from a digital camera. This can be accomplished either with a built-in memory card reader or over a provided cable or via wireless technology, in which case the printer and camera communicate via infrared beam.

Privacy policy A legally binding statement by any entity (such as a Web site) that collects personal information from users, as to how that information will be used and protected from misuse or dissemination. It's often accompanied by a means for users to "opt out" of commercial use of their information.

Privileges, rights, or permissions Granted to a user by a system administrator, the set of operations that the user may perform on a system, such as the ability to access, change or delete files in certain directories, or change the configuration of the system. They are usually tied to a user's login ID.

Processor The "brain" of a computer or other "smart" device.

Productivity software Applications for the office, such as word-processor, spreadsheet, and database software.

Program A logical sequence of instructions designed to accomplish a specific task, written in such a way that it can be read and executed by a computer. Also, to construct a program.

Program file A file that contains a program. Program files may also be data files if they serve as the input or output for other programs.

Programmed recording Allows a camcorder to be programmed to start recording at a specific time.

Progressive scan A progressive-scan DVD player can provide a smoother, more film-like picture when used with compatible HD-ready TVs.

Prompt A character, symbol, sound, or message sent to the screen to signal the user that the computer is ready for input; also, to issue a prompt.

Proportional spacing The characteristic of some print fonts (such as this text) in which narrow characters such as I and J use less space than wider ones such as M and W.

Proprietary Incompatible with others of the same type, not adhering to any specific industry standard; also, exclusively owned by a company or individual.

Public-domain software Programs that are neither owned nor copyrighted by anyone and are available to all who want them without restriction.

These programs can usually be obtained for a small service fee.

Query A request for information from a computer database; also, to issue a query.

Quick review A camcorder feature that lets you view the last few seconds of a scene without having to press a lot of buttons. It's handy for helping you decide if you need to reshoot a scene.

Quicktime A multimedia extension to the Macintosh operating system. A version is also available for Windows-based multimedia applications.

QWERTY keyboard The traditional keyboard layout familiar to most typists and keyboard users. (It's named for the first six letters from the left on the top alphabet row.)

Radio buttons A set of on-screen options, only one of which is selectable at any one time. Once a selection is made (usually indicated by a dot or similar symbol), any previous choice is turned off (the dot is removed).

RAM Random Access Memory, a read/write type of memory that permits the user to both read the information that is there and write data to it. This is the type of memory available to the user in most computers.

Random play Allows you to have a DVD unit randomly play different titles or chapters of a DVD (or tracks of a CD).

Rapid-fire shots Allows you to take multiple digital-camera shots in quick succession with one touch of the shutter button; useful when shooting a subject in motion. The number of shots varies by camera and with resolution setting. It's also called continuous shooting or burst mode.

Rear-projection TV A TV display system in which the image is beamed from a projector onto the rear of a projection screen. You view the opposite side of the screen from that which faces the projector.

Recording modes. Like a digital camera, a digital video recorder can compress a recording so that it takes up less space on a hard drive or DVD, but at the expense of picture quality. Most recorders let you choose among several such recording modes. It's similar to choosing between SP and EP mode on a VCR. Here are three commonly available modes: **Fine mode.** Typically the highest quality mode, yielding picture quality nearly as good as that of a commercial-grade DVD. But it lets you store just one hour of video on a blank, 4.7-gigabyte DVD or the fewest hours of video on a hard drive. **SP mode.** Not as high in quality as fine, this lets you store two hours of video, enough for a full-length movie, on a blank DVD. **EP mode.** The most space-conserving mode, it lets you typically store six hours of video on a DVD or the most hours on a hard drive. The picture quality is comparable to the quality of EP mode for a run-of-the-mill VCR.

Recording time (min.) Most answering machines store messages electronically. Recording time of 15 to 20 minutes is typical. In many cases, recording time may include not only incoming messages, but greetings, memos, and saved messages, so the total may be misleading. Most answerers maximize capacity by detecting pauses in a message and not storing them in memory.

Red-eye reduction With a digital camera, this reduces the chances that the pupils of your subject's eyes will appear red in flash photos. With red-eye reduction, the camera emits a burst of light just before the main flash, causing the pupils to contract. Most cameras with a flash have this feature. Image-editing software often offers red-eye correction as well.

Redial button Found on almost all cordless-phone models, this feature lets you automatically dial the last number called.

Refresh rate The number of times each second that a CRT monitor redraws the image on the screen. A refresh rate below about 72 Hz can appear to "blink" as the image fades between refreshes.

Remote control A remote control is now standard with most TVs, and most do more than turn on the power and switch channels. Here's what's available: The familiar standard remote controls only the TV and can't operate any other component. A **unified remote** will operate other equipment of the same brand. The more common **universal remote,** the code-entry or learning type, will operate other brands and types of equipment; it requires you to select the appropriate code for your equipment. A **learning remote,** less frequently offered, can determine the codes of remotes belonging to other systems, so you don't have to look them up. Some remotes offer illuminated buttons for easier operation in dimly lit rooms.

Remote control, camcorders A remote control is handy for operating a camcorder from a distance (say, to allow the user to be in the picture). It's also useful in playback mode since all the buttons are readily at hand.

Remote control, digital cameras Allows you to take a picture without touching the camera; an alternative to using a self-timer.

Remote control, MP3 players Some MP3 players include a wired or infrared remote control to access the player's function controls.

Remote handset For cordless phones with an answerer, this lets you listen to messages from the handset and may allow access to other answerer functions, such as recording your greeting.

Repeat play Allows you to repeat, from the beginning, an entire DVD—or a DVD's title or chapter—that is currently being played. The same feature can be used to repeat an entire CD or CD track.

Replaceable battery Some digital cameras use two or four AA batteries. Nonrechargeable batteries, such as alkaline and lithium, or rechargeable batteries, such as nickel-metal hydride (NiMH) or lithium-ion, may be used. Some cameras that use rechargeable batteries come with a charger and a set of rechargeable batteries.

Replaceable battery, camcorders All camcorders come with a rechargeable battery and an AC adapter. The adapter can recharge the battery or power the camcorder if an outlet is nearby (but generally not at the same time). Most models let you install a more-powerful battery than the original. Commonly used battery types are lithium-ion, nickel-cadmium, and nickel-metal hydride. A nickel-cadmium or nickel-metal hydride battery that's repeatedly recharged when not totally drained may lose the ability to recharge completely. A refresh switch on the adapter lets you fully drain the battery before recharging, to help maintain full running time.

Resolution Indicates the degree of detail that can be perceived—for example, in a displayed or printed image. The higher the resolution, the finer the detail.

Resolution, digital cameras A digital image is made up of hundreds of thousands or even millions of tiny dots called pixels. The resolution of a digital camera's sensor is the number of pixels horizontally multiplied by the number of pixels vertically. The more pixels the sensor has, the sharper and more detailed the picture. High resolution is expensive and requires much more memory per picture.

Resolution modes The number of levels, or modes, of resolution a digital camera offers.

Resume play Allows you to stop playing a DVD and later resume playback from where you left off.

Reverse frame by frame Most DVD players let you view a movie frame-by-frame in the forward direction. This feature allows you to do so in reverse as well.

Reversible charging With this feature, a cordless-phone handset battery can charge in the charging cradle with the handset face up or down.

Ribbon cable A flat, multiword cable design that is commonly used to connect devices, such as disk drives, within a computer.

ROM Read-Only Memory, storage that permits reading and use of data but no changes. ROMs are preprogrammed at the factory for a specific purpose and are found on many boards such as graphics and in many systems that automatically boot when they are turned on.

ROM BIOS A BIOS routine contained in a ROM chip, enabling a computer device to boot. The system BIOS on a PC's motherboard is one example; however, some components have their own ROM BIOS chips.

Rotatable lens A digital-camera lens that tilts up or down. Some can rotate nearly 360 degrees, allowing you to compose a self-portrait while viewing yourself on the LCD monitor.

RSI Repetitive Stress Injury, a disorder of the

hands, arms, back, neck, and even eyes that can arise from very heavy computer use.

Run To execute a program.

S-video inputs These split the video signal into two parts, color and luminance. In general, an S-video input will provide better picture quality than either an antenna/cable or composite-video input. These are often used with digital-cable boxes, satellite receivers, and DVD players. Many sets have front-panel S-video inputs, which let you make temporary connections to certain camcorders, game systems, and other devices with S-video output.

SACD discs One of two new, competing music formats. SACD (for Super Audio CD) discs contain a stereo (and possibly also a multichannel) version of the music content. Both this and the other competing format, DVD-Audio, also claim to offer better sound quality than CDs can deliver. Note that while SACD-formatted program material will only play on models that specify SACD capability, some "hybrid" SACD discs contain another version, in standard CD format, of the same program material. Such discs should be playable on any DVD or CD player.

SAP Secondary Audio Programming (SAP) reception, offered on many TV sets, is valuable for those who want to tune into the alternate sound versions sometimes available, such as a Spanish-language soundtrack or a specially designed audio track for the blind.

Save To store a file on a disk-storage device.

Scan velocity modulation This regulates the electron gun that fires electrons at a TV screen, creating the picture. Although having this feature can provide greater apparent sharpness, it can also produce unnatural-looking edges in the images.

Scanner A peripheral device that digitally translates and then transfers photos, graphics, and/or text onto a computer's hard drive.

Screen dimmer or saver, computer An applet that produces a moving image on a CRT monitor screen to prevent permanent ghost images from being burned into the phosphors by lingering, unattended displays. This does not really save the screen on modern monitors, which are better served by use of the power-saving standby mode.

Screen dimmer or saver, DVD players Over time, long-term pausing of movies or displaying the player's menu or logo may cause parts of those images to "burn" into the screen. A screen dimmer helps stave off this effect by dimming the screen whenever the picture is motionless for a long period; a screen saver substitutes a moving image in the same situation.

Screen size (in.) The size of the television's screen, measured diagonally in inches. In general, the larger the screen size, the farther away you need to sit for optimal picture quality. It's best to sit approximately 11 feet from a 36-inch set, 10 feet from a 32-inch set, and 8 feet from a 27-inch set. For HD (high-definition) sets, the distances can be halved.

Scroll To move onscreen graphics or text up, down, right, or left in a smooth, usually continuous and reversible action.

Scroll bar A computer screen element consisting of a horizontal and/or vertical bar with a slider that moves within the bar, both to control scrolling and to indicate position in a document.

Scrolling channel preview Provides, on some higher-end TVs, thumbnail images of what's on other channels besides the one you're currently watching.

Secure Digital (SD) card The Secure Digital (SD) card is a highly secure stamp-sized flash-memory card that weighs approximately two grams.

Secure grip Denotes cameras designed with room for your fingers, so you can hold the camera steady and keep your fingers clear of the flash, lens, or auto-focus sensor. The grip is especially important on the smallest cameras, which by their nature, have little room for a handhold.

Secure site A Web site that uses encrypted pages that cannot be read by unauthorized persons such as hackers. Many commercial and financial Web sites have secure sections for exchange of personal information with customers.

Selectivity Your TV's ability to tune channels without interference from adjacent channels, important only if you use your TV, not a cable box or other device, for tuning.

Self-timer A digital camera's self-timer lets you take shots that include yourself. A countdown timer delays the shot by 10 seconds or more, giving you time to get within its field of view. A remote control provides the same function without the rush.

Sensitivity Your TV's ability to pick up relatively weak signals and still display a picture, important only if you receive off-air broadcasts far from transmitting antennas.

Sensor type The sensor is the chip (CCD or CMOS) that records light falling on it as it travels through the digital camera's lens. It is the device that actually captures the image.

Serial port A type of computer connection that transfers data one bit at a time. Serial ports are commonly used by older input/output devices.

Server A computer in a network, the resources of which are shared by part or all of the other users.

Set-top box Also referred to as an external tuner or, for digital types, a receiver/decoder, it's a small box that converts incoming TV signals into a signal that a TV can accept and display. Common examples are a cable box, satellite box, and off-air tuner. There are also digital and HD versions of each. Some also have a hard drive for recording programs and watching at a later time (time-shifting).

720p-capable 720p refers to an HD signal based on 1280 pixels horizontally by 720 pixels vertically, progressively scanned (the "p"). Some broadcasters use the 720p format, but 1080i (1920x1080 pixels, interlaced) is a more common HD display mode. 720p-capable HD sets can display images using this type of signal without requiring an external set-top box, such as a digital-cable box or satellite receiver, to convert it to a resolution it can display.

Shareware User-supported software that is copyrighted and typically available on the Internet; the author usually requests a ($10 to $50) fee from those who decide to keep the program after trying it.

Sheet feeder A device attached to some computer scanners that automatically feeds a stack of sheets, one at a time, through it for scanning, thus eliminating the need to hand-feed the pages. Useful for large printed documents.

Shift key A key that changes the function of a character printed by another key when pressed along with that key.

Short cut An icon on a computer operating systems' desktop or program list that launches a program or document when activated. There can be many shortcuts to one program.

Shutter range The minimum and maximum shutter speeds available for a digital camera.

Signal-to-noise ratio Abbreviated S/N or SNR, it represents the ratio, expressed in decibels (dB), an undistorted maximum audio signal and the noise present in the signal. Audio signals typically contain some noise or background from electronic parts. A system's maximum S/N is called the dynamic range. For audio, the higher the number, the cleaner the sound. This number is useful when comparing like products.

Signal type The typical analog type of video signal comes out of older cable boxes, DVD players, camcorders, and VCRs. It can be carried over a composite-video, S-video, or component-video connection. When superimposed on a radio frequency, it can be broadcast over the air and picked up via antenna, or sent via cable to the cable box. If it's digitized first, then superimposed on a radio frequency, it can be delivered over the air as DTV (digital television), by DBS (direct broadcast satellite) to the satellite receiver, or as the digital portion of your cable service. Note: these three delivery methods use different digitizing and usually must be decoded by different tuners.

Simultaneous record/playback For DVD recorders, the ability to watch one program while recording another, or to begin watching a recording from the beginning, pause, reverse, or fast-forward while the recording is still in progress. Only models that record to the DVD-RAM format or include a built-in hard drive offer this function.

Single-side DVD recording times For a DVD recorder, the minimum and maximum hours of content that may be recorded onto a single side of a disc—using, respectively, the least and most compression.

Six-channel decoder A multichannel (usually six-channel) audio decoder is useful in a DVD player only if you plan to pipe the player's audio signal into a full home-theater system, and the system's digital receiver does not itself have multichannel (also known as 5.1 channel) decoding capability. The decoder separates audio into up to six true channels: front left and right, front center (for dialogue), two rear (also called surround) speakers with discrete wide-band signals, and a subwoofer for bass effects. Some DVD soundtracks even have additional channels beyond the expected six.

Sleep timer If you like to fall asleep with the TV on but don't want to leave it on all night, a sleep timer can be set, usually in 15-minute increments, so that the TV will turn off within a specific time. Such timers are included on many sets.

Slim-and-light laptop A laptop PC that contains only the components needed to run installed applications, operate on stored documents and files, and communicate with external devices. Removable-disk drives are connected externally when needed, as the focus of the design is on reducing travel size and weight.

Slot Similar to a port in a computer, but usually used for internal expansions such as memory, graphics, and so forth, by the addition of boards.

Smart card A plastic card, containing memory and a processor, that communicates with a computer through a reader into which it is inserted. The data on the card may authenticate a user, and/or may provide personal or financial information enabling a transaction. The memory on smart cards can be updated by the system as part of the transaction.

SmartMedia Also known as Solid State Floppy Disk Cards (SSFDC), they are a form of flash memory. They are roughly the size of a large postage stamp and about as thick as a credit card.

SMTP Simple Mail Transfer Protocol, the usual protocol for outgoing Internet e-mail.

Software The programs that are run on a computer for various purposes.

Sound, TVs Three different types of sound system are available. Many smaller TVs have **mono** sound, meaning that all the audio is processed through a single channel. The next step up is **stereo** sound, which splits the audio between two channels for a more lifelike sound. For an "expanded" audio experience, look for a TV equipped with **virtual surround** sound. Using only the TV speakers, this system simulates the "ambient" sound effects of home-theater systems. On most, however, you can turn off the ambience if you don't like the effect.

Sound board/card A component of multimedia PCs that can realistically reproduce (through attached speakers or headphones) almost any sound, such as music, speech, and sound effects. Sound boards can also connect to other sound equipment.

Sound format, camcorders Camcorders may record with mono, stereo, or PCM stereo formats. Mono records onto only one channel; stereo, onto two channels (left and right). PCM stereo, found on digital camcorders, can either record at SP speed with 16 bits of information on two channels (CD-quality sound, in theory) or divide the audio into four tracks by recording 12 bits on two channels, leaving another pair of tracks free for post-production audio editing and recording.

Sound technology, cordless phones Cordless phones transmit their signals between the base and handset wirelessly in the 900-MHz, 2.4-GHz, and/or 5.8-GHz-frequency bands using analog (the least expensive), digital, or digital spread-spectrum (DSS) technology.

Spam Slang term for unsolicited commercial e-mail, thought to come from a skit by the Monty Python comedy troupe in which the word spam was repeated over and over until it became annoying. Spam is the Internet's equivalent of junk mail and proliferates despite many efforts to reduce it.

Spam filter A feature built into e-mail programs or installed as an add-on that attempts to identify spam messages and remove them from your main inbox. Spam filters on individual PCs have mixed success. Some ISPs also offer a spam-filter option.

Speaker wattage, TVs The audio-output power is expressed in watts, ranging from less than 1 watt to as much as 7 watts. Higher wattage, offered on many sets, may provide a louder sound but will not necessary improve overall audio quality.

Speakerphone A speakerphone feature on a cordless phone offers a hands-free way to converse or wait on hold and lets others chime in. A base speaker lets you answer a call without the handset; a handset speaker lets you chat hands-free conveniently anywhere in the house.

Speech synthesizer A computer output device that simulates human speech using phonetic rules. When used with the appropriate software, a speech synthesizer can "speak" the words that are displayed on the monitor screen.

Spreadsheet A software package, such as Lotus 1-2-3 or Microsoft Excel, that allows the user to enter, into "cells," numbers and equations that the program automatically calculates. Spreadsheet software eases the development of financial applications.

Spyware Software that often rides in on a useful program but runs in the background and transmits statistics about your Internet activities to a marketing database for their use and resale.

Standard Agreed-upon industry design guidelines for a hardware or software product intended to make it work with the products of different manufacturers. Given the choice, it's usually wise to choose a standards-based product rather than a proprietary one.

Standby A computer's power-saving state in which some subsystems are shut off but can resume full-speed operation almost immediately when a key or the pointing device is touched. PCs in standby can also respond to modem-ringing signals or timed events by resuming. It's also called suspend or sleep mode.

Start menu A feature of the Microsoft Windows desktop that provides a single pop-up menu to launch any installed program and access other features of the operating system.

Status bar An onscreen area, usually at the top or bottom of a window, that provides information on the current operation of the software in use.

Still image file formats File output, (Extension) that the camera generates. TIFF and JPEG are the most common.

Still image resolution settings The number of levels, or modes, of resolution the camera offers.

Storage Any disk (fixed or removable), tape, CD, or online service that stores data.

Storage size (MB) Digital cameras store images as data files, like those on the hard drive of a computer. The more storage space available, the more images the camera can store. Most cameras have a few megabytes of internal storage, but many also accept removable memory cards or other media that can store as much as 1 gigabyte (GB).

Streaming Playing an audio or video presentation directly from an Internet Web site without your first having to download it. Streaming requires cooperation between the Web server and a "media player" applet on the user's PC.

Stretch and zoom modes On 16:9 sets, such display modes will expand or compress an image to better fill the screen shape. This helps to reduce the dark bands that can appear above, below, or on the sides of the image if you watch content formatted for one screen shape on a TV that has the other shape. The picture, however, may be distorted or cut off a bit in the process of stretching and zooming.

String On a computer, a set of characters treated as a unit.

Subwoofer output The ability, found in a few TVs, to output the lower-frequency portion of the audio directly to a powered subwoofer.

SuperVGA See "SVGA."

Surge suppressor or protector An electrical device, often built into a power strip, that is designed to prevent damage to the computer resulting from voltage spikes from the power source.

Surround-sound formats, DVD players Surround sound refers to the ability of your DVD player to play one or more varieties of multichannel audio through your home-entertainment system. Several different surround formats exist, each with distinct advantages and disadvantages. The main format choices are Dolby Pro Logic, Dolby Digital, and DTS.

SVGA SuperVGA, a high-resolution (800 x 600 pixels) graphics display mode.

S-VHS-C Marketed as a premium variant of VHS-C, it promises a sharper camcorder picture, though performance varies widely. This format uses a cassette that's about the size of a cigarette pack, but more expensive and less widely available than VHS-C.

S-video inputs An alternative to composite-video input. In general, using an S-video input will provide better picture quality than using either an antenna/cable or composite-video input.

S-video outputs An S-video connection from a DVD player's S-video output to the TV provides a picture with more detail and fewer color artifacts than you can get using the TV's composite-video or RF (antenna) connection. S-video output is also used to connect a camcorder to a television or VCR to watch and/or record information saved on a camcorder's tape (or disc).

Swap black for photo ink The photo ink for some printers comes in an extra cartridge. To use these photo inks, you must remove the black ink cartridge and replace it with the photo-ink cartridge. To go back to printing text or graphics, the photo-ink cartridge must be removed and replaced by the black ink cartridge. This can get tedious. Models that hold all the inks simultaneously minimize the hassle.

SXGA Super XGA, a very high-resolution (1280 x 1024 pixels) graphics display mode. SXGA+ provides 1400 x 1050 pixels.

System A single computer, or any group of interconnected computers and the network itself.

System disk, drive or volume The currently active data-storage device that contains the critical operating-system files for a running computer.

System software Programs required for the basic operation of the computer and its components. For PCs, this normally consists of the operating system and any associated utilities.

System utilities Programs usually supplied as part of the system software that permit and assist in basic control and maintenance of the computer and its components.

T

Tablet A computer input device often used by designers. Tablets consist of a sensitive membrane, movement (using a stylus or sometimes even a finger) upon which is transferred to corresponding positions on the screen.

Tablet PC Microsoft's name for a pen computer, a portable computer that uses a pressure-sensitive flat-panel screen for control and data input. A tablet PC can convert handwritten notes to electronic text.

Tabletop/console Most TVs are placed on top of or inside a piece of furniture (say, an entertainment center), but some TVs are consoles, meaning they have their own cabinetry and can stand directly on the floor. Rear-projection TVs in particular are often consoles, although newer "microdisplay" models typically require a stand.

Tape, computers A magnetic data storage or backup medium on which files are stored in a predetermined and rigid sequence. Updating a tape usually requires making a new copy of the entire tape.

Tape format, camcorders Format is based on the type of recording tape a camcorder uses (some newer models record to disc) and whether the model records in analog or digital mode. Currently, there are at least seven tape formats: 8mm, Hi8, MiniDV, Digital8 (D8), VHS, VHS-C, and S-VHS-C. Key differences among these formats include picture quality, size of camcorder, and compatibility with a VCR.

Task Any process currently running on a computer. An application may have several tasks running simultaneously.

Taskbar On the Microsoft Windows desktop, a bar with icons and window titles that is used to launch programs, switch between running tasks, and display the status of programs running in the background.

Technology, TVs All rear-projection TVs project their images onto a mirror, which reflects the image onto the screen for you to see. Projection TVs use one of several display technologies to project the image initially onto the mirror. **CRT or cathode-ray tube** is the traditional method, using three 7-inch picture tubes (one each for the red, green, and blue portions of the image). **LCD or liquid-crystal display** is a newer method that uses three LCD panels, each about an inch in size. **DLP, or digital light processing,** is a new technology that uses a microchip, which contains a microscopic array of pivoting mirrors, and a spinning color wheel. **LCoS** is the newest technology. It uses three microchips, each of which contains a microscopic array of mirror-like LCD elements.

Telecommunications Communications between devices that are not located near each other and must make use of a data communications channel. This occurs when PCs link to a host computer for an exchange of data.

TeleZapper Some cordless phones have a built in TeleZapper, which reduces the number of computer-aided telemarketing calls you receive.

Template A document guide on a computer, similar to a paper form, that permits the user to simply fill in the blanks to create a new document.

Text display A feature that displays text encoded on certain discs, giving you information such as song titles on CDs.

Text file A file that usually contains only ASCII characters, readable by practically any program that uses text.

TFT LCD Thin film transistor LCD, an active-matrix LCD display that is commonly used on top-line, color notebook computers.

35mm equivalent zoom ratio All digital camera manufacturers publish this "35mm equivalent" focal length simply because people are used to hearing it and knowing what kind of image a 28mm lens produces compared to a 50mm lens.

3:2-pulldown compensation A feature on HD sets (and on progressive-scan DVD players) that can make moving images look less jerky, with less jaggedness around the edges. It affects only the smoothness of movies converted from film to video. This feature is sometimes referred to as film, cinema, or movie mode, or by brand-specific names such as CineMotion.

Thumbnail A miniature reproduction of an image, usually for display.

THX-certified THX is an enhancement to Dolby Digital (DTS) sound processing that further processes the multichannel sound to simulate the acoustics of a movie theater. To hear the benefit, you must use the certified DVD player with a receiver and speakers that are also THX-certified.

Time and date stamp A camcorder feature with which the time and date are displayed in the viewfinder or on the LCD, and can be set to record on the tape.

Time code An automatic (and accurate) camcorder feature that records the frame reference on the tape in hours, minutes, seconds, and frames. The information, which is recorded separately from the video and audio signals, makes editing easier. The time and date are displayed in the viewfinder or on the LCD, and can be set to record on the tape.

Titling Like the time and date, titling can be programmed to record on a camcorder tape. Most models now have this feature, but its sophistication varies. Some camcorders simply provide a list of pre-made or built-in titles, such as "Happy Holidays," to choose from. Others let you set and save your own custom titles, such as "Sam's First Birthday Party."

TiVo and ReplayTV Trademarks for two hard-drive recorder brands that use sophisticated onscreen TV program guides to manage the recording of programs.

Toner A very fine, powdery ink, supplied in a cartridge, that is used in copy machines and laser printers. Toner particles become electrically charged and adhere to the pattern of an image defined by charges on a plate or drum.

Tower case A computer case design that employs an upright (stacked) arrangement of drives. Tower cases can sit on a tabletop, but more frequently they are placed on the floor or a low stand adjacent to the work area. The term is often prefixed by full, mid-, mini-, or micro-, indicating the case's relative size and expansion space.

Trackball A computer pointing device similar to a mouse; it uses a ball mounted on a fixed base to control onscreen cursor movement. You roll the ball with your fingers or thumb in the direction you want the onscreen pointer to go.

Transfer rate An estimate of how quickly an MP3 file can be transferred from a computer to the player. Transfer rate is usually measured in kilobytes or megabytes per second and can vary depending on the player, the interface type, the computer platform, operating system, configuration requirements, file size, and other factors.

Trojan or Trojan horse A general class of computer programs that gain system entry by riding in on legitimate-appearing programs or e-mail attachments. The best-known examples are malicious programs that provide hackers remote access to infected systems; however, not all Trojan horses are necessarily destructive.

Tube shape Direct-view television picture tubes are available in three types of front surface: spherical, cylindrical, and flat. Flat screens show the least amount of annoying room reflections. Spherical and cylindrical tubes are considered standard.

TV type As digital television has grown, the choice of TV types has expanded. Most models, known as standard or conventional, receive only the traditional analog TV signal. Digital TVs are available in HDTV (high-definition TV), EDTV (enhanced-definition TV), and SDTV (standard-definition TV) formats. HDTVs can display exceptional picture quality in a 16:9 aspect ratio. EDTVs offer a lesser picture quality than HDTV but have a picture that's roughly equivalent to that of progressive-scan DVD players. SDTVs may not measure up to the HDTV sound and picture standards, but they're similar to high-quality standard TVs. (For each type, the term "ready," as in "HD-ready," refers to the need to connect an external tuner to decode the incoming digital signals.) Even regular TVs will be usable with an external digital TV tuner/decoder.

Two-way intercom For models with a base speakerphone, it allows for conversation between the handset and the base speakerphone. For multiple-handset-capable models, it allows for conversation between one handset and another. Also referred to as Two-way Paging.

Typeface The design or style of a set of print characters, such as Arial, Helvetica, or Times Roman.

UI User interface, the means through which a user controls a computing device.

Ultra DMA or UDMA A further enhancement to the EIDE disk-drive interface that can transfer data as fast as 133 MB per second in bursts. A compatible drive is required.

Uninterruptible Power Supply See "UPS."

Universal remote Controls not only your DVD player, for example, but also other components, such as many different brands of TVs.

Unix A popular but not user-friendly operating system that runs on many platforms from mainframe to microcomputer. It employs cryptic but powerful commands, shells, and pipes, and has TCP/IP protocols built in; good for use in Internet servers.

Update or upgrade The process of changing software or hardware to a newer, more powerful, or possibly less-buggy version.

Upgradable A system whose components are designed to be easily upgraded to newer ones, usually by simply unplugging the old one and inserting the new one.

Upgrade path Refers to the means for a computer, hardware component, or software application to be changed to a more powerful or newer version without adversely affecting the remainder of the system or any pertinent files.

Upload To transfer a copy of a file from one computer, usually a PC, to another computer. In the opposite direction, it's a download.

UPS Uninterruptible Power Supply, an electrical device that contains a battery pack and will supply adequate power to a system for a short time in the event of a power failure, permitting it to be shut down in an orderly manner.

URL Uniform Resource Locator, an Internet/intranet address, such as http://*www.consumerreports.org*. Every place on the Web has such an address. Most Web addresses begin with http://, and most Web sites start with "www." Site URLs end with a "top-level domain" (TLD) suffix: commercial sites end in ".com," organizations in ".org," educational sites in ".edu," and government sites in ".gov." Other TLDs have been established, such as ".info" and ".biz." URLs can also address FTP and other types of sites, along with resources on a LAN.

USB Universal serial bus, a high-speed external interface on newer PCs, used to connect peripheral devices like printers, and digital cameras. A recent enhancement, USB2, has a much higher speed, with enough bandwidth for digital video and external hard drives. On PDAs, this connection synchs data in your PDA to your desktop and transfers it faster than a serial-cable or infrared link.

USB2 Most Windows and Macintosh computers purchased since the fall of 2002 have universal serial bus 2.0 ports (USB2). They can be used with printers that have either USB2 or USB connections. The speed for transmitting data with USB2 can be up to 40 times faster than with USB. Check which connections your computer has before purchasing a printer.

Usenet A large but informal collection of Internet servers that host groups of users known as newsgroups to exchange news and information on specific topics.

User interface Any device, either hardware or software, that provides a bridge between the computer and the user. Examples include the keyboard, mouse, and menu programs.

User-supported software See shareware.

V.90 A standard for 56-kbps modems. A later standard, V.92, alleviates some of the shortcomings of dial-up Internet access, such as lengthy call-setup times, slow upload speed, and phone-line tie-ups.

V-chip A parental-control feature, found in all TVs with screens 13-in. or larger, that can block specific programs based on their content rating. To override the restriction for a given program, you must enter a code.

VCR capability Some hybrid DVD players have a built-in VCR that lets you play and record videotapes as well as play DVDs. Note that such models do not permit the recording of copy-protected DVDs onto videotape.

VCR Plus+ For DVD/VCR combo units, a capability that simplifies time-shift recording by letting you punch in a program's code (from TV listings) rather than the program's date, time, and channel. Gold and Silver versions do most of the setup work for you once you enter your ZIP code.

Version number A number, such as 3.2, indicating an application or driver's place in the history of its development. In general, the higher the version number, the longer the program has been around and under development, and the more revisions it has undergone. Also, the greater the difference between two version numbers, the greater the change in the program.

VGA IBM's Video Graphics Array, a medium-resolution, 640-by-480-pixel color graphics system. VGA was originally designed for professional applications on top-of-the-line PCs; however, it is now considered to be standard equipment.

VGA/SVGA input Some TVs have VGA or SVGA inputs, which let your TV double as a computer monitor.

VHS-C A format for a camcorder using a cassette that's about the size of a cigarette pack–inexpensive and widely available. The tape can be played back in a VHS VCR, using the supplied adapter, or in the camcorder.

Video D/A conversion Most standard DVD players use a 10-bit/27-MHz digital-to-analog converter. Progressive-scan models use a 10- or 12-bit/54-MHz digital-to-analog converter.

Video inputs, TVs Video inputs provide a better picture than the antenna/cable input (which combines audio and video), and most TVs are equipped with at least one video input. There are generally three types. **Composite-video inputs,** the most common, provide minor improvement over antenna/cable. **S-video input,** at least one of which is found on most sets 27 in. or larger, is a further improvement. And **component-video input** separates the video signal into three component parts to offer the potential for even finer picture quality; they are useful mostly with a DVD player or other equipment that has component-video output. Digital video inputs–HDMI, DVI or FireWire–are found on HD and ED TVs. Front-panel inputs permit easy connection of an external device, such as a camcorder or game system, to the TV.

Video-noise reduction setting May reduce the effects of noise due to poor reception, although this feature may sacrifice some picture detail.

Video out Allows you to connect a digital camera directly to a TV or VCR and view your images on the TV screen or record your images onto a videotape.

Video output, DVD players The type of video output you use with your DVD player depends on the type of inputs on your TV or receiver. DVD players come with at least composite and S-video outputs. Both S-video and component-video outputs, however, provide an increase in picture quality.

Videoconferencing Teleconferencing in which video images are exchanged. Although this traditionally involved using video cameras and monitors, routine video conferencing via computer over the Internet is starting to become reality.

Viewfinder Found on virtually all digital cameras,

this optical device lets you look through an eyepiece to frame the subject before taking a picture.

Virtual reality A computerized simulation of three-dimensional space in which the user can interact and manipulate objects in the virtual world.

Virtual surround sound, TVs Television audio systems by themselves do not offer the true surround sound of a home-theater system, but produce a similar effect by special audio processing. Systems offered on some sets include 2-speaker surround, Matrix, Matrix/SRS, and SRS.

Virus A typically small, malicious computer program embedded in a legitimate-appearing "host" file, often a downloaded program or e-mail attachment. A computer becomes "infected" with the virus when a user runs the host file. Viruses replicate themselves in an attempt to infect other computers and attach to user files, causing annoyance or damage to the infected system.

Virus signature The unique machine code (binary) pattern of a computer virus program. Most antivirus programs include a search for known virus signatures as a means for quick detection.

Virtual surround sound, TVs Produces a simulation of the surround-sound effect using just two speakers.

Voice mail indicator A visual indicator on a cordless phone's handset or base that notifies you that you have new messages on your telephone company's message-waiting service.

Voice recognition The ability of a computer to accept input commands or data using the spoken word. Voice-recognition technology has advanced greatly and is likely to become a common alternative to keyboard control and data entry.

Voice recording An MP3 player feature with which the unit has a microphone that's useful for recording interviews, lectures, etc.

Voice synthesizer See speech synthesizer.

Voltage spike A sudden jump in electrical power. These can be very dangerous to data and, if large enough, to computer hardware as well.

VRAM (vee-ram) Video RAM, memory dedicated to handling video processing and output.

W

Wall-mountable Some TVs, particularly plasma sets, can be mounted on a wall, although we recommend you hire a professional because of their need for adequate support and ventilation. LCD TVs are also wall-mountable, though mounting makes sense mostly for larger models.

Warm boot To restart a computer from the keyboard. This method does not always completely clear and re-initialize the system; and a "cold" boot may be required.

Warranty, TVs The length of time the television is covered by its manufacturer for defects or repairs. Most warranty coverage is divided into parts and labor, typically one year for parts and either 90 days or one year for labor–and, for CRT-based TVs, 24 months for the picture tube.

Warranty excludes image burn-in Most TVs, with the exception of LCD-, LCoS, and DLP-based sets, are subject to burn-in, an uneven wearing of the screen's phosphors that results from leaving stationary images on-screen–such as the news, stock-price, or sports-score "zippers" that run across the top or bottom of the screen on many TV channels–or viewing images sized for a different aspect ratio (see "Aspect ratio") than that of your set. Manufacturers typically do not cover image burn-in in their TV warranties, considering it misuse.

Water resistance A printer's ability to produce output that will not run or smear if it gets wet. Water-resistance for a printer's ink (or dye, in the case of a dye-sublimation photo printer) may apply to black, color, or both.

WAV Also known as a wave file, this is a file format for storing uncompressed digital audio.

Webcam Web camera, a small camera connected to a computer, intended to send still or moving pictures to others over the Internet.

Webmail E-mail account access through a Web-page interface, which allows the mail user to send and receive mail anywhere an Internet connection is available.

Webmaster The individual responsible for maintaining a Web site's content and links. Usually, the Webmaster operates remotely and does not have (or need) direct control of the computer that serves the Web site.

Wi-Fi Nickname for a medium-range (150 feet) wireless connectivity standard, officially known as IEEE 802.11. Wi-Fi enables secure networking of PCs in either a peer-to-peer or a workstation-to-base configuration. 802.11b operates in the 2.4-GHz radio-frequency band and provides data throughput of about 5 Mbps. 802.11a operates above 5 GHz and has about five times the throughput over a somewhat smaller radius.

Wildcard A generic symbol (such as * or ?) that can stand for either a single character or several characters. Wildcards are frequently used in system commands.

Window A portion of a computer screen set aside for a specific display or purpose.

Windows A multitasking, graphical user interface developed by Microsoft for IBM-compatible systems. The program gets its name from using movable and resizable windows in which applications are displayed. Windows supports multimedia, common printer management, TrueType fonts, and copy and paste between Windows applications.

Windows XP (Home, Professional, Server, etc.) The latest versions of Windows 2000. Windows XP Home replaces prior versions of Windows, bringing many of the features of the Windows 2000 operating system to the consumer.

Wireless One of any communications link that doesn't use wiring as a transmission medium. Examples are Wi-Fi networking and Bluetooth.

Wireless frequency Cordless phones transmit their signals between the base and handset wirelessly in the 900-MHz, 2.4-GHz, and/or 5.8-GHz-frequency bands using analog, digital, or digital spread-spectrum (DSS) technology.

Wizard A program that takes you one step at a time through a complex process, such as setting up a home network, asking simple questions to set up configuration options.

Word processor A software application, such as Corel WordPerfect or Microsoft Word, that is designed to accept and process normal text (words) as data. Word processors range from simple programs that are little more than screen typewriters to those with complex screen handling, editing, and assistance features. Also refers to a stand-alone machine dedicated to word processing.

Workgroup A named group of computers connected as a peer-to-peer network.

World Wide Web (WWW or W3) A global, multimedia portion of the Internet featuring text, audio, graphics, and moving image files. The Web is the most popular part of the 'Net and is accessed using a program called a browser.

Worm A type of malicious computer program that, once released into a computer, is designed to repeatedly and rapidly reproduce itself without the user's knowledge or consent. One effect is that the system may soon have all available disk, memory, and other resources gobbled up, leading to a system crash. Worms can also spread to other connected systems over a network.

XYZ

X, as in 24X Denotes the rate at which a CD- or DVD-ROM drive reads or writes data, in multiples of the speed of the earliest models of that type of drive. For a CD-ROM, 1X is 150 kilobytes per second. For a DVD-ROM, 1X is about the speed of an 8X CD-ROM.

xD-Picture Card Ultra-compact memory media, (20.0x25.0x1.7-mm size), developed jointly by Fuji Photo Film and Olympus Optical.

XDS Extended Data Services. Some broadcast signals include additional information about TV programs, such as the channel label, program title, program length, and elapsed time, but the service is not available everywhere. This feature lets the TV display this information when it is transmitted.

XGA IBM's eXtended Graphics Array, a high-resolution, 1024x768-pixel color graphics mode that is very similar to SVGA.

XML Extensible Markup Language, a "superset" of HTML that allows Web page designers to incorporate new, interactive objects into their pages.

Zip drive A removable-disk drive whose cartridges can hold 100, 250, or 750 MB each.

REFERENCE INDEX

A
Answering machines, 125
Antenna, for HD TV, 77
Anti-virus software, 34-41

C
Cable-Internet service, 41-45
Camcorders, 9, 22, 27-30
    features, 28-30
    formats, 28
    Ratings, 129
Cameras
    digital. See Digital cameras
    phones. See Cell phones.
CD player/recorders, 104
    vs. CD burners, 103
CDs, do-it-yourself, 103-104
Cell phones, 111-112, 120-123
    batteries, 120
    bills, 115
    cameras, 122
    carriers, 110-111, 114-117
    features, 121-122
    headsets, 113-114
    Ratings, 154-155
    test messaging, 122
    Video services, 116
Computers
    brand repair history, 50
    desktop. See Desktop
        computers
    laptop. See Laptop

    computers
    moving files, 48
    networking, 13-16
    printers. See Printers
    protecting, 34-41
    recycling, 52
    software. See Software.
    technical support, 32
    where to buy, 10-12

D
Desktop computers, 32, 46-49
    brand re[air history
    configuring, 47
    features, 46-47
    monitors. See Monitors
    Ratings, 132-133
Digital cameras, 9, 17-19, 23-25
    features, 23-24
    making prints, 21
    photo-editing software, 19
    Ratings, 136-141
    reflex models, 24
Digital video recorders (DVR),
    84-85, 93-95
    features, 94-95
DVD formats, 90
DVD players, 85, 88-91
    brand repair history, 89
    features, 89-90
    portables, 88
DVD recorders, 84-85, 91-93
    features, 91-92

E
Electronics stores, 8-9
    Ratings, 9
E-mail, 8-9
    PDAs, 45
    security, 34-41
    switching providers, 45
Ethernet, 14-16
Extended warranties, 12

F
Firewall software, 35

H
Hackers, 16, 34-41
Headsets, 113-114
Home theater, 86-87, 95-96
    receivers, 96-99
    speakers, 99-100
    surround sound, 88
    theater-in-a-box, 95-96
        features, 95-96
        Ratings, 145

I
Internet
    broadband access, 41-45
        vs. dial-up, 42-43
    DSL, 42-43
    phoning (VoIP), 117-18
    protection, 34-41

Index (continued)

service providers, 41-45
    Ratings, 43

L

Laptop computers, 32-33, 49-52
    brand repair history, 50
    configuring, 47
    features, 50-51
    hidden costs, 132
    Ratings, 134-135

M

Monitors, 33, 52-54. *See also* Computers
    CRTs, 33, 52
    features, 53-54
    flat-panel LCDs, 12, 33, 53-54
    music, 103, 104
    recycling, 52
MP3 players, 101-103, 106-108, 148-151
    features, 107
    Ratings, 148-151
Music recording,
    legal issues, 102

N

Networking, home, 13-16

P

Passwords,
    protecting, 35
PDAs (personal digital assistant), 55-56, 152-153
    features, 56
    Palm OS models, 55
    Pocket PC models, 56
    Ratings, 152-153
Printers, 21, 57-62,
    costs, controlling, 67
    features, 81
    ink cartridges, 59, 62
    inkjet, 59

laser, 60
multifunction, 61-62
photos, 21, 58, 61
Ratings, 160-163

R

Receivers, 96-99
    features, 97

S

Satellite
    Internet service, 42-43
    radio, 104-105
    television, 77
Scanners, 20, 26-27, 164-165
    copying photos, 20
    features, 26-27
    Ratings, 164-165
Software
    photo, 20, 21
    protection, 34-40
Speakers, 99-100
    features, 100

T

Telephones
    Cellular. *See* Cell phones
    corded, 119
    cordless, 119, 123-126
        features, 124-126
        interference, 119
        Ratings, 156-159
Television sets, 62-82, 166-181
    front projection, 65
    LCD, 65, 68. 73-75, 166-168
        features, 74-75
        Ratings, 166-168
    picture-tube, 65, 67, 71-73, 172-177
        brand repair history, 67
        features, 72-73
        Ratings, 172-177
    plasma, 65, 69, 75-79
        features, 78

        Ratings, 178-181
    rear-projection, 65, 70, 79-82
        brand repair history, 80
        features, 80-81
        Ratings, 173

V

VCRs, 89
Videos
    preserving, 22
Voice over Internet Protocol (VoIP), 117-118

W

Wi-Fi, 13-16
    PDAs, 56
    vs. Ethernet, 14-15

Z

Zoom lenses, 24, 29
    optical vs. digital, 25